A

■   ■   ■

B O O K

The Philip E. Lilienthal imprint
honors special books
in commemoration of a man whose work
at University of California Press from 1954 to 1979
was marked by dedication to young authors
and to high standards in the field of Asian Studies.
Friends, family, authors, and foundations have together
endowed the Lilienthal Fund, which enables UC Press
to publish under this imprint selected books
in a way that reflects the taste and judgment
of a great and beloved editor.

The publisher gratefully acknowledges the generous contribution to this book provided by the Philip E. Lilienthal Asian Studies Endowment Fund of the University of California Press Foundation, which is supported by a major gift from Sally Lilienthal.

Speaking to History

Speaking to History

THE STORY OF KING GOUJIAN
IN TWENTIETH-CENTURY CHINA

Paul A. Cohen

With a Foreword by
John R. Gillis

中田

UNIVERSITY OF CALIFORNIA PRESS

BERKELEY   LOS ANGELES   LONDON

University of California Press, one of the most distinguished university presses in the United States, enriches
lives around the world by advancing scholarship in the
humanities, social sciences, and natural sciences. Its
activities are supported by the UC Press Foundation
and by philanthropic contributions from individuals
and institutions. For more information, visit
www.ucpress.edu.

University of California Press
Berkeley and Los Angeles, California
University of California Press, Ltd.
London, England
© 2009 by The Regents of the University of California

Library of Congress Cataloging-in-Publication Data
Cohen, Paul A.
    Speaking to history : the story of King Goujian in
twentieth-century China / Paul A. Cohen ; with a
foreword by John R. Gillis.
        p.   cm.
    Includes bibliographical references and index.
    ISBN: 978–0–520-25579-1 (cloth : alk. paper)
        1. China—History—20th century.   2. Goujian,
d. 465 B.C.   I. Title.   II. Title: Story of King Goujian
in twentieth-century China.
DS774.5.C8 2009
931'.03092—dc22   2008013446

Manufactured in the United States of America
17 16 15 14 13 12 11 10 09
10 9 8 7 6 5 4 3 2 1

The paper used in this publication meets the minimum
requirements of ANSI/NISO Z39.48–1992 (R 1997)
(*Permanence of Paper*).

FOR ELIZABETH

CONTENTS

ILLUSTRATIONS

FOREWORD

WHILE WESTERN CULTURES HAVE THEIR HEROES—Moses, King Arthur, Joan of Arc, George Washington—none are comparable to King Goujian, whose story circulates widely within China and is also known to many Chinese living in other parts of the world. Yet the tale of this ancient monarch is virtually unknown to Western scholars of twentieth-century China. Paul Cohen had not been aware of its significance until he began studying popular Chinese responses to national defeat and humiliation. Initially he found inspirational references to Goujian in both late imperial and early republican literature. But soon he was discovering the story of King Goujian everywhere he looked: in operas, school texts, and every form of mass media. That a figure who lived two thousand five hundred years ago should be remembered at all is remarkable, but that King Goujian has been upheld as a model for modern collective and personal behavior is truly astonishing, at least to those of Western background whose revered figures remain distanced. As Paul Cohen's book demonstrates in great detail, the king who survived utter humiliation to rebuild his kingdom and defeat his enemies has been a compelling, if sometimes invisible, presence in the mental life of modern China.

The tale of the ancient king is complex and not without its ambiguities, but at its center is the striking image of Goujian, the king of Yue, who, utterly defeated by the powerful ruler of the neighboring kingdom of Wu, survives and ultimately triumphs over humiliation by submitting himself to the practice of "sleeping on brushwood and tasting gall" *(woxin chang-dan)*. This extended ritual of self-denial and self-renewal at least symbolically allowed the kingdom of Yue to regain the strength necessary to defeat its rival and subsequently became a rallying cry in each of modern China's moments of defeat and humiliation from the late Qing period onward. For over one hundred years, it served the purposes of dynastic as well as nationalist renewal, used by both the political left and right, providing an apparently inexhaustible resource for private as well as public goals. King Goujian's overcoming defeat and humiliation proved relevant to the defenders of the old empire as well as their republican rivals. It was central to both Guomindang and Communist Party ideologies during the struggles against the Japanese. And when Chiang Kai-shek retreated to Taiwan, the story went with him and translated readily into the struggle between the island and the mainland. *Woxin changdan* remained a powerful reference even after Chiang's death in 1975, but it also buttressed Mao's efforts to strengthen the People's Republic of China against its cold war antagonists.

But "sleeping on brushwood and tasting gall" did not end when both Taiwan and the People's Republic of China put aside their immediate hostilities and redirected their energies to economic development. Today, *woxin changdan* is no longer practiced in preparation for war, but it is still invoked in preparation for exams and business competitions. It has migrated from public to private discourse to become a part of the drive to rebuild the two Chinas on capitalist principles of competitive individualism. Always a part of popular culture, especially the opera, the story of King Goujian finds expression in comics, film, television, and, most recently, tourism, which has made of the ancient capital of Yue, Shaoxing, a place to visit for those who know its story. No doubt this book will inspire foreign visitors, for, as Paul Cohen argues, the story of Goujian deserves to be known in the West, not so much for its narrative merits, but because it has played such a vital role in contemporary history, events that have affected the lives not just of Chinese but of the entire world.

The value of Paul Cohen's book lies in his willingness to cast aside the blinkers that historians have willingly worn since the establishment of their academic discipline in the second half of the nineteenth century. Since that time, stories like that of King Goujian have been left to the literature expert or the folklorist. Ever since history and *belles lettres* parted ways, historians have treated that which they regard as fiction as entertaining but insignificant. Universities police these disciplinary boundaries, making it difficult for scholars to make connections that might illuminate their subjects.

There was a similar divorce between history and memory. From the nineteenth century onward, historians have been at pains to correct what they regard as the failings of memory. In the academy, myth, ritual, and folktales are considered appropriate subjects for anthropologists, folklorists, or scholars of premodern societies, but are virtually ignored when they are documented in more recent periods. Yet, as Cohen shows so convincingly, the power of stories has by no means diminished in recent times. Indeed, there is abundant evidence that the potency of myth, ritual, and memory has increased and that what were once regarded as survivals, soon to be extinguished in the great march of progress, are, in fact, vital parts of modernity itself.

Ever since the Enlightenment, the Western academy has been dedicated to placing stories like that of King Goujian out of sight and out of mind. The most common hiding place has been that vast, empty container called the past, which in the West is thought of as a "foreign country," thoroughly distanced from the present. Another convenient closet is spatial rather than temporal. Anthropologists and folklorists look for myth, ritual, and collective memory in rural backwaters, in exotic places, and among the lower orders of society, ignoring evidence of their existence much closer to home.

As Paul Cohen puts it, stories like that of King Goujian form an "undercurrent of meaning flowing beneath the surface of conventionally recounted history." The goal of his book is to bring this wellspring of Chinese politics and culture to the surface of consciousness, making it speak to and enrich history. The remarkable ways in which the story of King Goujian has animated twentieth-century Chinese life and politics suggest that the Western Enlightenment project that resulted in the radical separation of history from folklore, literature, and memory never had the same impact in China. While subject to defeats and disasters as far reaching as anything that ever happened in the West, the sense of rupture with the past has been absent. The Chinese notion of history as a series of long cycles, essentially continuous in character, encouraged a turning to the historical record as a treasure trove of examples that has no real parallel in Western academic thinking. Even the Maoist version of Marxism sustained a dialogue with the past. While the Western tendency has been to distance the past, to make it strange, the Chinese have insisted on making it familiar.

The Chinese capacity to turn to a two-thousand-five-hundred-year-old story for inspiration has no parallel in the West, except within the context of religion. In both Judaism and Christianity, memory of distant events can come alive within certain liturgical and prophetic contexts. The story of Moses leading his people from exile has inspired remarkable modern movements like Zionism and the African-American liberation movement, but these are essentially faith based and do not resonate within the wider secular culture. There is no real parallel to the way that the story of King Goujian has entered into the public and private lives of Chinese; there is no historical figure who evokes the personal identification that ordinary Chinese people feel with Goujian, despite the fact that he was a monarch who lived in such a vastly different time and place.

China has not been immune to millennialism or cultic behavior, but the identification with Goujian bears no resemblance to the Taiping movement or the cult of Mao. What makes his story so appealing are those embodied details and images of a man who slept on what amounted to a bed of nails and rose each morning to taste the bitterness that motivated him to persist in the ultimate goal of avenging himself. The West has its tales of self-denial and perseverance, but its hero worship is of a very different order. Moses, Joan of Arc, and George Washington share many qualities with Goujian, but they remain figures enveloped with a sacred aura.

We do not identify with them in the same way as the Chinese do with Goujian. No American student would think of drawing inspiration for his exam preparation from Moses's ordeal in the desert, Joan's burning at the stake, or the miseries of overwintering at Valley Forge. Those experiences all belong to a past that is perceived as admirable but essentially inaccessible. The only Western figure who evokes emulation in the same way as Goujian is Jesus Christ, but those who explicitly identify with the pain of his crucifixion (flagellants, for example) are barely tolerated by the church itself, which maintains that the worship of Christ is supposed to stop well short of personal identification, normally regarded as a form of heresy.

What is striking about the story of King Goujian to someone outside the Chinese tradition is how utterly secular it is. The humiliation of the monarch is not divinely ordained, nor is his ultimate triumph anything but the result of human effort, his own and that of those around him. Paul Cohen does not tell us how his story has been inflected by Chinese Christianity, but it would seem that Goujian has never been invested with the sacrality with which both Judaism and Christianity have cloaked their particular heroes. In the West, folk memory has been systematically appropriated by established religion for its own purposes. Pagan heroes became saints, and oral traditions turned into sacred texts. Christianity has been at war with popular memory almost from its beginnings, regarding it as pagan or heretical, always in need of correction or censure. By and large, the written and archival practice of academic history has served the interests of both the church and the state, thereby cutting itself off from other approaches to the past.

The absence of a monolithic religious establishment in China may be one reason why popular secular memories not only survived, but had enormous purchase on popular consciousness. The Chinese practice of history seems to have been much more capacious, less dismissive of what Westerners consider to be "mere memory." Indeed, Paul Cohen's account would suggest that from the late nineteenth century onward Chinese historians have been active collaborators in the elaboration of stories like that of King Goujian. The Chinese practice of history seems not to have distanced itself from popular memory. Quite the contrary, it has consistently sustained and promoted it in various ways. If, in the West, folk memory was ignored and marginalized, in China it has been at the center of public and private discourse. This particular tale did not so much erupt from some suppressed oral tradition, but was long present in well-known texts. Goujian was never exiled from the present, nor was the ancient kingdom of Yue seen as a "foreign country." On the contrary, both were welcomed into the present to support a variety of political and personal agendas.

Today, memory has become a fashionable subject in both Europe and America. Everywhere historians are attempting to bridge the gap between their own approaches to the past and the consciousness embodied in popular memory. Scholars like Pierre Nora, Michael Kammen, and David Lowenthal have already challenged us to cross the divides between folklore, literature, mythology, and history, to question the disciplinary boundaries that have enforced their segregation from one another. To those, like myself, who have been involved in this project, the Chinese example provides many interesting insights. Clearly, the institutional contexts of history and memory remain very different in the West than they do in China, but Paul Cohen's illuminating treatment shows us how we might rethink our academic boundaries. With this book as an example, it should be easier to explore the hidden wellsprings of our own political and personal cultures.

John R. Gillis
October 24, 2007

PREFACE

ARTHUR MILLER ONCE OBSERVED IN REGARD to his 1953 drama *The Crucible:* "I can almost tell what the political situation in a country is when the play is suddenly a hit there—it is either a warning of tyranny on the way or a reminder of tyranny just past."[1] The reason for Miller's observation, of course, is that his play, although dealing with the late-seventeenth-century witch hunt in Salem, Massachusetts, was also a thinly disguised reflection of the playwright's outrage at the witch hunt of his own day (McCarthyism), thus making it serviceable as a metaphor for political oppression wherever or however it might occur. This resonance between story and situation, between a narrative and a contemporary historical condition that prompts those living in it to attach special meaning to that narrative, is what this book is mainly about.

Although such narratives can in theory be ancient or modern, fictional or factual, indigenous or foreign, the most potent ones are often those that derive from a culture's own past. Certainly this has been true in the case of China, where, from ancient times to the present, people have demonstrated a strong affinity for stories dressed in historical garb. The tale of Goujian (r. 496–465 B.C.E.), king of the southeastern state of Yue in the Eastern Zhou period, provides an intriguing example of just such a story, one that, in a wide array of circumstances, spoke to Chinese with exceptional force throughout the twentieth century. Although I first encountered the story while reading materials pertaining to national humiliation *(guochi)* in the first half of the century, it did not take long for me to discover that the narrative related to many other concerns as well. Prior to the late Qing, the main vehicles for transmitting the Goujian story, apart from the ancient texts themselves, were opera, historical romance, and other forms of literary endeavor (oral and written). After the turn of the twentieth century, however, the story began to be disseminated by a wide range of other means, including the newspaper and periodical press, school primers, mass education materials, spoken drama, and, later on in the century, radio, film, and television.

Although the story's core structure has persisted with little change from its first emergence in ancient times right up to the present day, like most ancient Chinese historical narratives, it evolved over time, some elements being reworked, others dropped, and still others added.[2] A favorite diversion of opera fans that was not part of the original story, for example, is the alleged romance between Fan Li, Goujian's top minister, and the ravishing beauty Xi Shi. The text of the story, in other words, in contrast with the relatively stable texts of a Chekhov play or a Jane Austen novel, was a soft or pliable one. In fact, to even speak of a "text" in the case of the Goujian saga is probably misleading. Oral transmission was still strong in China during the period when the story first emerged. And in subsequent times, much as in the trail of stories inspired by so many other historical figures about whom there is little reliable information (Joan of Arc comes to mind), the narrative was recycled almost continuously in response to the requirements of different audiences, different historical moments, and different authorial predilections.[3] The importance of the recounting of Goujian's life and career for Chinese during the past century and more, it is clear, has resided less in its embodiment of historical truth than in its many-faceted allure as a story.

During the so-called century of humiliation, lasting from the Opium War (1839–1842) to the Communists' 1949 victory in the civil war, a broad spectrum of Chinese, ranging from high Qing dynasty officials (Lin Zexu and Zeng Guofan) and major twentieth-century political leaders (Chiang Kai-shek) to lowly immigrants detained at the Angel Island Immigration Station in San Francisco Bay or struggling to make ends meet in the Philippines, found the Goujian story unusually compelling and, when faced with seemingly intractable personal or political problems, often looked to it as a source of inspiration and encouragement.[4] Even in the very different environments that prevailed after the Communists came to power and the

Nationalists retreated to Taiwan, the story continued to be influential. For example, it periodically emerged in Communist theatrical productions as a vehicle for the dissemination of political messages of one sort or another, and in post-1949 Taiwan it offered psychological and political support for the Nationalist goal of retaking the mainland.

One thing that this last assertion points to—and it merits underscoring—is the degree to which narratives like the Goujian story functioned as a shared *Chinese* cultural resource that went much deeper than political divisions. This struck home with particular force while I was leafing through the 1974 editions of the Nationalist government's Chinese-language textbooks for primary and middle school students. These were published in Taiwan while the Cultural Revolution was still in progress on the mainland and the ideological conflict between the Communists and Nationalists was at its most intense. One of the lessons in each work contained a rendering of "The Foolish Old Man Who Removed the Mountains" ("Yu gong yi shan"), an ancient fable the point of which was that, with sufficient resolve, any goal could be achieved, no matter how great the difficulty. Another lesson in the elementary school primer applied the fable to the engineering challenges presented in the construction of the Zengwenxi Reservoir in southern Taiwan.[5] What struck me was that this same fable was well known for having been promoted by Mao Zedong (1893–1976) during the Cultural Revolution—it was one of "Three Essays" that everyone was supposed to memorize—to encourage the Chinese people to tear down the twin "mountains" of feudalism and imperialism.[6] Different historical settings. Different meanings. But the story, part of China's cultural bedrock, was identical.

The Goujian story was as familiar to Chinese schoolchildren as the biblical stories of Adam and Eve or David and Goliath are to American youngsters—the story is "in our bones," a scholar from China said to me not long ago. Yet, despite its far-reaching impact throughout the Chinese cultural world, among American students of the recent Chinese past (those, that is, not of Chinese descent) it appears to be mostly unknown, while scholars of ancient Chinese history or literature, who know the Goujian story well, are unlikely to be aware of its salience for Chinese in the twentieth century. Manifestly, the story of King Goujian is one of those artifacts of cultural knowledge, found in every society, that "insiders," people who have been raised and gone to school in the society, are apt to have instilled in them from an early age as part of their cultural training, but that "outsiders," those who learn about the culture mainly from books or from having lived in the society for brief periods as adults, almost never run into (or don't notice when they do). As a result of this curious situation—a situation that suggests the existence of two quite different tracks for learning about a culture—the place of the Goujian story in the history of China over the past century has been omitted entirely from the work of American historians (and, as far as I know, Western historians generally).

What is odder still is that Chinese historians also appear to have overlooked it. Let me be absolutely plain here. Chinese students of the twentieth century, unlike many of their American counterparts, are intimately familiar with the Goujian story and keenly aware of the pervasiveness of accounts of (and references to) it, especially at certain historical junctures.[7] But I have found little indication that they see the relationship between story and situation *in itself* as a fit object for serious historical inquiry. A possible reason for this, in the case of the Goujian story in particular, is that such scrutiny might, in certain respects and at certain moments in time, be too sensitive politically. But a more fundamental reason, I suspect, is that most Chinese simply accept the existence of the story-situation relationship as a given. It is not, in other words, something that they have a high degree of self-consciousness about. The notion that stories even from the distant past can speak in meaningful ways to what is going on in the present is something that has been inculcated in them from childhood. They pay attention to such stories, therefore, for the guidance or inspirational value they may offer in the present, but there is little likelihood of their stepping back and interrogating the distinctive importance of the story-situation relationship *as such,* either in China or in other cultural settings.

There is another reason as well for the failure of historians to include the Goujian story in their accounts. This is that the story, for all its importance in other respects, contributes little to the history of twentieth-century China when this history is framed as a narrative of interconnected events. Indeed, it can be omitted from this narrative almost entirely—as it has been— without significantly altering the overall picture. (This is of course also true of many other aspects of intellectual and cultural history.) However, when we shift our attention to the ways in which the Goujian story has affected Chinese perceptions of their experience—a more interior perspective on the Chinese past—we get a very different sense of things. As the psychologist Jerome Bruner has stated, we "cling to narrative models of reality and use them to shape our everyday experiences. We say of people we know in real life that they are Micawbers or characters right out of a Thomas Wolfe novel." Such stories become "templates for experience." What is astonishing about these templates, he adds, "is that they are so particular, so local, so unique—yet have such reach. They are metaphors writ large" or, as he puts it in another place, "root metaphors of the human condition."[8] When the Goujian story is understood, in Bruner's sense, as a root metaphor—or as several such metaphors—it assumes a far more imposing historical presence than we would ever guess from the standard narrative accounts of twentieth-century Chinese history. It is this presence that I will be probing in the following pages.

The basic plan of the book, after an opening chapter introducing the Goujian narrative as it was known in ancient times, is to examine the ways in which the story functioned—the parts it took—as it percolated through Chinese history from the late Qing to the present. My interest, I want to be perfectly clear, is not primarily in how the story evolved *as a story.* That is a job best left to the student of Chinese literature. Rather, it will be directed to the rich variety of ways in which Chinese, sometimes instinctively, at other times more self-consciously, adapted the contents of the Goujian story to the requirements of different historical situations—and why this mating of story to history was deemed so critically important.

ACKNOWLEDGMENTS

THIS BOOK, AS SOMETIMES HAPPENS, began as another one. Initially, I wanted to probe Chinese sensitivity to national humiliation over the past century. However, in pursuit of this goal, I kept running into the story of King Goujian, which spoke not only to national humiliation but to much else as well. Clearly, if I stayed with the original plan, I would have to omit vital parts of the Goujian story's engagement with recent Chinese history, something I was increasingly reluctant to do. Elizabeth Sinn, to whom this book is lovingly dedicated, helped me out of this quandary by proposing that, instead of national humiliation, I consider writing on the impact of the Goujian story in all its facets. A simple suggestion, but also a radical one, as it meant a shift both in the book's specific focus and in the broader issues that would ultimately form its intellectual core—above all, the relationship between story and history. Although only half realizing at the time the scholarly adventure that was in store for me, I eagerly accepted Elizabeth's idea. In the years since then, she has responded patiently to my pestering about countless specific matters pertaining to the book, for which I am immensely grateful. But my main debt to her is for opening my mind to the possibilities of taking a turn in the road that I otherwise might not have chosen.

I benefited from the assistance of many other people also. Timothy Brook, Keith Schoppa, and an anonymous reviewer read through the entire manuscript and, in addition to offering much encouragement, pointed to ways in which the book might be improved. Parks Coble, Perry Link, Rudolf Wagner, Roderick MacFarquhar, and Merle Goldman supplied useful advice on parts of the whole. I also profited from audience comments following talks at Indiana University, Harvard University, the Chinese University of Hong Kong, the University of Hong Kong, and Wellesley and Carleton colleges.

Once word got around that I was writing a book on the Goujian story in twentieth-century China, a number of colleagues alerted me to references to the story that I otherwise would surely have missed; I thank each of these individuals at the appropriate place in the backnotes. Special mention must be made here of the kindness of my old friend Wang Xi of Fudan University, who, in addition to sending me periodic e-mails containing useful information on the Goujian story, prevailed on a Fudan graduate student, Qin Ling, to scour the Shanghai Library for unusual sources on the story. Qin Ling supplied me with a list of more than two dozen items, for which I am much in his debt.

I want to extend warm thanks to Lisa Cohen for photographing in Shaoxing the artwork that appears on the cover and for her skillful preparation of the digitized images for the book's black-and-white illustrations; Hue-Tam Ho Tai and Bonnie McDougall for helpful insight into the Goujian story and its influence; David Pillemer for leading me to some of the literature on storytelling in the field of cognitive psychology; John Ziemer for his usual judicious counsel on an array of bookmaking matters; Christopher Pitts for his deft copyediting; and Suzanne Knott for her expert handling of all phases of the book's production.

It has been a very special pleasure to work at last with Sheila Levine of the University of California Press. Sheila responded with keen interest when I first told her about the Goujian story over a meal some years ago and, once the manuscript was accepted, oversaw its transformation into a book with sensitivity and skill.

I am indebted, finally, to the staffs of the Harvard-Yenching and University of Hong Kong libraries for facilitating my use of their fine collections, which formed the basis for much of my research; the Fairbank Center for Chinese Studies at Harvard for the supportive and stimulating intellectual environment from which, much to my good fortune, I have benefited for almost half a century; and the University of Hong Kong's Centre of Asian Studies, which, during my frequent visits to Hong Kong over the past decade, has been my home away from home, generously providing me with a congenial place to work and making it possible for me to take full advantage of the university's rich offerings.

ONE

The Goujian Story in Antiquity

BEFORE LOOKING AT THE VARIETY of ways in which the figure of Goujian assumed meaning for Chinese in the twentieth century, we need to examine the story itself. In reconstructing the Goujian story, I have not been unduly concerned with the historicity of particular incidents or details.[1] The impact of the story in the twentieth century, as noted in the preface, derived not from its accuracy as history but from its power as narrative.[2] Nor have I attempted to trace the evolution of the story as it wended its way from ancient times on up to the end of the imperial era. This is not an exercise in Chinese literary history. What I want to do in this opening chapter is establish a rough baseline for what was known about the Goujian narrative in the first century C.E., the time when the first full-fledged version of the story (of which we are aware) appeared. To this end, I have consulted, either in the original or in translation, such basic ancient sources as *Zuozhuan* (Zuo's Tradition), *Guoyu* (Legends of the States), Sima Qian's *Shiji* (Records of the Historian), and *Lüshi chunqiu* (The Annals of Lü Buwei).[3] However, I have relied most heavily on the later (and highly fictionalized) *Wu Yue chunqiu* (The Annals of Wu and Yue), originally compiled by the Eastern Han author Zhao Ye from 58 to 75 C.E.[4] I have done this for two reasons. First, in comparison with the earlier sources, it is (as David Johnson correctly observes) "far more detailed and coherent" and contains "major new thematic elements."[5] Second, it had a seminal influence on accounts of the Goujian story written during the remainder of the imperial period and was a principal source, directly or indirectly, for many of the versions of the narrative that circulated in the twentieth century.[6]

The setting for the Goujian story was the rivalry beginning in the latter phase of the Spring and Autumn period (722–481 B.C.E.) between the neighboring states of Wu (in modern Jiangsu) and Yue (in modern Zhejiang), two newly ascendant powers on the southeastern periphery of the contemporary Chinese world. In 496 B.C.E. the king of Wu, Helu (alt. Helü), took advantage of the opportunity created by Yue's preoccupation with funerary observances for its recently deceased king to mount an attack. The new Yue ruler, Goujian, at the time only in his early twenties, counterattacked and employed exceptionally brutal tactics to defeat the forces of Wu. Helu was mortally wounded in the fighting, but before dying he summoned his son and successor, Fuchai (alt. Fucha), and asked him to never forget that Goujian had killed his father. Accordingly, after assuming the kingship, Fuchai devoted himself energetically to planning his vengeance against Yue. Goujian saw what was happening and, overconfident after his earlier triumph, asked his trusted minister Fan Li what he thought about a preemptive strike against Wu.[7] Fan Li, observing that Yue was not nearly as strong as Wu, urged the young king to be patient. However, convinced that he knew best, Goujian went ahead and attacked Wu anyway. The year was 494 B.C.E. It did not take long for Fuchai's armies to inflict a severe defeat on Yue at Fujiao (in the northern part of Shaoxing county in modern Zhejiang), forcing Goujian and a remnant army of five thousand men to retreat to Mount Kuaiji (southeast of modern Shaoxing city), where they were surrounded by the forces of Wu.

This was a critical point in the sequence of events. Goujian, facing certain defeat, was fully prepared, we are told, to fight to the finish, but his high officials remonstrated with him, arguing the case for a less suicidal course. In the interest of saving Yue from extinction, they contended, Goujian should do everything possible to bring about a peaceful resolution to the conflict, mollifying Fuchai with humble words and lavish gifts and even evincing his willingness to go with his wife to Wu as slaves of the Wu king. Swallowing his pride, Goujian, with much misgiving, acquiesced in this strategy. It was also decided that Fuchai's grand steward *(taizai)*, Bo Pi (alt. Bo Xi), well known for his greed and lust, should be secretly bribed with beautiful women and precious gifts in order to gain internal support for Yue at the Wu court.[8]

Goujian's servitude in Wu, together with his wife, began in the fifth year of his reign (492 B.C.E.). Fan Li accompanied them while the other top official of Yue, Wen Zhong, remained at home to look after the state's governance during the king's absence. During the ceremonial leave-taking that took place prior to Goujian's crossing of the Zhe River (the modern Qiantang River) into Wu, his official counselors, in an effort to console and encourage him, pointed to the historical precedents of King Tang of the Shang dynasty, King Wen of the Zhou, and other sage rulers of antiquity, all of whom had experienced great setbacks and painful humiliations in their day, but had ultimately managed to turn defeat into accomplishment and calamity into good fortune so that their merit was passed down through the ages. Goujian was encouraged not to berate himself or view his predicament as the result of personal failings; rather, he should endure humiliation for the sake of Yue's survival.[9]

Upon reaching the Wu capital and being brought into the presence of Fuchai, Goujian immediately knelt to the ground and performed a *ketou*** before the Wu ruler. He then acknowledged the shame he felt over his actions in the fighting against Wu and expressed his profound gratitude to Fuchai for sparing his life and permitting him, as a lowly slave, to sweep the dirt from the palace. He also asked Fuchai's forgiveness for his part in the death of the Wu king's father.

Fuchai's prime minister, Wu Zixu,[10] unable to contain his fury over the scene unfolding before him, admonished Fuchai, stating his disbelief that, in light of Goujian's wanton behavior at Mount Kuaiji, the king did not have him killed forthwith. Fuchai responded that he had heard that if one put to death someone who had surrendered, misfortune would be visited on one's family for three generations. His reason for not killing Goujian was not that he felt any affection for him but, rather, that it would be an offense against Heaven. The grand steward, Bo Pi, now stepped forward and, after criticizing Wu Zixu for his small-mindedness and lack of comprehension of the larger principles for ensuring a state's safety, spoke in support of the Wu king's position. In the end, Fuchai did not have Goujian killed; instead, he issued orders that the king of Yue was to serve as a car-

---

*Also *koutou,* a ubiquitous Chinese ritual denoting respect for a superior and involving knocking the head on the ground while in a kneeling position; the origin of the English word *kowtow.*

riage driver and tend to the horses. Goujian, his wife, and Fan Li were domiciled in a humble stone cottage in the vicinity of the palace.[11]

In their daily lives, Goujian and his wife wore the coarse clothing of working people. The husband collected forage and took care of the horses; the wife brought water for the animals to drink, cleared away the manure, and washed out and swept the stables. They went on in this fashion for three years, showing not the slightest sign of anger or resentment. When Fuchai climbed a tower in the distance to spy on them, he saw Goujian, his wife, and Fan Li seated by a mound of horse manure. He was greatly impressed that, even in these straitened circumstances, the proper protocol was observed between ruler and minister and the proper etiquette carried out between husband and wife. He turned to Bo Pi and remarked that Goujian was a man of integrity and Fan Li a dedicated and upright minister, and that he felt sad on their behalf. Bo Pi expressed the hope that the king of Wu would display a sage's heart and feel compassion for these poor, miserable souls. Fuchai then announced that he had made up his mind to pardon Goujian. Three months later he chose an auspicious day on which to issue the pardon and asked Bo Pi what he thought of the idea. The granting of grace was always rewarded, Bo Pi responded, and if Fuchai dealt generously with Goujian now, Goujian would be sure to repay his kindness in the future.[12]

When Goujian learned of Fuchai's plans, he was delighted. But he was also worried that something would go awry, and so he asked Fan Li to look into the matter by means of divination. Fan Li, after so doing, reported that he saw harm arising out of the situation and did not predict a happy outcome. As if on cue, Wu Zixu now approached the king of Wu and, arguing as he had before, urged him to have Goujian killed, lest Fuchai repeat the calamities suffered by the Xia and Shang dynasties. After taking into consideration the opposing advice of his high officials, Fuchai finally announced that when he had recovered from the illness that had long been plaguing him, he would pardon the king of Yue in accordance with the recommendation of his grand steward.[13]

One month later, Goujian summoned Fan Li and observed that in three months' time Fuchai had not gotten better. He asked Fan Li to use his divination arts to foretell the likely outcome of the Wu king's illness. Fan Li reported back that Fuchai was not going to die and that on a specified date *(jisi)* his illness would abate. He urged the king of Yue to take careful note of this. Goujian, announcing that his survival during captivity was entirely owing to Fan Li's stratagems and recognizing that the time had come for him to act decisively, asked Fan Li to suggest a plan. Fan Li outlined a strategy that he said was certain to succeed. Goujian should request permission to inquire after the condition of Fuchai's illness. If permitted to see the king, he should then ask leave to taste Fuchai's stool and examine his facial color. After so doing, he should kneel to the ground and offer his congratulations to the king of Wu, informing him that he would soon get well and would not die. When this prognosis proved correct, Goujian need have no further worries.

The following day Goujian asked Bo Pi to arrange an audience with Fuchai so that he could ask about his health. Fuchai summoned Goujian into his presence. As it happened, at the very moment Goujian arrived at the palace, the Wu king had just moved his bowels and Bo Pi was carrying the stool out when he encountered Goujian at the entranceway. Goujian greeted Bo Pi and asked if he might taste Fuchai's stool in order to make a prognosis concerning his illness. He then proceeded to stick his finger into the container and taste the stool, after which he went inside and announced to the Wu king: "The captive servant Goujian offers his congratulations to the great king. The king's illness will begin to improve on *jisi*. On *renshen* of the third month he will be completely well." Fuchai naturally wanted to know how Goujian knew all this. Goujian explained that he had formerly studied with an expert who made prognoses on the basis of the smell and taste of fecal matter and had learned about the correspondence between the taste of stool and the taste of cereal grain. When the taste of a person's stool was not in harmony with the seasonal taste of grain, the person was certain to die, but when the two were in harmony the person would live. He informed Fuchai that he had just tasted the king's stool and that the taste was bitter and sour. Since this taste was in keeping with the taste of grain in spring and summer, he knew that the king would make a full recovery.[14] On hearing this, Fuchai was overjoyed and announced to Goujian: "Truly you are a man of virtue." He pardoned him on the spot and told him he could leave the stone cottage and move into the palace, but he was still to tend to the horses and carry on with his other duties as before.[15]

Fuchai's illness began to improve exactly as Goujian said it would. Stirred by Goujian's loyalty and honesty, the Wu king ordered a banquet to be held with Goujian seated in the place of honor. On the following day Wu Zixu, appalled at Fuchai's conduct, went to the palace to admonish him. He warned the king about people who were outwardly friendly but harbored harmful designs in their hearts. He then went into a lengthy account of the real motives behind Goujian's behavior. Goujian "has started out by drinking the

Figure 1. Goujian tastes Fuchai's stool. Source: *Wu jiejie jiang lishi gushi* (Taibei, 1979).

great king's urine, but he will end up eating the great king's heart; he has started out by tasting the great king's stool, but he will end up devouring the great king's liver." The very existence of the state of Wu hung in the balance, Wu Zixu remonstrated. Fuchai must open his eyes to what was taking place. Having heard enough, Fuchai advised his prime minister to forget the entire matter and not to mention it again. He then went ahead with his plan to pardon Goujian, escorting him personally through the Serpent Gate on the south side of the capital and asking him, on his return to Yue, to always bear in mind his goodwill in forgiving him. Goujian performed a *ketou* and vowed before Heaven that he and his high officials would forever remain loyal to the Wu king and never turn against him. He performed another *ketou*. Fuchai raised him up and helped him into his carriage. With Fan Li holding the whip, they drove off.

As they arrived at the ferry crossing, Goujian raised his face toward Heaven, sighed, and remarked that he had not expected to live to cross the Zhe River again. During the crossing, he and his wife, overcome with emotion, covered their faces and wept, as the people of Yue greeted them joyously and the high officials of the state stepped forward to welcome them and offer their congratulations.[16]

Goujian's return to Yue took place in the winter of the seventh year of his reign (490 B.C.E.). The king of Wu had restored to Yue a piece of land one hundred *li** in circumference, with the boundaries carefully specified. Goujian remarked to Fan Li that for three years, as a prisoner of Wu, he had submitted to constant humiliation and that it was only because of his prime minister's wise counsel that he had been able to survive and eventually return to his native land. Now it was his wish to restore stability and calm to Yue and build a new capital on Mount Kuaiji. He asked Fan Li to take full charge of the undertaking. Fan Li ingeniously incorporated into the new capital's design a number of features that appeared to signify Goujian's continued loyalty to Fuchai. For example, in the construction of the outer wall, he left a portion of the northwestern side (the side facing the state of Wu) open in order to signal to Wu that Yue remained subordinate to it and had not built the wall for defensive purposes. But in keeping with Goujian's ultimate goal of vanquishing Wu and becoming overlord *(ba),*†

---

*A unit of length equal to about 1/3 of a mile.

†The *ba,* sometimes translated as "hegemon," was the top holder of real power in the declining Zhou dynasty.

Figure 2. Graphic depiction of "sleeping on brushwood and tasting gall." Although hundreds of variations on this image have been created, the bed of brushwood and suspended gallbladder are constants. Generally, such images contain only Goujian, but occasionally, as in this figure, other elements are added, in this instance the image of Goujian's wife at her spinning wheel. Source: Chen Heqin and Zhu Zefu, *Woxin changdan.*

Fan Li also secretly incorporated certain features reflective of this goal into the capital's design.[17]

After resuming his rule over Yue, Goujian, a different man from the headstrong, self-indulgent youth of only a few years before, governed in a respectful and circumspect manner, practicing strict economy and avoiding extravagance. Knowing that taking revenge against Wu was something that required elaborate preparation and could not be accomplished overnight, he worked incessantly, never resting his mind or body. When overcome with sleepiness he would use the sharp smell of knotweed *(Polygonum)* to keep his eyes from closing. When the soles of his feet were cold, he would soak them in even colder water to lift his spirits. In the winter, when it was freezing, he would often carry ice and snow in his arms, while in the heat of summer he would hold a hot brazier in his hands. Although the proverb *woxin changdan* ("to sleep on brushwood and taste gall") that became so closely associated with the Goujian story in the late imperial era does not appear to have come into use until the Song dynasty, already in ancient times we are told that Goujian hung a gallbladder in his room, licking it every time he went in or out in order to guard against complacency and to remind himself of the bitter suffering he had undergone.[18]

Since Goujian knew that Fuchai liked to wear comfortable, loose-fitting garments, he conceived the idea of dispatching people into the hills to gather kudzu vines *(ge)* and then having women use the fibers to weave cloth to present to the Wu ruler as a means of currying his favor. His ministers all thought this was a good idea, and orders were given to carry it out. But before the project was consummated, it had already come to Fuchai's attention that Goujian, since returning to Yue, had shown himself completely content with his circumstances. He was so impressed with Goujian's behavior that he decided to confer more land on him, augmenting Yue's territory to eight hundred *li* in circumference. To repay the king of Wu for this kindness, Goujian sent him one hundred thousand bolts of hemp cloth *(gebu),* nine wooden containers of honey, seven multicolored square-shaped vessels, five pairs of fox pelts, and ten boats constructed of bamboo. Fuchai, who had always regarded the remote and insignificant state of Yue as possessing little if anything of value, was struck by this tangible expression of Goujian's loyalty and consideration.

Wu Zixu, after learning of these developments, went home, lay down on his bed, and expressed to his attendants his forebodings concerning the future consequences of the enlargement of Yue's territory. But Fuchai, upon receiving the hemp cloth tribute from Yue, carried out his promise to enlarge Yue's land and also presented Yue with a banner adorned with feathers, a crossbow, and ceremonial garb appropriate to a feudal lord. The officials and populace of Yue were extremely pleased with the way things were going. All understood the Yue king's strategy for handling Fuchai and fully supported him in his efforts.[19]

Goujian made it clear to everyone high and low that they were not to talk openly of Yue's long-term plans. He led his people in replenishing the granaries and armories and in opening up new lands and plowing the soil, so that the populace might be enriched and the state strengthened. He also established a "brain trust" consisting of eight ministers and four friends, whom he regularly asked for advice on matters of governance. On one such occasion, Wen Zhong argued that the key to good governance was for the ruler to concern himself first and foremost with the well-being of the people *(aimin).* In response to this advice, Goujian relaxed the severity of Yue's

Figure 3. Graphic depiction of "sleeping on brushwood and tasting gall."
Another variation. Source: Zhao Longzhi, *Goujian*.

laws and punishments and reduced taxes and levies, with the result that the conditions of the populace improved and all were willing to "buckle on their armor" and go to war to advance Yue's interests.

In the first month of the ninth year of his reign (488 B.C.E.), the king of Yue summoned his five top ministers into his presence. He reminded them of Yue's past defeat at the hands of Wu, the abandonment of the Yue ancestral shrine, and his own captivity—humiliations that were known among all the states. His thoughts were constantly fixed on seeking revenge against Wu, just as a lame person thinks constantly of being able to stand up and walk or a person who has lost the sight in both eyes thinks constantly of being able to see again. But he did not know what strategy was best and appealed to his ministers for guidance. Although there was some variation in the advice now proffered him, the general consensus was that Goujian should not reveal his intent to seek revenge against Wu until the time came to strike. Fuchai was an arrogant man, consumed by self-love. The conflict between Bo Pi and Wu Zixu was a fatal flaw that, in combination with Fuchai's weaknesses as a ruler, would eventually bring about Wu's fall. But, for the time being, Wu remained militarily powerful. Yue, therefore, should build up its strength in secret while continuing outwardly to demonstrate its loyalty to Wu, waiting patiently for the time when Wu, having exhausted itself in fighting against its rivals, Qi and Jin, was vulnerable and could be safely attacked. Goujian, after listening to the advice of his ministers, concluded that the right time to attack Wu had not yet come and expressed the hope that all would continue to carry on with their duties as before.[20]

In the second month of the tenth year of his reign (487 B.C.E.), Goujian assembled all of his ministers. Still weighed down by his past humiliation and hunger for revenge, he had accepted the advice of his highest officials and begun the process of enriching the populace and strengthening the state. But it was now several years since his return to Yue,[21] and he had not heard of any warriors who were prepared to lay down their lives for him or officials who were able to avenge the wrongs and wipe out the humiliations he had suffered. Venting his impatience and frustration, Goujian faulted his ministers with being easy to get but hard to use.[22]

Jiran (alt. Jiyan), a young, low-ranking official seated toward the rear, raised his hand and walked quickly up to the Yue king. "Wrong," he said, boldly challenging Goujian, "the king's words are wrong. It isn't that ministers are easy to get but hard to use; rather, the problem lies in the king's failure to use his ministers properly." Goujian was not happy to hear this and a look of shame crept over his face. He asked the other officials to withdraw and proceeded to question Jiran alone. Jiran observed that Fan Li had an excellent understanding of internal affairs while Wen Zhong was farsighted and skilled at prediction in external matters. He expressed the hope that the king would summon Wen Zhong and engage him in a full and comprehensive discussion, which he was sure would result in a plan for realizing Goujian's ultimate goal of becoming overlord.[23]

Goujian called Wen Zhong in and, noting that this minister's advice had saved him from difficult situations in the past, asked him to recommend a plan for taking revenge against Wu. Wen Zhong replied that if Goujian wished to destroy Wu, the first thing to do would be to determine Fuchai's desires and indulge them; only after so doing would it be possible to acquire Wu's land and wealth. More concretely, there were nine stratagems for the king to consider—stratagems that had been used by King Tang of Shang and King Wen of Zhou in the course of their efforts to become kings, and by Duke Huan of Qi and Duke Mu of Qin in the course of their efforts to become overlords. As a result of their use of these stratagems, the conquest and occupation of a city or town had been as easy for them as removing their shoes. Wen Zhong hoped that Goujian would adopt the same measures himself.

The nine stratagems were as follows: (1) venerate Heaven and Earth and serve the ghosts and spirits respectfully so as to obtain the blessing and protection of each; (2) make gifts of valuable and expensive goods to the ruler of the enemy state and use large quantities of gold, jade, cotton, and silk to curry favor with the enemy state's ministers; (3) deplete the enemy state's granaries by purchasing fodder and grain from it at a high price and debilitate its population by indulging the enemy's desires; (4) present the enemy ruler with beautiful women in order to confound his thinking and disrupt his plans; (5) send skilled artisans and craftsmen and high-quality wood to the enemy state to enable it to construct palaces and towers and thereby exhaust its financial resources; (6) buy off enemy officials who are good at flattery to weaken the enemy's defenses against attack; (7) embolden enemy officials who dare to voice outspoken criticism to their ruler's face so that the ruler will force them to commit suicide; (8) bring prosperity to the king's own land and equip its armies with the best weapons; (9) train the king's own soldiers well so that they are ready to attack when the enemy forces have weakened.

If the king of Yue kept these nine stratagems secret, Wen Zhong concluded, and if he used his intelligence to gain complete mastery over them, the whole world was his for the asking. What difficulty, then, should he have in bringing the lone state of Wu to its knees? Goujian was delighted with Wen Zhong's advice and immediately set about implementing the first stratagem, establishing shrines in a number of places to make sacrificial offerings to the gods in order to secure their support. During the many months in which he made such offerings, Yue was protected against adversity.

When Goujian asked Wen Zhong what stratagem he should try next, Wen Zhong observed that Fuchai was obsessed with constructing palaces and towers and had his workmen engage in such construction nonstop. The king should therefore make a selection of the finest wood and present it to Fuchai. Goujian had his woodworkers scour the hills for such wood and, once located, instructed his workmen to cut, shape, polish, and decorate it. He then sent Wen Zhong to Wu to present the timber to Fuchai, who was, of course, overjoyed.

Fuchai's prime minister, Wu Zixu, on the other hand, was not pleased at all and entreated the king of Wu not to accept the wood. Formerly, he said, when Jie, the last ruler of the Xia dynasty, constructed the Ling Tower, and Zhou, the last ruler of the Shang, erected the Lu Tower, these actions caused *yin* and *yang* to be out of joint, winter and summer to come at the wrong times, and the grain not to ripen in the fields, resulting in calamities that brought privation to the people and misfortune to the state. In the end, these two rulers occasioned their own destruction. If Fuchai accepted the presentation from Yue, it would surely spell the end for the state of Wu.

Fuchai, predictably, paid no heed to Wu Zixu's remonstrance. He accepted the timber from Yue and incorporated it into the Gusu Palace,* which took five years to complete. The tower was so high that from the top one could see two hundred *li* in every direction. The workers recruited to construct it underwent enormous hardship and suffering. The common people were in a state of utter exhaustion, unable to earn a livelihood; the nobility were overcome with anguish. "Excellent," exclaimed Goujian, elated by how well the second of Wen Zhong's stratagems had worked.[24]

In the eleventh year of his reign (486 B.C.E.) Goujian was still fixated on taking his revenge. He summoned Jiran and told him that although he wanted to attack Wu, he was worried that he might not be successful and therefore sought his guidance. Jiran responded with general advice about

---

Gusu tai in Chinese. The primary characteristic of the building was its great height; *tai* can be translated as "tower," but since the *Gusu tai* appears to have been used primarily as a royal dwelling, I have translated it as "palace."

preparing well in advance, making sure to select an auspicious time, and so on. When Goujian pressed him for more specific direction, Jiran elaborated on the four rules of death and the four rules of life, explaining them in terms of the relationship between the changing of the seasons and the agricultural cycle. Goujian asked Jiran how it was that one so young in years was so full of wisdom, to which Jiran, with characteristic immodesty, replied that ability and virtue had nothing to do with age. Goujian put his young minister's views into operation, and in three years' time the supply of grain in Yue increased fivefold and the state was well on the way to prosperity. The king exclaimed that if he became overlord, it would be because of Jiran's sage counsel.[25]

In the twelfth year of his reign (485 B.C.E.) Goujian told Wen Zhong that he had heard that Fuchai had a weakness for beautiful women and that, when indulging this passion, he completely disregarded the administering of his realm. The Yue king wondered whether by exploiting this failing it might not be possible to undermine Wu's defenses. Wen Zhong replied in the affirmative and, adding that Yue could count on the eloquence of the grand steward Bo Pi to weaken Fuchai even further, urged Goujian to select two beautiful women for presentation to the king of Wu. Accepting this advice, Goujian dispatched someone skilled at reading faces to scour the land. At Ningluo Mountain this person discovered two beautiful maidens, Xi Shi and Zheng Dan, and brought them back to the capital, where they were fitted with silk clothing and taught how to move gracefully and convey feeling in their facial expressions. Housed in a place several *li* east of Kuaiji, they practiced these things for three years, at which point they had become proficient enough to be presented to the king of Wu.[26]

Goujian ordered Fan Li to escort the two beauties to Wu, where Fuchai received them with delight, seeing the gift as yet another sign of Goujian's loyalty. Wu Zixu remonstrated with Fuchai, warning him of the trouble that would ensue if he accepted Goujian's gift. The Wu prime minister described Goujian as a man who, day and night, thought of nothing other than his desire to destroy the state of Wu, a man who paid heed to good advice and surrounded himself with men of virtue and ability. Goujian had already assembled a force of tens of thousands of men who were prepared to die for Yue. In the heat of summer he donned garments made of fur and in winter he fended off the cold with nothing more than light cotton clothing. If a man of such resilience and determination were allowed to remain alive, he would surely become the instrument of Wu's destruction. Men of virtue and ability were a state's treasure, beautiful women the source of a state's ruin. Fuchai should take warning from the fact that beautiful women had brought about the downfall of the Xia, Shang, and Western Zhou dynasties.

Fuchai, ignoring Wu Zixu's cautionary advice, accepted the gift of Xi Shi and Zheng Dan. When this was reported back to Goujian, the Yue ruler exclaimed, "Excellent! That takes care of the third stratagem."[27]

In the thirteenth year of Goujian's reign (484 B.C.E.), the Yue king told Wen Zhong how pleased he was with the efficacy of the tactics thus far used to weaken Wu and asked what stratagem he should avail himself of next. Wen Zhong advised him to inform Fuchai that Yue had suffered a severe crop failure and wished to purchase grain from Wu. Goujian dispatched Wen Zhong to Wu with this message. Fuchai was strongly inclined, in light of the constancy of Goujian's allegiance to him, to grant Yue's request. Wu Zixu, convinced that the request was a trap, argued vehemently against accepting it. But his advice fell on deaf ears, leading the prime minister to solemnly predict that he would surely bear witness to the fall of Wu. Bo Pi now entered the fray, countering Wu Zixu's argument at every turn and accusing him, in Fuchai's presence, of being a small-minded official who in the past had consistently deceived the Wu king in order to satisfy his own interests and desires. Fuchai, finding Bo Pi's reasoning agreeable, announced that he was prepared to lend Yue ten thousand *dan* of grain, to be paid back when Yue experienced a bumper harvest. On Wen Zhong's return to Yue, Goujian gave the grain to his officials to distribute among the people. The following year, after the grain had ripened, the Yue king issued orders for the finest seeds to be selected and boiled. A quantity of grain equal to ten thousand *dan* was then transported to Wu. Fuchai was most pleased and gave instructions for the seeds to be planted. The farmers of Wu sowed the Yue seed, but since it had been sterilized it produced no crop, resulting in a severe famine.[28]

Goujian, observing that Wu was in straitened circumstances, thought that this might be a propitious time to attack his nemesis. More than a decade had elapsed since his humiliating defeat at Mount Kuaiji and he was impatient for revenge. Wen Zhong, however, advised against any immediate action. Although it was true, he said, that Wu had begun to feel the pinch of poverty, it still had loyal ministers at court and Heaven had yet to give a clear signal concerning its fate. It was best, therefore, to wait for a more opportune moment.

Goujian then spoke with his prime minister. Fan Li had assembled boats and chariots for combat, the king noted, but these were defenseless against swords, spears, and bows and arrows. Was it possible, he wondered, that Fan Li in his military planning had omitted something important? Fan Li replied that the great rulers of ancient times had all excelled at warfare, but in such specific matters as the arrangement of battle formations, the commanding of troops, and the beating of drums to signal advance and retreat, the difference between success and failure hinged entirely on the military skills of the troops themselves. Fan Li knew of a maiden from the forests of southern Yue whose swordsmanship was praised by all, and he urged the Yue ruler to send for her. Goujian thereupon sent emissaries to invite the maiden to come to the capital to demonstrate her skill in the use of the sword and halberd.

When the maiden arrived at court, Goujian asked her about her sword-handling skills. She told him that she had grown up in a wild, sparsely inhabited area, where there was no opportunity for formal study, but that her secret passion had always been swordplay. Nobody had instructed her. Her mastery had come all of a sudden out of nowhere. Goujian asked her for a detailed account of her technique. The maiden said that her technique was subtle yet quite simple, but that the meaning was veiled and profound. She then supplied a more elaborate explanation, concluding that after attaining proficiency in her technique one person could subdue a hundred persons in combat. Goujian was so delighted to hear all of this that he instantly gave the girl the name "Maiden of Yue" (Yue nü). He then issued orders for the commanding officers and best soldiers in his army to take instruction in sword-handling skills from her and, after achieving mastery, transmit them to the rank and file. Everyone at the time acclaimed the swordsmanship of the Maiden of Yue.[29]

Fan Li next recommended an outstanding archer from the state of Chu named Chen Yin. When Chen Yin arrived at court, the king plied him with one question after another. He wanted to know about the origins of the bow and arrow, the history of its construction, the design of the crossbow, the methods for achieving accuracy in shooting, the rules for aiming at a target from a distance, and the techniques for releasing several arrows simultaneously or one arrow at a time. Chen Yin supplied detailed answers to all of Goujian's questions, holding nothing back. The king was elated and asked him if he would teach everything he knew to the warriors of Yue. Chen Yin replied that the secret to archery was hard work. If a person practiced diligently, he would be successful. Goujian thereupon sent Chen Yin to the capital's northern outskirts to give instruction to the Yue army, and after three months had passed the entire army had mastered the techniques.

Figure 4. The Maiden of Yue teaching swordsmanship to a Yue soldier. Source: Xiao Jun, *Wu Yue chunqiu shihua* 2:467.

Later, when Chen Yin died, Goujian was greatly saddened. He had him buried on a hill west of the capital and named it Chen Yin Hill.[30]

In the fifteenth year of his reign (482 B.C.E.), Goujian told Wen Zhong that he had persuaded the people of Yue to fully support an attack on Wu and asked him whether Heaven had yet provided a sign authorizing such action. Wen Zhong said that the source of Wu's strength all along had been the presence of Wu Zixu at court. Now, as a result of Wu Zixu's blunt and forthright remonstrations, Fuchai had ordered him to commit suicide.[31] This was a sign from Heaven indicating that the time was ripe for Yue to attack Wu. Wen Zhong expressed the hope, therefore, that the king would devote himself wholeheartedly to preparing the people for war.

Goujian launched into a lengthy summation of all the things he had done over the years to win the hearts of the Yue people.[32] He had begun, he reminded Wen Zhong, by publicly apologizing for having recklessly made an enemy of a large state (Wu) without first taking adequate account of Yue's own military circumstances (referring to Yue's catastrophic defeat at Fujiao). He assumed full responsibility for this failure, which had resulted in large-scale casualties among the people, and promised to amend his policies and methods of governing in the future. A major facet of the ensuing change had been his concerted effort to identify with the people of Yue and become intimately involved in their lives. He buried those who had died in battle, expressed sympathy and solicitude for the wounded, offered his condolences to the families of the bereaved and his congratulations to those marking happier occasions, saw people off who left for other states, and welcomed those who came from elsewhere to Yue.

After having brought an end to the disasters his people had suffered, Goujian had humbled himself by going to Wu to serve under Fuchai. Then, following his release from servitude and his receipt from the Wu king of a small piece of territory, one of his first acts had been to call the elders of the area together and announce policies designed to rehabilitate Yue. Seeking to increase Yue's population, he had forbidden young men to take older women as wives and older men to enter into marriage with women in their prime; he had made it a punishable offense for parents if a daughter, on reaching the age of seventeen, had still not been married off, or a son, on turning twenty, had still not taken a wife; he had made medical help available to pregnant women about to give birth; had rewarded the families of women who gave birth to two boys with a jug of wine and a dog, and the families of women who produced two girls with a jug of wine and a piglet; had provided a wet nurse to any family with a woman who had given birth to triplets and, in the case of families with women who had borne twins, had offered assistance in raising one of the children. To ease the lot of those who had suffered misfortune, Goujian had exempted from taxes and corvée families that had lost sons (the exemption lasting for three years in the case of eldest sons and three months in the case of younger ones),[33] and buried the deceased with tears as if they were his own offspring; he had also provided for state assistance in the raising of children who had been orphaned or whose parents were sick or impoverished; and when, on his tours of inspection, he encountered poor children wandering about, he had given them food to eat and soup to drink and shown them kindness and asked their names.

Goujian went on to note that he ate only grain he himself had grown and wore only clothing his wife had made with her own hands. For ten years he had collected no land tax from the people and every household had a three-year supply of grain stored up.[34] The men of Yue sang for joy, the women wore smiles on their faces. Every day the family elders beseeched him: They recalled that Fuchai had disgraced him before the other feudal lords and that the people of other states had long ridiculed him. Now that Yue had, owing to his efforts, become prosperous, wasn't it time for him to permit them to take revenge on his behalf and wipe clean the old humiliation? Goujian at first had rejected the plea of his people, saying that the humiliation he had suffered in the past was no fault of theirs and that therefore it would be inappropriate to ask them to avenge it. They had persisted, however, likening themselves to the king's children and arguing that it was as natural for subjects to avenge a hatred on behalf of their ruler as it was for children to avenge an enmity on their father's behalf. Goujian at last gave in to their urging.

Wen Zhong, reversing his earlier advice, now argued that the time was still not ripe for Yue to launch an attack against Wu. Formerly, he had thought that once Wu achieved its goals against Qi and Jin, it would next attend to Yue. But a year had gone by and Fuchai seemed to have forgotten about Yue. His armies were exhausted and his people were faced with such privation that, with the onset of winter, they would likely have to migrate to the shores of the Eastern Sea in search of food to fend off starvation. Wen Zhong's divination made it clear that, despite all of this, if Yue sought to take advantage of Wu's present difficulties to attack it, it would provoke Fuchai's anger and not turn out well for Yue.

Goujian was caught between the advice of one of his highest officials and the sentiment of his people, which for three years had favored war with

Wu. The elders of Yue now once again implored him to attack Wu, arguing that even if Yue proved unable to defeat its nemesis, the fighting would further exhaust Wu's forces, Fuchai would sue for peace, and Yue could form an alliance with Wu that would significantly enhance Goujian's standing among the feudal lords. Goujian gave his consent to this. He then convoked a meeting of all his ministers and issued a command to the effect that henceforth all talk opposing an attack on Wu would be severely punished. Wen Zhong and Fan Li consulted together and agreed to submit to the king's command, even though it went against their advice. Goujian assembled his armies and delivered a warrior's exhortation. The family elders of Yue were overjoyed.[35]

However, when Goujian again summoned Fan Li and asked him whether this was a good time to attack Wu, the prime minister said it would be better to wait until the following spring. Fuchai, he said, had gone north to Huangchi (in modern Fengqiu county, Henan) for a meeting with the other rulers and had taken his best troops with him, leaving the crown prince behind with a force of old and weak soldiers to defend Wu. But since he had left very recently and was still not far from Wu's borders, were it to be reported to him that Yue had taken advantage of his absence to launch a surprise attack, it would be an easy matter for him to turn around and come back. Better, therefore, to hold off until spring.

That summer—it was still the fifteenth year of Goujian's reign (482 B.C.E.)—the king again inquired of Fan Li whether the time was ripe to attack Wu; this time, Fan Li said yes.[36] Goujian thereupon dispatched a force totaling almost fifty thousand troops and engaged the Wu defenders in battle. The Wu crown prince was captured and immediately put to death. Yue forces then entered the Wu capital and set fire to Fuchai's beloved Gusu Palace. Messengers were sent north to report this news to Fuchai. But Fuchai, fearing that he would never be chosen overlord if the other kings got wind of what had happened, kept everything quiet until the meeting was over. At that point he sent emissaries to Yue to sue for peace, which Goujian, recognizing that he was not yet strong enough to annihilate Wu, welcomed.[37]

Six years now passed, and in the seventh month of the twenty-first year of his reign (476 B.C.E.) Goujian had once again readied the Yue military for a punitive expedition against Wu. But before acting, he sought advice from his top ministers and from a visiting official from the state of Chu concerning the factors most likely to ensure the success of his endeavor.[38] After hearing their recommendations, he withdrew to prepare himself for the offering of sacrifices to his ancestors and the gods. He sent an emissary to the Zhou court to announce his intention to punish an unprincipled state so that the rulers of the other states would not begrudge him. Then he issued a formal command to the people of Yue, announcing that those who reported for action within five days were his subjects in good standing, while those who took more than five days to report were not his subjects and would be punished with death.

After issuing this command, Goujian went into the palace to give final instructions to his wife. Henceforth, he told her, internal palace matters were not to be reported outside and external military matters were not to be communicated to people in the palace. If something disgraceful happened in the palace, that was her responsibility; if, far away from Yue, his armies were humiliated in battle, that was his responsibility. He warned her not to take lightly what he had said. After leaving the inner palace, Goujian met with his ministers in the outer court. He warned them that if they were not equitable in their provisioning of the scholar class and if the agricultural lands were not brought under cultivation properly, resulting in a disgrace to him on the home front, the onus would be on them; if his soldiers did not engage the enemy or if when fighting they were afraid to die, resulting in the humiliation of Yue before the other feudal lords and the sullying of its past achievements before the world, the responsibility for that would be his. Henceforth, matters of domestic governance were not to be communicated outside Yue and external military matters were not to be reported to people at home.[39]

Goujian took seriously the need to instill fear into the Yue army. In the course of reviewing his forces prior to leaving the capital, he had three criminals publicly beheaded and then announced to the troops that this was the treatment that would be meted out to those who disobeyed his orders. The following day, in the countryside outside the city, he had three more criminals put to death and repeated the same announcement. He then invited family members who had come from other parts to bid their sons and brothers farewell and ordered those who lived in the capital to come out and say good-bye to their sons and brothers. Those present, grieving in the knowledge that they were likely never to see their loved ones again, composed a song to boost the men's spirits and remind everyone that the object of the expedition was to wipe clean the humiliation their king had suffered years before. The following day, with his army camped at the Yue border, Goujian again had three criminals beheaded in the presence of all as a warning to those who did not submit to his commands. Three days later, after taking his forces to Zuili (in modern Jiaxing county, Zhejiang), he again had three criminals beheaded, announcing to the troops that this was how those whose thoughts and behavior were wicked and who were unable to withstand the enemy were to be dealt with.

Then the Yue king, showing his more compassionate side, ordered his officials to make a survey of the entire army to find out the names of all soldiers with parents but no brothers. Because of the important punitive expedition in which they were taking part, he had caused them to be separated from the parents who had raised them and family members of the older generation who had nurtured and loved them to throw themselves into the task of meeting a grave danger to the state of Yue. He wanted them to know that if, during the time that they were engaged in fighting the enemy, one of their parents were to fall ill, he would deal with it as if it were his own parent, and if a parent were unfortunately to die, he would carry the coffin and bury that parent as if it were his own.[40] A few days later, Goujian, after moving his armies to Jiangnan, demonstrated both the hard and soft sides of his complex character. After having five more criminals beheaded, he declared to his warriors that he cherished them as much as if they were his own sons, but that if someone committed a capital offense, even if it were his own son, he could not pardon it.

For all his severity, Goujian worried that if his warriors were motivated only by fear of punishment and not by heartfelt conviction, it would be hard to mold them into an effective fighting force. He felt that he had still not succeeded in instilling in them a true spirit of willingness to risk their lives for something larger than themselves. Just as he was mulling this over, he spied a frog by the roadside, beating its belly in anger and filled with the spirit of one about to do battle. Goujian stood up in his carriage and saluted the frog. When one of his soldiers asked him why he was showing respect for a miserable little creature, he said that he had long hoped for an expression of anger on the part of his men but had not yet found any who were in full concurrence with his mission. The frog he had just seen was an ignorant animal, but when it encountered an enemy it became infuriated, and so he had shown it a sign of respect. Upon hearing of this incident, all of the warriors committed themselves to a spirit of sacrifice and resolved to lay down their lives for their king.[41]

In the ensuing months, Yue, with Goujian in command, engaged Wu in battle after battle, each time emerging victorious, and finally besieging Fuchai's forces in the western part of the Wu capital. Initially Goujian wanted to enter the Wu capital via the Xu Gate (the entrance on the south side of the city). As his men approached the gate, however, they looked up and saw suspended from the top of the south wall the head of Wu Zixu, as large as a chariot wheel, with flashing eyes and hair hanging downward on all sides, so incandescent that it could be seen from a distance of ten *li*. Terrified, the Yue armies stopped and camped for the night by the roadside. At midnight a terrific storm suddenly struck, causing grave damage and forcing the troops to retreat to Songling. The bodies of the dead lay all about and the troops scattered in every direction, yet there was no way to bring the devastation to a halt.

At this juncture, Fan Li and Wen Zhong, removing their upper garments and performing a *ketou,* expressed their gratitude to Wu Zixu and begged him to show them a way out of the disaster consuming the Yue force.* Wu Zixu then appeared to them in a dream. He told them that he had long known that the Yue armies were certain to attack the Wu capital and therefore, just before dying, had requested that his head be placed atop the south wall of the city so that he could personally witness the destruction of Wu. His only thought at the time had been to put Fuchai in a difficult position. But when the Yue force was on the point of entering the Wu capital, it was too painful for him to bear and so he had created a horrific storm to frighten Yue into retreating. The fact was, however, that Yue's punishment of Wu was Heaven's will and was not something he could stop. If the Yue army wished to enter the Wu capital, it should alter its plan and go in via the east gate, which he himself would open. The following day, acting on Wu Zixu's instructions, the Yue army made its way to the east gate and surrounded the army of Wu.[42]

Goujian's army persisted in the war against Wu for three years,[43] winning one engagement after another and eventually forcing Fuchai to hide away on the top of Mount Guxu (alt. Gusu or Guyu; located southwest of Suzhou in modern Jiangsu). The Wu ruler then sent an emissary to make peace with Goujian, recalling that years before he, Fuchai, had given offense to Goujian at Mount Kuaiji and that he would not now dare to flout the Yue king's command. If Goujian wished to lead his army forward to attack him, he would submit; alternatively, if Goujian was willing to pardon him, he was prepared, along with his ministers, to enter a condition of servitude under the Yue king, much as Goujian himself had earlier done in the aftermath of the Mount Kuaiji affair.

*To strip off one's upper garments was a ritual demonstration of submission, used to apologize for an offense and request forgiveness. See Huang Rensheng, *Xin yi Wu Yue chunqiu,* 344, n. 5.

After hearing this, Goujian did not have the heart to treat Fuchai with the ultimate sanction and seemed on the point of accepting his offer of peace negotiations. However, Fan Li, observing that his king was softening, interjected that at the time of the Mount Kuaiji defeat, Heaven had bestowed Yue on Wu, but Wu had not accepted it. Now Heaven was bestowing Wu on Yue. Could Yue possibly go against the will of Heaven? What was more, the Yue king every day from morning until night had held court and attended to governmental matters, gnashing his teeth in pent-up anger. Was not the strategizing that he had engaged in for twenty long years directed precisely at bringing about the present state of affairs? Now that the object of all his efforts was in his grasp, how could he consider throwing it aside? If he did not accept what Heaven had bestowed on him, he would surely suffer Heaven's punishment. The king must not forget the misery he had suffered at Mount Kuaiji.

Goujian told Fan Li that it was his intention to follow his advice, but that he could not bear to respond to Fuchai's envoy in such a direct fashion. On learning this, Fan Li sounded the war drums and called in soldiers. He announced that the Yue king had entrusted him to deal with the matter and instructed the Wu envoy to leave at once or risk his displeasure. The envoy left in tears. Taking pity on Fuchai, Goujian then sent an envoy to Mount Guxu to tell the Wu king that he was willing to arrange for him and his wife to go to Yongdong (Zhoushan Island in modern Zhejiang) to live and would allot them three hundred families to wait upon them for the rest of their days. Fuchai rejected Goujian's offer, saying that the calamity that Heaven had unleashed on Wu had taken place while he was on the throne. His altars to the earth and grain gods and his ancestral temple had been destroyed and Wu's land and people already incorporated into the state of Yue. He was an old man and unable to become Goujian's servant. He then took a sword and killed himself.[44]

After Yue's destruction of Wu (473 B.C.E.), Goujian led his armies north across the Yangzi and Huai rivers. He met with the rulers of Qi and Jin in Xuzhou (in the state of Qi, south of Teng county in modern Shandong) and also presented tribute to the Zhou court. After his new status was confirmed by the Zhou king, he returned with his troops to Jiangnan. He conferred territory in the Huai River valley on Chu; he restored to Song the lands originally belonging to it that Wu had conquered; and he conferred on Lu an area one hundred *li* in circumference in the southeastern part of modern Shandong. At this point in time the Yue armies had free run of the entire area encompassed by the Huai and Yangzi river valleys.

The rulers of the other states offered their congratulations to Goujian and proclaimed him overlord.[45]

As he was about to lead his army back to Wu, Goujian turned to Fan Li and asked his prime minister how it was that his advice always accorded with the Way of Heaven. Fan Li replied that it was because his counsel was based on the theories of the goddess Su Nü (an alleged contemporary of the Yellow Emperor). After he had elaborated further on this, Goujian asked whether, if he were to proclaim himself *wang* (king),[46] Fan Li could predict the outcome. Fan Li replied that the Yue ruler must not proclaim himself *wang*. Formerly, Fuchai had done that, exceeding his proper status and transgressing on the title of the Son of Heaven (the Zhou king), and as a result there was an eclipse of the sun. If Goujian now, instead of leading his army back to Yue, decided to follow in Fuchai's path, it was to be feared that there would again be an abnormal heavenly event.

Paying no heed to Fan Li's words, Goujian led his troops back to the Wu capital and gave a great banquet at Wen Tower for all his ministers. He asked the musicians to compose a song in honor of Yue's destruction of Wu. After the musicians began, Fan Li and Wen Zhong joined in; Wen Zhong then offered a toast to the Yue king, the overall effect of which, while celebratory, was to emphasize closure: it was now time, he intimated, to return home and reward all the meritorious officials who had contributed to Yue's triumph. The other ministers, jubilant, all smiled, but Goujian, hoping to extend his successes still further, remained silent, a look of displeasure crossing his face.

Fan Li understood that what Goujian coveted was territory, and that for the sake of territory he was prepared to sacrifice the lives of his ministers. Originally Fan Li had intended, while they were still in the Wu capital, to take his leave of the Yue king at that point. But he decided that it was his duty to accompany Goujian back to Yue first. On the way back he tried to persuade Wen Zhong that he too should leave, as Goujian was surely going to have him killed. Wen Zhong was unconvinced. So Fan Li wrote him a letter in which, characteristically, he likened the ups and downs of human life to the cyclical course of nature. Just as spring was the season when things grew and winter the time when things perished, when the fortunes of men reached their high point, they were bound to move in the opposite direction. Although he, Fan Li, had no special aptitude, he understood well the principle of advance and retreat. When the soaring birds have been felled, the archer puts away his trusty bow; when the cunning hares have been snared, the good dog is thrown into the pot. Goujian was mean and sinister in appearance (literally, "long necked and sharp tongued"), with hawklike eyes and the movement of a wolf. You could share hardship and adversity with such a man, but not peace and happiness. Therefore, if Wen Zhong valued his life, he should leave. Wen Zhong, after reading Fan Li's letter, still was not persuaded.

On the day *dingwei* of the ninth month of the twenty-fourth year of Goujian's reign (473 B.C.E.) Fan Li requested of the Yue ruler that he be permitted to take leave of him. After listening to his prime minister's long, self-deprecating farewell speech in which he reviewed the high points of his service, Goujian, overcome with sadness, said that Fan Li's departure would be a terrible blow both to the state of Yue and to him. If he would reconsider, Goujian proposed to confer half of his state on him so that they could rule Yue together. If he remained steadfast in his decision to leave, however, his wife and offspring would be punished with death. Fan Li said that his decision was firm, but asked Goujian why it was necessary to punish his wife and children. He urged the king to make every effort to act in a moral way and bade him farewell. Fan Li boarded a small boat and left; to where, no one knew.[47]

After Fan Li's departure, Goujian was most unhappy. He summoned Wen Zhong and asked him whether he should try to convince Fan Li to return. Wen Zhong said that that was impossible, that Fan Li could not be made to come back, and went into an elaborate cosmological justification as to why. Goujian, apparently persuaded, placed Fan Li's wife and children under his own care, conferring on them a piece of territory one hundred square *li* in size and announcing that anyone who made trouble for them would suffer the punishment of Heaven. He also had his artisans fashion a bronze statue of Fan Li, which he had placed next to where he sat so that he could discuss governmental affairs with him from dawn to dusk.[48]

Subsequently, Jiran pretended to go mad while the other ministers became more and more estranged from Goujian and no longer attended court in person. Wen Zhong, who was very concerned, also failed to appear in court. Someone then slandered Wen Zhong, saying to Goujian that, after having wholeheartedly assisted the Yue ruler in his quest to be proclaimed overlord, he was resentful about the fact that he had neither been promoted to a higher official position nor granted additional titles. Because he could not keep his anger from showing in his expression, he stayed away from court. At a later point, Wen Zhong himself came before Goujian and asked him, now that he had achieved his long-term goal of destroying the state of Wu, whether there was anything else that he was worried about. Goujian remained silent. In point of fact, there was indeed a problem. Duke Ai of Lu, who faced a revolt within his state, had sought Yue's assistance, but Goujian, worried that Wen Zhong might be plotting against him, had been reluctant to send his army away from Yue.

In the twenty-fifth year of Goujian's reign (472 B.C.E.), the king summoned Wen Zhong to court and asked him what sort of man he thought he was. Wen Zhong knew that this spelled trouble. He enumerated some of his qualities that he suspected had rubbed the king the wrong way, but said that he was not the kind of person who loved life and feared death so much that he would fail to speak his mind just because it might give offense. Formerly, Wu Zixu, just prior to being forced to take his life, had said to Fuchai that after the clever hares have been caught, the hound is thrown into the kettle to boil, and when the enemy states have been destroyed, the ministers whose planning brought this result about are inevitably put to death. Fan Li, on the way back from Wu to Yue, had told him much the same thing. Wen Zhong concluded by informing the Yue king that he understood his real intention. When his remarks were met by silence, he felt he had nothing more to say and withdrew.

When Wen Zhong returned to his residence his wife asked him what was wrong. Wen Zhong told her that the king failed to recognize his worth. The nine stratagems that he had outlined to Goujian and that had played such a critical part in Yue's ultimate triumph over Wu were evidence enough of his loyalty, but were completely overlooked by Goujian. He told his wife that he was certain to be called back to court and that that would doubtless be the last she would see of him.

Goujian did indeed summon Wen Zhong to court again and, as expected, handed him a sword with which to take his life. Wen Zhong, before doing so, caustically observed that in the future, during times of decline, loyal ministers would be sure to treat him as a trope for the devoted but unappreciated official. He then drew the sword and killed himself.

Goujian provided Wen Zhong with an elaborate burial in the hills west of the capital. After he had been in the ground for a year, Wu Zixu came from the sea and, passing right through the hillside, carried Wen Zhong back with him. Thereafter, the two men floated together on the surface of the ocean's waters. When the tide came in the first wave was Wu Zixu; the second wave following close behind was Wen Zhong.[49]

After forcing death upon the loyal Wen Zhong, Goujian was proclaimed overlord of the area east of the Hangu Pass (in modern Henan province) and moved the capital of Yue to Langye (in the eastern part of modern Shandong). Here he built an observation tower measuring seven *li* in circumference so that he could see the Eastern Sea and gathered around him eight thousand brave soldiers and three hundred warships outfitted with axes and spears. Before long he put out a call for men of virtue to come to Yue. Confucius, hearing of this, led his disciples to Langye to perform music on ancient instruments for the Yue king.[50] Goujian, in full military regalia, met him at the entrance to the capital, along with an honor guard of three hundred soldiers. When Goujian somewhat impatiently asked what Confucius could teach him, Confucius replied that he could convey the principles of governance followed by the Five Emperors and the Three Kings, and that it was his intention to do so through a performance of the instruments used in their day. Heaving a long sigh, Goujian said that the men of Yue were by nature coarse and without grace. When they went places they went by boat; at home, they lived in the hills. Boats were their carts, oars their horses. When they charged forward they were as swift and violent as a whirlwind; when they withdrew they were impossible to pursue. They were fond of weaponry and were unafraid to die in battle. What, he wondered, did Confucius have to teach such men? Confucius did not respond. He bade farewell and left Yue.

Goujian sent some men to Mount Muke (in modern Shaoxing, Zhejiang) to exhume the remains of his father, Yuanchang (alt. Yunchang), so that they could be reinterred in Langye. But when after three attempts the gravediggers finally penetrated the burial chamber, a violent wind blew forth sending sand and stones flying in all directions and preventing them from entering. Concluding that his late father did not wish to have his remains moved, Goujian abandoned the project.

The remaining years of Goujian's time as overlord were spent in military and diplomatic activities of one sort or another. In 465 B.C.E., when he was in his midfifties, he fell seriously ill. Summoning the crown prince into his presence, he recounted how Yue, with the support of Heaven and the gods, had grown from a wretched little state to its then triumphant position, destroying along the way the state of Wu and asserting its authority over Qi, Jin, and the other states to the north. But accomplishments of this sort, he cautioned, invariably carried their own warning. It was extremely difficult for the successor of an overlord to perpetuate his successes, and so the crown prince must exercise the greatest vigilance. After he finished speaking, Goujian breathed his last.[51]

The Goujian we encounter in Chinese antiquity is nothing if not compli-cated. In his treatment of the people of Yue following his defeat at Mount Kuaiji and again after returning from his three-year internment in Wu, Gou-jian demonstrated considerable sensitivity and compassion, introducing so-cial, economic, and legal measures designed to ease the lot of his subjects, enrich them, and earn their support. But he was also capable of unbeliev-able cruelty, not only toward his enemies but even toward his own people. The instances of this contained in *The Annals of Wu and Yue* are fairly tame compared to some of the stories that circulated closer to Goujian's day. Here, for example, is what the philosopher Mozi (468–376 B.C.E.), who was born around the time that Goujian died, had to say:

> King Goujian of Yue admired bravery and for three years trained his sol-diers and subjects to be brave. But he was not sure whether they had under-stood the true meaning of bravery, and so he set fire to his warships and then sounded the drum to advance. The soldiers trampled each other down in their haste to go forward, and countless numbers of them perished in the fire and water. . . . The soldiers of Yue were truly astonishing. . . . Con-signing one's body to the flames is a difficult thing to do, and yet they did it because it pleased the king of Yue.[52]

Another instance of Goujian's cruelty toward his own people came early in his reign when, in responding to the attack of King Helu of Wu, he sent three waves of convicted criminals toward the Wu front lines, where with a great shout they proceeded to cut their own throats. While the Wu forces stood stupefied, the Yue army launched a surprise attack from another di-rection, defeating Wu and mortally wounding Helu himself.[53]

As these examples suggest, Goujian was, perhaps more than anything, a man of war. The encounter with Confucius dramatically attests to this, as does much else in *The Annals of Wu and Yue*. But "warfare" for Goujian was not just a matter of bravery and brutally enforced discipline, of war-ships and swordsmanship and archery. As important as these things were, his strategizing also placed a great deal of emphasis on weakening his ad-versary in every conceivable way: economically, politically, socially, and psy-chologically. And, in the pursuit of this objective, guided by his ministe-rial advisers, he was not above (indeed, he took a certain ghoulish delight in) resorting to such tactics as deception, trickery, lying, and bribery.

Unlike his archenemy Fuchai, Goujian did not crave luxury. Both during his confinement in Wu and after, he demonstrated his willingness and ability to engage in the most humble forms of physical activity. He also acquired a reputation for his capacity to endure privation and discomfort, whether enforced or self-imposed. And, again in dramatic contrast to the king of Wu (and many another Chinese ruler over the centuries), he seemed impervious to the distractions of sex.

Perhaps the most intriguing dissimilarity between Goujian and Fuchai was in their relationships to their top ministers. Where Fuchai again and again rebuffed the tough-minded, unsentimental, truth-speaking counsel of Wu Zixu and followed that of the corrupt and self-serving Bo Pi, Goujian, both during and after his captivity, attached great weight to the advice of Fan Li and Wen Zhong and repeatedly expressed his gratitude to them for their loyal service. He did not, moreover, rely solely on these two dedicated officials; he also showed himself ready and willing to accept instruction from other less likely sources. After voicing his complaint that ministers were easy to get but hard to use, he listened attentively when the brash, young, low-ranking minister Jiran told him that the problem was not that his ministers were hard to use but, rather, that he needed to learn how to use them better. He also welcomed with enthusiasm the contributions of people of unusual talent, regardless of their social background or gender, as long as they had skills that could be of benefit to Yue. In brief, Goujian exemplified in his behavior one of the qualities that Chinese political thought has always viewed as indispensable to successful rule: the recognition and proper use of people of ability.

But the relationship between Goujian and his ministers also had its problems. It became instantly clear to Fan Li—but not, alas, to the less-prescient Wen Zhong—that, once the Yue king had succeeded in the consuming goal of avenging himself against Wu, he would have no further use for either him or his other leading ministers. A few centuries later, after General Han Xin, through exceptional merit and cunning, had played a key role in enabling Liu Bang to defeat his rivals and save the newly established Han dynasty, a wise man from Qi, alluding to the earlier example of Goujian's treatment of Fan Li and Wen Zhong, tried to persuade Han Xin to revolt against the new emperor: "Your position is that of a subject, and yet you possess power enough to make a sovereign tremble and a name which resounds throughout the world. This is why I consider that you are in danger! . . . Merit is difficult to achieve and easy to lose. The right time is hard to find and easy to let slip. The time, my lord, the time! It will not come twice! I beg you to consider carefully!"[54] Han Xin was not persuaded. Fan Li also had no desire to revolt against Goujian. But he knew his master well and sensed, after the demise of Wu, that the unbridled ambition and envious nature of the Yue king would make life extremely dangerous for anyone in his entourage who had accumulated great merit. And so, demonstrating the resoluteness and sense of timing that were two of his most striking qualities, Fan Li left Yue and reinvented himself in another life.

The central story line that threads through the saga of Goujian is, of course, the quest for revenge.[55] This theme extends beyond Goujian himself. Fuchai, after Goujian's soldiers had mortally wounded his father, vowed to avenge this act—a vow that was consummated in 494 B.C.E. with his humiliating encirclement of Goujian's forces at Mount Kuaiji. And Wu Zixu, originally from Chu, left his native state and placed himself at the service of Chu's enemy Wu after the king of Chu had had both Wu Zixu's father and elder brother put to death. When the army of Wu eventually vanquished Chu, Wu Zixu (according to a number of accounts) dug up the king's body and "whipped it three hundred times before he stopped," in symbolic retaliation for the earlier wrong.[56] In both of these instances, resentment and hatred were triggered by the death of a father (as well as, in Wu Zixu's case, an older brother), so that the act of revenge may be viewed as an expression ultimately of filial feeling and obligation. By contrast, in the case of Goujian, it was an affront to the young king's pride and dignity, rather than the killing of an immediate family member, that was the triggering event. Instead of filial piety, it was personal humiliation that fueled Goujian's desire for revenge.[57]

Humiliation, as we have seen, is one of the more involved and complicated aspects of the entire Goujian story. As something externally imposed on the Yue king—the original defeat by Wu—it served as a crucial driving force behind Goujian's quest for revenge against Fuchai. But it also had a self-imposed aspect, insofar as Goujian, in order to realize his immediate and long-range objectives, willingly submitted to becoming a prisoner-slave in Wu; to cleaning his master's stables and driving his chariot; and, most stunningly, in an elaborately concocted ruse designed to soften Fuchai and win his confidence, to tasting the Wu king's urine and excrement for prognostic purposes. The self-inflicted dimension of humiliation also carried over to the period after Goujian's release from captivity, when, in order to build Fuchai's trust and allay any fears he might entertain concerning Yue's growing prosperity and strength, Goujian became the very picture of the submissive, ingratiating lesser lord. The core idea here, nicely encapsulated in the proverb *renru fuzhong* (literally, "to endure humiliation in order to

Figure 5. Wu Zixu whipping the corpse of King Ping of Chu. Source: *Shibao* (The truth post), Aug. 30, 1934.

carry out an important task"), is that there is a higher order of courage that will cause an exceptional individual to acquiesce in the most degrading forms of humiliation or indignity, if, by so doing, the possibility of attaining some greater end will be enhanced.[58]

Chinese history is filled with examples of this kind of courage. In the *Shiji* biography of Han Xin, we are told that in Han Xin's youth, when he was still a poor commoner, a butcher taunted him one day saying, "You are big and tall and love to carry a sword, but at heart you're nothing but a coward!" He insulted Han Xin before a crowd of people and then said, "If you feel like dying, come on and attack me! If not, then crawl between my legs!" Han Xin bent down and crawled between the young butcher's legs, prompting a roar of laughter from the crowd at his expense. Years later, after Han Xin had become one of the most important people in the empire, he summoned the man who had humiliated him and made him a military commander. "'He is a brave man,' Han Xin told his generals and ministers. 'At the time when he humiliated me, I could of course have killed him. But killing him would have won me no fame. So I put up with it and got where I am today.'"[59]

Another example, well known to every student of Chinese history, is that of the great historian Sima Qian (145–90 B.C.E.). As a result of his spirited defense of the general Li Ling (who after defeat in battle had surrendered to the Xiongnu), Sima offended the reigning emperor (Han Emperor Wu) and was offered a choice of punishments: suicide or castration. Although in such circumstances it was expected that someone of Sima's high standing would choose suicide, he opted instead for the dishonorable alternative of castration, preferring, as he wrote in a moving letter to his friend Ren An, to go to prison and live out his life in shame in order to be able to complete his magisterial *Shiji*.[60] "A man has only one death," Sima observed in the letter. "That death may be as weighty as Mount Tai, or it may be as light as a goose feather. It all depends upon the way he uses it."[61]

Sima Qian's comment on Wu Zixu's avenging of his father's death is interesting in this connection. King Ping of Chu, holding Wu Zixu's father, Wu She, hostage, had summoned Wu and his older brother, stating that if they came he would spare their father, but that if they failed to come he would kill him. When the brothers consulted, Wu Zixu said: "When the two sons arrive, father and sons will die together. How can this save father from death? If we go, it will only make it impossible for us to avenge this wrong. It would be better to flee to another state and borrow its strength to wipe out father's disgrace. To perish together is of no avail." Moved by

Figure 6. Han Xin crawling between the butcher's legs. Source: *Ertong shijie* 24, no. 11 (Sept. 14, 1929).

Wu Zixu's hard choice, which, although the circumstances were different, was not entirely unlike his own, Sima Qian ventured the following thought: If Wu had "accompanied [his father] She in death, how would he differ from an ant or mole-cricket? Casting aside a lesser duty, he wiped clean a great disgrace, and his name has endured through later generations."[62]

An example of a quite different sort, drawn from the more recent period of Chinese history, is supplied by Zhou Enlai. In May 1927 a left-wing Guomindang commander ordered his men to fire on strikers in Changsha, killing over one hundred Communists. His commissar, a Communist named Liu Ning, mounted a vigorous propaganda campaign to denounce the commander as a murderer. When Zhou, who was head of the Communist Party's Military Department at the time, saw Liu's posters in Hankou (where the left-wing Guomindang and the Communists had set up a rival government), he chastised him for exacerbating the already strained relationship between the Communists and the left-wing Guomindang. "What do you mean?" Liu protested. "Are we somebody's concubine? Are we to accept their spitting and beating without any right to speak up in protest?" "Comrade Liu," Zhou admonished, "we must be patient. For the sake of our revolution we must be very patient. For the sake of our revolution we can play the role of a concubine, even of a prostitute, if need be."[63]

Implicit in all of these examples is a distinction between two modes of behavior. One is marked by impetuosity and shortsightedness. Those who display it, unable to abide even for a moment an insult or affront, respond hastily and without reflection, satisfying an immediate emotional need or moral imperative, but in the process relinquishing (or at least jeopardizing) the possibility of achieving some larger, more important objective. In the other mode, which is completely different in nature, the emphasis is on forbearance and self-control. Its practitioners demonstrate infinite patience and thoughtful consideration of long-term consequences, coupled with a willingness to accept any indignity or humiliation or privation or embarrassment, provided that by so doing the chances of realizing an ultimate goal are enhanced.[64] Despite his periodic bouts of impatience, it was this latter sort of behavior that Goujian personified, enabling him over many years to rebuild Yue to the point where it was able to triumph over a far larger and more potent rival and thus avenge the wrongs it had repeatedly suffered at Wu's hands. Two and a half millennia later, this trajectory of success, so improbable at the outset, made the Yue king a powerful example for embattled Chinese in the twentieth century.

TWO

The Burden of National Humiliation
Late Qing and Republican Years

PATRIOTIC CHINESE IN THE LATE Qing and republican periods referred endlessly to the humiliations *(guochi)* their country experienced at the hands of foreign imperialism beginning with the Opium War. Indeed, in the republican era they even established days of national humiliation or shame *(guochi ri)* to mark the anniversaries of these painful episodes.[1] Such days, along with the sensitivity to national humiliation they reflected, constituted a major form of collective remembering and became the implicit or explicit focus of a vast *guochi* literature. Given the persistence of this open wound—a sense of grievance that not only failed to abate but kept being revisited—it is scarcely surprising that the Goujian story should bulk large in the minds of Chinese throughout these years.

THE LATE QING: POSING THE PROBLEM

The recurrent pain of national humiliation was one facet of the Chinese scene in the late Qing—and certainly it was the most important—that invited special interest in the Goujian story. But there was another aspect, less well known, that we should at least take note of. This was the widespread sense among Chinese intellectuals that the larger world into which their country had been thrust paralleled the Spring and Autumn (722–481 B.C.E.) and Warring States (403–221 B.C.E.) periods of China's own history in striking ways.[2] One reason for this perception was that from the late Spring and Autumn period until the Qin unification in 221 B.C.E., the Chinese culture area was not coterminous with anything that could properly be called a Chinese state but, rather, was divided up into a number of autonomous political units, much as has been the case with the European culture area in the modern era.[3] Another reason was that, as in the Spring and Autumn period and, even more conspicuously, the Warring States period, there was no effective restraint on the behavior of the individual political units.[4] In the world of the late nineteenth century, as it appeared to Chinese observers, might was the ultimate arbiter in interstate relations, not right.

The distinguished historian Lei Haizong's observation on the late Zhou conflict between Wu and Yue is worth noting in this regard. Lei saw Fuchai and Goujian as symbolizing an important shift taking place in the Chinese world at the end of the Spring and Autumn period. Fuchai, justifying his actions with the chivalric values of an earlier day, treated Goujian generously, not killing him and repeatedly resisting Wu Zixu's advice to obliterate the state of Yue; Goujian, in contrast, foreshadowing the harsher conduct that was to become commonplace in the succeeding Warring States period, availed himself of every conceivable stratagem to deceive his archenemy and, in his single-minded quest for revenge, was not satisfied until Fuchai was dead and the state of Wu had been completely destroyed.[5]

The parallel between the late Zhou and contemporary world situations would not, in and of itself, have prompted late Qing commentators to look to the Goujian story for guidance. The substance of the saga was all-important. A major theme of the story, as we saw in chapter 1, was Goujian's fear that the memory of the humiliations he had suffered would fade with time. He therefore took a variety of measures to ensure that this would not happen and managed, through such steps, to overcome the threat of complacency, eventually destroying the state of Wu and becoming the dominant leader of the China of his day. Forgetfulness and indifference, however, were not problems amenable to permanent solution. During the late Qing and the early years of the republic, they reemerged in a major way, and commentators, in their desperate efforts to awaken the Chinese public to this lamentable state of affairs, looked again and again to the example of Goujian.

An early instance of this was an article published in 1904 in the newly founded general magazine *Eastern Miscellany (Dongfang zazhi)*, the central theme of which was China's unresponsiveness to the repeated humiliations it had experienced at the hands of the foreign powers. The article, written by a member of the journal's editorial staff (under the pseudonym Fang-shi), begins by positing a number of broad theorems concerning states. It is in the nature of states, he asserts, to contend with one another, and in all such contention there are winners and losers. When a state is defeated and disgraced, it is deeply pained. This pain, however, serves as a constant admonition to seek revenge; the desire to be victorious never fades. He then observes: "It took twenty years [for Yue] to destroy Wu [*nian nian zhao Wu*]. . . . This is what is meant by the determination to lie on brushwood and taste gall [*woxin changdan*] and to never forget past humiliation [*wuwang qian chi*]." But for such resolve to be carried to a successful conclusion a people must maintain its moral fiber and persevere even in the face of great difficulties. Hence, if one wants to know whether a state will flourish or decline, one must look to the character of its inhabitants.

That such was the case, Fangshi continued, was evident from China's current situation, which was marked by external troubles of unprecedented severity. The heart of the problem, which he referred to as the "white peril," was not that China was historically unique in being subjected to repeated humiliation; other countries had been exposed to comparable indignities. The problem lay in China's failure to react. When the Muslims in the tenth century [*sic*] seized the place where Jesus was buried in Palestine, Christians viewed this as a great humiliation. In response, showing a willingness to die for their religion, they launched the Crusades lasting for almost two hundred years, and, subsequently, the countries of Europe underwent vigorous development. Again, when the Japanese, after shedding blood to obtain the Liaodong Peninsula in the War of 1894, were forced by Russia [*sic*] to return it, the entire population of Japan viewed this as a great humiliation. Never for a moment did they forget their hatred of the Russians, and now they have been victorious over them (referring to Japan's early triumphs in the Russo-Japanese War).

The contrast with China was stunning. When German soldiers violated the Temple of Confucius in Shandong in 1897, something the entire Chinese people should have experienced as the most egregious insult, there was not a whisper of protest. When the Russians occupied Manchuria, the final resting place of the rulers of the dynasty and an area of strategic importance, China offered no resistance. With no sense of shame in the face of humiliation, it treated a hostile act as if it were a friendly one. Even Korea, when Russian cavalry had recently violated its borders, attacked the Russians and forced them to retreat. If such a paltry little country could behave in this way, how was it that China was incapable of doing so? The answer,

Fangshi concluded, lay in China's imperviousness to insult and humiliation. If the Chinese people were to avenge themselves against their enemies, they must first develop a clear sense of national shame.[6]

There are two things that are of particular interest about Fangshi's piece. First, the author makes it plain early on that in his view the Goujian story—Yue's destruction of Wu after twenty years of patient preparation during which Goujian goes to great lengths to keep from forgetting the earlier humiliation Wu inflicted on Yue—supplies the prototypical model for how China should respond to foreign imperialism in the early twentieth century.[7] Second, Fangshi argues that the most serious problem facing China is not the humiliation it has endured at the hands of the foreign powers—this was something all countries at one time or another experienced—but its failure to recognize humiliating acts as humiliating. This was a note sounded with growing urgency by Guo Songtao, Wang Tao, Liang Qichao, and other Chinese in the last decades of the Qing.[8] It suggested in no uncertain terms that the people of China, by not heeding the example of Goujian, bore substantial responsibility for their country's troubles.

Later in 1904, a writer using the pseudonym Kexuan published an article (also in *Eastern Miscellany*) that pursued some of these same themes. Chinese, Kexuan began, had much to be ashamed of, but loss of territory and military defeat were not among them, for these were things that happened to all countries. What was unique to China, and truly cause for shame, in his view, was the deplorable state of the individual, the family, society, the nation, and religion, a situation that in each instance was due to the failure of Chinese education. In the conclusion to his piece, Kexuan revisited the point with which he had begun: "Taiwang moved to Mount Qi and became king *[wang]*; Goujian safeguarded Kuaiji and became overlord *[ba]*. Loss of territory and defeat in battle are only momentary humiliations. There is nothing in them to be ashamed of."[9]

In both the Fangshi and Kexuan essays, we have examples of terse allusions, which the readership of the day would be expected instantly to decode, on the basis of their familiarity with a common fund of stories from the Chinese past. Fangshi's use of the set phrase *nian nian zhao Wu* (literally, "it took twenty years to destroy Wu") does not mention Yue, but every reader knows that it is Yue that destroyed Wu after twenty years of preparation. Again, all will know that the phrase *woxin changdan* ("to sleep [or lie] on brushwood and taste gall") refers to the measures Goujian is alleged to have taken to keep his mind concentrated on the goal of achieving revenge. In the case of Kexuan's piece, Taiwang (Great King) was the honorific title later bestowed on Gu Gong Danfu, who was the grandfather of King Wen, the founder of the Zhou dynasty. According to the traditional account (found in the "Basic Annals of Zhou" in Sima Qian's *Shiji*), Gu Gong Danfu and his people originally resided among the Rong and Di tribes in a place called Bin in modern Shaanxi. At some point, after being attacked by his neighbors, he led the Zhou people on a great migration to Mount Qi in the central Wei River valley (also in Shaanxi), where he built a city, established a government, reclaimed wasteland, and developed manufactures, enabling the Zhou gradually to become strong and to prosper.[10] The equally telescoped phrase, "Goujian safeguarded Kuaiji and became overlord," refers of course to the whole train of developments that began with the Yue king's decision, when encircled on Mount Kuaiji, to sue for peace with Wu instead of fighting to the bitter end, thus establishing the groundwork (or at least a necessary precondition) for his eventual emergence as the most powerful leader of North China. The reason Kexuan puts Taiwang and Goujian forward as models is that, through foresight, intelligent planning, and persistent effort, they were able to turn their peoples' fortunes around in a dramatic way.[11] In like manner, in his own day, the author was convinced that the foothold imperialism had gained in China was in no way due to impersonal fate. It was entirely the result of the internal failings of the Chinese people—failings that, in his judgment, it was well within their power to correct.[12]

Although Fangshi, Kexuan, and others complained about the indifference to humiliation they saw all about them, there were many educated Chinese at the turn of the century who were anything but indifferent to China's plight. Such individuals also drew support from the Goujian story. Newspaper editorials referred to it in their critiques of Japanese and Russian territorial ambitions in East Asia.[13] A writer named Li Liangcheng reworked the story into a forty-chapter knight-errant novel titled *Traces of Righteous Ardor (Rexue hen),* which appeared in 1907. Deeply distressed by the inroads of foreign imperialism, Li made it plain in the very first chapter that his motive for creating this work was to encourage his compatriots to avenge the humiliations imposed on China.[14]

Late Qing observers, of course, in addition to being troubled by the foreign menace, also had other concerns, and the nature of these concerns had a direct bearing on what stories from the Chinese past they looked to for moral support. Dedicated anti-Manchu revolutionaries, to cite a prominent instance, were more apt to turn to the examples of the Ming loyalist Zheng Chenggong (1624–1662) or the Song patriotic hero Yue Fei (1103–1142) than to that of Goujian. Zheng (also known as Koxinga), who had used Taiwan as a base to resist the Manchu conquest in the mid-seventeenth century, was transformed by revolutionaries from a symbol of loyalty to a fallen dynasty into one of national self-determination.[15] Something very similar happened to Yue Fei, another icon of undying dynastic loyalty. In a famous poem that Yue is said to have written to the tune "Man jiang hong" (Red Filling the River), he referred to the "shame" *(chi)* of *jingkang* (1126; the year the Jurchen Jin wrested control of northern China from the Song) as "not yet wiped away" *(you wei xue)*. Good Goujianesque language. But then he went on to write, "My fierce ambition is to feed upon the flesh of the Huns / And, laughing, I thirst for the blood of the Barbarians"—images that had nothing to do with the Goujian story but resonated powerfully with the heavily mythologized, often extremely violent anti-Manchu rhetoric of the revolutionaries.[16] It was entirely fitting, therefore, that when Chen Duxiu, later to become a cofounder of the Chinese Communist Party, established a secret revolutionary organization in Anhui in 1905, he named it after Yue Fei (Yue wang hui).[17]

THE REPUBLICAN ERA: REMEMBERING NATIONAL HUMILIATION

The Qing dynasty was finally overturned and a new order brought into being in 1911–1912. In the years after 1912, however, China lurched from one crisis to another—Yuan Shikai's sabotaging of the young republic, Japan's issuance in 1915 of the Twenty-One Demands, the rejection of China's claims at the Versailles Peace Conference, the years of warlordism from 1916 to 1928, the impact of the world depression, the first civil war between the Communists and Nationalists (Guomindang) in the early thirties, and finally the Sino-Japanese War and the second civil war, lasting from 1937 to 1949. Although there were positive developments as well during the republican period, this was, for vast numbers of Chinese, a wretched time in which to be alive.

During these years of anguish and almost continually frustrated hope, one persistent theme was nationalism, a familiar expression of which was the appropriation, reshaping, and wide dissemination of stories of heroic figures from the past, with a view to shoring up sagging Chinese spirits in the present. As in the late Qing—and indeed as had been the case in China since remotest antiquity—there was a strong, almost instinctive tendency in these circumstances to match specific stories to specific situations. In the

Figure 7. Patriotic heroes venerated in the early 1930s. In the aftermath of
the Manchurian crisis of the early 1930s, there was an observable increase in the
children's magazine press of illustrated stories about historical figures who gave
their lives in defense against foreign invaders. This figure portrays the iconic
image of Yue Fei's mother inscribing the words "Absolute Loyalty in Service
to One's Country" *(jinzhong baoguo)* on her son's back. Source: *Ertong shijie* 31,
no. 10 (Nov. 16, 1933).

Figure 8. Patriotic heroes venerated in the early 1930s. Wen Tianxiang rejecting the Mongol emperor Khubilai Khan's (r. 1260–1294) request that Wen abandon the Song and become a high official on the Mongol side. Source: *Ertong shijie* 31, no. 11 (Dec. 1, 1933).

wake of mounting Japanese aggression in the 1920s and 1930s, interest was naturally revived in Zheng Chenggong, who had liberated Taiwan (since 1895 a Japanese colony) from foreign (Dutch) control in 1662;[18] and equally predictable, the Ming general Qi Jiguang (1528–1588), famous for having led the fight against Japanese pirates off the Zhejiang and Fujian coasts in the 1550s and 1560s, was now reconstituted as a Chinese nationalist hero.[19] Other figures from the Chinese past who were celebrated in the republican era for their heroic resistance to external invasion were the Southern Song scholar-official Wen Tianxiang (1236–1283), who was executed by the Mongols for refusing to capitulate to them; Shi Kefa (1601–1645), a Ming loyalist who died at the hands of the Manchus;[20] and, of course, Yue Fei, who was widely praised for his patriotism in Guomindang party propaganda and whose stirring words, "Give us back our rivers and mountains" (from the "Man jiang hong" lyric), were scrawled on walls all over occupied China during the Sino-Japanese War.[21]

The Goujian story, although also adapted in important ways to the anti-Japanese nationalism of the first half of the twentieth century, is not part of the above grouping. Why? One reason, surely, is that unlike these other patriotic heroes, Goujian lived at a time prior to the establishment of China as a recognized political entity. True, we think of the Zhou as a Chinese dynasty, and when leaders like Goujian acquired the status of overlord (ba) they regularly acknowledged the ritual paramountcy of the Zhou in a symbolic Chinese world. But China's political unification still lay far in the future in Goujian's day. We would never identify the Yue king as a "Zhou loyalist," and we certainly would not conceptualize the periodic conflicts between Yue and Wu as conflicts between a "Chinese" and a "non-Chinese" state.

It has been observed in regard to China that "whenever invasion threatened this otherwise civilian-oriented society, military heroes were resuscitated."[22] This applies to most of the patriotic heroes apotheosized in the republican years, including Goujian. But once again there was a crucial difference between Goujian and the others: Goujian alone was a king. Where, for the others, the quality of loyalty to ruler and dynasty was of overriding importance and lay at the very core of the original heroic image, it was a complete nonissue for Goujian (although, of course, it was very much an issue in the Goujian story writ large). This had an important bearing on how the story functioned in political China. Chiang Kai-shek (1887–1975) could admire Yue Fei greatly,[23] but as we shall see further on in this chapter, during the 1920s and 1930s it was with Goujian that he *identified;* the figure of Goujian, moreover, was widely perceived in post-1949 Taiwan as a stand-in for the Guomindang leader (see chapter 3). Conversely, as will be argued in chapter 5, the darker, more brutal Goujian who emerged after the triumph over Wu could be used to attack the despotic style of Maoist rule. In other words, because Goujian was the top person in the state of Yue and subsequently in North China as a whole, it was natural to link him, either positively or negatively, to the top person in either Guomindang or Communist China.[24]

One further reason for distinguishing Goujian from the other patriotic heroes canonized during the republican years was the prominence in his story of the theme of *guochi*. Although during the Spring and Autumn period *guochi* referred to the humiliation not of a nation but of a ruling house,[25] by the late nineteenth century the former meaning had already gone far toward displacing the latter. As national humiliation became increasingly central to Chinese political discourse, other heroic figures—an early example was Zheng Chenggong[26]—were also linked to this theme, but none anywhere near as consistently or steadfastly as Goujian. Consequently, during the years from the establishment of the republic in 1912 to the outbreak of the Pacific War in the late 1930s, as China experienced one humiliating setback after another (mostly at the hands of an increasingly assertive Japan), the example of Goujian was called upon again and again as a morale booster and guide to proper thinking.

A landmark event in this process was the Japanese government's secret presentation to Beijing of the Twenty-One Demands on January 18, 1915. The demands were originally divided into five groups, the fifth of which if assented to would have required the virtual transfer of Chinese sovereignty to Japan. As a result of intense Chinese opposition and international pressure, Japan eventually withdrew the fifth group. But on May 7 Tokyo presented the remaining demands in the form of an ultimatum and on May 9 the Yuan Shikai government acceded to them.[27] Yuan's own position at the time, not unlike that of Chiang Kai-shek less than two decades later, was deeply rooted in Goujianesque thinking. At a cabinet meeting on May 8, he acknowledged that although everyone would view the government's capitulation as a great humiliation, China's only course, in the face of Japan's greater military strength, was to root its actions in the spirit of "sleeping on brushwood and tasting gall" *(woxin changdan)* and apply itself in all spheres to national renewal in preparation for the future.[28]

The China of 1915 was very different from that of a decade before—between the early 1900s and the 1911 Revolution there had been a tremendous

Figure 9. The pain of national humiliation. This is the image that appears on the cover of an anonymous work titled *Guochi tongshi* (The painful history of national humiliation). The ax blade bears the characters for May 9, the date of China's acceptance of the Twenty-One Demands. Source: *Guochi tongshi* (1920?).

expansion of activist opposition to foreign encroachment[29]—and the public's immediate reaction to the Japanese demands and the Yuan regime's acquiescence in them was anything but indifference. The problem in 1915 was one not of indifference, but of staying power: how long the Chinese people (a term that I use here mainly to refer to the inhabitants of China's cities) could sustain a mood of anger and resentment and carry out actions built around these emotions.[30] Chinese newspapers began reporting the Japanese demands in late January 1915. By the end of February, telegrams of protest against Japan and in support of the Chinese government were pouring into Beijing from the provinces. Chambers of commerce, educational associations, and the press were particularly active in encouraging resistance to Japan. Boycotts against Japanese goods were launched. In February Chinese students in Japan and America held rallies and submitted petitions. In March there were mass protest rallies in Shanghai and other cities. In April prominent bankers and businessmen in Shanghai established a National Salvation Fund, to which Chinese from all sectors of society, including the very poorest, made contributions.[31]

It did not take long in this heated atmosphere for Chinese to begin to portray the Japanese demands as a "national humiliation" *(guochi)* and to enshrine either May 7 or May 9 as "National Humiliation Day," to be commemorated annually.[32] The slogan "Do Not Forget the National Humiliation" *(wuwang guochi)* was disseminated all over the country. At a meeting of students in Changsha, Hunan, a resolution was passed to request that newspaper and magazine publishers print the slogan above their newspaper or magazine's name, that shops be urged to place it on the paper they packaged their products in and on their signs, that theaters print it on their programs and paper manufacturers on their stationery, that major publishers (such as Shangwu and Zhonghua) stamp it on the covers of their textbooks, and that schools inscribe it on their signs and flags.[33]

What seems especially noteworthy about all this talk of "national humiliation" is that it was concerned above all not with the rallies, boycotts, petitions, and fund-raising efforts in progress at the time, but with people's consciousness. As early as May, in fact, intellectuals began to ponder seriously the question of how best to keep the memory of the Twenty-One Demands alive in the future. The educator Hou Hongjian (ca. 1871–1961) published an article in July in which he urged that the issue of national humiliation be incorporated into every part of the school curriculum.[34] At a meeting of Jiangsu school principals in June it was resolved that schools should hold assemblies devoted to the issue of national humiliation and make national humiliation souvenirs *(jinianpin).*[35] In Beijing the Japanese ultimatum was read aloud to students every day so that they "would not forget the humiliation." Finally, to spread awareness of the national humiliation beyond the confines of the schools to the general public, it was proposed that popular "national humiliation songs" *(guochi ge)* be composed, that students on vacation travel about the countryside reading texts on *guochi* to illiterate farmers, that plays be performed to stimulate people's patriotism, and so forth.[36]

The flip side of this fixation on remembering was that, as the more immediate and direct expressions of China's response to the Twenty-One Demands ran out of steam, contemporaries began to worry about Chinese "forgetfulness." Clearly, they did not think that their compatriots would literally forget the recent crisis. In point of fact, in the years after 1915, the social, political, and even economic landscape of China was fairly saturated with reminders of the Twenty-One Demands. My sense is that what really worried a host of Chinese intellectuals in the period from 1915 to the eve of the Sino-Japanese War was the *quality* of the remembering, the persistent indifference and passivity that they detected in the mood of the Chinese public.[37]

It is no wonder, in these circumstances, that the Goujian story, a central thread of which was the fragility of memory and the consequent importance of taking concrete measures to keep from forgetting past humiliation, should occupy an increasingly central place in Chinese consciousness. Explicit references to the story were encountered with great frequency in the press and elsewhere in discussions of the Twenty-One Demands and other humiliating national experiences. But even when writers were less than explicit, a link to the story was implicitly established. When people used phrases like "Do not forget the national humiliation" or "Do not forget May 9," the Goujian story lay just beneath the surface.[38] The story's contents resonated with China's contemporary experience—and the rhetoric used to describe it—in such palpable and powerful ways that it did not have to be explicitly alluded to for an association to be implied.[39]

SHARED CULTURAL KNOWLEDGE: DISSEMINATION
OF THE GOUJIAN STORY IN REPUBLICAN CHINA

A German correspondent in Shanghai in the fiercely anti-imperialist 1920s observed that whenever "an occidental resident of Shanghai, particularly of the older generation, mentions hatred of foreigners, the memory of the Boxer outbreak always lurks somewhere in the background of his mind, like a mediaeval incomprehensible spook."[40] The correspondent used the phrase "particularly of the older generation" in order to make the point that Westerners in Shanghai who had actually lived through the Boxer events of 1900 were more likely than their younger contemporaries to construe the treaty-port rhetoric of the mid-1920s (which tended to be harshly dismissive of the "new nationalism") in light of those events. They had direct access, in other words, to a special body of remembered historical experience that enabled or at least made it easier for them to interpret contemporary Chinese behavior in a certain way. The relationship between the Goujian story and the rhetoric of not forgetting past humiliation bears some resemblance to this. Only in this instance it was a body of shared cultural *knowledge* rather than of past personal *experience* that made possible an implied connection.

There were, of course, other differences as well between the two cases, the most salient being the fact that the Boxer-shadowed rhetoric encountered in the treaty-port press in the mid-1920s was deployed for the express purpose of discrediting Chinese nationalism,[41] whereas the Goujian story's impact on the rhetoric of remembering past humiliation functioned more as a positive guide, a model for Chinese to bear in mind and emulate in their encounter with foreign imperialism. What was common to both cases—and this was critically important—was the prior existence in people's minds of a paradigmatic narrative, a kind of template, that shaped (or at least colored) the ways in which they processed contemporary experience.

The impact of the Goujian story during the period stretching from the Twenty-One Demands of May 1915 until the Chinese civil war in the late 1940s may be measured in a number of ways. First, there was the sheer abundance and variety of vehicles used to disseminate it, including everything from children's literature to opera librettos to posters to commercial ads. Second, a number of publications containing the story went through frequent printings, indicating a wide reading public. Third, these publications were often accompanied by some form of official seal of approval: endorsement by the Guomindang Ministry of Education, compilation and printing by a provincial government, and so on. And fourth, a major effort was made to include the Goujian story in popular and mass education materials and to incorporate it in the school curriculum at all levels.

The frequent use of the Goujian story in popular, mass education, and general teaching materials was of paramount importance in establishing it as an artifact of shared cultural knowledge. Between 1917 and 1921 one of the top Shanghai publishing houses brought out a series entitled Short Works of Fiction *(Xiao xiaoshuo)*, intended both to entertain and to provide moral instruction. The series included a story in easy literary Chinese entitled *Sleeping on Brushwood and Tasting Gall (Woxin changdan)*, which was reissued frequently in later years. The story's focus is largely on Goujian's period of incarceration in Wu. Much detail is supplied on the Yue king's behavior as a prisoner, the degrading work he and his wife were required to do, his apparent total submission to Fuchai (including a full account of the stool-tasting stratagem), the recurrent conflict between Wu Zixu and Bo Pi over how Fuchai should deal with his prize captive, and so forth. The twenty-year period devoted to the rebuilding of Yue after Goujian's return is, however, only referred to obliquely, and there is no reference at all to the growing tension between him and his top ministers after the destruction of Wu. The conclusion of *Woxin changdan* highlights the main message of the Goujian story. It begins with an exchange between Goujian and Fan Li following the king's move to the new capital city Fan Li designed for him at Kuaiji:

> Goujian said to Fan Li: "I acted improperly, resulting in the loss of the state. If it were not for the help and support of the prime minister [referring to Fan Li] and the other ministers, how could we possibly have arrived at the present favorable situation?" Fan Li responded: "This is the good fortune of the great king, not the meritorious achievement of his servants. If only the great king will never forget the hardships endured in the stone cottage, then Yue may flourish and the wrongs inflicted by Wu may be avenged." Goujian said: "Your advice is respectfully accepted." From that point on, Goujian exerted himself to make the state prosper and day and night gave thought only to avenging the wrongs inflicted by Wu. After twenty years Wu was finally destroyed by Goujian.

This is followed by an articulation of the story's key moral: "If one can endure a great humiliation, later one will be able to accomplish a great revenge. The plan to destroy Wu had been decided upon long ago in the stone cottage. Truly Goujian was a man of outstanding capacity!"[42]

One of the more intriguing aspects of the *Woxin changdan* narrative just summarized is that the publisher chose to categorize it as a work of fiction, seemingly underscoring the point (made in chapter 1) that what was primarily important about the Goujian story was its mythic power, not its historicity. The mythic power of the story was also implied in a lesson entitled "National Humiliation" ("Guochi") in the *Textbook of One Thousand Characters for Townspeople (Shimin qianzi ke)*, originally issued in March 1927 by the National Association for the Advancement of Mass Education.

This primer, which was endorsed by the Nationalist Ministry of Education, went through numerous printings and had a circulation in the millions.[43] As the lesson's title suggests, the Goujian story is directly linked in it with the broader issue of national humiliation.[44] The text, which is very brief, reads as follows:

> The citizens of China are filled with the desire to avenge the humiliations to which they have been subjected. Therefore, when they hear the story of how the king of Yue, through perseverance and self-imposed privation [literally, "lying on brushwood and tasting gall"], avenged himself against Wu and wiped out his disgrace, their faces light up with joy. But how many times greater than the humiliations suffered by the king of Yue in those days are the manifold indignities to the nation—the ceding of territory, the payment of indemnities, the forfeiting of sovereign rights, and so on— that China has endured in recent decades? We citizens of China, what shall we do?[45]

Although the target reading audience of the mass education movement primer consisted of illiterate youth and adults in China's cities,[46] the reach of the movement extended beyond urban China to the rural population, where spoken drama took a critical part in its activities. The person most responsible for this was the American-educated playwright Xiong Foxi (1900–1965), an early believer in the power of theater to bring about social change. Appointed to run the drama program at the movement's center in Dingxian (in central Hebei province), Xiong was, according to Chang-tai Hung, "the pivotal figure in the mass education and rural reconstruction campaign" from 1932 to 1937.[47]

In November 1931, two months after the Mukden Incident of September 18 that sparked the Japanese takeover of Manchuria, Xiong Foxi completed a spoken drama on the Goujian story entitled *Sleeping on Brushwood and Tasting Gall (Woxin changdan)*. The play, which was first performed in the county seat of Dingxian on Chinese New Year's Day 1933, was noteworthy for several reasons. First, it was written in very colloquial language, making it fully accessible to a rural audience with rudimentary education. Second, although adhering faithfully to the Goujian story's core humiliation-revenge structure, it modified many of the details in a fairly radical way. Third, and most interesting for our purposes, Xiong made a considerable effort to adapt the play's contents to the multiple problems facing China in the early 1930s, even sprinkling the text with vocabulary and phrases widely used at the time.

In the first scene of the second act, for example, Goujian and his wife are sitting late at night in the humble dwelling they have made their home since returning from captivity in Wu. They hear the Yue people outside shouting, "Down with [dadao] Wu!" "Everyone unite!" "Strive to build up national strength!" and the like. Goujian's wife says that, given the high spirits of the people, perhaps the moment has arrived to "declare war" (xuanzhan) on Wu. Goujian, echoing a complaint heard almost daily in the contemporary Chinese press, responds that slogans do not win wars; real preparations must be made first.[48] He goes on to identify the four great enemies that have to be rooted out before Yue can take revenge against Wu. The first enemy is ignorance. Since learning is the foundation of a strong state, with 80 percent illiteracy, how can Yue wipe away the humiliation that has been inflicted on it? The second enemy is poverty, the third is poor health, and the fourth is selfishness, the majority of the Yue people having no conception of nationhood. Goujian, after itemizing these failings—which just happen to coincide closely with the mass education movement's view of the foremost problems afflicting Chinese farmers[49]—resolves to take a stronger leadership role in the future in combating them.[50]

Patriotism is another contemporary theme that is highlighted in the play. The second scene of act 2 takes place in a village tea and wine shop operated by the father of the beautiful Zheng Dan together with his daughter.[51] Father and daughter both express anger and hatred toward Wu and regret that they cannot join the Yue army, he because of age and she because of gender. Furious, Zheng Dan exclaims: "Daughters can't serve as soldiers? Females aren't people? Females aren't one component of the citizenry [guomin]? Females shouldn't be patriotic [aiguo]?" Goujian, disguised as an ordinary farmer, enters the shop and orders a cup of tea. Zheng Dan asks him if he wouldn't like some wine as well. He asks her what kind of wine they serve. She says "bitter wine." They used to sell sweet wine, but they switched to bitter wine to encourage customers "to bear in mind the national humiliation" and "not forget to avenge the country and wipe clean the shame inflicted on it." Goujian, deeply impressed with the patriotism of Zheng Dan and her father, confides to them that he is their king and asks whether they would be willing to go to Wu as spies for Yue. Father and daughter, announcing that they are prepared to do anything for the benefit of the country, return with the king to the Yue capital.[52]

The third and final act of Xiong's play takes place at Goujian's field headquarters. Wu has just been soundly defeated by Yue and the Wu king Fuchai has been brought into Goujian's presence. Fuchai pleads for mercy. Xiong

Foxi, plainly alluding to recent events in Manchuria, has Goujian lecture Fuchai about "invading and occupying" *(qinzhan)* the territory of another: "It isn't at all that I, Goujian, wish today to take revenge against you, Fuchai; it's only that an overweeningly ambitious man like you needs to be taught a lesson: people who want to invade and occupy the territory of others will inevitably be invaded and occupied themselves; people who contemplate the destruction of the nations of others will inevitably suffer the same fate themselves!"[53]

As has often been noted, the experience of migrating from the world of the unlettered to that of the lettered can be immensely empowering psychologically—one of the first lessons in the mass education primer discussed earlier likened those who could not read to blind people[54]—and the first things one learns to read can make an unusually strong impression. This is no less true of children in the early stages of their lives. As Chiang Kai-shek put it in *China's Destiny:* "The character of young students is not yet definitely molded; their knowledge is still scanty and easily susceptible to outside influence, like a piece of white paper that can be painted red, black, gray, or yellow."[55] During the republican era the Goujian story was included in the Chinese curriculum at all levels, from lower primary to upper middle school. A version of the story for lower primary school pupils that I have seen appeared in an eight-volume *Chinese Primer (Guoyu duben),* first published by the Shanxi provincial government in 1935. To give some idea of its range of contents, in addition to the Goujian story, it included chapters (mostly two or three pages in length) on patriotism, a New Life Movement song, the life of Sun Yat-sen, a letter to an elder brother, the Yangzi and Pearl rivers, the Ming loyalist Zheng Chenggong, the Opium War, reforestation and hydroelectric power in Shanxi, and so forth. The chapter entitled "King Goujian of Yue" went as follows:

> During the Spring and Autumn period the states of Yue and Wu were neighbors, and because they were in contention for supremacy they fought constantly. On one occasion Yue was defeated by Wu, and Goujian, the king of Yue, being powerless to hold out, had no choice but to capitulate to the Wu king, Fuchai.
>
> After surrendering to Wu, Goujian and his wife personally entered into servitude under the Wu king. All the things that other people cannot bear to do, Goujian was able to endure the humiliation of doing. After a few years, the king of Wu saw how devoted he was and let him return home.
>
> After going back to Yue, Goujian settled upon a plan consisting of "ten years of building up the population and economy, ten years of instruction

and training." Determined on a course of revenge, he immersed himself in hard work, wearing simple clothing, eating plain food, and sharing directly in the grueling lives of the people. At night he slept on brushwood; also, in the doorway he hung a gallbladder, which he licked every time he passed through in order to guard against complacency and as a reminder of the suffering he had undergone.

Twenty years passed in this fashion. The country became prosperous and the population multiplied. All, moreover, were determined to avenge the earlier wrong. Goujian therefore led his armies in an attack on Wu, which ended in the destruction of the state of Wu and the wiping out of the national humiliation.[56]

The story of Goujian presented to lower primary school students was at best an appetite-whetter. The bare outlines of the story are limned, but there is no detail at all and little indication of what Goujian and Fuchai were like as individuals. The leading ministers in fuller versions of the saga (Fan Li, Wen Zhong, Wu Zixu, and Bo Pi), with their distinct personalities and vitally important parts in the story's development, are not even mentioned. While we can surmise that the better teachers would likely fill in these gaps in class, some students at least might have to wait until they were older to encounter a more detailed version of the Goujian story.

One such rendering, aimed at the upper primary level (ages eleven and twelve), appeared shortly after the victory over Japan in the Sino-Japanese War and went through a number of reprintings. Part of a series of two hundred booklets on all subjects designed to supplement the regular course work of children in the primary school grades, it is distinctive in several respects. First, over three-quarters of its forty pages are concerned with the preliminary period from Goujian's defeat of Helu to the start of the Yue ruler's servitude in Wu under Helu's son and successor, Fuchai. Special attention is paid to the details of Goujian's efforts to persuade Fuchai to accept his surrender. Second, the arguments used by the various ministers to persuade either Goujian or Fuchai are well-framed and do much to enliven the story. Here, for instance, is Wen Zhong in his second effort to convince Fuchai to accept Goujian's surrender (after the first had been rejected):

This lowly minister Wen Zhong was commanded by Goujian to come to Wu to beg to surrender, but the great king did not permit it; this lowly minister went back and reported this to Goujian. Very disappointed, Goujian reflected that, well, anyway, he could only die once; so he decided that, after killing his wife and children and setting fire to Kuaiji, turning it into scorched earth *[jiaotu]*, he would lead his five thousand remaining soldiers in a last-ditch battle. I think that although five thousand men are not a large number, since Goujian will have already killed his wife and destroyed all his possessions by fire, he will certainly be determined to fight to the finish. If these five thousand men are truly prepared to risk their lives in a decisive engagement, I fear that it will not be so easy to deal with them. Therefore this lowly minister's venturing once again to request an audience with the great king is not entirely for the sake of Goujian; half of my motive is to get the great king to give some thought to his own interests. I hope the great king will mull this over carefully![57]

A third feature of this rendering of the Goujian story is that although some effort is certainly made to capture the flavor of the late Spring and Autumn period, a certain number of modern terms and phrases, along with occasional allusions to the recently concluded war against Japan, are also built into the text (as in Xiong Foxi's play). When Wu, early in the narrative, is confronted with Goujian's preemptive invasion, Wu Zixu advises Fuchai that since Yue is the "aggressor" *(qinlüezhe)* and Wu the "victim of aggression" *(bei qinlüezhe),* as long as Wu bolsters the morale of its forces and mobilizes all able-bodied soldiers for a fight to the death, it is certain to prevail. When Wen Zhong presents Bo Pi with eight beautiful women and eight rare treasures in support of his request for a second audience with Fuchai, Bo Pi, delighted with the gifts, thinks to himself that if he arranges another meeting with the king, it will be no big deal and surely cannot be described as a "treasonable act" *(maiguo xingwei;* literally, "selling out the country behavior"). Fan Li, after Goujian has decided to seek surrender unconditionally *(wutiaojian touxiang),* calls on the people of Yue, if they are true patriots *(zhen aiguo de ren),* to turn over any valuable possessions they may have and to sacrifice their lovely sisters and daughters for their country and their king. Wen Zhong, as we have seen, tells Fuchai that if Goujian's offer of surrender is not accepted, the Yue king is prepared to resort to "scorched earth" tactics to deny Wu the enjoyment of his palace and possessions. And, we are told, Goujian, after his return from Wu, although adopting long-term plans for making Yue prosperous and strong and taking a variety of measures to keep himself from becoming soft and complacent, is unable to proclaim publicly such slogans as "overthrow Wu" *(dadao Wu guo)* and "rejuvenate the nation" *(fuxing minzu)* for fear of arousing Fuchai's suspicion.[58]

Phrases such as *maiguo, qinlüezhe, wutiaojian touxiang, aiguo,* and *dadao* (the last frequently used in the phrase *dadao diguozhuyi*, or "down with imperialism") had become an important part of the vocabulary of political rhetoric during the first half of the twentieth century in China, and references to scorched-earth tactics (which had been employed by Chiang Kai-shek during the early phases of the Sino-Japanese War) and unconditional surrender (the demand imposed on both Germany and Japan by the Allied forces) clearly enhanced the relevance of the Goujian story to the searing historical experience through which young readers, along with other Chinese, had just passed.

Fourth, although in most tellings of the Goujian story, including this one, what tends to be emphasized is the *contrast* between Goujian and Fuchai, there is also an important parallel between the two kings. I refer to the adverse consequences for both rulers of not heeding the remonstrances of their top ministers. There is a critical difference, to be sure, between the two cases: Goujian, although he suffers mightily for his failure early in his royal career to abide by Fan Li's advice not to attack Wu, ultimately triumphs (after learning to listen to his prime minister), while Fuchai, after following Wu Zixu's counsel at the start of his kingship and achieving a victory over Yue, subsequently turns a deaf ear to Wu's repeated urgings to destroy his rival and ends up losing all. But this neat contrast in the fortunes of the two kings masks a deeper parallelism reflective of the minister-centered (as opposed to king-centered) interpretive thrust of early Chinese historiography: ministers like Fan Li and Wu Zixu knew what they were talking about—that is, they knew how to read the intentions of Heaven accurately. Kings who heeded their advice, therefore, were almost certain to be successful, while kings who followed their own impulses, defying the counsel of their top advisers, faced a high risk of failure.[59]

These examples of the dissemination of the Goujian story in the 1920s, 1930s, and 1940s constitute only a very partial sampling, and there is some risk in attempting to generalize on the basis of it. I would like, nevertheless, to do so, in order to identify, however tentatively, a few broad characteristics of the story as it was presented to Chinese during these years. First, although different writers chose to focus on very different parts of the Goujian narrative, a number of key themes recur. Goujian is consistently depicted as a man who, in order to avenge past humiliation, is ready to undergo severe personal deprivation and humiliation while preparing patiently for the day when Yue will be in a position to exact its revenge. The emphasis in the examples discussed is not on the measures adopted by Yue to enrich and strengthen itself; rather, invariably, it is on the mind-set of the

Yue king—his state of consciousness—and in particular the lengths he is willing to go to to not forget the indignities he has suffered or the mission of revenge he has set for himself. Second, the behavior of both Goujian and Fuchai underscores the importance, as limned in the previous paragraph, of kings heeding the advice of their official advisers if they are to reap success in their endeavors.

And finally, the story, in all of the examples, terminates with Yue's destruction of Wu and the consummation of Goujian's mission of revenge. The growing tension between Goujian and his top ministers after Yue's triumph—an important part of the saga as it circulated in antiquity—is omitted entirely. This way of concluding the story makes much sense from a literary point of view: the final destruction of Wu constitutes a natural end point. It also makes sense in terms of the historical and political context of the first half of the twentieth century, a context admirably suited to a paradigmatic story incorporating a simple pattern of humiliation and revenge, not humiliation, revenge, and then conflict between a triumphant king and the brilliant ministers who had made his triumph possible.[60] Under the very different historical circumstances that prevailed later in the twentieth century, as we shall see in chapters 5 and 6, this missing last episode of the story of Goujian would reappear.

REVERBERATIONS OF THE GOUJIAN STORY IN THE PRESS AND ELSEWHERE

The widespread diffusion of the Goujian story in republican-era educational materials and popular literature—its establishment as shared cultural knowledge—meant that shorthand allusions to it in connection with national humiliation in newspapers, magazines, posters, and even advertisements, although unlikely to make sense to outsiders, would be instantly deciphered by virtually the entire Chinese reading public. Two examples of pictorial images from the 1920s demonstrate this nicely. The lesson on national humiliation in the National Association for the Advancement of Mass Education's *Textbook of One Thousand Characters for Townspeople,* introduced in the preceding section, is accompanied by two illustrations, one of which shows a despondent man reclining on a hard brushwood bed, deep in thought, with a dark oval-shaped object suspended from a string in front of him. It is doubtful that this image would be understood by someone with only a vague and superficial familiarity with the Goujian story. I use myself as an embarrassing case in point. Since the text of the lesson, al-

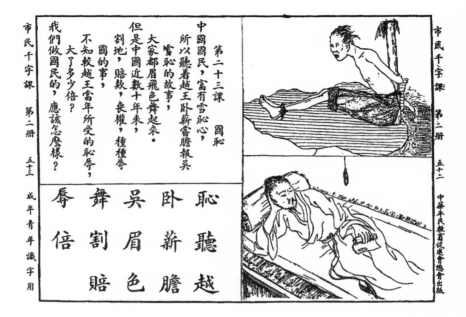

Figure 10. Goujian as portrayed in a mass education primer lesson on "national humiliation." The lesson appears on the left-hand side, along with new vocabulary to be mastered (bottom section). The top image on the right shows a man seated on an outline map of China, his feet tied together, his arms bound to a post behind him, and his upper body uncovered, symbolizing China's oppressed condition; the other image depicts Goujian as described in the text. Source: *Shimin qianzi ke,* 20th ed. (Shanghai, 1929).

though briefly alluding to the Yue king's revenge and incorporating the telltale phrase *woxin changdan,* was mainly about the humiliating treatment Chinese had received at the hands of foreign imperialism, and since I was unaware that the illustration in question was the standard visual representation of *woxin changdan* that accompanied numerous published renderings of the Goujian story in the twentieth century, the first thought that crossed my mind when I looked at the unhappy figure portrayed in the picture was that it was perhaps an opium addict. When I asked another China historian—also a Westerner and no better acquainted than I with the *woxin changdan* story and its customary graphic depiction—he agreed that that was a plausible reading of the image. Unsure of my understanding, I subsequently asked a Chinese friend to tell me what she thought the picture

Figure 11. Advertisement for Golden Dragon (Jinlong) cigarettes. Source: *Shenbao*, May 7–11, 1925; May 9, 1926. Also in *Shibao* (The eastern times), May 7–12, 1925; *Shishi xinbao*, May 8–10, 1925, and May 9, 1926.

was about. She immediately identified the figure as Goujian and the mysterious suspended object as a gallbladder.

The second example, quite different in nature and even more opaque to a viewer with only passing knowledge of the Goujian story, consists of an advertisement for Golden Dragon cigarettes (a brand manufactured by the Nanyang Brothers Tobacco Company) that appeared in May 1925 and May 1926 in a number of Shanghai dailies. The ad, which ran in several consecutive issues of each paper, was timed to appear around May 9, the anniversary of National Humiliation Day. In addition to asking people not to forget May 9, it explicitly identifies the smoking of Golden Dragon cigarettes as a patriotic act. An inset at the far left-hand side of the ad shows a group of people standing under a tree on the branches of which are hung strips of paper with *guochi* written on them. At the bottom of the ad, just to the left of center, is a modern-day Goujian seated uncomfortably on a pile of brushwood, holding a gallbladder up to his mouth, his gaze directed toward the paper strips on the tree. What is interesting is that although the purpose of the ad, apart from marketing Golden Dragon cigarettes, was to establish a clear connection between Goujian and the admonition not to forget China's humiliation, the ad's creators obviously saw no need to indicate to readers who the seated figure was or what he was holding in his hand.[61]

Allusions in writing to the Goujian story during the republican years are often just as spare as the pictorial representations just described and assume prior knowledge on the part of the reader. (This was also true of the late

Qing, as pointed out at the beginning of this chapter.) In the immediate aftermath of the Twenty-One Demands, an editorial appearing in the Shanghai daily *The Eastern Times (Shibao)* opened with the fairly obscure line: "The present day is a time for Goujian to show respect for the frog, not one for the snipe and the clam to grapple with one another." The first allusion referred to the angry frog Goujian used as an example to motivate his army for the upcoming battle against Wu (see chapter 1); the point of the second one was that when the snipe and the clam fought, it was the fisherman (or some other third party) that stood to benefit. The key message of the editorial was that Chinese must not rest easy now that the Japanese had withdrawn the fifth group of demands and the immediate crisis had passed, but must pull together, cease all internal wrangling, and seize the opportunity to fortify themselves in every sphere, so that in the future the country would be respected and feared and no adversary would again try to follow Japan's example.[62]

A more accessible (though equally brief) allusion to the Goujian story was made by the minister of education, Tang Hualong, in a speech at a meeting of the provincial educational associations of China in the spring of 1915. Tang emphasized that thereafter Chinese educators would have to pay more attention to moral issues, encouraging the youth of the country to discard petty resentments and private grudges, become more public-spirited, place love of country before love of family, and take pleasure in engaging in good acts, "strengthening the foundations of the nation in the present, while putting up with temporary pain and discomfort [*woxin changdan*] in order to wipe away China's shame in the future."[63]

Although such coded allusions to the Goujian story as *zhao Wu* (to destroy Wu), *shi nian shengju* (ten years to build up the economy), and *shi nian jiaoxun* (ten years to train the military) are encountered with some frequency in twentieth-century writing (all originally derived from the version found in the *Zuozhuan*), the proverb *woxin changdan* is by far the most common, emblematic, and widely recognized reference to the story. Although I have sometimes rendered it by such phrases as "putting up with temporary pain and discomfort" or "persistence and forbearance," I have often translated it literally as "sleeping (or lying) on brushwood and tasting gall" or simply left it untranslated. I have done this mainly because the phrase encompasses a spectrum of meanings, including (in addition to the above) not forgetting past humiliations, being determined to seek revenge and erase earlier grievances, exercising patience in the face of humiliation while preparing carefully for the day when Yue/China will be strong enough to prevail, and so forth. Sometimes *woxin changdan* is explicitly linked with one or another of these meanings, but more often the meaning or range of meanings is left vague. In such instances, it has seemed to me that the prudent thing is to signal this to the reader by translating the phrase literally or not translating it at all.

Frequently, of course, references to the Goujian story went well beyond such elliptical phrasing. Shortly after Tang Hualong's address, for example, another educator, Jia Fengzhen, published an article in which he contended (as did many at the time) that China's salvation lay in education and that the first task of education was to inculcate an understanding of shame *(ming chi)*. After citing passages from Confucius and Mencius on the importance of having a sense of shame, Jia provided two historical examples of proper responses to humiliation. The first related to Goujian: "Goujian was surrounded at Kuaiji and submitted to the rule of Wu. Over three years his spirits never flagged. Afterward he built up Yue's economy for ten years *[shengju shi nian]* and trained the military for ten years *[jiaoxun shi nian]*, and then he avenged the humiliation of Kuaiji." As an indication of the new worldliness spreading across urban China during the first decades of the twentieth century, for his second example, Jia pointed to France, which, after suffering a humiliating defeat at the hands of Prussia in 1870, rallied its people to help in paying the huge indemnity imposed by the victors and before ten years were out had again become a first-rank power.[64]

In general, Goujian was put forward as a model for Chinese to emulate, or, alternatively, as a yardstick for measuring the degree to which contemporary behavior fell short. Typical was a manifesto delivered at a student meeting in Shanghai on May 9, 1924: "Is it possible that our four hundred million compatriots can't smash Japanese imperialism? How did King Goujian of Yue years ago avenge the wrong done him? I think everyone knows the answer. We must at once, grabbing hold of the spirit of 'sleeping on brushwood and tasting gall,' take revenge and erase the humiliations heaped upon us!"[65]

In an example of a quite different sort, an editorial in the Nanjing daily *People's Livelihood News (Minsheng bao)*, written by the paper's founder, Cheng Shewo, a few days after the Japanese military's alleged massacre of Chinese in Ji'nan (Shandong) on May 3, 1928, argued that Chinese should not be concerned about the wrong done them on this occasion; rather, they should be concerned about drifting along in the same old ways, forgetting all about what happened. Cavour had to tolerate all sorts of indignities and setbacks, but eventually Italian unification was achieved. After their defeat in the Franco-Prussian War, the French "slept on brushwood and tasted gall" for fifty years before Alsace and Lorraine were finally restored to them. And it was much the same in Chinese antiquity: "Cao Mo [or Gui] was not ashamed to fail three times,* Goujian eventually destroyed mighty Wu." The important thing—and this was a rule that pertained to modern times as well as ancient, to foreign history as well as Chinese—was to learn from the bitter experiences of the past, to be farsighted, and to plan ahead.[66]

Often, as observed earlier, references to the Goujian story were closely tied to the injunction to remember the humiliations China had experienced and to keep these in the forefront of one's consciousness. The trouble was that over the years, if we are to credit the repeated expressions of concern by patriotic Chinese intellectuals, memory of these humiliations had become attenuated as a result of a process of routinization or repetition overload. The famous publicist Liang Qichao wrote a penetrating indictment of this process in an editorial in the Shanghai paper *China Times (Shishi xinbao)* in May 1925.[67] Many (including Liang) charged that the National Humiliation Day anniversary observances, in particular, while providing an opportunity for emotional venting, had begun to function less as true vehicles for the recalling of the Twenty-One Demands than as a disguised form of forgetting. Time and again, the complaint was heard (internalizing a criticism originally voiced by foreigners) that Chinese had "an enthusiasm for things that only lasted five minutes" *(wu fenzhong zhi redu)*. One reader of the leading Shanghai daily *Shenbao,* alluding to this, wrote in 1921 that there were people who did not even remember the date of the May 9 national humiliation. The whole point of marking the May 9 anniversary and holding commemorative meetings, he insisted, was to keep Chinese from forgetting this great national humiliation and to arouse them to exert themselves to wipe it clean, following the example of Goujian's lying on brushwood and tasting gall. But, instead, in six years' time the anniversary of May 9 had come to be observed as a happy occasion, as if it were China's National Day. It was time, therefore, to abandon National Humiliation Day entirely and establish in its stead an Avenge Humiliation Day *(xuechi ri).*[68]

---

*Cao Mo was a commoner from the ancient state of Lu who served as a general under the Lu ruler Duke Zhuang. After suffering three defeats at the hands of the larger and more powerful state of Qi, at the peace conference between the two states he forced the Qi ruler to return the captured Lu lands. Takigawa, *Shiki kaichū kōshō,* vol. 8, *juan* 86 ("Cike liezhuan"), 2–4; also Schaberg, *A Patterned Past,* 186–88.

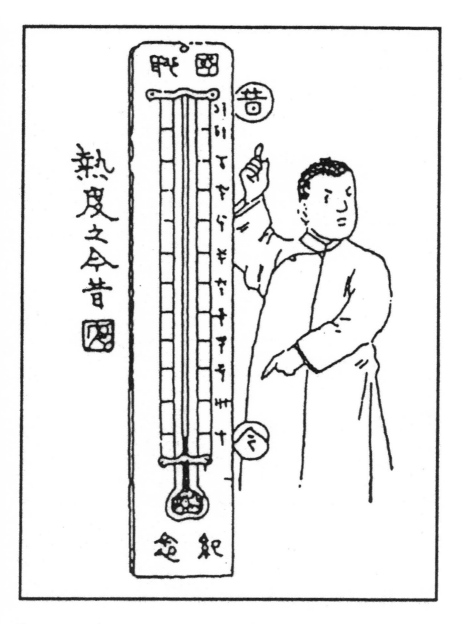

Figure 12. Weakening response to National Humiliation Day. Published on the seventh anniversary of China's acceptance of the Twenty-One Demands, this cartoon dramatizes the cooling of popular concern over time. At the top and bottom of the thermometer are the characters for "national humiliation anniversary"; the man's right hand points upward to the character for "formerly," his left hand to that for "now." Source: *Shenbao*, May 9, 1922.

This sharply judgmental stance toward Chinese failure to follow the path forged by Goujian was also reflected in an article that appeared in the same paper in May 1924 on the ninth anniversary of National Humiliation Day (which the writer, using the traditional Chinese method of reckoning time, treated as the tenth anniversary). In the piece the author assumed the identity of a deadly parasite implanted by a very short child (Japan) in the body of "the sick man of the East" (China). At first China did not know it had become the host to this parasite. But later, as it became weaker and weaker, it became aware of the parasite's existence and named it *guochi*. Then there was a lot of talk about "lying on brushwood and tasting gall" and wiping the humiliation clean. But a decade had passed, little if any progress had been made, and now the deadly parasite was to be honored by a celebration of its tenth birthday.[69]

Not all *Shenbao* contributors adopted such a bitterly sardonic tone. A few years earlier, another reader had argued that China, as a weak nation, was not in a position to rely solely on "right" as a protective talisman. The consequences of its participation in World War I had made this plain enough. The only path for the Chinese people to follow, therefore, was Goujian's lying on brushwood and tasting gall, by which the author meant a genuine rebuilding process, involving the active involvement of all sectors of the population. If China contented itself with merely giving lip service to wiping away the national humiliation and did not supplement this with practical measures, its efforts would never amount to anything.[70]

Echoing this concern on a more individual level, in May 1922 a contributor to *Shenbao* proposed that on National Humiliation Day, along with the lowering of flags, the meetings, and the speechmaking—all things that took place in public view—Chinese should take actions in their personal lives that would have an immediate practical effect. Just as Goujian, following his defeat at Kuaiji, slept fitfully and ate without pleasure because of what was on his mind, Chinese citizens of all occupational groups, male and female, young and old, should abstain on this day from fish and meat and only consume bean curd, vegetables, and coarse or brown rice. If in the past Goujian could subject himself day in and day out to such deprivations, surely Chinese in the present could become vegetarians for a single day. What was more, if enough individuals followed this suggestion, it would significantly benefit the Chinese economy, as the money saved could be contributed to such things as famine relief and education.[71]

The issue, touched on in the piece just discussed, of the personal quality of the remembering that should take place on National Humiliation Day anniversaries, and in particular the part that the symbolism embedded in the Goujian story should play in such remembering, was explored in much greater depth in an interesting short story by the celebrated cartoonist, writer, and devout Buddhist Feng Zikai (1898–1975). Published in September 1936 in the newly launched magazine *New Youth (Xin shaonian)*[72] and titled "The Night of September 18" ("Jiu yiba zhi ye"), Feng's story takes place at a school and begins with a morning assembly in the school's memorial hall. In the opening speech the principal described the Mukden Incident of September 18, 1931, and subsequent national humiliations and exhorted the students to go all-out, unite, and struggle, until "Jiu yiba" (9/18) had become a thing of the past. The next speaker, the person in charge of moral education, after telling the story of Goujian's sleeping on brushwood and tasting gall, asked the students not to forget that they lived in a time of hardship and struggle, not one of pleasure seeking and creature comforts, and urged them henceforth to be more serious and diligent in their studies.

That evening it was the turn of the drawing instructor, Teacher Qin, to supervise self-study. She entered the classroom grinning, sat down on the chair on the lecturer's platform, and looked at the students as if waiting for someone to ask a question. The students put away the math exercises many of them had been working on and started to ply her with questions relating to art. One student, Lin Peizhen, posed a particularly timely question. She observed that that morning the head of moral education had told them not to forget that they lived in a time of hardship and struggle, not one of pleasure seeking and creature comforts. She agreed with that and wondered whether, in such circumstances, students should be spending time on things like drawing that gave pleasure to the eye and the mind. Why, she asked, did the school still teach drawing and painting?

While Teacher Qin was pondering this somewhat provocative question, another student, Wu Wenying, stood up and said that, contrary to Lin Peizhen, he felt that drawing was of great practical value. For example, if students were to try to portray in drawing the "sleeping on brushwood and tasting gall" referred to by the moral education head earlier that day, it would encourage them to struggle. A lot of the students responded favorably to this suggestion, saying, "Not bad, not bad."

Teacher Qin now spoke. She said that the two viewpoints that had been expressed were simultaneously correct and incorrect. Lin Peizhen's view that students should not spend time on things that gave pleasure to the eye and the mind and Wu Wenying's view that drawing was of practical use were both correct. But Lin Peizhen's belief that drawing was something that gave pleasure to the eye and the mind and Wu Wenying's belief that drawing was an instrument of struggle were also both incorrect. As the students pondered her words in puzzled silence, Teacher Qin in a louder voice asked them to remember two things of fundamental importance about the study of drawing: first, that drawing was not simply something that gave pleasure to the eye and the mind, that in fact it involved painstaking effort; and, second, that the practical value of drawing did not consist in its functioning directly as an instrument of struggle, but rather in its functioning indirectly to train people's minds, enabling them to perfect their lives. Then, raising one hand, she said to Lin Peizhen:

> You think that drawing is entirely a pleasurable thing that requires no great effort? If I now ask all of you to draw a hand, the most ordinary hand, out of more than thirty of you there will not be a single one able to draw it with complete "accuracy." If you want to draw it with complete accuracy, you must expend several years of hard work, and if you want it to be not only "accurate" but also "pleasing to the eye," you will have to expend several more years of hard work. The goal of the study of drawing is to train the capacity to draw all images both accurately and beautifully. How is this not hard work?

Everyone now extended their hands in front of them and examined them carefully, expressing tacit approval of what the teacher had said. Next, Teacher Qin turned to Wu Wenying and said:

> You believe that the practical application of useful drawing is to draw something like sleeping on brushwood and tasting gall? Such drawing does indeed have utility, but its utility is too circumscribed. . . . The larger utility of drawing is indirect and consists in developing our abilities. We must use hard work to train our visual powers, our manual dexterity, and our mental strength, nurturing the capacity to observe with sensitivity, describe with accuracy, and express ourselves in an aesthetically pleasing way. Then, we must apply this capacity to all aspects of our lives, so that our lives are well intentioned, genuine, and beautiful, like a fine work of art. This is the indirect value of drawing. . . . Conversely, if you want to put drawing to immediate practical use, without using hard work to train your hands, eyes, and minds, you will inevitably fall short. For now, let me just ask who among the thirty or forty students in this room can produce out of thin air a decent image of *woxin changdan?* For-

get about the rest; even if you were to just draw one of Goujian's hands, I fear that not one of you would be able to render it with accuracy!"

Below the lecturer's platform, a sound of satisfied laughter could be heard, as a lot of white hands were extended and rotated this way and that beneath the electric light.

"Therefore," Teacher Qin summed up, "I say to you: We do indeed live in a time of hardship and struggle. But under no circumstances can the study of art be abolished, and we also must not mechanically use art as an instrument of struggle, coveting a small benefit and losing a large one. Starting today, all of us should work hard to train our visual, manual, and mental powers, in the hope that in the future each one will become a complete citizen and a complete person. When we have reached that point, we will have nothing more to fear!"[73]

Feng Zikai's piece is of particular interest because, unlike most of the other examples we have looked at, it does not draw on the Goujian story to jog people's memories of past humiliations or to arouse them to strengthen China in preparation for a future day in which revenge will be exacted against the country's enemies. Nationalism is only referred to obliquely in "The Night of September 18," and despite the piece's title Japan is not mentioned at all. On one level, a major theme of Feng's story is that art, far from being unserious or merely pleasurable, is a source of valuable knowledge that can be applied to all phases of one's life. On a deeper level, however, what is mainly noteworthy about the story is that in it the notion of *woxin changdan*—of persistent hard work and patient preparation—is transferred from the all-too-familiar humiliation-revenge cycle to a broader canvas, where it is employed metaphorically to encourage people to shape their lives in more productive and satisfying ways, to seek fulfillment as citizens and as human beings. It is not surprising that Feng Zikai should want to develop this deeper meaning of the Goujian story. The same humane spirit was demonstrated in his famous wartime cartoons, which, reflecting his deeply held Buddhist views, went beyond appeals to his fellow countrymen to resist Japanese aggression to present "a powerful indictment of the senseless waste of human lives" that all war represented.[74]

Again and again in the 1920s and 1930s, as the foregoing examples suggest, probings of the Goujian story, generally brief and elliptical but occasionally (as in Feng Zikai's story) of a more extended nature, found their way into the Chinese newspaper and magazine press, suggesting that the story and the symbolism it embodied had become an important part of public consciousness concerning China's present situation and future outlook. Another major arena within which the story took a significant part during these years was that of Guomindang ideology and, in particular, the mind-set of the Guomindang leader, Chiang Kai-shek.

GUOMINDANG IDEOLOGY,
CHIANG KAI-SHEK, AND THE EXAMPLE OF GOUJIAN

The Goujian story, beginning in the 1920s, became a regular and prime feature of Nationalist rhetoric and propaganda. In 1996 the Guangzhou Municipal Government invested 36 million yuan (over US$4 million) in the restoration of the complex of buildings that had housed the Whampoa Military Academy (Huangpu junxiao) on an island in the Pearl River just west of Guangzhou's commercial port.[75] The original academy, which was destroyed by Japanese bombing in 1938, had been founded in 1924 with Chiang Kai-shek as commandant, its purpose being to train a new generation of Chinese military officers who would be indoctrinated in the tenets of Guomindang ideology, loyal to the party and its leaders, and fundamentally different from the warlord model then widely prevalent in China. Significantly, the front entrance of the original (as well as the restored) academy shows, on either side, the flags of the Republic of China and the Guomindang, and at the top center, draped across the archway, a large light-colored banner on which is written in bold black characters the proverb *woxin changdan*.[76]

Allusions to the Goujian story were a standard part of the official ritual repertoire of the Guomindang after its attainment of national power in 1927. For example, at Guomindang-sponsored National Humiliation Day anniversary observances in Nanjing on May 9, 1928, a party official, in a speech, referred to *woxin changdan* as part of what Chinese must do to prevail against the Japanese.[77] This was just days after the Ji'nan Incident of May 3, in which Chinese soldiers taking part in the Northern Expedition for the reunification of the country engaged in a bloody clash with Japanese troops in Ji'nan, Shandong, resulting in several thousand Chinese deaths (including that of a diplomatic official, Cai Gongshi).[78] On May 9, 1929, a newspaper notice placed by the Propaganda Department of the Executive Committee of the Guomindang's Shanghai Branch called on Chinese "to sleep on brushwood and taste gall" and vow to wipe clean the national humiliation.[79] At Guomindang Central Committee and National government observances of the May 9 anniversary in the same year, Chinese were enjoined to ad-

Figure 13. Front entrance of Whampoa Military Academy (ca. 1925). Source: Zhongguo geming bowuguan, *Huangpu junxiao shi tuce;* original source: National Museum of China.

here to the spirit of *woxin changdan* if they wanted to expunge the national humiliation and make the country strong.[80] Two years later, an announcement of the May 9 anniversary meeting, to be held under the auspices of the Shanghai Branch of the Guomindang, stated that the focus of the meeting would be on how Chinese, holding fast to the spirit of *woxin changdan,* must erase the humiliations of the Twenty-One Demands and the more recent Ji'nan Incident.[81]

In the aftermath of the Mukden Incident, the Commercial Press in Shanghai came out with a volume entitled *National Humiliation Illustrated (Guochi tu)* that, like so many other books published subsequent to the Guomindang's assumption of national power, clearly reflected the ruling party's point of view.[82] The book contained ten large full-color foldouts of charts, maps, and other pictorial material pertaining to China's victimization at the hands of imperialism. One of the foldouts, titled "A Chart of the Different Kinds of National Humiliation," superimposes a list of the wrongs China has suffered as a result of the unequal treaties over the proverb "to sleep on brushwood and taste gall" *(woxin changdan)*, drawn in large block characters. On either side of the foldout is depicted a sword passing through a crown of thorns—a symbol, interestingly, derived from Christian iconography, where it represents the mocking humiliation of Christ by the Roman soldiers who placed the crown on Jesus's head. From each crown of thorns is suspended a gallbladder dripping bile into the open mouth of a Goujianesque figure clad only in shorts and lying against a pile of brushwood.* As in many of the other shorthand allusions to the Goujian story that we have previously encountered, it is taken for granted that Chinese readers will know that *woxin changdan* refers to the story of Goujian and the burden of suffering and shame (including the mockery) he endured and will interpret the contents of the image accordingly.[83]

Although it cannot perhaps be demonstrated in a categorical way, it is certainly plausible to argue that the strong identification of the Guomindang with the example of Goujian during these years reflected the profound sense of connection that Chiang Kai-shek himself felt with the Yue king. This sense of connection doubtless had something to do with the fact that the Guomindang leader hailed from the same geographical area—the modern province of Zhejiang—in which the ancient state of Yue had been situated. But I wouldn't put undue emphasis on this.[84] Far more important, in my judgment, were the personal qualities exhibited by the Yue king—the forbearance in the face of repeated humiliations, the willingness to absorb temporary setbacks for the sake of achieving ultimate victory— and the appeal to Chiang of the larger strategy adopted by Goujian over time in his dealings with the state of Wu.[85]

These aspects of the Goujian story so attracted Chiang that in spring 1934, two years after his appointment as chairman of the Nationalist government's Military Affairs Commission (Junshi weiyuanhui weiyuanzhang), his Nanchang Field Headquarters, which had a lead role in the military's political indoctrination,[86] ordered the compilation of biographies of Goujian and his two top ministers, Fan Li and Wen Zhong. The Goujian biography was put out in two versions, one in literary Chinese, the other in a more colloquial style for popular consumption.[87] Following *The Annals of Wu and*

---

*In ancient China, as pointed out in chapter 1, the removal of one's upper garments was a ritual expression of submission, used to apologize for an offense and request forgiveness. The bare upper bodies of the Goujian figures in this foldout clearly indicate a state of oppression and victimization rather than an admission of fault. An analogous example is found in the top illustration accompanying the "Guochi" lesson in the mass education movement primer discussed earlier (figure 10).

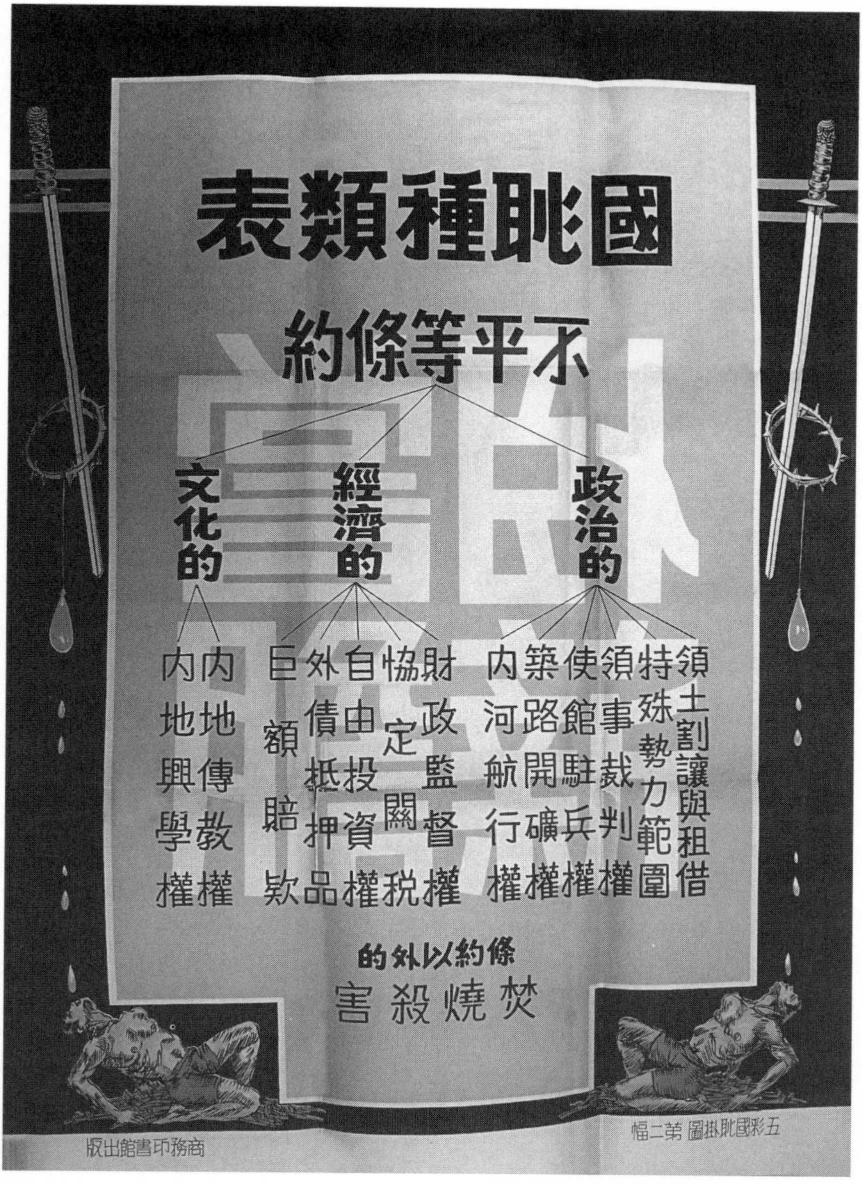

Figure 14. Illustrated chart of different kinds of national humiliation. Source: *Guochi tu,* 2nd foldout.

Yue (Eastern Han) version fairly closely (although it is of course much shorter), it devotes particular attention to episodes with a military bearing: the engaging of the Maiden of Yue and Chen Yin to instruct the Yue army, the motivational story of the angry frog by the roadside, Goujian's training of his soldiers (including the severity of his disciplinary regime), and so on. The stool-tasting episode is omitted, the role of Xi Shi and Zheng Dan is alluded to only in passing, and although the account briefly notes that after the destruction of Wu Goujian was appointed overlord of North China, there is no hint of postconquest tension between the Yue ruler and his ministers. This version of the story—what was included and what was omitted or deemphasized—conformed to the contemporary needs of the Nationalist military, which at the time the order was given for the story's compilation was engaged in the final "extermination" campaign against the Communist forces in Jiangxi province; it also conformed to the puritanism and military discipline that were conspicuous features of the New Life Movement, which Chiang launched in 1934 in an effort to refashion China into a modernized, secular Confucian society.[88]

The PRC historian Yang Tianshi, in an article on Chiang Kai-shek's Japan strategy in the years leading up to the outbreak of war between China and its neighbor, based mainly on Chiang's unpublished diary, has written that the rare "power of restraint" Chiang exhibited at the time "can only be related to the influence of Goujian."[89] During this period, Chiang insisted that, given China's comparative weakness militarily, before engaging Japan it was crucially important, first, to achieve domestic political unity, and second, to await the emergence of a more favorable international environment. After the outbreak of the Mukden Incident and the ensuing Japanese takeover of Manchuria, Chinese societal pressure to resist Japan mounted and Chiang's stance became increasingly difficult to maintain. He faced particularly vocal opposition from students, intellectuals, and writers. When, for example, Chen Dabei's play *Xi Shi* was staged in Nanjing in the mid-1930s, winning high praise from the Nationalist authorities, the left-leaning playwright Tian Han, who was in Nanjing at the time, wrote a blistering critique in which he lambasted the government's policy of nonresistance and its Goujian-like advocacy of "forbearance" *(woxin changdan)*. Tian had only recently been released from a Guomindang jail. His review, in which he disparaged the credentials of Goujian as a popular leader and contended that any plan for saving China would have to rest on the masses and not on some ravishingly beautiful woman, was a thinly concealed attack on Chiang Kai-shek and his wife.[90]

In this difficult and decidedly unfriendly environment, Chiang often bolstered his spirits by recalling the attitude and conduct of Goujian, who also, faced with a far more powerful adversary, had to postpone indefinitely the gratification of his consuming desire for revenge. Two days after the Mukden Incident, Chiang wrote in his diary: "Goujian slept on brushwood and tasted gall, expanding the population and wealth of his state and instructing and guiding its people, as a result of which Yue became overlord; today it is my time to do the same."[91] A week later, deeply burdened by the loss of Manchuria, Chiang, alluding more indirectly to the Goujian story, elaborated on these themes, expressing the wish that all Chinese would unite under the leadership of the Nationalist Party, that they would "increase in numbers and economic strength and be properly indoctrinated [shengju jiaoxun], observe strict order and submit to discipline, in the hope that within ten years, we will wipe away the supreme humiliation of the present and bring to fruition the great cause of the national revolution."[92]

When the headstrong young Goujian, shortly after succeeding to the Yue throne, attacked Wu against the advice of his ministers and suffered a humiliating defeat, Fan Li scolded him, making the key point (as interpreted by commentators) that "if the opportune moment has not arrived, you cannot force things; if conditions are not ripe, you cannot force a successful conclusion." Chiang liked this interpretation and copied it into his diary.[93] He also had great admiration for Goujian's capacity to withstand the most horrific abuses and indignities: "During Goujian's captivity, not only did he lie on brushwood and taste gall, he also drank urine and tasted excrement. Compared with me today, his ability to put up with hardship and tolerate humiliation was many times greater!"[94] According to Yang Tianshi, Chiang also absorbed into his thinking Laozi's dictum that it was necessary to yield in order to gain and the ancient Daoist notions of "retreating in order to advance" and "overcoming hardness with softness." Repeatedly in his diary and other writings of the 1930s, he alluded to such ideas in order to remind himself that China, in its response to Japan, "must exercise the greatest patience," "accept the unacceptable and endure the unendurable."[95]

These ideas also formed an important part of Chiang's more public pronouncements. At the time of the Ji'nan Incident of May 3, 1928, when (according to Chiang) "the Nationalist Government and the Revolutionary Army were thoroughly humiliated by Japan and severely criticized by the people," he issued the following directive to the officers and men of the army: "In order to avenge our country's humiliation, you must free China from imperialist oppression and must attain the objectives of independence and liberty. Today you can only endure insults and prepare yourselves for vengeance. It will take ten years to train the population in the firm belief of our forefathers that the lost territories can and must be recovered and the national humiliation avenged."[96] This is a loose rendering of the original Chinese text of Chiang's speech, which used such phrases as *woxin changdan, shi nian shengju,* and *shi nian jiaoxun,* directly taken from the story of Goujian.[97]

In less formal remarks to subordinates, delivered in Zhejiang on February 5, 1934, Chiang was more explicit in his adulation of Goujian: "We must emulate King Goujian of Yue, everyone must become a King Goujian of Yue. . . . In all our actions, all our methods, we must follow his example. . . . With such a model as Zhejiang's King Goujian of Yue, if we are unable to save the nation, truly we will be unable to face our ancestors."[98]

Up until the middle of the 1930s, Chiang Kai-shek mainly pursued a policy toward Japan of accommodation and concession. Although this policy began to stiffen perceptibly in the fall of 1936, owing partly to further Japanese encroachment in the north and partly to the Nationalists' suppression of anti-Nanjing rebels in Guangdong and Guangxi and an upturn in the Chinese economy (two developments that gave Chiang renewed confidence),[99] criticism of the government's policy from within the Guomindang as well as outside it had for years been unrelenting. This was especially so in areas, such as the far south and the northwest, where Nanjing's capacity to exert control over the press was weakest.[100] In 1935 Zou Lu, a veteran Guomindang member and chancellor of Zhongshan University in Guangzhou, penned a searing critique in which he noted that ever since the Mukden Incident of September 1931 Nanjing had steadily surrendered China's territory and rights to the Japanese, to the point where everyone likened the authorities to the Song dynasty traitor Qin Gui, a man reviled through the ages for his involvement in the killing of the patriotic hero Yue Fei. Nanjing, according to Zou, disputed this characterization, describing itself as a Goujian that tolerated temporary humiliations for the sake of long-term goals *(renru fuzhong).* Zou did not buy this analogy at all, claiming that Nanjing had not done a fraction of the things Goujian had done to strengthen the country and that in any case China's current adversary Japan was hardly to be equated with the weak and bumbling Fuchai. Even the depiction of the government as a Qin Gui was, in his view, inappropriate, since Qin Gui, by pursuing a policy of peace toward Jin, had at least managed to get some of China's territories returned, while the Nanjing authorities had accomplished nothing in this regard.[101]

Some of the themes in Zou Lu's critique were developed in 1936 in an article entitled "We are Goujian, but the Other Side Isn't Fuchai" ("Wo wei Goujian, ren fei Fuchai"), which appeared in the newly established Xi'an paper *Northwest Guide (Xibei xiangdao).*[102] Written by one Lin Guanghan, the gist of the article was that "Goujianism" (Goujianzhuyi), whatever its strengths (and Lin acknowledged these to be considerable), was wholly inadequate as a response to China's current crisis. The main precondition for the success of Goujian had been the ineptitude and muddleheadedness of Fuchai, and, bluntly put, Japan was no Fuchai. The only policy for dealing with the Japanese, therefore, was immediate resistance. Responses to Lin's piece in subsequent issues of *Northwest Guide* were enthusiastically supportive.[103]

One thing that Chiang Kai-shek's unabashed exaltation of Goujian, together with the criticism of this exaltation as misguided, clearly suggests is that on all sides of the political divide in the mid-1930s there was a general recognition that the example of Goujian—what Lin Guanghan called "Goujianism"—was the guiding spirit underlying Nanjing's Japan policy. More broadly, both the adulation and the denigration it provoked supply fascinating instances of Bruner's point about stories serving as "templates for experience." In Chiang's remarks to his subordinates and the criticisms of Zou Lu, Lin Guanghan, and others, Goujian, Fuchai, and Qin Gui are each deployed as metaphoric touchstones for defining and assessing contemporary historical situations.

Contrary to what one might expect from the strident criticisms of Chiang Kai-shek's Japan policy, the Nationalist leader, even before the fall of 1936, was by no means completely unreceptive to a strategy of resistance. Indeed, in the years after the Mukden Incident, Chiang, even while being forced repeatedly to give ground to Japan, simultaneously intensified his planning for war. In two respects these preparations echoed strategies that Goujian himself had pursued more than two millennia earlier. First, Chiang, operating from a position of relative military weakness, engaged in a succession of diplomatic efforts designed to bring about an international environment favorable to the Chinese cause (an alliance, for example, with the Soviet Union against Japan),[104] much as Goujian, in his plans for avenging himself against Wu, had paid close attention to Yue's—and Wu's— relations with the large northern states of Qi and Jin. Second, just as Goujian took care to conceal Yue's military ambitions from Wu, Chiang's hot pursuit of the Communists during the Long March in 1934 and 1935 was intended in part to divert Japanese attention from the secret preparations then being made to create a rear base in the southwest for eventual Chinese resistance against Japan.[105] Thus, Yang Tianshi concludes, "at the same time that Chiang Kai-shek made one concession to Japan after another, he also went ahead with preparations for military resistance, drawing inspiration from the spirit of self-imposed hardship and restraint in the face of provocation shown by Goujian."[106]

THE WAR OF RESISTANCE AND
THE AVENGING OF CHINA'S HUMILIATION

The publication of Chiang Kai-shek's *China's Destiny* in 1943 was intended to celebrate the signing on January 11, 1943, of new treaties between China and its two wartime allies, Britain and the United States, ending the unequal relations embodied in the previous treaties with these nations and bringing to a conclusion China's "century of humiliation." This was a momentous symbolic event: "It is our good fortune," Chiang proclaimed to the citizenry of China, "to witness this day the end of our humiliation and the beginning of a new stage in our struggle for independence and freedom."[107] But it scarcely masked the fact that China was still at war with the country that had caused it the most harm and suffering in the first half of the twentieth century. During the war years the Goujian story was drawn on in ways that differed somewhat from its uses in the prewar period.

Prior to the outbreak of the Sino-Japanese War, the story was all about self-denial, hard work, keeping alive memory of the repeated humiliations of the past, and preparing patiently for the day when it would be possible to wipe these humiliations clean. With the inception of actual fighting against the Japanese and the ensuing occupation of eastern China, the question of what to do with May 9 and other national humiliation anniversary days, the focus of which had been centered on the remembering of past hurts, was naturally raised. In the early stages of the war, many Chinese still felt that it was appropriate to acknowledge national humiliation days, even though for political reasons it was not always possible to do so in public ways. On May 9, 1938, flags throughout Hankou were still lowered to half-mast and people were asked to refrain from costly entertainment and recreational activities. By the following year, however, it had been decided that in Shanghai flags should not be flown at half-mast on this day and that people should confine their observance of the May 9 anniversary to refraining from meat.[108]

One *Shenbao* reader was inspired by this ruling to write an extended essay on the virtues of vegetarianism that was very much in the spirit of the Goujian story. Formal public actions, such as the lowering of flags and gatherings of citizens, were not nearly as important, he reasoned, as having the right psychology, a psychology that emphasized putting up with humiliation for the realization of a larger purpose and that was sworn to avenge the wrongs done to the nation. In the existing circumstances, there was no more appropriate way for Chinese to erase the humiliations their country had sustained than by following the time-honored practice of abstaining from meat, which was akin to "lying on brushwood and tasting gall." In order to remove the disgrace of the Versailles Peace Treaty, the German people had stopped eating butter, meat, and other costly items and used the money saved to manufacture ships, airplanes, and artillery. This was the equivalent of long-term vegetarianism. If Chinese—and here the author echoed a point others had made previously—were to refrain from eating meat on May 9 and donate the money saved to the nation, the amount would surely be significant and the contribution to the war effort substantial. It would be even better if people fasted completely on this day, following the example of the Jewish people on the anniversary of the destruction of their nation.[109]

As late as 1940, various sectors of the Shanghai populace continued, of their own volition, to consecrate May 9 to the memory of the Twenty-One Demands and to mark the date by not going to the theater or eating lavish meals, by economizing and giving aid to those in distressed circumstances, and by saving money for the purpose of rebuilding the nation. Chinese radio stations in the city, by not broadcasting programs of entertainment on May 9, showed that they too had not forgotten the events of 1915.[110] But the general tendency, after the beginning of the war, was for May 9 to recede in importance and to be replaced by July 7, the date on which the war between China and Japan commenced in 1937. A *Shenbao* editorial of May 9, 1939, entitled "From the 'Twenty-One Demands' to the 'New Order in East Asia,'" gave voice to the thinking that had now become increasingly common: "The lessons of history, lessons written in blood from twenty-four years of Japanese aggression against China, have finally awakened the 450 million people of China. The War of Resistance [the Chinese name for the Sino-Japanese War] China is now waging has taken the place of 'May 9' and constitutes a positive response to the 'Twenty-One Demands' of 'May 7.' Otherwise put, in the past Chinese society memorialized 'May 9' with anger and indignation and the shedding of tears, but now Chinese armies with bravery and iron and blood have rendered 'May 9' a thing of the past."[111] One year later, in May 1940, the Nationalist government in Chongqing (to which it had retreated in the face of the Japanese advance) formally abolished National Humiliation Day, reasoning as follows: "The May 9 anniversary was originally for the purpose of prodding the populace to recall Japan's ambition to commit aggression against China. Now, ever since July 7, 1937, the entire nation has been engaged in the War of Resistance, and July 7 has been established as the anniversary of the War of Resistance. There is no longer any need, therefore, to commemorate May 9."[112]

The change in the psychological climate in China implied in these statements had a direct bearing on how the Goujian story played during the war years. Actually, some renderings of the story in an explicitly anti-Japanese context began to appear almost immediately after the Mukden Incident. In 1932, the Guomindang's provincial branch in Hebei published a group of nine plays under the title A Collection of Dramas for Resisting Japan and Saving the Country (Kang Ri jiuguo xiju ji); one of the plays, which unfortunately I have not been able to examine, was entitled Woxin changdan.[113] The war years proper witnessed a diverse array of material relating to the Goujian story, much of it expressly targeting the masses. One item, which again I have not seen, was an opera, also titled Woxin changdan, that was performed by professional opera actors for the entertainment of the armed forces in Hankou in 1937, before the Japanese moved into that city.[114]

In November 1937 the National Association for the Advancement of Mass Education, forced by the war to move from Hebei to the Hunanese city of Changsha and now actively engaged in anti-Japanese propaganda work, came out with a popular collection of pamphlets called Peasant Resistance (Nongmin kangzhan congshu). Included in the series, apart from items on such war-related topics as Sino-Japanese relations before September 18, Qi Jiguang's pacification of Japanese pirates, and air and poison-gas defense, were several historical stories highlighting patriotic themes. One of these, written by Xi Zhengyong in simple colloquial language, was Goujian Avenges Past Humiliations (Goujian xuechi). Perhaps the most significant part of Xi's rendering, in terms of its bearing on the war against Japan, is its treatment of Xi Shi and Zheng Dan. Both women are portrayed as deeply distressed by the calamities that have struck Yue and only regret that, as females, they are unable to go out and fight the enemy. When they hear that a search is under way for meinü (beauties) to go to Wu and undermine the position of Fuchai, they respond with eagerness, thus conveying the message to Chinese women in 1937 that there were many ways to be patriotic and that, even if women could not join the army, they could still contribute to the war effort in meaningful ways. The broader lesson of the account is stated in the concluding paragraph: "Because Goujian was mindful of the humiliations his country had experienced, he worked hard to make Yue strong. Although his country was beset with difficulties on all sides, owing to the fact that the leaders and the populace were of one mind and put forth great effort, after only ten years of enriching the populace and ten years of training the military, they had their revenge and wiped clean the national humiliation [guochi]. Truly this is a fine example for us later generations to follow."[115]

Another version of the Goujian story aimed at the common people and clearly linked to the war was Chen Heqin and Zhu Zefu's *Woxin changdan*, first published in August 1938 and promptly reissued two months later. Brought out by the People's Bookstore (Minzhong shudian) in Shanghai, it was part of a series of stories from the Chinese past explicitly dedicated to highlighting the role of the masses in history. One of the objectives of the series was described as "to study the spirit of struggle displayed by our nation in the past in order to arouse our national consciousness and strengthen our faith in China's salvation."[116] In line with this goal, there are several places in the story that clearly point to the current situation. As Goujian and his wife are leaving to go to Wu as Fuchai's prisoners, the king tearfully addresses the Yue people who have come to see them off, telling them that although they will have to put up with much suffering and humiliation in the near term, the day will come when they will wipe clean the national humiliation, when their hatred will be avenged, when their land will be returned to them, and when their blood debt will be cancelled in one stroke.[117] As in Xiong Foxi's 1931 play and the upper primary level primer of 1947 discussed earlier, the text of *Woxin changdan* is dotted with contemporary phrasing, heightening the relevance of the account to the war against Japan. When Goujian leaves for Wu, it is pointed out that before parting he has formulated a plan and that therefore this is not a true "surrender" *(touxiang)*. A few years later, upon hearing that their king will soon return from Wu, the people of Yue are overjoyed that the leader of their "war of resistance" *(kangzhan)* is coming home. After Goujian's return, he institutes a "general mobilization" *(zong dongyuan)*, recognizing that the people must be brought to understand the national humiliation before they can fight and that if Yue is to avenge itself and erase its humiliating condition, first priority must be given to instructing and training the masses. "Male, female, young, and old—the entire population must be totally mobilized."[118]

The populist thrust of this rendering of the Goujian story is underscored toward the end, where the Yue king wavers momentarily in response to Fuchai's plea for a peaceful resolution of the conflict between Yue and Wu. There was no way, we are told, that Fan Li and Wen Zhong, who had borne hardships together with Goujian, were going to make peace; there was no way that the soldiers on the front lines who had risked their lives were going to accept peace; and the people of Yue who had suffered so greatly at the hands of Wu, "how could they consent to peace?" Goujian, pressured from all sides, saw that compromise was out of the question, that the fight must be carried through to the finish, until Wu was utterly destroyed and the great humiliation suffered by Yue had been completely eradicated.

The contemporary bearing of Chen and Zhu's account is made explicit at the very end: "The wheel of history moves forward, not in reverse, and the situation at present is very different from that of ancient times. But the lesson of perseverance in the face of difficulty [*woxin changdan*] that we learn from this story continues to have relevance for the current quest of the Chinese nation for independence and for the liberation of our 450 million people."[119]

The linkage of the Goujian story with China's War of Resistance was most intense in the city of Shaoxing, located on the site of the ancient Yue capital, Kuaiji. The author of an introduction to a collection of historical materials relating to the revolutionary culture of Shaoxing described the "spirit of Goujian" as having for centuries been a fundamental feature of the moral character of the city's inhabitants, prompting them "in time of national crisis to donate the family fortune to the state" *(huijia shunan)* and lay down their lives for their country.[120] Among the materials contained in this work were songs and poems written by Shaoxing people during the years just prior to the Japanese seizure of the city in April 1941. The authors repeatedly refer to the inhabitants of Shaoxing with such phrases as "Brave men of Yue," "Sons and daughters of Yue," and "Descendants of the King of Yue."[121] A few examples will convey the songs' militant spirit: One, entitled "A Paean to the Defense of Shaoxing" ("Baowei Shaoxing ge"), began as follows: "Defend Shaoxing, defend Shaoxing, Shaoxing is the ancient city of the king of Yue. Our people, one million two hundred thousand strong, emulating the *woxin changdan* spirit of our ancestor, vow to destroy the Japanese slaves."[122] Another's lyrics follow:

One million two hundred thousand strong,
We are the descendants of King Goujian of Yue;
Qiu Jin and Xilin* are our martyrs,
Our spirit is tasting gall and sleeping on brushwood.
One million two hundred thousand strong,
We have hearts as tough as iron;
We fear not the enemy's fire and are determined to defend great
  Shaoxing.
One million two hundred thousand strong,
Righteous ardor boils over in our hearts;
We will defend the south shore of the Qian River,
And we won't let a single Japanese bandit slip past our blockade.
Forging ahead, one million two hundred thousand strong,
We descendants of King Goujian of Yue will exert ourselves to the
  utmost.
We will not, we absolutely will not be slaves;
We will overthrow, we will overthrow savage Japan.[123]

The strong identification of the people of Shaoxing with Goujian was also reflected in the titles of periodical publications launched in the city in the late 1930s as part of the anti-Japanese war effort. These included the semimonthly *Spirit of Shaoxing's King of Yue* (*Shaoxing Yue wang hun*; established by the Shaoxing County Political Work Group), *The Ten-Day Bulletin of the Spirit of the King of Yue* (*Yue wang hun shiri tongxun*), and the *Spirit of the King of Yue Wall Newspaper* (*Yue wang hun bibao*).[124]

In late March and early April 1939, Zhou Enlai visited a number of places in Zhejiang, including Shaoxing, to boost anti-Japanese morale. Although he had been born in Jiangsu, Zhou's ancestral home was Shaoxing and he often referred to himself as a "Shaoxing person." On the evening of March 28, in the question-and-answer period following a talk he gave to a group of some two hundred united front supporters, he cited the example of King Goujian of Yue's "sleeping on brushwood and tasting gall" to encourage everyone to bolster the moral courage of the nation, unite in carrying forward China's War of Resistance, and defeat the Japanese bandits. Two days later, at an informal evening discussion with young workers from a local electrical company, Zhou spoke about the anti-Japanese situation and, draw-

*Qiu Jin (1875–1907) and Xu Xilin (1873–1907) were two celebrated revolutionaries from Shaoxing, both of whom were martyred in the late Qing.

ing on the story of Goujian's "devoting ten years to building up the economy and ten years to training the military," urged his listeners to work hard to make China strong and, in emulation of the spirit of "sleeping on brushwood and tasting gall," vow to erase the national humiliation and bring about a final victory in the War of Resistance.[125]

Just as the story of Goujian was a *cultural* resource for Chinese of all political hues, Communists as well as Nationalists, it was also a *national* resource in spite of its local Shaoxing origins. Toward the end of the war, the Tianjin-born playwright-director Mei Qian (b. 1916), experiencing political persecution at the hands of enemy and collaborationist elements in the Beiping-Tianjin area, returned to Shanghai, where he had gone to school, and soon after arriving wrote a play entitled *The Spirit of a Party Member (Dangren hun),* with the alternate title *Qiu Jin and Xu Xilin (Qiu Jin yu Xu Xilin).* Deeply moved by the martyrdom of the two Shaoxing revolutionaries, Mei poured his intense feelings into the script, assuming that in Japanese-occupied Shanghai it would never be performed. He got lucky, however, and a rich young capitalist who read the play liked it and decided to back it. Since it was a historical drama and contained nothing overtly anti-Japanese, it got by the censors and opened in January 1944 at the Carleton Theater (Ka'erdeng daxiyuan).

Owing to its ability to stir up the patriotic feelings of audiences and call forth their sense of national pride, Mei Qian's drama was enthusiastically received and played to a full house at every performance. Although the dialogue may seem stilted and overwrought to readers today, it is not hard to see how the following exchange between Qiu Jin and Xu Xilin (apparently taking place at the time of the Boxer War of 1900) might be decoded by Chinese theatergoers in 1944:

QIU JIN: When I left the capital, the city was in flames, the Westerners were killing people like flies, bodies were scattered along the road leading to the Qian Gate, large numbers of women had been raped. Truly it was a situation where in every family there were people who threw themselves into wells and in every household people hung themselves from the beams. . . .
     . . . Ever since ancient times, our Kuaiji has been noted as a place for the avenging of wrong and the eradication of humiliation. In that period long ago, King Goujian of Yue right here at this spot slept on brushwood and tasted gall, and after taking ten years to build up the population and resources and ten years to instruct and train the military, gave

Yue a new lease on life. . . . We too, following in the footsteps of our ancestor, must arouse the spirit of the nation and make deliberate plans for the avenging of wrong and the eradication of humiliation. . . .

XU XILIN: . . . Better to be a dog without a home than a slave without a country. . . . We descendants of Yan Di and Huang Di [i.e., the Chinese people], under the dark rule of the Manchu Qing dynasty, have for three hundred years suffered untold hardships; the rot and decay of the court, the corruption of the officials, today the ceding of territory, tomorrow the payment of indemnities, the utter destruction on a daily basis of our national rights, the dividing up of China by the powers—the day is not far off when China will become extinct! . . . This fine expanse of rivers and mountains that make up our China, that successive generations of our ancestors have used their blood and sweat to clear for cultivation and to irrigate—can we let it go to ruin in this way? . . . The ordinary people of China can be humiliated no more!

After the initial performances, Mei Qian turned the play over to a theater group under the direction of the Communist underground in Shanghai. In the spring of 1945, on the eve of China's victory in the Sino-Japanese War, it was staged ten times at three of the city's top theaters. The response of the more than thirteen thousand people who saw it was again one of rapt appreciation.[126]

Just as, in the early stages of the war against Japan, May 9 as an anniversary date was superseded in importance by July 7, in one book-length account of the Goujian story that I have seen (published in Chongqing toward the end of the war), the emphasis on the remembering of past humiliation gave way to a new stress on Yue's war against Wu, which the author, Wei Juxian (1899–1989), as had by now become commonplace, referred to as a "war of resistance" (kangzhan). Wei was a prolific, if somewhat maverick, writer on archeology, history, and many other subjects.[127] In his rendering of the Goujian story, the details of the king's humiliating three-year-long captivity in Wu are passed over entirely, much greater weight being placed on the work of rejuvenating the state of Yue. Indeed, Goujian's rebuilding his state in response to a "national crisis" (guonan) is expressly portrayed at the end of the account as a model for contemporary Chinese to emulate and is submitted by the author as his main justification for compiling the volume.[128]

Wei Juxian's telling of the Goujian story, unlike the more accessible versions examined earlier, is pretentiously academic, placing more emphasis on the piling up of historical citations than on the construction of a readable piece of literature. Also different from the other examples discussed, the author does not stop with Yue's destruction of Wu, choosing instead to incorporate the friction and mistrust that developed after this event between Goujian and his top ministers. Intent on recounting the whole story, he then goes on to discuss Goujian's death, his descendants, and historical traces and relics concerning Yue and its famous king.

Wei Juxian's book, simply entitled *Goujian,* was part of a collection called Stories of Famous Chinese Worthies through the Ages. In an emotional and heavily nationalistic prefatory statement (by series coeditor Pan Gongzhan) describing the objectives of the collection as a whole, a number of themes are highlighted. The individuals whose stories are included—among them, the sage king Yu, Confucius, Qin Shi Huang (the first emperor of Qin), Chinggis Khan, and Sun Yat-sen—are presented as the embodiment of China's fine cultural traditions and national spirit. These traditions and spirit, which are latent in the blood of every Chinese, were forsaken in the nineteenth century, as a result of which China suffered repeated humiliation at the hands of the foreign powers and almost expired as a nation. After the revolution led by Sun Yat-sen, however, they blazed forth once again, becoming the wellspring of China's rebirth in the twentieth century. This rebirth remained incomplete, however, as indicated by the continued existence in the country of "cultural slaves"—people lacking confidence and self-respect, who had the bodies of Chinese but had lost their Chinese souls. For this reason, it was necessary for those engaged in cultural work to redouble their efforts. Hence the decision to compile a collection of accounts of great Chinese of the past.[129]

In this chapter I have explored an aspect of China's history in the first half of the twentieth century that has been almost entirely overlooked in the accounts of historians. Western historians of this period have overlooked the Goujian story, I suspect, because they have not generally been aware of its existence; certainly they have not recognized its importance. Chinese historians, although clearly aware of the existence, even pervasiveness, of renderings of or allusions to the story in contemporary materials, have not given it the prominence it deserves, perhaps because they have taken it too much for granted, like a picture on a wall that one has seen so many times one ceases to be aware of it. The one exception to this that I have encountered is the illuminating article by Yang Tianshi earlier cited. But even here the emphasis is entirely on Goujian's influence on the thinking of Chiang Kai-shek as an individual—an influence possibly deriving, Yang implies, from Chiang's having hailed from Zhejiang province[130]—rather than the impact of the story on the consciousness of Chinese generally during these decades.

It is this general impact of the Goujian story on Chinese consciousness that I find interesting and compelling. J. D. Y. Peel has argued that for Protestant missionaries operating in West Africa in the nineteenth century, and even more for their African converts, the Bible was "their supreme paradigmatic history, through which they recognized new situations and even their own actions."[131] This connection appears to have carried over into the religious lives of millions of people of African descent in America. Barack Obama describes his profound emotional response to a Sunday morning sermon he heard as a young man in Chicago: "Inside the thousands of churches across the city, I imagined the stories of ordinary black people merging with the stories of David and Goliath, Moses and Pharaoh, the Christians in the lion's den, Ezekiel's field of dry bones. Those stories—of survival, and freedom, and hope—became our story, my story."[132] In a similar vein, Gabrielle M. Spiegel, following the groundbreaking work of Yosef Hayim Yerushalmi in his little book *Zakhor: Jewish History and Jewish Memory,* maintains that "for Jews, historical experience is incorporated into the cyclical reenactment of paradigmatic events in Jewish sacred ritual," recent or contemporary experiences acquiring "meaning only insofar as they can be subsumed within Biblical categories of events."[133] Others have made similar observations about "the capacity of stories to structure behavior" (Elvin) or "shape our experience" (Bruner).[134] Did the Goujian story function in this way in China in the first half of the twentieth century? That is, did it actually shape, even define, Chinese memory of past humiliations and how these humiliations should be responded to, supplying them with meanings they otherwise would not have had? Or was it simply a narrative that resonated with the memories and responses that people would likely have had anyway?

I'm not sure these questions are finally answerable. The cases discussed by Peel and Spiegel both deal with sacred texts that, at least for believers, are the embodiment of ultimate reality and truth. Naturally, therefore, these texts have a commanding influence on how subsequent human experience is perceived and understood. The Goujian story, it may be argued, is different from this. It is a powerful myth, but it is not sacred in the way that the Bible is sacred in the Judeo-Christian tradition. Yerushalmi, in a postscript to *Zakhor* entitled "Reflections on Forgetting," suggests that, at certain historical junctures, peoples are capable of anamnesis, of reaching "back into an often distant past to recover forgotten or neglected elements with which there is a sudden sympathetic vibration, a sense of empathy, of recognition."[135] This, it seems to me, more accurately captures the Chinese situation in the first half of the twentieth century. Not that the Goujian story had ever been completely forgotten or neglected in China. But at a certain point in time—as far as I can see, it was the final decades of the Qing—growing numbers of Chinese began to discern a close correspondence between the basic structure of the story and China's contemporary experience. This sense of "sympathetic vibration" became, in time, quite general, developing into a perception that was widely shared among Chinese during the years of the republic.

It was not, however, a fixed, stable connection. The mating of ancient story to contemporary experience was a contingent one, with the result that, as Chinese concerns changed over time, the Goujian story—or at least the meanings gleaned from it—also underwent significant modification. The clearest instance of this in the republican period was perhaps the shifting emphasis of the story during the war years, including the insinuation into it of terms and concepts derived from the Sino-Japanese War experience. During the second half of the twentieth century this process of story transformation became far more pronounced.

THREE

The Plight of Chiang Kai-shek's Taiwan

FOR THE COMMUNISTS, SUCCESSIVE VICTORIES in the Sino-Japanese War and the ensuing civil war (1945–1949) created a fundamentally new historical situation in which the major humiliation of foreign imperialism had become a thing of the past. But for Chiang Kai-shek's Nationalists, after their retreat to the island province of Taiwan (which had been restored to China in 1945 after Japan's defeat), the most salient change, arguably, was that the area under direct government control had drastically shrunk. The Guomindang still faced the task of eliminating foreign imperialism (now in the guise of the Soviet Union) and its Chinese accomplices.[1] There remained, in other words, a major humiliation to be eradicated, requiring the same qualities of forbearance, hard work, belt-tightening, and tireless effort—of *woxin changdan*—that had been staples of the Goujian story as it had been articulated in earlier decades. Predictably, in these circumstances, the story was from the outset widely disseminated among all sectors of Taiwan's population.

THE TAIWAN SETTING AFTER 1950

To better understand the pertinence of the Goujian story to Taiwan's circumstances in the middle of the twentieth century, a few of the more distinctive characteristics of these circumstances need to be delineated. Territorially minuscule in comparison with the Chinese mainland, Taiwan embraces an area roughly half the size of Ireland. Its population, as of 1950, was less than ten million (including an infusion of some two million refugees during the civil war years), as contrasted with a mainland population at the time of close to six hundred million. In late 1949 and early 1950, Chiang Kai-shek's embattled government was readying itself for an amphibious Communist invasion that appeared imminent and that the American government assumed, given the deplorable state of the Nationalist military, would be successful. Then, in June 1950, the Korean War broke out and the East Asian world changed overnight. Communist forces, which had been assembling in southeastern China in preparation for the final act of the civil war, were redeployed to the northern part of the country, and the United States, determining that Taiwan was now an important part of its defense perimeter in East Asia, moved its Seventh Fleet into the Taiwan Strait. "For the Nationalist Chinese," Nancy Tucker writes, "the struggle in Korea had come as if by magic at the last possible moment before disaster engulfed them."[2]

Provided with the breathing space it had previously been denied, the Chiang government during the 1950s moved in a number of broad directions that were to distinguish the Taiwan scene for the next three decades. After an examination of past errors evocative of the pained self-scrutiny Goujian engaged in following his humiliating defeat at Mount Kuaiji,[3] the Nationalists reorganized and rebuilt their armed forces, fashioning a military that by the end of the 1950s was six hundred thousand strong and bore "little resemblance to the disorganized, demoralized units" fleeing the mainland in 1949. Huge in relation to the size of the population, this military was fed by a system of two- or three-year universal conscription that, for the male members of society, constituted an additional period of formal training on top of their prior educational experience. The latter was also nearly universal, with some 93 percent of children of primary school age enrolled in school as of the late 1950s.[4]

During the 1950s a number of important economic and social developments also took place, laying the groundwork for the vigorous economic growth that Taiwan experienced in the 1960s and 1970s. A much-praised land reform program was initiated in 1949, which dramatically reduced the power of the landlord class in the countryside and transformed Taiwan's agriculture into an owner-cultivator system. The infrastructure the Japanese had created during the colonial era, substantial American economic aid from 1950 on, and the actions of an impressive group of Western-educated Chinese technocrats who had migrated to Taiwan in the final stages of the civil war were additional factors favoring the island's economic growth. As incomes rose, educational opportunities expanded, including increased access to schooling for girls. Literacy rates, already relatively high at the end of the Japanese colonial period, rose still further. Compulsory teaching in the "national language" (guoyu) from 1946 on facilitated over time a lessening of tension between native Taiwanese and immigrants from the mainland. This latter result was also encouraged by examinations for admission to secondary school, college, and the civil service that were honestly administered and scrupulously fair.[5]

The foundational policy that drove these developments and that, for several decades after 1950, was enunciated incessantly was the goal of retaking the Chinese mainland. The manifestations of this goal, succinctly embodied in such slogans as fangong fuguo (launch a counterattack and recover the nation) and fangong dalu (launch a counterattack against the mainland), were encountered everywhere: on billboards in public venues, in magazines and books, in school primers, in political speeches, on radio and television, and in the press.[6] The remarks of Chiang Kai-shek in 1963 in his annual October 10 (Double Ten) message, celebrating the anniversary of the beginning of the 1911 Revolution, were typical:

> On our shoulders lies the heavy responsibility of delivering our compatriots, recovering the mainland, and destroying the Chinese Communist regime, that scourge of mankind. . . . It may not be possible for us to attain our goal in one leap. But the return to the mainland is what all of our people, military and civilian, at home and abroad, are awaiting. If we are united in deed and thought, and if we strive unceasingly, we shall reach our objective of national recovery in the near future. . . . To us recovery of the mainland is a sacred mission. . . . It is our duty to launch a punitive expedition against the rebels, to deliver our compatriots from tyranny, and to recover the mainland. . . . The time to begin counteroffensive action may now come at any minute.

Chiang's speech concluded with three cheers, the first of which was "Victory in our counteroffensive and mainland recovery!"[7]

The ideological handmaiden to the core political objective of retaking the mainland was a spirited emphasis, in the school system and elsewhere, on the inculcation of "Confucian" values.[8] This was partly for the purpose of refurbishing the Republic of China's credentials as the repository of the authentic traditions of Chinese culture at a time when, from the Nationalist perspective, these traditions were being foreignized, falsified, and destroyed under the Communists.[9] It was doubtless also aimed at the Taiwanese majority on the island who had recently spent a half century living under Japanese colonial rule. Many mainland Chinese viewed the Taiwanese as wartime collaborators in dire need of being reintroduced to such time-honored Confucian precepts as loyalty and integrity.

The supreme Nationalist goal of counterattack and recovery, reversing the stinging humiliation of defeat in 1949, resonated in a powerful way with the story of Goujian. It is no surprise, therefore, to learn that in one form or another, the story was widely encountered in educational materials in Taiwan, as well as in juvenile literature, opera, spoken drama, fiction, film, television, and radio. The narrative was often tailored, either implicitly or explicitly, to the specific circumstances in which the Nationalists found themselves. Indeed, although it was hardly necessary, given its central theme, some renderings actually incorporated the phrase *fuguo* in their titles, thereby underscoring the intimate association between the Goujian story and Nationalist government policy.[10]

ADAPTATION AND POPULARIZATION: SPOKEN DRAMA AND OPERA

Beginning in the 1950s, the Goujian story was a frequent theme in opera, spoken drama, fiction, and film in Taiwan. Since the fiction and film treatments of which I am aware tended to place as much emphasis on the famed beauty Xi Shi as on Goujian, I will confine myself here to spoken drama and opera. One of the most interesting of the former, in terms of the author's conscious endeavor to adapt the story to Taiwan's contemporary plight, was *Goujian and Xi Shi (Goujian yu Xi Shi),* written by the screenwriter, playwright, and director Chen Wenquan.[11] The date of completion of Chen's five-act play—October 1958—was significant, as the offshore islands of Quemoy (Jinmen) and Matsu (Mazu), which were part of the Republic of China (ROC), had come under fierce Communist bombardment from late August into early October, resulting in a sharp increase in tension in the Taiwan Strait. In these circumstances, when the author of one of the play's prefaces referred to the important part theater had to take in supplying spiritual nourishment to the army and the people in "the great age of anticommunism," we may assume that consumers of theater in Taiwan read this as something more than mere rhetorical flourish.[12]

Chen Wenquan spelled out his aims in the play very clearly in his own preface. "The warp of this play's subject matter," he wrote, "is the recovery of one's country [*fuguo*]; loyalty, filial piety, integrity, and righteousness [*zhong xiao jie yi*] are the woof." The play, he went on, contained behavioral models for people of the present day—negative models for them to be on guard against (Fuchai's unfilial conduct, for example) and positive ones for them to emulate (such as Xi Shi's integrity and righteousness and Fan Li's trustworthiness). The recovery of Yue, in Chen's view, was due only partly to the personal virtues of Goujian. No less important were the qualities of loyalty and courage demonstrated by the entire Yue populace. Indeed, it was this synergism between ruler and ruled that was the key to the state's successful rebirth.

Chen proceeded to list a number of ways in which he had modified the story as customarily recounted. It was most unlikely, for example, that the love between Fan Li and Xi Shi would have reached the stage of their having "improper" *(aimei)* relations. And certainly, Xi Shi would not (as tradition sometimes suggested) have had a baby whom, on the journey to Wu, she abandoned in a river. Fan Li and Xi Shi lived in a time when the teachings of Confucius were much in vogue. Since Xi Shi was well raised and Fan Li was an important state official, their behavior could not possibly have been so reprehensible. Moreover, the tradition that, after Yue's conquest of Wu, Fan Li changed his name and, taking Xi Shi with him, floated off among "the three rivers and five lakes" was not to be credited. Given a woman of Xi Shi's high moral character, it was most unlikely that she would have agreed to remarry. The fact is, for one in her position, the only recourse was to commit suicide.[13]

Apart from Chen Wenquan's insistent literalness and his exaggerated portrayal of early fifth-century B.C.E. China as a world profoundly shaped by Confucian values (hardly an apt characterization of the conduct of the contending states of the day), what is most fascinating about the play is the degree to which the author holds its main characters up to the highest standards of Confucian teaching. This is true above all of the depiction of Goujian and Xi Shi.

The treatment of Goujian is plainly in line with classical Confucian precepts concerning the ideal ruler of a state; it is also noteworthy for its incorporation of language and themes that resonate with the contemporary situation of the Nationalists on Taiwan (and, arguably, the behavior and self-image of the Nationalist leader Chiang Kai-shek, who as we saw in chapter 2 strongly identified with Goujian). At the beginning of act 2, when Goujian returns to Yue after his three-year incarceration in Wu, the first thing he does is approach the Yue ancestral shrine at Mount Kuaiji. He looks up and asks himself plaintively: "Goujian! Have you forgotten the humiliation you suffered at Mount Kuaiji?" With tears in his eyes, he kneels before the shrine, then bemoans his past errors and the shame he has brought on Yue. He then arises slowly and, after announcing that Yue must undergo thorough reform, states that he wants the capital moved to Mount Kuaiji, to prompt him to be forever vigilant. He also orders a gallbladder to be hung up in his bedroom, so that the bitter taste of his experience in Wu will not weaken over time. Goujian then, like a model Confucian ruler, asks his high officials what advice they have to give him and, after accepting their recommendations, goes out to speak to the throng of ordinary Yue people who have gathered to welcome him home.[14]

Elsewhere in the play, Goujian's humane Confucian impulses are highlighted. Years later, in the midst of frenzied preparations for the long-postponed attack against Wu, he pauses to console a hunter, whose son has just died in an accident and is about to be buried. This prompts Wen Zhong and Fan Li to heap praise on him as a king who, while denying himself all material comforts, is close to his people and shares with them their personal afflictions. Shortly thereafter, Goujian demonstrates in a more formal way his commitment to the centrality of the family unit when he instructs Wen Zhong to announce to the army that if a father and son are both serving, the father need not take part in the Wu campaign; if elder and younger brothers are both serving, the eldest need not take part; in the case of only sons whose parents are still alive, they should return home to care for their parents; and if there are soldiers who are ill and unable to march, they should stay in Kuaiji to nurse their illness.[15]

Never lost sight of in Chen's play is the crucial fact, forming a partial parallel to the late 1950s mainland-Taiwan contrast, that Wu is a large and prosperous state with a strong army, while Yue is small, poor, and weak.[16] Yue cannot vanquish Wu, therefore, merely by increasing its own military strength and economic well-being. It must also do everything possible to weaken and impoverish its rival. To this end, just as Wu had planted spies in Yue, Yue made use of the grand steward Bo Pi as a spy at the Wu court. It also scoured the country for the loveliest maidens to present to Fuchai, partly to divert him from conscientiously attending to his responsibilities as king and partly to strengthen Yue's undercover operations in Wu. In addition, every conceivable stratagem was used to deplete Wu's resources and weaken the support of the Wu people for their king. And since Yue was well aware that the hardheaded and perspicacious prime minister of Wu, Wu Zixu, saw through all of its stratagems, a major objective of the Yue leadership was to drive a wedge between Fuchai and Wu Zixu and thereby bring about the destruction of the man it admired above all others at the Wu court.

Fuchai, in this regard, certainly did his best to accommodate Yue, since from the outset he showed himself irritated by Wu Zixu's badgering and far more amenable to the counsel of Wu's archrival at court, the deeply corrupt and traitorous Bo Pi. The play opens at the Wu court. Fuchai has just recovered from his long illness and the question of what to do about Goujian has arisen. Fuchai asks what has happened to the servant whose job it is to remind him repeatedly of his filial obligation to avenge the death of his father, Helu. After being told that the man stopped doing this during his illness, Fuchai orders his return. The man returns and, as in the past, shouts out, "Fuchai, have you forgotten the grudge you bear toward the Yue king for having killed your father?" Fuchai responds, "I dare not forget." The routine is repeated and the king becomes annoyed. When the man shouts out the same question a third time, Fuchai explodes, calls the man a bloody fool *(hundan),* and asks him why he keeps shouting the same thing over and over, when his instructions are to shout only once daily upon seeing him. The man replies that, since he has not shouted for three months, he is making up for the long dry spell. Fuchai again calls him a bloody fool and tells him to get lost.[17]

From this rather comical episode, we immediately learn that the Wu king is cranky and ill tempered and, more important, that he does not take his duty to avenge his father's death with the proper degree of seriousness. Wu Zixu enters and pleads with Fuchai not to be taken in by Goujian's subservient behavior. He is a dangerous man, and the Wu king must seize this opportunity to have him killed, thereby on one hand fulfilling the pledge not to live under the same heaven as the killer of one's father, and on the other hand eliminating a mortal threat to Wu. Fuchai, exasperated, finally yields to Wu Zixu's nagging and orders him to have Goujian done away with. But at this point, Goujian, his wife, and Fan Li are ushered into the king's presence and Fan Li attempts to dissuade Fuchai, for the sake of his good reputation, from having Goujian killed. Bo Pi and Wen Zhong (who has just arrived at the head of a Yue tribute mission) also try to get the king to exonerate Goujian and allow him to return to Yue. Wu Zixu enters the fray, and the arguing goes back and forth, mainly between Wu and Bo Pi. Fuchai eventually decides to reverse his earlier order and set Goujian free. The latter, with mock obsequiousness, expresses his gratitude and undying loyalty to the Wu king. Everyone leaves except Fuchai. The servant reminder once again appears and shouts out, "Fuchai, have you forgotten the grudge you bear toward the Yue king for having killed your father?" Fuchai angrily tells him to get out: "Bloody fool! Everyone's gone. What's the point of shouting now?"[18]

The interaction between Fuchai and the servant shouter is more than a simple dramatic device. Of far greater moment is the signal it sends to the reader (or audience) about the authenticity of Fuchai's sense of filial obligation. When Goujian, immediately after returning from Wu, kneels before the Yue ancestral shrine and asks himself whether he has forgotten the shame he suffered at Mount Kuaiji, the occasion is marked by solemnity, the question laden with deep feeling. For Fuchai, by contrast, the parallel question called out by his servant assumes the guise more of an empty ritual—a formality that the king has staged to demonstrate his filial feeling to the rest of the court, but that he doesn't care to be truly guided by in his behavior.

Fuchai's small-mindedness and weak, vacillating behavior are revealed in other ways as well in the play, nowhere more conspicuously than in his infatuation with Xi Shi, which causes him again and again to place the gratification of his own emotional needs ahead of the interests of Wu. This is especially marked after the forced suicide of Wu Zixu, which takes place at a fairly early point in the action. Thereafter, Xi Shi fulfills her duties as a patriotic daughter of Yue in a range of ways, taking a major part in bringing about the progressive deterioration of Wu's position and in setting it up for its ultimate destruction. But as a deeply moral individual, the part Xi Shi is called upon to play does not rest easily with her. At the beginning of the final act, in an exchange with another Yue palace woman, she gives voice to the tangle of conflictual feelings burdening her. She does not love Fuchai, but she is enormously grateful to him for all the things he has done to please her. Although she loves Fan Li, she is married to Fuchai. Yet, although married to Fuchai, she loves her country still more.[19]

The concluding scene of the play takes place three years later. The final Yue assault on Wu is now in full swing and chaos reigns. Fuchai enters. Wu soldiers come in reporting one reverse after another and Fuchai is advised to flee. Xi Shi tells Fuchai of her deep remorse, since she repeatedly encouraged him to believe that Goujian was a loyal subject. As a Yue person, she says she is now too ashamed to face him. Fuchai tells her she is being silly, that she has long since become a Wu person. She offers him one goblet of wine, and then another. As the reports of approaching disaster keep coming in, Fuchai laments the fact that he did not listen to Wu Zixu and destroy Yue when he had the chance. The king calls for more wine, then asks Xi Shi to dance, saying that he is willing to sacrifice everything—his country, the altar to the gods—as long as he can be with her always. Xi Shi, sensing the inappropriateness of the king's behavior, with tears in her eyes beseeches Fuchai to let her die so that she will no longer stand in the way of his larger obligations. Fuchai persists in his request that she and the other palace women present sing and dance for him. At this point the servant shouter, who has been seriously wounded, is helped in by two Wu soldiers and reports to Fuchai that the Yue army has broken through the east gate of the capital and captured the Wu king's three sons. The servant then intones, "Fuchai, have you forgotten the grudge you bear for the killing of your father?" one last time and falls to the ground dead.[20]

The top Wu commanders enter and announce that, violating their king's orders, they requested peace talks with Goujian but that the Yue king had turned them down. Yue's rejection, they report, came in the form of a message sent by arrow into the Wu camp. The message listed five great faults of Fuchai, among which were his killing of the loyal minister Wu Zixu and his failure to avenge the death of his father. Given these breaches of the cardinal virtues of loyalty and filial piety, the message concluded, Yue had no choice but to destroy Wu. Fuchai confesses to all present that he has indeed been an unfilial son and that after having Wu Zixu killed there is no way he can face him. He picks up his sword, readying to kill himself, but is stopped by Xi Shi and a Wu general. The general urges Fuchai to try to rescue the three princes. Xi Shi beseeches Fuchai to flee with her and hide instead, but after assuring her that he will come back he accedes to the general's urging and the two of them exit. Xi Shi, weeping, prostrates herself and (presumably alluding to all of the actions she has taken to bring about the present situation) says that she has injured Fuchai too cruelly.[21]

At this point a Wu soldier reports that Fan Li's army has fought its way to the palace and that the Wu defenders are preparing to surrender. The Yue palace women are overjoyed. One of them says that she hears Xi Shi is going to marry Prime Minister Fan Li and asks if the rest of them can remain with her. Xi Shi replies: "Oh? Don't you know that a woman of virtue *[lienü]* does not wed a second husband? We have already received the favors of Fuchai. How can I have the face to marry another!" At this point the temple attendant of Yue enters and, addressing Xi Shi, reports that Fan Li has been slightly delayed. He adds that he has heard that Fuchai, after being surrounded by Yue forces, fled to the hills and committed suicide. As Xi Shi, stunned at this piece of news, covers her face and weeps, the temple attendant tells her that she has truly rendered outstanding service to Yue, that without her help Yue's resurrection would not have been possible. She responds modestly that, no, Yue's revival has been owing to the persistence of Goujian and the combined efforts of the army and people of the entire country.[22]

Fan Li at this point enters and begins to address Xi Shi. The others exit, leaving the two alone onstage. Fan Li tells Xi Shi of the jealousy and resentment that have warred in his breast over so many years, almost driving him to suicide, until he recalled that the wrong done to Yue had not yet been redressed and that his responsibilities remained unfulfilled. Now, finally, Yue's goal has been accomplished and the two of them have been reunited and can grow old together. Xi Shi acknowledges having had similar sentiments, but now that Yue has attained its revenge against Wu, she is a fallen woman. Having already served Fuchai, her moral sense will not permit her to serve Fan Li. She hopes, therefore, that he will permit her to commit suicide in order to preserve her virtue.

Fan Li objects to this. Then Xi Shi pretends that Goujian is entering and, when the prime minister turns around to welcome the king, picks up a sword and cuts her throat. The stunned Fan Li gathers her in his arms, crying out, "Xi Shi, Xi Shi!" She asks his forgiveness, saying that she has now avenged her country's shame and also paid off her personal debt to Fuchai. Fan Li, she adds, should be happy for her, happy that the citizens (guomin) of Yue possess such high-minded morals. She then closes her eyes.[23] Fan Li summons attendants and orders that Xi Shi, who is still alive, be placed on a boat. When Goujian enters and asks for her, Fan Li informs him that Xi Shi has fulfilled her loyalty to her country and, in order also to fulfill her sense of integrity, has cut her throat. He tells Goujian that he has given orders for her to be taken to Kuaiji for medical attention.

A Yue soldier comes in and announces Fuchai's suicide. Goujian says he already knows and issues orders that the Yue army construct a large tomb for him. Bo Pi enters, announces that Fuchai's three sons have been brought in, and asks whether they shouldn't be decapitated outside the city walls in order to forestall future trouble. Goujian says that since Yue already has possession of all of Wu, it is unnecessary to also sever the Wu ancestral line; he then orders the release of Fuchai's sons. When Bo Pi cites the authority of his archenemy Wu Zixu on the need, in such situations, to cut off the family line completely as insurance against subsequent problems, Goujian replies that Wu Zixu as a man was overly cruel and brought on his own death as a result. He then orders the execution of Bo Pi for having deceived his king and endangered the realm of Wu.

At this point, a Yue soldier comes in and reports that Xi Shi has leapt into the river and that they can't find her body. Fan Li addresses Goujian. He tells him about the pact made years before between Xi Shi and himself to the effect that when Yue had recovered its country *(fuguo)*, he would request permission to retire from public life. Now Xi Shi is gone and, wishing to honor his end of the agreement, he asks Goujian to allow him to resign from his position. Goujian, expressing regret, says that Yue's ability to rejuvenate itself hasn't just been due to the achievement of ten years spent enlarging the population and ten years devoted to training the army; the most important thing has been the achievement of the whole country acting as one, deeply conscious of the righteousness of its cause, and carrying its mission through to the end. The Yue ministers, kneeling, exclaim that the country's triumph has been entirely owing to the inspiration of their king's moral conduct, as embodied in *woxin changdan*. The top Yue commander enters and announces to Goujian that the army has gathered outside the palace and is waiting for the king to speak. The play concludes with Goujian's telling the assembled multitude that the people of Yue must in the future continue the accomplishments of this day, all working together to build "our new country."[24]

The Confucian virtues—loyalty, filial piety, integrity, and righteousness—that Chen Wenquan referred to as the thematic woof of his drama are put on full display in the final act. Wu Zixu, Fan Li, and Xi Shi are represented as paragons of loyalty, Bo Pi as the extreme opposite. There is no positive example of filial piety as such, but Fuchai more than makes up for this—initially, by his failure to fulfill his filial obligation, and later, by his pained acknowledgment of this failing. In the end, ironically, it is the Wu king's nemesis Goujian who punishes him both for his filial transgression and for the killing of his most loyal minister, Wu Zixu.

The fullest embodiment of integrity and righteousness in the play is, of course, Xi Shi, who is also by far Chen's most complex character. Xi Shi's loyalty to Yue is never in doubt. But the tasks she is asked to perform in the fulfillment of this loyalty place a huge burden on her psychologically. First of all, she must win the affections of the man who is the chief enemy of her state and whom, at least at the outset, she does not love. Second, although she becomes the wife of Fuchai, which by her stringent moral code means she must serve him faithfully throughout her life (even if he predeceases her), she also acts deliberately in such a way as to undercut his interests again and again; in other words, Xi Shi repeatedly betrays the man who, in her mind, is her husband. This is extremely painful for her, but up until the point at which Yue has consummated its mission of revenge against

Wu, there is nothing she can do about it; she cannot kill herself because that would render her unable to act any longer in Yue's behalf. Once Yue has triumphed over Wu and Fuchai has taken his life, on the other hand, the obligation for Xi Shi to remain alive is no longer operative. At this point, the reappearance of Fan Li in her life activates the other conflict burdening her. As much as she loves Fan Li, she cannot marry him because, to her way of looking at things, she is already married. Unlike the earlier conflict, which Xi Shi was not in a position to resolve, this one can be resolved—indeed, it can only be resolved—by her committing suicide, an act that, once achieved (but not before), Fan Li appears able to accept.

Goujian, in his role as the victorious king, acts in such a way as to reinforce the importance of the positive values embodied in the play's main characters and to censure the negative ones. He heaps praise in the penultimate act on the patriotic actions taken by Xi Shi to advance Yue's cause.[25] In the final act, in addition to condemning Fuchai's faults, he punishes the traitorous Bo Pi with death and acknowledges the great contributions of Fan Li and others to Yue's final victory. But what is most interesting about Goujian's actions in the play's dénouement is their embodiment of a Confucian virtue that is not specifically mentioned by Chen in his preface. I refer to his humanity. We have already seen instances of this earlier. Now his humanity is reflected in the generosity he shows in his moment of triumph. Goujian orders the army to give Fuchai a burial proper to the king of a state and, contravening the extreme advice of the late Wu Zixu (as articulated hypocritically by Bo Pi), he sets the Wu king's sons free instead of having them needlessly killed.

Although we have in Goujian and Xi Shi two variants of the Confucian moral code—the former representing the broadly humane virtues of classical Confucianism, the latter a more puritanical, straitlaced form of Confucian behavior that was to become especially influential after the Song period—both characters affirm behavioral models that Chiang Kai-shek's Nationalists were intent upon instilling in Taiwan's population in the years after 1950. Another play that sought to accomplish a similar end was Tan Zhijun's *Goujian Recovers His Country (Goujian fuguo)*, which, although published in 1971, was in all probability written in the 1950s or early 1960s.[26] Prior to following the central government to Taiwan in 1949, Tan had worked in the Ministry of National Defense, was involved in literature and artwork in the army, and took an active part in anti-Communist activities within the Chinese film and theater world. After getting to Taiwan, in addition to his efforts in spoken drama, he wrote the lyrics for such patriotic choral works as *Counterattack Cantata (Fangong dahechang), Our Great Leader (Weida de lingxiu),* and *Our Great China (Weida de Zhonghua).* He also wrote numerous plays for radio, a medium that as late as 1970 was still three times more prevalent than television in Taiwan homes.[27] Tan's theatrical productions in general, not surprising in light of his background, were rich in military themes and consciousness. Indeed in 1956, while still a young man (he was born in 1921), he was honored for his accomplishments by none other than Chiang Kai-shek himself.[28]

Implicitly recalling the situation in Taiwan in the aftermath of the catastrophic Nationalist defeat in the civil war, Tan Zhijun's play opens in 494 B.C.E. at Mount Kuaiji, where some five thousand defeated Yue soldiers have assembled. The atmosphere is one of bleakness and total devastation. Several Yue soldiers, exhausted, are onstage talking about the huge loss they have just sustained. Two Yue generals enter. One of them remarks on what a great shame it is that a leader as wise as Goujian should experience a defeat of such tragic proportions. "Heaven," he cries out, "you are too unfair!" The other general expresses a more optimistic perspective: "A momentary setback means nothing. There's no way our great king will be vanquished in the end. Although today we have met up with defeat, before long we will again be triumphant. Although today our country has been weakened, as long as we don't willingly suffer humiliation, before long Yue will become strong once again."[29]

Goujian and Fan Li come onstage. Goujian is despondent and filled with remorse over the suffering his rashness—the attack against Wu in defiance of the advice of his top ministers—has caused his generals and officials, as well as the population of Yue and the Yue army. The two generals respond that their fault is greater still and voice their loyalty to the Yue ruler. As an indication of the depth of their sense of personal failure they make a move to slit their throats with their swords and are only prevented from doing so by the intervention of Goujian and Fan Li. The generals exit. Goujian then turns to two of the soldiers still onstage and, taking note of the extreme hardship they have suffered the past few days, tells them to return to camp to get some rest. After the soldiers leave, Goujian remarks to Fan Li on how truly likable the generals and soldiers of Yue are. Fan Li responds: "That is entirely a result of the fact that the great king treats them with sincerity, caring for them as if they were his own sons. Your minister is confident that, as long as the great king is on the throne, the state of Yue can count on a resplendent future."[30]

Apart from Goujian's compassionate treatment of his people and his receptivity to the advice of his ministers (following the initial setback at the hands of Wu), two other Confucian values that are underscored in *Goujian Recovers His Country* are loyalty to king and country (patriotism) and filial devotion. In an incident that appears, in one form or another, in many retellings of the Goujian story, an effort is made to seduce Fan Li into leaving Goujian and going over to the Wu side. In Tan's play, this episode takes place toward the end of the three-year incarceration in Wu. Wu Zixu approaches Fan Li one day and tells him that Fuchai is greatly impressed by Fan Li's talent and, if he were willing to transfer his loyalty to Wu, would give him an important position in the Wu government. Fan Li rejects the invitation out of hand. Then Wu asks him whether it would make any difference if Goujian were no longer in the picture and confides to him that Fuchai has accepted his (Wu Zixu's) recommendation that Goujian be put to death. Fan Li announces to Wu Zixu that, in that case, he is prepared to go with his king to the grave, following the adage that "a loyal minister does not serve two rulers; a virtuous woman does not serve two husbands."[31]

Fan Li's exemplary sense of loyalty (forming a stark contrast to the character of Bo Pi in the play) is presented in this episode in a nonconflictual way. In other scenes, the demands of loyalty to king and country stand in potential conflict with those of filial piety. In such instances, loyalty, because of the situation Yue is in, has clear priority in *Goujian Recovers His Country*. When Fan Li is searching for lovely maidens to send to Wu, he asks the father of Xi Shi how he feels about his daughter sacrificing herself for her country. The father replies that he understands there are times when one must place the needs of one's country before those of one's family *(wei guo wang jia)*. Later he makes the same point directly to Zheng Dan, telling her that "everyone bears a share of responsibility for the fate of the country" *(guojia xingwang renren you ze)*.[32] Here, Xi Shi's father taps into a theme—the injunction to put country ahead of family and public service before private interest—that was fairly ubiquitous in Nationalist discourse both before and after 1949 and constituted an important ingredient in the citizenship training carried on in republican schools.[33]

Filial piety was a sacred requirement in the Confucian scheme of things. Therefore, it helped immeasurably, in situations where another obligation was to be given precedence over it, for paternal support and encouragement—a kind of parental release—to be supplied. This was clearly illustrated in the episode just cited involving Xi Shi's father. Another example occurs in the first scene of the final act of Tan's play, as Yue at last is readying itself to make war on Wu. Goujian instructs Fan Li, in almost the same language as that used in Chen Wenquan's play, that if a father and son or elder and younger brother are both serving in the army, the father or elder brother need not take part in the attack; if an only son is serving and his parents are alive, he also needn't take part and can go home to look after his parents; and so on. A man whose two elder brothers were both killed in the fighting against Wu sixteen years before and who is the lone remaining son of his parents appears with his father before Goujian. The father begs Goujian to allow his son to participate in the impending attack, so that he can avenge his brothers' deaths and wipe clean the country's earlier humiliation. The son then makes the case for himself, arguing that by taking part in the war he will be able at once to fulfill his sense of loyalty to his country and also to exercise his filial duty by heeding his father's wishes. Goujian agrees to make an exception in this instance.[34]

In my discussion of the plays of Chen Wenquan and Tan Zhijun, I've highlighted Confucian themes in order to show how these works, often quite intentionally, reinforced a major thrust of Nationalist policy in post-1950 Taiwan: the effort to portray the Nationalists as the true inheritors of the Chinese past, as contrasted with the Communists, whose rejection of much of this past, in particular its Confucian teachings and values, made them, from Taibei's perspective, traitors to Chinese culture.[35] As important as this Confucian emphasis was, however, it was not the central theme of the plays. The central theme—the warp, in Chen Wenquan's words—was *fuguo* or recovery of the country. *Fuguo* was closely linked to *xuechi,* the eradication of an earlier humiliation. It was the focal point of the expressions of patriotic sentiment so often encountered in the plays. And, of course, in its contemporary sense of recovery of the mainland, it was the overriding political objective of the Nationalists themselves after 1950.

Fuguo was part of the title not only of Tan Zhijun's play but also, according to the opera authority Zhang Daxia, of a good many Chinese operas that also took the title *Goujian fuguo.* Dissatisfied with the older librettos, Zhang in 1982 published his own version, in which he made a number of changes. One of these was in direct response to the current political context. The earliest operatic renderings of the story of Xi Shi, he noted, laid special emphasis on the *dan* (female) parts. Since this was not in keeping with the requirements of the existing situation in Taiwan, he cut out unnecessary episodes and reduced the number of female roles, while augmenting the role of the *laosheng* (mature male)—Goujian—in the opera, so as to accord with the principal theme of "Goujian recovering the country."[36]

Zhang also made an important change in regard to the Xi Shi part as such. The Xi Shi role is one of the most pliable in the Goujian story generally. In Chen Wenquan's play, as we have seen, Xi Shi, although her patriotism is never in doubt, is torn by a conflicting web of moral obligations from which, in the end, she is able to escape only by taking her life. In Tan Zhijun's play, as in Chen's, Xi Shi and Fan Li fall in love and she performs with skill her patriotic functions as spy and seductress at the Wu court. There is none of the emotional and moral conflict found in Chen's play, however. When Yue has completed its conquest of Wu and Fan Li is finally reunited with Xi Shi, he tells her that she is pure and stainless and that he loves and respects her exactly as he did thirteen years earlier when they first met. She thanks him and reciprocates his sentiments. There is no hint of any emotional or moral claim exerted on her by Fuchai.[37]

Zhang Daxia was not happy with either of these treatments of Xi Shi. Although in the postface to his revised libretto he took note of the legend of Fan Li "carrying Xi Shi off and roaming hither and yon with her," he pointed out that in the earliest historical versions of the story, Fan Li's only motive for undertaking a search for lovely maidens was to eradicate the humiliation Yue had suffered and recover the country *(xuechi fuguo)*. The account in the earlier librettos of Fan Li and Xi Shi falling in love ran counter to the theme of the ancient story, and Zhang therefore eliminated it entirely from his libretto.[38] Even prior to the arrival of Fan Li in Ningluo village, Xi Shi, in his rendering, is presented as a young woman who, although all alone in the world and forced to wash silk to eke out a living, does not dwell on her own circumstances but is deeply anxious and distressed about the imprisonment of her king and the decline of Yue. When Fan Li appears on the scene and sees how beautiful Xi Shi is, his explanation of the mission he has in mind for her is framed entirely in patriotic terms. The task of recovering the country and obliterating Yue's humiliation *(fuguo xuechi),* he tells her, rests on her shoulders. She happily accepts the charge Fan Li outlines for her. At the end of the opera, after she has fulfilled her mission with consummate skill, Goujian summons her and tells her that Yue's success in avenging itself against Wu and eradicating its prior humiliation has been largely the result of her meritorious actions. He says that, after their return to Yue, he intends to reward her well. Xi Shi, predictably, responds (repeating the phrase from Tan Zhijun's play discussed earlier) that in matters pertaining to the life and death of the country, everyone bears responsibility *(guojia xingwang renren you ze)*. There should be no talk, therefore, of material reward. Goujian tells her she is truly a woman of honor and orders his army to return to Yue.[39]

Figure 15. Xi Shi and Zheng Dan washing silk in Ningluo. Source: Xiao Jun, *Wu Yue chunqiu shihua*, 2:417.

The complex character of Xi Shi is depicted in yet other ways in fictional works by Nan'gong Bo (1962) and Wang Chengpin (1974), both titled *Xi Shi*,[40] and in the award-winning 1965 film of the same title, made in Taiwan by the prominent Hong Kong director Li Hanxiang.[41] Since all three of these works, however, are principally concerned with Xi Shi herself and only marginally relevant to the core themes of the present chapter, I shall resist the temptation to discuss them here.

The other role in the Goujian story that has the potential to be treated in widely divergent ways is, of course, that of Goujian himself. As recounted in chapter 1, in ancient China the story did not end with Yue's triumph over Wu. The postconquest Goujian was presented as a man consumed by ambition and envy, who would not tolerate anything that stood in the way of his quest for more territory and power and who in time found ways to rid himself of those in his official entourage whose heroic achievements threatened to overshadow his own. What is interesting is that in the works discussed in this section, this ugly aspect of Goujian's character is completely passed over.[42]

After committing his one big mistake shortly following his accession to the kingship—a mistake that caused enormous suffering among the people of Yue and that he profoundly regretted—Goujian became an archetypically model ruler. He listened to the counsel of his official advisers. He made use of talent wherever it turned up. He lived an ascetic life and did not fritter away scarce resources. Never wavering in his commitment to avenge the earlier humiliations the king of Wu had inflicted both on himself personally and on Yue, he worked tirelessly over many years to enlarge the population of the state, rebuild its economic life, and strengthen its military. He adopted enlightened social policies. And he consistently demonstrated humaneness and compassion in his day-to-day dealings with the Yue people.

If we ask why the authors of these works chose to portray Goujian in this way, I don't think we have to search far for answers. For one thing, the central theme in all of them was the recovery of full control over the territory of Yue and the avenging of the humiliations the state had suffered as a result of its earlier defeat. These goals were achieved with the final victory over Wu and the suicide of Goujian's main antagonist, Fuchai. When the Yue king, still in the Wu capital, addresses his soldiers and officials at the end of Chen Wenquan's and Tan Zhijun's plays and tells them, in almost identical phrasing, that he hopes they will continue untiringly to work together in the building of their "new country" *(xin guojia),* there is a natural sense of ending.[43] This is the moment that both plays have been pointing toward from the beginning. We are not told what happens next, and from a dramatic point of view, it doesn't matter.

For another thing, given the almost perfect fit between the Goujian story, as developed in these works, and the supreme Nationalist goal after 1950 of returning to and reestablishing its rule over the Chinese mainland, it is safe to assume that readers or viewers of these plays would instinctively identify Goujian, the leader of Yue's *fuguo* mission, with Chiang Kai-shek, the dominant Nationalist figure associated with the policy of *fuguo* (mainland recovery) until his death in 1975. Certainly, it is not hard to imagine teachers in Chinese classrooms drawing such a parallel for their students. When we take into account that an authoritarian political system and police state environment prevailed in post-1949 Taiwan—the emergency decree of martial law, enacted in 1949, was not lifted until 1987, not long before the death of Chiang's son and successor, Chiang Ching-kuo—it may be inferred, given the likely identification with Chiang, that to portray Goujian as anything other than an exemplary ruler would be at best in poor taste and at worst a delicate and possibly risky business.[44] The use of historical literature to convey political messages was an age-old Chinese practice—it certainly wasn't invented by the Communists—and Chinese were accustomed to looking for such messages in much of what they read and viewed.

I do not, however, want to suggest that the process of creating such literature was an entirely manipulative one, cynically carried out by individuals who did not sincerely believe in the messages they transmitted. For most Chinese who fled to Taiwan in 1949, after all, the hope of returning to their homes and being reunited with family members on the mainland was a genuine one,[45] and if this hope could be kept alive and bolstered by stories from the Chinese past that touted the likelihood of success against great odds, provided one had the proper attitude and spirit, this was all to the good. It did not matter what one might think of Chiang Kai-shek personally. The fact was, one could not read such a story in the circumstances then prevailing in Taiwan without associating Chiang with the protagonist; it was desirable if not incumbent, therefore, that Goujian, like Chiang himself,[46] be depicted in an adulatory way.

THE GOUJIAN STORY AS EDUCATIONAL MATERIAL: HUANG DASHOU'S POPULARIZATION EFFORTS

The idealization of Goujian as a ruler applied not only to the world of theater but also to that of popular education. This is amply documented in the efforts of Huang Dashou to publicize and promote the story of the Yue king, starting in the 1950s. Born in 1920 in Jiangxi province and educated at Sichuan University, Huang became one of Taiwan's best-known and most-prolific writers on historical subjects. As of early 2000, not long before his death, he was said to have already produced some sixty to seventy books, many of them aimed at a broad, nonacademic readership.[47] He did his first rendering of the Goujian story in 1950, not long after arriving in Taiwan following the Nationalist defeat. It was entitled "Goujian Destroys Wu" ("Goujian mie Wu") and was published in a monthly magazine for young people. The same piece (slightly revised), along with other stories dealing with the theme of national revival, formed the basis for a series of radio broadcasts Huang made in 1952. Readers and listeners urged him to put the stories into book form, which resulted several years later in a little volume entitled *Historical Accounts of National Resurgence (Zhongxing shihua).*[48]

The connection between the contents of *Historical Accounts of National Resurgence* and the contemporary political situation in Taiwan in the early 1950s was made immediately clear by the picture on the book's cover, which showed a self-assured Chiang Kai-shek, his feet planted squarely on a raised base in the shape of Taiwan, with a drawn sword in his right hand and, in his elevated left hand, a lantern with the characters "fight [or oppose] communism" *(fangong)* emblazoned on the side. This connection was reinforced on the title page, at the foot of which appeared the slogans: "We need to launch a counterattack against the mainland! The mainland needs us to launch a counterattack against it!"

It was the historical episodes recounted in the book, however, that established the real link with the contemporary circumstances of Taiwan. In each of the chapters, Huang reconstructed in lively, informal prose encounters from China's past in which, by a combination of hard work, thorough preparation, unflagging determination, and astute leadership, a weaker adversary was able to prevail over a far more powerful one.[49] Following the first chapter, which dealt with the Goujian narrative, there was a story from the Warring States period (403–221 B.C.E.), recounting how, after the state of Yan had attacked the state of Qi and seized some seventy cities, the people of Jimo (in modern Shandong province), one of only two Qi cities remaining uncaptured, chose Tian Dan as their new commander. Tian Dan used a brilliantly unconventional stratagem to lead the Qi army in a surprise night attack against the encircling Yan force, routing it and recovering

Figure 16. Cover picture of Chiang Kai-shek. Source: Huang Dashou, *Zhongxing shihua*.

the captured cities.* The next chapter related the saga of Liu Xiu's restoration of the Han dynasty (in 25 C.E.), bringing an end to the ruinous civil disturbances that had erupted in the last years of the usurper Wang Mang's rule and establishing the prototype for later dynastic revivals. This was followed by an account of the celebrated battle of Red Cliff (Chi bi) on the Yangzi River (208 C.E.), at which the southern naval forces of Sun Quan and Liu Bei decisively defeated the far larger and more powerful army of the northern general Cao Cao, forcing Cao Cao to abandon his goal of extending his dominion over the entire country. A partly analogous episode was the subject of the succeeding chapter, which described another famous battle, that of Fei River (383 C.E.; in modern Anhui), in which the small but properly disciplined and well-led army of the Eastern Jin (317–420 C.E.), the reigning dynasty in the south, annihilated the much larger but poorly trained forces of the invading (Earlier) Qin, which had recently conquered North China and hoped to bring the south as well under its sway. The sixth chapter of *Historical Accounts of National Resurgence* related the achievements of the great general Guo Ziyi (697–781) in reestablishing peace and order to the Tang after the dire threats created by the An Lushan rebellion and other disturbances of the mid-eighth century. The book concluded with the story of Sun Yat-sen's revolution (also, of course, the triumph of a small group of dedicated individuals over a vastly larger and wealthier adversary).

Two former high officials under the Nationalists, Huang Jilu and Cheng Tianfang, each of whom wrote prefaces to *Historical Accounts of National Resurgence,* both underscored the parallels between the stories contained in it and Taiwan's current situation, Cheng praising the book as "the best extracurricular reading material for the youth of Free China."[50] Huang Dashou, in his own introductory statement, was equally explicit:

These were all events of epoch-making significance in Chinese history, and in each case the first phase of the event's trajectory may be said to bear a close correspondence to our present situation, in which we are

---

*Tian Dan collected more than a thousand oxen from within the city. He had multicolored dragons painted on them, swords tied to their horns, and grease-impregnated firewood and hay fastened to their tails. Several dozen holes were bored through the city walls. At midnight the oxen were driven through the openings, with five thousand Qi soldiers following close behind. The soldiers set fire to the oxen's tails, and the oxen, in great pain, charged straight into the Yan forces, who, in the light created by the burning tails, thought they were being attacked by dragons and in their fright were devastated by the Qi soldiers. Tian Dan's ruse is described in his biography in Sima Qian's *Shiji.* See Takigawa, *Shiki kaichū kōshō,* vol. 8, *juan* 82 ("Tian Dan liezhuan"), 5.

using Taiwan as a base for rejuvenation and for preparing our counter-offensive against the mainland. After reading these seven historical accounts, how can we not feel confident? As long as we are prepared to endure hardships and stick it out to the finish, how can we not be victorious in our struggle against the Communists and Russians? How can our recovery of the mainland [guangfu dalu] not be crowned with success?[51]

Although there is no need for a detailed summation of Huang Dashou's recounting of the Goujian story, some of its features, particularly those that most clearly resonate with Taiwan's dire situation in early 1950 (when Huang says he completed the work), are worth noting. The treatment of Goujian himself is, in some respects, even more highly idealized than that found in the theatrical versions of the story earlier discussed. Although the chapter opens with Helu's attack against Yue immediately after the death of Gou-jian's father, the brutal throat-slashing stratagem Goujian used to divert the attention of the Wu forces and pave the way for Yue's victory is omitted (the ruse is alluded to in Chen Wenquan's play). Also omitted is Fan Li's unheeded advice to Goujian a few years later that he sue for peace and not try to fight the far stronger army of Fuchai. This omission enables Huang to attribute Yue's disastrous defeat at Wu's hands to insufficient military preparation rather than to the foolish impetuousness of a headstrong young king. Additionally, although in the aftermath of this loss Goujian offers to place himself at the service of the Wu king, in the end Fan Li and another Yue minister go to Wu as hostages and Goujian remains in Yue, thereby conveniently removing from Huang's rendering aspects of the story that are especially degrading to the Yue ruler.

This sanitization of Goujian, especially noteworthy in light of the clearly implied effort in the book as a whole to link the heroes of the stories re-counted in it to an embattled Chiang Kai-shek, is coupled with a portrayal of the Yue king as a model ruler. In addition to dressing and eating simply, Goujian labors in the fields alongside his people, setting an example for hard work that the farmers of Yue emulate. He listens respectfully to anyone who proffers advice, even when it comes from the lowliest individuals. And local leaders follow the example set by him in the administration of their own areas.

Huang Dashou's account of the Goujian story, like the theatrical treat-ments dealt with earlier and in keeping with the title he gave it, concludes with Yue's conquest of Wu and ignores entirely the less appealing behavior of the postconquest Goujian. Two other aspects of the conclusion are also of interest. One, making up the final paragraph, is symbolically suggestive of the consummation of Chiang Kai-shek's dream of reestablishing Nationalist rule over the Chinese mainland: "On the next day, as the sun rose to the east, the Yue king and his ministers met in the Wu palace atop Mount Gusu to go over plans for the future administration of Greater Yue. Goujian, having taken the place of Fuchai, was the new ruler of Wu; the flag of Yue fluttered in the air above the Wu palace, reflecting in the golden splendor of the eastern sky the immeasurable glory of the moment."[52]

The other part of Huang's conclusion that is of special interest occurs just prior to the end and involves a departure from the conventional treatment of the demise of Bo Pi. The corrupt Wu minister, after Goujian has ordered his execution, is cursed by onlookers for having been disloyal to his king and betrayed his state. The executioner then asks him if he has any last words. Bo Pi responds that it is too late for him to express his repentance, but he has one thing to tell those looking on: whatever they do, they must not follow his example and sell out their country for personal gain; if they do, they will end up like him, dying under the executioner's sword.[53] What is interesting about this episode is that it is not customary in renderings of the Goujian story for Bo Pi, after being sentenced, to offer himself up as an explicit warning to others. Why does Huang have him do so here? The answer, it seems to me, has to do with the special salience of the dichotomy between loyalty and betrayal that existed in Taiwan in 1950. The Guomindang-supervised Chinese war crimes trials, at which such wartime collaborators as Chen Gongbo were brought to account, had taken place in Suzhou only four years before; and, at the trials, as Margherita Zanasi has demonstrated, the political atmosphere (as at the trial of Marshal Pétain in France) was such as to sweep aside all ambiguity and portray the issue of loyalty to country in starkly Manichaean terms.[54] This issue was greatly magnified by the Chinese civil war, still technically in progress in 1950, where, again, there was little official tolerance for the ambiguities that tend to characterize all such conflicts. In Taiwan at this time (and indeed for many years after) the question of whether you were Communist or anti-Communist—that is, whether you were loyal or disloyal to the Nationalist cause—was front and center and brooked no compromise. In this climate, Bo Pi's words of warning moments before his execution, arguably, take on added meaning.

The Nationalist forces that arrived in Taiwan in 1949 and 1950 included several hundred thousand unattached males, a sizable number of whom were beyond the normal fighting age. Since these men had "highly uncertain prospects of ever returning to their homes or of having a family of their own on Taiwan," Jay Taylor has written, "the theme of the counterattack was critical for keeping up their morale and retaining their political loyalty." It was also important, Taylor adds, that once discharged from the military "they did not become a social or economic problem and further alienate the local Taiwanese."[55] To address these and other possible trouble areas, a Vocational Assistance Commission for Retired Servicemen was established. Headed in the late 1950s by Chiang Kai-shek's son, Chiang Ching-kuo, and heavily funded at the outset by the United States, which recognized its importance for maintaining social stability, the commission did much to integrate discharged soldiers into the economy.[56]

The Vocational Assistance Commission for Retired Servicemen also made an effort to boost the morale of ex-soldiers. This was where Huang Dashou came in. Huang himself had served in the Nationalist army, apparently during both the war against Japan and the civil war. In February 1957 he presented a series of six talks to an educational study group attached to the commission. The talks, collectively titled "People in History Who Achieved Success by Dint of Hard Struggle" ("Lishishang kudou chenggong de renwu"), were designed as classroom lessons. The first five dealt with Goujian, Ban Chao, Fan Zhongyan, Wang Shouren,* and—to make the point that people who attained success through hard struggle were not confined to earlier times or to China—Benjamin Franklin. In the sixth and concluding lesson, entitled "The Road to Success" ("Chenggong zhi lu"), Huang distilled from the first five the methods that needed to be followed to achieve one's goals. The members of the study group to whom Huang made his presentations were leading figures in the commission. Afterward, branch groups were established in various locations and the lessons were disseminated to the veterans making up these local groups.[57]

What is fascinating is the detail Huang went into in the planning of the lessons and the instructions he provided for the benefit of the teachers who would be teaching them. Since all of the lessons followed the same pattern, we may take the one on Goujian for illustrative purposes. After a one-page

---

*Ban Chao (33–103), brother of the famous historian Ban Gu, almost single-handedly reestablished the Later Han dynasty's control over Central Asia in the first century c.e.; Fan Zhongyan (989–1052) was a famous Song dynasty statesman and reformer; Wang Shouren (alt. Wang Yangming; 1472–1529), the most influential philosopher of the Ming, was associated with the Neo-Confucian School of Mind.

summary of the story, ending with Yue's final triumph over Wu and the consummation of Goujian's revenge, Huang specifies the goal of the lecture (the gist of the Goujian story is presented in one long sentence), the time to be used for the class (fifty minutes in all, thirty-five to forty minutes for the telling of the story, ten to fifteen minutes for questions and answers, with more time spent explaining the notes in the case of classes of fairly high educational attainment), and proper lesson preparation (a summary of the contents of the lecture should be written on the blackboard or on a large piece of white paper affixed to the wall next to the blackboard).

Huang then spells out the procedure the teacher should follow in the class. The first item to be attended to is motivation. Before starting to lecture, the teacher should ask the class, "Do you know the story of King Goujian of Yue's sleeping on brushwood and tasting gall?" Some members of the class will surely be familiar with it and will reply that they know it. The teacher then asks, "After King Goujian of Yue was defeated by King Fuchai of Wu, what happened?" The class responds that he decided to surrender and put himself at the service of the Wu king. Then the teacher asks, "Did King Goujian of Yue continue serving the Wu king indefinitely? Did he give no thought to avenging himself and wiping out the wrong done him?" The class responds that he did want to avenge himself and eradicate the wrong done him. The teacher then asks if he achieved this goal, to which the class responds in the affirmative. The teacher then concludes: "Relying on patience, determination, and the spirit of hard work and struggle, he eventually fulfilled his hope. Now I'm going to talk with you about what he went through to achieve his goal."

Huang then lists six main points that the teacher should cover in the class: (1) explain the long-standing enmity between Wu and Yue; (2) explain King Fuchai's determination to avenge his father's death, his efforts to rebuild Wu and to train his army; (3) explain how after his defeat Goujian had no choice but to surrender to Fuchai and wait for an opportunity to resurrect Yue; and so on. This is followed by a diagram of the contents of the Goujian story and then a set of notes elaborating on such things as the origin of the term "Spring and Autumn," the modern geographical equivalents of the ancient states of Wu and Yue, the alternative ways of writing the "Gou" of "Goujian," the later emergence of the proverb *woxin changdan*, and the origin and meanings of the phrases *shi nian shengju* and *shi nian jiaoxun*.

The final part of the lesson plan presents six pairs of questions and answers, two examples of which follow:

"What was the nature of the relationship between Wu and Yue? Answer: Wu and Yue were two states of the Spring and Autumn period. Wu's state was situated in the southern part of Jiangsu, Yue's in Zhejiang province. The two states were always at odds and frequently attacked each other."

"What was King Goujian of Yue's life like during his incarceration in Wu? Answer: He and his wife, wearing prison garb that exposed their shoulders and upper backs, went to Wu as hostages, having requested to serve the king of Wu. The king of Wu made Goujian and his wife live next to his father's grave. Every day they cut grass and fed the horses. When the king of Wu went on tours of inspection, Goujian held the horsewhip and went in front of the king's chariot. This sort of chore was humiliating to King Goujian of Yue, but he put up with it respectfully and submissively and did not rebel."[58]

Several things are of interest in regard to Huang Dashou's lesson plan. First, there is a great deal of overlap and repetition in the content of the different instructional steps he outlines, although the format varies from step to step. In his introduction to the appendix, Huang makes it clear that this was entirely intentional on his part: "If you want to cause a person to have a deep impression of something, you mustn't fear repetition in teaching. Only in that way will you get the results you want. From the standpoint of learning psychology, teaching something only once isn't of much use."[59] Second, although Huang's lesson plan embodies a measure of flexibility, enabling the instructor to increase or reduce the degree of difficulty depending on the educational level of the class, it is on the whole fairly straightforward and simple, even in places patronizingly so (considering that the prospective student audience consisted of grown men). Third, and from my perspective most important, Huang teaches the Goujian story as a kind of set piece. The "discussion questions" don't really permit much discussion, since there is only one answer to each question. No effort is made to use the story, say, to get students to think about how they themselves might have responded to the problems Goujian faced or to indicate how they feel about the story's central theme of revenge.[60] The emphasis is entirely on the Yue king's exemplary behavior and the moral to be derived from it. The purpose of the lesson is to motivate and inspire, not to make people think.

Much the same is true of the sixth lesson, in which Huang details the ingredients that go into the making of a psychology and culture of personal success. "In the past," he says to the class in his introductory statement, "we served the nation in the armed forces, taking direct part in the wars against Japan and the Communists, discharging the obligations it was our duty to discharge. At present, we are no longer in the military, but we are still involved in production, reconstruction, and other kinds of work, doing our part on behalf of the nation to strengthen it in the fight against communism and Russia. We must preserve the glorious history of the past, we must advance along the great road that leads to success." To accomplish this, he continues, there are a number of qualities the students in the class need to possess. They need to have hope for the future and faith in themselves. They need determination, so that they won't fear setbacks and will be able to overcome adversity. They need to exercise patience and self-restraint. And they should not look down on the work they're currently engaged in—not a few demobilized soldiers worked in construction projects or had low-paying jobs as street hawkers and pedicab drivers[61]— since having a steady job is a far happier position to be in than having no job at all. "In brief," Huang concludes his opening statement, "if we are prepared to 'shoulder tasks others refuse to shoulder, take risks others dare not take, endure hardships others are unable to endure, and suffer wrongs others are unwilling to suffer,' if we emulate those figures of the ancient or recent past, from China or abroad, who by dint of hard struggle attained success, using sweat and toil to open up a path on which they were able to advance toward the light, there will surely come a day when we will achieve our hopes."[62]

Although the central theme of the first five of Huang Dashou's 1957 lessons was the success achieved on a national scale by renowned historical figures who refused to be cowed by difficulties and hardships, in the concluding lesson Huang's attention shifted to the personal life situations of a troubled—and therefore potentially troublesome—class of individuals in post-1950 Taiwan. Huang referred in passing to the national issue of opposing communism and Russia, but his aim clearly was to bolster personal rather than national morale. To make his presentation more effective, moreover, he deliberately employed the first person in this lesson, figuring that since he also was a retired serviceman, this would lend a more-personal, less-distant and academic-sounding quality to what he had to say and make it easier for the members of the class to accept.[63]

In 1964 Huang Dashou was invited by the Taiwan Television Corporation to host a lecture series on Chinese history. He based his own lectures on revised versions of the stories of national revival he had written ten years earlier. After the broadcasts, in response to the urging of numerous viewers, he had them published, initially in installments in a semimonthly magazine for young students and in 1965 in book form. In the same year, Huang was invited by a Taibei publisher to do a piece on Goujian for inclusion in the first volume of a publication entitled *Biographies of National Heroes and Revolutionary Martyrs (Minzu yingxiong ji geming xianlie zhuanji)*. According to Huang, the stated aim of this multiauthor work (which appeared in 1966) was to supply reference material for teachers of primary and middle school courses in citizenship, history, and Chinese *(guowen)*, and also reading matter for students in upper middle school and beyond.[64]

Huang's contribution, simply titled "Goujian," was very different from his earlier recounting of the Goujian story. Part of the reason for this is that when he wrote the earlier version in 1950, the situation in regard to research materials in Taiwan was extremely poor and the only ancient source he could lay his hands on was Sima Qian's *Shiji*. Forced (apparently) to rely to a great extent on memory, he insinuated numerous details into the account that were not in the older historical texts. For the later version, Huang had a full array of books at his disposal, with the result that although there was still some embellishment in places, the final product was both more complete and also more in line with the information known about the Goujian story in antiquity. A clear illustration of the difference between the two versions was seen in the author's treatment of Xi Shi, which was fuller by far in the 1950 rendering.[65]

Another reason for the difference between Huang's 1966 and 1950 renderings of the Goujian story had to do with the change in Taiwan's situation since the writing of the earlier version. To be sure, the Nationalists in the midsixties were no closer than before to achieving their ultimate goal of returning to the mainland as the legitimate government of China. But militarily and economically, the ROC had made impressive gains in the intervening sixteen years, and although the political environment in 1966 remained as authoritarian as ever (and no government of the cold war era was louder in its insistence on the central importance of opposing communism), the widespread sense of anxiety and despair prevailing in the immediate aftermath of the Nationalist retreat to Taiwan had given way to an increasingly stable and confident society.

One expression of this developing state of affairs was the importance attached to the training of the young. The state provided six years of free public education (in 1968 it was extended to nine), and a remarkably high proportion of young people were enrolled in school.[66] The educational system, in addition to imparting useful knowledge, expended a great deal of effort inculcating certain ideas and values, notably respect for authority and support for the government, filial piety and other generic Confucian ideals, patriotism, anticommunism, and the Three People's Principles of Sun Yatsen. Cutting across all of these zones of prescriptive instruction, moreover, were the stories of exemplary historical figures that constituted a central part of Chinese cultural tradition. These stories were a vital component of the formal instruction that took place in the classroom. They were also conveyed to young people informally via radio, television, films, magazines, and other extracurricular reading materials.

It was within this latter realm that Huang Dashou's 1966 telling of the Goujian story fell. Other chapters accompanying it in the first volume of *Biographies of National Heroes and Revolutionary Martyrs* were devoted to such heroic figures as Tian Dan, Liu Xiu, Ban Chao, Guo Ziyi, Yue Fei, Wen Tianxiang, Qi Jiguang, and Zheng Chenggong.* In his long epilogue to the work as a whole, Lu Yuanjun,[67] a representative of the publishing house, articulated the main premise on which the book was based, the compilers' goals, and the target readership the publishers hoped to reach. After noting the disastrous depths to which life on the Chinese mainland had sunk and applauding the remarkable economic and military progress that had been made in Taiwan under Chiang Kai-shek's wise leadership, Lu pointed to the great need for accurate and vibrant historical writing that conveyed the spirit of the many previous episodes of national revival in China and could serve as inspirational models for all those compatriots now engaged in the struggle to drive out the Communist bandits and recover the nation. The exemplars whose stories were included in the book were those who were fearless in the face of difficulties and danger and did not become disheartened when they met with failure, who were able to endure humiliation and undergo self-imposed hardships *(woxin changdan),* who demonstrated the utmost fortitude from start to finish and were able, beginning from a feeble territorial and demographic base, to restore the empire, taking ten years to build up the population and wealth of their realm and another ten years to teach their people to fight *(shi nian shengju, shinian jiaoxun).* These were the national heroes—and from Lu's itemization of their qualifications it

*On Tian Dan, Liu Xiu, Ban Chao, and Guo Ziyi, see above. The others are introduced in chapter 2.

was plain that Goujian, although unnamed, stood at the head of the pack—who merited the praise of the entire nation and should be taken as models to be emulated by Chinese of the present day.[68]

As for the work's projected readership, Lu Yuanjun, using physiological metaphors, argued that since youth were the blood cells of the present and children the backbone of the future, injecting the national marrow into the blood cells and backbones of young people and children should be an urgent educational priority. Today's youth and children, he contended, were potentially the heroes and inspirational leaders of the future. But in order for them to grow into these roles, they needed to be exposed to stories about the accomplishments of the heroes and martyrs of the past at an impressionable age. Such stories, if vividly presented, would circulate permanently in their hearts and minds, serving as a spiritual compass for their subsequent behavior and achievements. If the young people and children of China were educated and inspired in this way, how could the Chinese people of the future fail to flourish? How could the Chinese nation not prosper?

It was all the more important that these goals be realized, Lu added, because at that very moment youth and children on the Chinese mainland were being indoctrinated with a false conception of history that, with a view to covering up the Communists' own monstrous crimes, sang the praises of such villains as Qin Shi Huang (the first emperor of Qin), the usurper Wang Mang, and the late-Tang rebel leader Huang Chao (d. 884). A historiographical war was in progress, and it was plainly a war that the Chinese on Taiwan could not afford to lose. It was for this reason that *Biographies of National Heroes and Revolutionary Martyrs* had such a critical part to play; it supplied for Chinese youth and children a thoroughly rectified conception of history, one that had the potential to shape the destiny of the Chinese nation and its people. With this in mind, the publishers hoped that every teacher and student in every secondary and primary school history class throughout the island would have his or her own copy.[69]

The conception of history adumbrated in Lu Yuanjun's epilogue is not unfamiliar to people in the West, although, at least for professional historians, it has long been unfashionable to embrace it. Nor, certainly, was it as new and innovative in the Chinese cultural world as Lu made it out to be (a certain amount of promotional hype was, after all, to be expected from a publisher's spokesperson). As a matter of fact, the idea that historical writing should focus on the stories of heroic exemplars from the past and that these stories, because of their capacity to motivate and inspire, should be drummed into the heads of the young, to be internalized as a moral and spiritual resource used throughout their lives—this idea or cluster of ideas was already extremely influential in the Chinese cultural world of post-1950 Taiwan, as indeed it had been in China since time immemorial. What was particular to the stories found in *Biographies of National Heroes and Revolutionary Martyrs* was the specific goal to which they were coupled. They were linked not to female rectitude, filial virtue, official incorruptibility, or steadfastness in the pursuit of one's aspirations in life, but to the goal of national recovery and renewal, which was then, and would remain for years to come, the foundational dream of the ROC.[70]

Huang Dashou's conception of history was certainly broader than this. He had authored numerous historical works that organized the Chinese past in terms other than the centrality of heroic individuals. But when it came to the role that such individuals should play as models for people in the present, Huang's thinking was of a piece with Lu Yuanjun's. He continued to promote the stories of Goujian and other national heroes in the 1970s. In 1975 he came out with a book entitled *Stories of Great Chinese (Zhonghua weiren gushi)*, in which he reprinted unchanged the Goujian account he had published in 1966, along with accounts of Tian Dan, Liu Xiu, Ban Chao, Guo Ziyi, and other historical prototypes whom he had previously written about. As in the past, Huang, responding to Chiang Kai-shek's 1955 appeal for "literature for the sake of war" *(zhandou wenyi)*,[71] linked his popularization of these stories to the calamity that had befallen his compatriots on the Chinese mainland. For more than two decades, he noted, he had culled from among the many illustrious personages of Chinese history a small number who might offer encouragement and inspiration in the present situation and had composed biographies and stories about them. He had repeatedly published these in magazines for young people and books for people in the military, or broadcast them on the radio or television, using a range of methods to instill them in students, soldiers, and the members of society at large, with a view to encouraging future generations of exceptional Chinese to make manifest their capacities. For when one lived in an extraordinary age, the only way to triumph over danger and revive the fortunes of the nation was through the efforts of extraordinary individuals. As if to underscore the point, Huang began *Stories of Great Chinese* with accounts of two such individuals: China's most venerated teacher, Confucius, and (in his judgment) its most beloved and esteemed contemporary political leader, the recently deceased Chiang Kai-shek.[72]

The popularization efforts of Huang Dashou for the most part targeted youth of secondary school age and present and former members of the military. They were not really intended for children. But other writers who did direct their efforts toward the younger segment of the population seemed to operate on essentially the same premises and with similar goals in mind. In this section, I will look at three such accounts—a novel, a comic book, and a picture book—each of which shaped the Goujian story specifically for a juvenile readership.

The novel, a 1953 reprint of a 1940 work titled *Xi Shi,* was written by Chen Enhui and was part of a series of illustrated historical novels, all dealing with celebrated Chinese women.[73] Chen's book is written in a very informal, easy-to-read style, and he is skillful at imaginatively reconstructing the feelings and thoughts governing the characters in different situations. Here, for example, is his depiction of the ailing Fuchai's ecstatic reaction after Goujian has tasted his stool and pronounced confidently that he would soon get well, followed by Chen's sense of what must have been going through Goujian's own mind at the time:

> "Grand steward [Bo Pi], could you have done such a thing?" After Bo Pi was asked this, a look of extreme discomfort came over his face. He shook his head and, hemming and hawing, replied: "Although your servant is filled with love for his great king, this is something that, well, uh, I just couldn't bring myself to do." The Wu king then said: "It isn't only the grand steward who couldn't do it, even the heir apparent who is of my own flesh would, I fear, be unwilling to do it!" While the two of them were marveling in this way at Goujian's performance, poor Goujian himself was at the time beset by a cascade of mixed feelings, alternately sweet, sour, bitter, and stinging. It wasn't, after all, that he had been desirous of tasting the excrement of an enemy for whom he harbored the most profound hatred. He had submitted to such a humiliation only for the sake of his country and his own life, hoping that by so doing he would win Fuchai's trust.[74]

Despite the title of Chen Enhui's book, it isn't until the reader is two-thirds of the way through it that Xi Shi herself appears. Up to this point the focus is almost entirely on Goujian, a great deal of space in particular being devoted to the preparations for the Yue king's incarceration in Wu

Figure 17. Indignities suffered by Goujian while a slave in Wu. When Goujian drove Fuchai's carriage on his excursions, crowds of Wu subjects lined the roadside and mocked the man who was formerly a king and now a slave. Source: Chen Enhui, *Xi Shi,* illustration 4.

and the multiple indignities he suffered after getting there. It is clear from the preface, nevertheless, that Chen regarded a major purpose of the book as being to recast the persona of Xi Shi, so that the actions of this famous beauty spoke in a meaningful way to the discouraging situation in which Chinese found themselves in his own day. Like Chen Wenquan (and Nan'gong Bo and Li Hanxiang), Chen portrays Xi Shi as a conflicted figure. The nature of the conflict is, however, entirely different. There is no indication in the novel of any romantic involvement between Xi Shi and Fan Li; nor does Xi Shi get all worked up over her moral and emotional ties to Fuchai. (The novel ends with the heroine, an expression of joy on her face, standing by the body of the Wu king, who has just taken his life. Looking out at the early morning sky, aware that she has finally fulfilled her sacred duty as a citizen *[guomin],* she cannot restrain herself from exclaiming gran-

Figure 18. Indignities suffered by Goujian while a slave in Wu. This figure shows Goujian sampling the stool of Fuchai, who looks on from his sickbed (see also figure 1). Source: Chen Enhui, *Xi Shi,* illustration 6.

diloquently, "The land of the ancestors is bathed in brightness!"[75]) Xi Shi's conflictual feelings have to do almost entirely with her relationship to Wu Zixu. Here is how Chen describes them in the preface:

> In these times, spiritual nourishment for the national character is the very thing we need. Take Xi Shi. The history books only record her beauty and neglect her great sacrifice. When Wu Zixu failed to come to court to congratulate her on her birthday, she realized that he was a man of great perceptiveness and that he saw through the beauty trap *[meiren ji]* Yue had set for Fuchai. So, when she was in Fuchai's presence, she played the spoiled child and ingratiated herself with him in order to drive a wedge between ruler and minister. But Wu, deeply patriotic minister that he was, from start to finish refused to soften his harsh admonitions, and this resulted in his having to commit suicide by order of the Wu king. Wu Zixu's supreme loyalty was something that struck a deeply sympathetic chord with Xi Shi. But when she contemplated the revival of her

homeland, she couldn't help smiling through her tears. She understood that this loyal minister's ending up as he did had, however imperceptibly, dealt a mortal blow to the enemy of her mother country.

"If you read with care only this one part of the story," Chen went on, "it will offer inspiration enough. But there's also the section detailing the course of action undertaken by Xi Shi's ruler, Goujian, which will move you to tears and song and win your admiration and respect. It is just the thing for people of the present day to draw lessons from."

Chen saw his construction of the story of Xi Shi as being rich in material relating to the contemporary concerns of his compatriots, since such themes as the consequences of aggression, the importance of those in relatively weak situations relying on the strength of their own efforts, and the heroic martyrdom of people of unswerving loyalty to the motherland were thoroughly developed in the book and in such a way as to give young readers a sense of real encouragement. "If," he concluded, "there are people who speak of Xi Shi as one of those vicious beauties who wreck the country and ruin the people, they are really too blind. Assuming that Xi Shi, in the netherworld she inhabits, is percipient and sees the account of her in this book, she should be grateful to the author for the care and thought he has put into it."[76]

I observed earlier that stories of heroic figures had long been viewed in China as a cultural resource of the first importance—a resource that, once internalized, could serve as a guide to individuals in their thought and behavior. The Goujian story, whether focusing on Goujian himself or on Xi Shi, was, of course, a prime instance of this. What is interesting is that even *within* the Goujian story we often find the same phenomenon in miniature. That is, stories about past exemplars are related (almost always by ministers) in order to encourage or provide guidance to people (almost always kings) in the present. There are a number of examples of this in Chen Enhui's *Xi Shi*. In some instances, stories from the past are deployed to urge on either Goujian or Fuchai a specific course of action. Thus, when Wu Zixu hears the news that Fuchai has decided to set Goujian free, he hurries over to where the king is and, flushed and out of breath, with a stern look on his face, tries to get him to reverse himself: "Great king! Formerly, King Jie [the last ruler of the Xia dynasty] didn't put King Tang to death and King Zhou [the last ruler of the Shang] failed to kill King Wen, as a consequence of which King Jie was killed by King Tang and the Shang king was destroyed by the king of Zhou. In the present situation, if the great king, while holding the Yue ruler captive, does not put him to death and, worse still, contemplates letting him return to his state, I fear it will not be long before the disaster that befell Xia and Yin [Shang] will also be visited upon Wu."[77]

Fuchai was momentarily persuaded by Wu Zixu in this instance. However, because he fell ill, he did not take immediate action to have Goujian killed. This gave the Yue king an opening, and Fan Li, after determining by divination that Fuchai's sickness was not serious, concocted the excrement-tasting ruse to take advantage of it. Goujian, however, was not at all happy with the part assigned to him in the scheme, saying to Fan Li that, although he was unworthy, he had after all been the ruler of a state. How could he, on top of the humiliations he had already endured, suffer the still greater ignominy of tasting another man's stool? Fan Li, in his effort to overcome his king's false pride, drew on one of the more horrific of Chinese cultural stories: "Formerly, King Zhou [of the Shang] imprisoned Xibo [King Wen of Zhou] in Youli. After killing his son Boyikao, he boiled the body and, taking it to Xibo, made him eat it. Xibo, having no choice, reluctantly had to consume his cherished son's flesh." Goujian, Fan Li suggested, was a man who was capable of great things. He mustn't wrap himself in a cloak of self-importance and balk at having to do something that was ultimately trivial in nature. As for Fuchai, he was in all his actions "like a woman," completely lacking in the decisiveness of a real man. The Yue king therefore must agree to the excrement-tasting scheme, as this was the way to win Fuchai's sympathy and induce him to change his mind yet again.[78]

These stories in miniature firmly implanted in the minds of young readers the idea, reflecting an assumption that had been widely held in China for centuries, that situations recur in history, so that if you were familiar with how people had responded to a specific set of circumstances in earlier times, you would, if faced with like circumstances in your own day, sense what course of action to take. This same idea was embodied in the Goujian story as a whole. Goujian had suffered a serious setback that was extremely humiliating to him, but by responding to it in a certain way he had been able eventually to avenge himself and in so doing erase the humiliation. The story thus constituted a resource that could be drawn upon for encouragement and guidance in subsequent situations in Chinese history that were of a roughly comparable nature. One of these, explored in chapter 2, was the succession of humiliating setbacks China had experienced at the hands of foreign (mainly Japanese) imperialism in the first half of the twentieth century; another, probed in the present chapter, was the defeat the Nationalists had sustained in the civil war of the 1940s, resulting in their flight to Taiwan.

Since the Goujian story resonated so closely with the situation the Nationalist government found itself in after 1949 and the staple policy of *fangong fuguo* that it adopted in response, it comes as no surprise to learn that the story's dissemination was actively supported by the state in a variety of ways. This was blatantly evident in the case of the popularization efforts of Huang Dashou. Huang's accounts of the story were in books that, as often as not, contained prefaces by top-ranking former Nationalist officials.[79] His broadcasts of the story were aired over radio and television stations that were partly owned (and of course controlled) by the Guomindang party-state.[80] And his use of the story as a morale builder for ex-soldiers took place, as we have seen, under the auspices of the Vocational Assistance Commission for Retired Servicemen, which in the late 1950s was headed by Chiang Ching-kuo.

The government's imprimatur was even more explicit in the case of the comic book *Woxin changdan,* compiled and illustrated by Lan Hong.[81] Lan Hong's book was published in 1976 with the support and authorization of the powerful National Editorial and Translation Office (Guoli bianyi guan) and was awarded the office's first prize in the category of comic books for that year.[82] Although the pictures are drawn with expressiveness and vigor, the development of the story is fairly conventional. As in Chen Enhui's *Xi Shi* and many other renderings of the Goujian narrative, ministers often relate stories from the past in their efforts to persuade their kings. Thus, when Xi Shi and Zheng Dan are presented to Fuchai, Wu Zixu warns him: "The destruction of Xia was brought on by Moxi, the destruction of Yin [Shang] was brought on by Daji, the Western Zhou's ruin was brought on by Baosi. Beautiful women are a source of trouble. I request the king not to accept the two women Yue has presented."[83]

Xi Shi, after quickly becoming Fuchai's favorite, does all in her power to validate the wisdom of Wu's warning. The Wu king goes to great expense to build the Guanwa Palace for her. At her request, moreover, he has it constructed on Mount Lingyan, which just happens to be the location of the base camp where Wu Zixu drills the Wu army. The camp has to be moved elsewhere, which of course intensifies Wu Zixu's ill feeling toward Fuchai and breeds resentment among the soldiers. The palace's location also makes it more difficult for the top ministers of Wu to meet with their king.[84] In other ways as well, Xi Shi works with great resourcefulness to poison the relationship between Fuchai and Wu Zixu, ultimately resulting in the latter's death.

Figure 19. Wu Zixu's futile attempt to warn Fuchai of Xi Shi and Zheng Dan. In frame 269 Wu reminds his king of past dynasties that were destroyed by beautiful women. Fuchai, demonstrating his usual credulity, responds (frame 270) that Goujian's willingness to part with such beauties (instead of enjoying them himself) is a sure sign of his loyalty and submission. Source: Lan Hong, *Woxin changdan.*

The focus of Lan Hong's comic book is, however, not on Xi Shi but on Goujian, its main thrust being that with belief in one's cause, a willingness to endure repeated humiliation, and hard work over a span of many years, it is possible to achieve final victory, even when the odds are heavily stacked in favor of the other side. In addition to foregrounding these familiar features of the Goujian story, the comic book suggests clear parallels between the story and the contemporary circumstances of Taiwan. It does this in part by the use of well-known code phrases in post-1949 Taiwan. Thus when Goujian learns to his delight that Fuchai has fallen passionately in love with Xi Shi, he steps up the drilling of the Yue army so that it will be battle ready when the moment arrives to "launch a counterattack and recover the country" *(fangong fuguo),* and when shortly thereafter he hears that Fuchai has taken his best troops north to the Huangchi conference (where he is to meet with the other state rulers of the day to choose a new overlord), he announces to his top advisers that "the time has come to counterattack and avenge the wrong done us" *(fangong xuechi).*[85] The tie-in between the Goujian story and Taiwan's situation in the 1970s is established with even greater explicitness at the comic's end, where Lan Hong articulates for his youthful readership the following moral: "This is an example from our country's

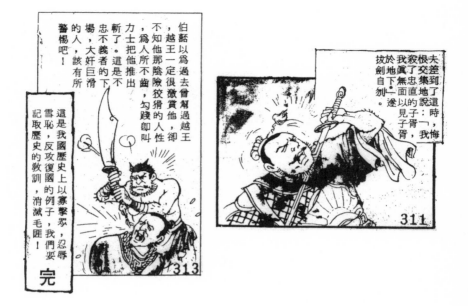

Figure 20. Propagation of Nationalist government policy via a comic book. At the very end of Lan Hong's comic, the author explicitly links the Goujian story with Taiwan's current situation (in a boxed message). Also shown are images of Fuchai's suicide and Bo Pi's execution. Source: Lan Hong, *Woxin changdan.*

history of the few attacking the many, of enduring humiliation and wiping out disgrace, of launching a counterattack and recovering the nation *[fangong fuguo]*. We must bear in mind the lessons of history and obliterate the Mao bandits!"[86]

The emphasis on the past as a storehouse of lessons for young people in the present is also the dominant theme of *Sleeping on Brushwood and Tasting Gall: Goujian (Woxin changdan: Goujian),* a short, illustrated rendering of the Goujian story for very young children published in 1978. Written by Su Shangyao and illustrated by Wen Kai, the book's pages are made of stiff cardboard rather than paper, the illustrations (on every page) are in bright color, and the Chinese text is extremely simple and accompanied by the national phonetic alphabet *(guoyin zimu)* to help with pronunciation. The focal point of the story is on the early battles between Yue and Wu. But the author still manages in the last few pages to present a lively (if much abridged) account of the rest of the tale's high points: the humiliating incarceration of Goujian and his wife in Wu, the Yue king's determination on returning to Yue to rebuild his country and expunge the shame of defeat, the hard life he subjects himself to in the process, his ritual practices of sleeping on a bed of kindling and daily tasting of a pig's gallbladder for self-motivation ("compared to being the slave of a defeated country," he remarks, "the bitter taste of bile really is no big deal"), the rejuvenation of Yue after more than a decade's hard work, and the final destruction of Wu, consummating Goujian's goal of wiping out the earlier disgrace and recovering his country (xuechi fuguo).[87]

Su Shangyao and Wen Kai's Goujian picture book was part of their collection of similar works entitled *Yibaige lishi mingren gushi* (One hundred tales of famous historical figures). The collection as a whole, as introduced on the outside rear cover of each volume, aimed at familiarizing children painlessly with the long Chinese past: "In former times, people often said that to read ancient books and understand ancient affairs one had to 'regard the ancients as friends' [shangyou guren]. I think what they meant by these words was simply that we must make it a practice, when perusing the stories of history, to engage the people of the past and understand them, at the same time taking their words and actions as models and treating the ancients as friends and mentors." The stories in the collection were intended to supply material for just this kind of reading, in the hope that children not only would find the study of Chinese history less daunting but also would draw closer to the people of ancient times, find out what made them tick, befriend them, and take them as examples to be followed in their own lives.

Much the same could be said of the other two books for young people examined in this section. Although their authors understood very well that stories about celebrated figures from the past must be enjoyable and entertaining in order to attract young readers, they were also deeply committed to the idea that these stories should embody moral (as well as political) instruction and guidance, that the lives of the ancients were as relevant today as they were in the remote past. Such stories, as we have repeatedly seen, constituted an important part of the pedagogical training of children growing up in Taiwan in the decades after 1949. The messages they contained, however, were closely attuned to a specific set of circumstances. And as these circumstances changed, especially after the mid-1980s, the stories had to be either reshaped or replaced by other stories that resonated more closely with the new situation. This was largely owing to the fact that the old messages had lost much of their currency. But it was also because, in the more relaxed atmosphere prevailing in Taiwan after the mid-

1980s, people no longer felt constrained for political reasons to produce a certain kind of story.

Chiang Kai-shek died in 1975. Although in a titular sense he was succeeded in the presidency by Yen Chia-kan (Yan Jiagan), real power was wielded by Chiang Ching-kuo, who had been made premier in 1972 and was elected president in 1978. Like his father, the younger Chiang was resolutely opposed to communism and "steadfastly refused to yield the Nationalist claim to jurisdiction over all of China."[88] Also, it was not until 1987, shortly before his death, that the emergency decree of martial law was finally lifted. Despite these policy continuities, vitally important changes did take place during Chiang Ching-kuo's years in power. The loss of the ROC's seat in the United Nations to the PRC in 1971 and the subsequent "derecognition" of the ROC by numerous countries, including the United States (in 1979), represented serious diplomatic setbacks for the Nationalists and did much to undermine their claim to be the sole legitimate government of China. At the same time, the end of the Mao era on the mainland in 1976 and the emergence of a new leadership in Beijing dedicated more to economic modernization than to revolution, combined with a series of PRC-initiated peace overtures and the emergence of a less-threatening atmosphere in the Taiwan Strait, created a new external environment for the Nationalists.

Partly as a result of these developments and partly as a result of internal economic and social changes, the 1980s witnessed the beginnings of a radical political transformation in Taiwan. Already in the early 1980s there were signs of growing political activism on the island.[89] Shortly after the middle of the decade, Chiang Ching-kuo presided over the legalization of opposition political parties (1986) and the granting of permission for residents of Taiwan to visit relatives on the Chinese mainland (1987). Although Chiang Ching-kuo died in January 1988, under his successor, the Taiwan-born Lee Teng-hui (Li Denghui), there were further advances in the process of democratization and political opening. Many more native Taiwanese now rose to top positions in the Nationalist Party and government, economic and other contacts with the Chinese mainland expanded exponentially, and important constitutional reforms were undertaken. Most pertinent, as far as the argument of the present chapter is concerned, Lee presided over a fundamental change in Taiwan's attitude toward mainland China. Already in the early 1990s, the ROC made it clear that it no longer considered itself the lawful government of the whole of China. The policy of national mobilization for "Suppression of the Communist Rebellion," which had been adhered to for four decades, was formally terminated in May 1991. No longer considering Beijing "an illegal rebel," Taibei's stance toward the PRC changed, in Immanuel Hsü's (somewhat optimistic) formulation, "from one of confrontation and cold war rhetoric to one of peaceful competition and cultivation of mutual trust."[90]

In 1996 Lee became the first person to be elected president by popular vote, and four years later Chen Shui-bian became the first non-Guomindang president of the ROC. Chen, who was reelected in 2004, heads the Democratic Progressive Party, which has traditionally favored greater political independence for Taiwan—a position that Chiang Kai-shek and Chiang Ching-kuo both staunchly opposed and Lee Teng-hui, whatever his private feelings, was pragmatic enough not to espouse openly during his years as president. Because Beijing has repeatedly made it clear that an official declaration of Taiwanese independence would be regarded by it as a casus belli and, equally important, because a sizable proportion of the Taiwan electorate, mindful of Beijing's stance, has consistently favored preservation of the existing ambiguous situation, Chen Shui-bian during his years in power, although obviously preferring an independent Taiwan and periodically proposing actions that (at least symbolically) advance this preference, has stopped short of demanding Taiwan's formal separation from China.

From the foregoing, it can be readily seen that during the two decades or so from the early 1980s to the present (2007) a remarkable shift has taken place in Taiwan's situation. At the beginning of this period, Taiwan still regarded itself as the rightful government of all China and remained officially committed to a policy of reconquest of the mainland. Although there were many who objected to such a policy as unrealistic, it remained dangerous to state such disagreement publicly. By the end of the period, the goal of retaking the Chinese mainland by force had long since been disavowed, and the choices facing Taiwan were reunification with the mainland, formal declaration of independence, or prolongation for an indefinite period of the existing indeterminate status. Since there were—and are—huge obstacles to realization of either of the first two options, the third alternative has received wide support from a large segment of the public on Taiwan and at least tacit acceptance from the major governmental actors involved.

The substantial change that has taken place over the past twenty years in the political relationship between Taiwan and mainland China has been matched by even more dramatic changes on the people-to-people level. In the early 1980s, apart from illicit trade and travel, there were no cultural, academic, journalistic, or economic contacts between the mainland and Taiwan. Since that time, cultural exchanges have developed in both directions. Scholars from the mainland have for some years regularly attended conferences, carried out research, and had their books reprinted in Taiwan, as has also been the case in reverse. Journalists from Taiwan began early on to cover developments on the mainland; mainland journalists, developments in Taiwan. Most remarkable, there has been a rapid growth in economic interdependence between Taiwan and the mainland. Cross-strait trade, according to one source, went from virtually zero in 1984 to US$68.65 billion in the first eight months of 2006, with China becoming Taiwan's largest trading partner.[91] As of 2005, there were roughly a million people from Taiwan living in the PRC, as compared to none twenty years earlier. This included some five hundred thousand Taiwanese businessmen and -women resident in the lower Yangzi region alone. The Taiwanese have established thousands of factories and invested billions of dollars in China, and, of course, large numbers of people from Taiwan have traveled to the mainland as tourists, spending in the initial five-year period (1987–1992) "an average of US$4,000 apiece on gifts, travel, hotel, and the like" and "injecting an estimated US$20 billion" into the mainland economy.[92]

Thus, one by one, the features that characterized Taiwan's stance toward the Chinese mainland in the early decades after 1949 and that, from the perspective of the island's mainlander refugee population and Nationalist party-state, made the story of Goujian so compelling, have faded from the scene. It is interesting to note what has happened as a result. Most important, with the abandonment of the foundational policy of retaking the mainland, the core theme of the Goujian story—the theme of a small state, through patience, hard work, shrewd planning, and thorough preparation, triumphing against all odds over a much larger one and avenging thereby an earlier humiliation—has been drained of relevance. And as a result, beginning in the 1980s, a major change became apparent in both the number and nature of Taiwan publications dealing with the story. In comparison to the abundance of material on the Goujian story published in the period from the early 1950s to the early 1980s, for the two decades from the mid-1980s to the first years of the present century, I have been able to identify only five books with a significant focus on either Goujian or the *woxin changdan* theme. The tenor of these books, moreover, differs sharply from that of writings on the Goujian story from the 1950s, 1960s, and 1970s.[93]

In order of date of appearance, the first of the titles was a Taiwan edition of some of the plays of the controversial PRC literary figure Bai Hua (b. 1930), which included his *The Golden Spear of the King of Wu and the Sword of the King of Yue (Wu wang jin ge Yue wang jian)*, first published in the early 1980s.[94] The second was a reprint of the mainland scholar Yang Shanqun's full-scale scholarly reconstruction of the Goujian story. Yang's book, first published in Shanghai in 1988 under the title *A New Biography of King Goujian of Yue (Yue wang Goujian xin zhuan)*, was reprinted in Taiwan in 1991 under a slightly different title and again in 1993 under yet another title.[95] The next books on the Goujian story, published in 1995 and 1997, were two historical novels, both with the title *Goujian and Fuchai (Goujian yu Fuchai)*, one of which again was authored by a PRC writer.[96] The final item, which appeared in 2001, was a study, jointly written by Japanese and Chinese scholars, of the overlord *(ba)* phenomenon of the late Zhou period, focusing on Duke Wen of Jin, Fuchai, Goujian, and Qin Shi Huang.[97]

The mere circumstance that at least three of the foregoing works were by mainland writers was in itself symptomatic of the vast changes that, by the 1990s, had taken place in the relationship between Taiwan and the Chinese mainland. Also of interest is the fact that in the three literary writings the repellent side of the figure of Goujian is given full play, something that almost never happened during the Chiang Kai-shek years. In Bai Hua's play (which will be discussed in chapter 5), Goujian, after his conquest of Wu, turns into a veritable Fuchai look-alike. The first of the two novels, by the remarkable Naxi writer Wang Pizhen (ca. 1921–2003),[98] contains a number of interesting features. Xi Shi is depicted as an uncompromising, hard-bitten patriot, who, during her years at the Wu court, takes an aggressive part in advancing the interests of Yue. When her closest friend, Zheng Dan, falls ill and threatens, in her fevered mutterings, to spill the beans to Fuchai about the Yue spying operation, she forestalls this by poisoning her. After the victory over Wu, Goujian is oddly unappreciative of Xi Shi's great sacrifice, and when his wife writes him, describing Xi Shi as a "*wangguo zhi wu*" (a femme fatale who can bring a country to ruin), he comes to the conclusion that, however necessary the beauty trap *(meiren ji)* may have been, it was a shameful stratagem that did not look very good for one now in a position to become the dominant political figure of North China. Following his wife's suggestion, therefore, he resolves to eliminate Xi Shi by having her drowned in a river. Luckily, Xi Shi is rescued at the eleventh hour by Fan Li (to whom she had been betrothed before going to Wu) and they go to Qi, where they live out their days together under assumed identities. But meanwhile, after this grizzly episode, matters go from bad to worse at the Yue court.[99]

In the second novel, by Li Cheng, there is no relationship at all between Fan Li and Xi Shi. Zheng Dan and Xi Shi are very close, and when Zheng Dan has an opportunity to escape from Fuchai's palace, secretly return to Ningluo, and marry her foster brother and longtime sweetheart, Zhuan Yi, Xi Shi is completely supportive of the arrangement. Despite these and numerous other differences from Wang Pizhen's novel, however, the treatment of the postconquest Goujian in Li Cheng's work is strikingly similar. Initially, Goujian plans to commend Xi Shi at the victory banquet upon the return of the Yue army to Kuaiji. But his wife, on hearing of this, objects strenuously. As in Wang Pizhen's novel, she refers to Xi Shi as a "*wangguo zhi wu*" and asks what good can possibly come from keeping her around, especially since, during their captivity in Wu, Xi Shi was at the Wu court, knew all the details of the shameful things they had had to submit to at that time, and was therefore in a position to sully Goujian's good name in the future. Goujian extols his wife for her shrewdness and, after exclaiming with relief that he had just missed becoming a second Fuchai, gladly turns over the task of disposing of Xi Shi to her. She thereupon arranges for Xi Shi to be taken secretly to the lake outside the city and drowned. This time, however, it is Zheng Dan's husband, Zhuan Yi, who comes to Xi Shi's rescue. She returns with him to Ningluo, where she spends the rest of her days in domestic bliss, living as a sister to Zheng Dan and Zhuan Yi and a third parent to their children. After the victory banquet, at which Goujian again puts his lack of generosity on display by failing to announce rewards to his meritorious ministers and generals, Fan Li leaves to seek his fortunes elsewhere, while Wen Zhong, not heeding his longtime colleague's warning, stays and meets with an unhappy end, consoling himself before taking his life that at least subsequent generations will mention him and Wu Zixu in the same breath.[100]

Among the works dealing centrally with the Goujian story printed in post-1985 Taiwan, the one that is perhaps of greatest interest for our purposes is Yang Shanqun's biographical study. Yang's book was based on a wide and critical reading of the written sources on Goujian, as well as a range of pertinent archeological findings. What he wrote in his preface to the first Taiwan edition was especially revealing. After noting that it was a matter for rejoicing that it was now possible for a book like his to be published in Taiwan, he continued:

The Chinese nation possesses a vast and remarkable historical and cultural heritage, and the story of King Goujian of Yue sleeping on brushwood and tasting gall is an outstanding example of it. It is an awe-inspiring story, which motivates people to go all-out, in the belief that no matter what the difficulties and hardships, if they persist and are not afraid of hard work, and if they vow to stay the course, seeking out and consulting with people of worth and ability and relying on the masses, they can change things around and in the end bring their great undertaking to a successful conclusion. This story imparts philosophical inspiration to people, providing them with encouragement and strength. It is the common spiritual treasure of compatriots on both shores of the Taiwan Strait.[101]

What I find particularly interesting about these remarks, conventional as they might seem, is that they underscore the inherent adaptability of the Goujian story. In the body of this chapter, I have repeatedly discussed the story in terms of its capacity to speak to the situation Taiwan was in (as well as the policies adopted by the Nationalists in response) during the first several decades after 1949. The context was explicitly anti-Communist. The emphasis, both in the stories and in the wider Taiwan environment, was consistently on counterattack *(fangong)*, national recovery *(fuguo)*, and the avenging of humiliation *(xuechi)*. What Yang Shanqun does in his preface is remove the Goujian story from a parochially ideological environment (us against them) and reposition it within an all-encompassing nationalist one (Chinese, rather than Guomindang or Communist). Although Yang's stance was by no means entirely devoid of ideological bearing, inasmuch as it was in accord with Beijing's one-China policy, it differed clearly from the earlier stance of the Nationalists by being inclusive and nonconfrontational.

A similar shift also took place among those individuals on the Taiwan side whose patriotic instincts naturally pointed them, after the changed situation that emerged beginning in the mid-1980s, in the direction of reunification with the mainland and the creation of a single, unitary China. An especially poignant example was supplied by none other than Huang Dashou. Huang was probably the most active and effective popularizer of the Goujian story in the Taiwan of the 1950s, 1960s, and 1970s, and his activities in this regard were carried on within an unequivocally anti-Communist framework. How surprising, then, to find Huang in 1992 taking a lead role, along with the PRC historian Shi Shi, in the launching of a collaborative effort to compile a new history of the Chinese nation *(Zhonghua minzu shi)*. This is a large-scale, multiauthor undertaking that has already been the focus of several conferences in China and that, based partly on new archeological, anthropological, and folkloric evidence, proposes a substantial revision of the history not only of ancient China but also of the historical relationship between the Chinese mainland and Taiwan.[102]

Those participating in the project, believing that it is time to break out of the framework established by Sima Qian more than two thousand years ago, maintain that Chinese civilization did not have its origins solely in the North China plain, centering on the Yellow River valley, but was also the product of influences from other cultural and geographic areas, including notably the far south. They argue, on the basis of archeological discoveries, that Chinese history is ten thousand, not five thousand, years old. And, particularly interesting for us, they contend, again on the basis of recent archeological findings, that the main branch of the original inhabitants of Taiwan, the Gaoshan people, were a seafaring people who hailed from the ancient Yue area (thus challenging the commonly held belief that they are of Austronesian descent). Some scholars pinpointed it even further, claiming they hailed from the area around Shaoxing, the modern site of the ancient capital of the state of Yue.[103]

The scholarly merits of this undertaking do not concern me. I am interested mainly in the political context within which it has taken place. This context, of course, has to do with the contested nature of Taiwan's relationship to the Chinese mainland, not a few individuals having taken the position that this relationship is of relatively recent standing, that Taiwan was not a part of China in any meaningful sense until a few hundred years ago. If, contrary to this, it can be demonstrated that the first human inhabitants of Taiwan in fact came from the Chinese mainland and that they did so as much as six thousand years ago, this lends strong support, it is argued, to the view that "Taiwan" has been part of "China" literally for millennia.[104] Huang Dashou bought into this logic completely. It was embodied in a book he published together with Shi Shi in 1999 entitled *A History of the First Inhabitants of Taiwan (Taiwan xian zhumin shi)*.[105] In an interview he gave in China that appeared early in 2000, he stated that he profoundly hoped for the reintegration of Taiwan with the mainland and, although close to eighty years of age and in not very good health, he was prepared to use whatever strength he had left to accomplish this goal. This was the reason for his wholehearted support of the collaboration of mainland and Taiwan scholars in the writing of a new history of the Chinese nation. "Writing history," he stated, "is for the sake of creating history. A historical work of this kind is just the thing to promote the peaceful unification of the motherland and the unity of the Chinese nation."[106]

Had Huang Dashou really changed his stripes since the early post-1949 decades? Perhaps. But I'm inclined to think not. Huang was from start to finish a "political" historian, in the sense that he consistently felt comfortable placing his historical work in the service of political goals. He was also, it seems clear, unfailingly nationalistic, although the negative target of his nationalism did not remain constant over time. During the earlier post-1949 years Huang was clearly convinced, as were many others who had fled to Taiwan, that Chinese communism in its Maoist guise was a profound threat to Chinese national aspirations. To oppose communism was therefore for Huang the patriotic thing to do, and propagating the story of Goujian was an appropriate way to give expression to this stance and to encourage it in others. During the post-Mao years, however, this all changed. Common ground gradually began to open up, on which Chinese in Taiwan and Chinese on the mainland were able to act in concert. Over time, this common ground widened further, as a result of the increased strength of proindependence sentiment in Taiwan—sentiment that, even if it could not be acted on immediately, was bound to be unsettling to people like Huang who had been born and raised on the mainland and were deeply committed to the idea that Taiwan was a part of China. Looked at from this vantage point, it is not hard to understand how, at the turn of the twenty-first century, scholars like Huang Dashou and Yang Shanqun, although residing on opposite shores of the Taiwan Strait, one in a communist state, the other in a state whose government had for years been avowedly anticommunist, could arrive at a common position in regard to their hopes for the future.

In the decades after 1949, while one set of circumstances was playing out in Taiwan, a vastly different set of circumstances came into existence on the Chinese mainland. The saga of King Goujian of Yue, nevertheless, was as highly valued and widely disseminated in the People's Republic of China as it had been in Taiwan. Although thus confirming Yang Shanqun's assertion that it was a "common spiritual treasure of compatriots on both shores of the Taiwan Strait," as we shall see in the following chapters, the ways in which the story was appropriated by people on the mainland—and the reasons for its appropriation—were a good deal more diverse than had been the case in Taiwan.

FOUR

Crisis and Response

The Woxin changdan *Fever of the Early 1960s*

IN THE PEOPLE'S REPUBLIC OF CHINA, numerous intellectuals, including some of China's most prominent literary figures, gave serious attention to the story of Goujian, beginning for the most part around 1960.[1] In the aftermath of the Anti-Rightist Campaign, the Lushan Conference, the rift with the Soviet Union, and in the latter phases of the Great Leap Forward and accompanying famine—all events of the late 1950s and early 1960s—the Wu-Yue conflict and Goujian's part in it became for a few years a major preoccupation of Chinese writers.[2] The well-known historian Wu Han and others introduced the story in newspapers, magazines, and short books, calling attention in particular to the themes of "self-reliance" *(zili gengsheng)* and "working hard to strengthen the country" *(fafen tuqiang)*, both much emphasized at the time by the central leadership of the party.[3] The longtime minister of culture Mao Dun (1896–1981), who published a little book on the Goujian story in 1962 (it first appeared in article form in late 1961), asserted that from late 1960 through the spring of 1961 theaters and acting groups all over the country put on performances on the *woxin changdan* theme.[4] Also at this time Cao Yu (1910–1996), widely viewed as China's leading playwright of the twentieth century, ventured for the first time into historical drama with a five-act play on the story entitled *The Gall and the Sword (Dan jian pian)*. The play was first performed in Beijing in 1961, when Cao Yu was at the height of his prestige.[5]

How do we account for this upsurge of interest in the Goujian story, especially given the sharply different circumstances of mainland China as compared to Chiang Kai-shek's Taiwan? One broad factor that certainly played an important part was the tendency of many playwrights, in the aftermath of the Anti-Rightist Campaign of 1957 and 1958, to reach back into the past for thematic material. The Anti-Rightist Campaign, which Mao Zedong launched in June 1957 in response to the unanticipated outpouring of criticism of the Communist Party during the Hundred Flowers Movement of 1956 and 1957, had traumatized intellectuals, and in light of the severe criticism leveled during the campaign against plays on contemporary themes, it often seemed safer for authors to refocus their efforts on historical subject matter.[6] This created another set of problems, however, since it necessarily involved the extensive use of material from a "feudal" past that the Communists had tried hard to put behind them and did not wish to see resurrected. The shift toward historical drama therefore resulted in an extended—and highly contentious—debate in theatrical and historical circles on the relationship between history and historical drama and the whole involved question of how the past could be made to serve the present.[7]

THE GROUNDSWELL OF OPERAS ON THE GOUJIAN STORY (1960–1961)

This historical turn in the world of Chinese theater was an important precondition for the increased attention given to the Goujian story. It was not, however, sufficient. The content of the story, if it was to invite special notice, had to relate in meaningful ways to what was going on at the time. As one writer in the early 1960s put it:

Because of differences in the political tasks faced, certain types of historical dramas are relatively popular at certain times. For example, in the initial days after the country's liberation, *Li Zicheng Enters the Capital (Chuang wang ru jing)*, by warning people not to get carried away with success, had great educational value;* during the Resist-America Aid-Korea period, *The General and the Prime Minister Make Peace (Jiang xiang*

---

*The army of the late Ming rebel leader Li Zicheng—he styled himself the "the dashing king" *(Chuang wang)*—occupied Beijing in April 1644. Li declared the founding of a new dynasty, but by early June he had fled the capital under pressure from the combined forces of Wu Sangui and the invading Manchus, and a new Manchu emperor was installed on the Chinese throne.

he) showed us how to become more effectively united when confronting a formidable enemy;* and in the present day, when the party has called on us to engage in arduous struggle *(jianku fendou)* and to work hard to strengthen the nation *(fafen tuqiang)*, the story of King Goujian of Yue's sleeping on brushwood and tasting gall has appeal for large numbers of viewers.[8]

As illustrated by this statement, a fundamental premise of virtually all historical drama at this time was that it had to be of immediate practical relevance. Playwrights should not aspire to portray historical conditions simply for the sake of portraying historical conditions; their work must have educational importance in the present, providing models for contemporary Chinese to emulate in their lives.[9] This was the basic meaning of the slogan "making the past serve the present" *(gu wei jin yong)*. It points to a remarkable commonality in terms of core cultural assumptions between mainland China in the early 1960s and Chiang Kai-shek's Taiwan, although the contextual, ideological, and stylistic differences separating the two Chinese worlds were immense, and (as we shall presently see) mainland writers, unlike those on Taiwan, faced deeply ambiguous political strictures and often had to tie themselves up in knots simply in order to survive.

The underlying assumptions were similar, but the ways in which they played out could not have been more different. For one thing, in Taiwan the immediate political reason for the widespread diffusion of the Goujian story was, as often as not, made absolutely clear. Again and again, highlighting the theme of *fuguo* (recovery of the country), the story was explicitly cast as part of the ideological armament of the Republic of China in its ongoing battle against Communist rule on the mainland. In the PRC in the early 1960s, by contrast, the construction of the story in opera librettos and plays and its extensive discussion in theatrical journals and the press were

---

*During the third century B.C.E., Zhao, a weak state, had to contend with Qin, a strong one. When the Zhao diplomatic official Lin Xiangru, after outwitting the king of Qin, was rewarded with promotion to the office of prime minister, which placed him above Lian Po, the top Zhao general, Lian took offense and was intent on teaching Lin a lesson. He therefore confronted Lin on the road outside the latter's home. Faced with this provocation, Lin, despite his higher rank, ordered his driver to back into a side alley, yielding to Lian's carriage. He acted in this way not out of cowardice but, rather, out of the fear that Qin, if it learned that the top civil and military officials of Zhao were on bad terms, would exploit the fissure and put Zhao at a disadvantage. When word of Lin's patriotic motive got back to Lian, he was deeply ashamed and apologized to Lin. Henceforth, the two men cooperated fully in their efforts on Zhao's behalf.

consistently focused not on recovery of the country (which would have had little meaning) but on self-reliance *(zili gengsheng)*, on Chinese depending on their own efforts to build up the strength and prosperity of the nation *(fafen tuqiang)*. Communist writers, moreover, unlike those in the ROC, never at the time (to my knowledge) explicitly articulated their understanding of the story's underlying political message. This message, partly reflective of Mao's increasing emphasis on Chinese independence from the Soviet model (a prime reason for the Great Leap Forward in the first place),[10] and partly (as scholars outside the PRC have observed) a response to the growing tension with the USSR and the recognition that China could no longer depend on its former ally for help in its economic and military buildup,[11] was too sensitive to express openly in the absence of a fully adversarial relationship with the Soviet Union.[12]

For another thing, in Taiwan during the Chiang years, Goujian was almost always treated in a positive way, and although the specifics of his behavior differed from one rendering of the story to the next, the overall question of how he should be portrayed—which side of his character should be accentuated, which downplayed—seldom if ever came up for discussion. (Much more attention, as we have seen, was devoted to the issue of how to characterize Xi Shi.) In the PRC in 1960 and 1961, it was a very different matter. There was a great deal of divergence over how the figure of Goujian should be handled, and differences of viewpoint were openly articulated, vigorously contested, and widely disseminated in print.

A key issue on which opinions differed was the question of how to assess heroic personages like Goujian (Yue Fei was another) who were members of the feudal ruling class. Most writers maintained that since class standing was only one factor among several and that the impact of an individual's actions on the development of society and the condition of the broad masses should also be taken into account, it was perfectly legitimate to treat such figures as models for the present. A minority position was, however, sometimes advanced. The critic Qi Hong, for example, in discussing a *woxin changdan* opera put on by the Qingshan Opera Company of Shanghai, flatly denied the educational value of the Goujian story, arguing that the contradiction between Wu and Yue was nothing more than a contradiction within the feudal ruling class, focused on rivalry over population and territory and the reach of personal power and influence. No matter which of the two states triumphed, it would not be of benefit to the people. Goujian therefore should not be viewed as praiseworthy and could not serve as a positive figure in historical dramas.

Another contentious issue relating to the evaluation of heroic figures of feudal class background had to do with the limitations under which such persons operated. Should these limitations be made manifest, and if so, how? And how should the notion of "limitations" be understood? Qian Yingyu, like Qi Hong, had attended the Qingshan Opera Company's staging of the *woxin changdan* story in 1960. His take on the opera, however, was very different. Rather than denigrating Goujian himself, he criticized the producers of the opera for their portrayal of the Yue ruler as a weak-willed, ineffectual individual who because of his limitations was unable to advance convincingly the central ideas of *fafen tuqiang* and hard struggle. This stress on Goujian's limitations probably stemmed, in Qian's view, from the concern of the opera's creators that if they elevated the Yue king too high it would deviate from the principle of historical materialism. Qian felt that such fears were excessive, that when writing historical dramas about the efforts of members of the feudal ruling class to strengthen their states, there was no need for playwrights to put such great emphasis on their subjects' limitations. A slightly different view was advanced by another critic, Fu Jun, who argued that a distinction must be made between a character's limitations and his shortcomings. Limitations of time and place must absolutely be dealt with, he maintained, but there was no need to put undue emphasis on personal shortcomings. Unfortunately, because many of the creators of the *woxin changdan* operas confused the two, they imposed unnecessary constraints on Goujian, making him into a figure dominated by shortcomings and incompetence and therefore unable to fulfill the educational purpose of making the past serve the present.[13]

The drama critic Zhang Zhen alluded to a number of other issues in his published reply of early 1961 to a letter from an unnamed writer who was contemplating creating a drama on the *woxin changdan* theme. Among the problems troubling the writer in question was the matter of how to depict the process Goujian engaged in to make his state strong without making it sound like a stand-in for twentieth-century modernization. Zhang began his response by noting that, while class contradictions necessarily existed in Yue, when it came under attack by Wu and the ruling class of Wu became the main exploiter and oppressor of the Yue people, the contradiction between the ruling class of Wu and the people of Yue superseded the internal contradiction within Yue between rulers and ruled. At such a time, even though the people of Yue remained unhappy about certain abuses of power by the Yue ruling class, it was in their interest to support Goujian's economic and military policies and the measures he took to throw off the shackles of Wu's oppression.

This did not at all indicate, however, that Goujian was incapable of acting in an oppressive way toward his own people. The Yue king was indeed a heroic figure with many strengths. He had willpower and ambition; he was able to put up with hardships; and he was successful in his efforts to rebuild Yue and make it strong. But he never lost his ruling-class world outlook, and the steps he took to mobilize and unify the people of Yue clearly reflected this. Although it was only after the defeat of Wu that Goujian's kingly behavior—the wallowing in luxury and pleasure, the arrogance, and so forth—manifested itself in a conspicuous way, it had been there all along, suggesting an internal consistency between the preconquest Goujian and the postconquest one. If Zhang's correspondent could manage to portray this accurately, he should have no trouble showing how the Yue ruler's actions differed from present-day efforts to make the country strong.[14]

Underlying Zhang Zhen's position was the assumption, made explicit in another letter a few months later, that history was a progressive process and that the people of a given period could not possibly rise above the constraints of the time in which they lived. This was true not only of rulers like Goujian, but also of ordinary individuals. It was entirely understandable, therefore, that the people of Yue did not struggle against landlords and that peasants who historically took part in armed uprisings still supported "good emperors." Zhang took sharp issue with those writers who, oblivious to the progressive nature of history, assumed that the only way to give the past contemporary relevance was to superimpose on historical figures the behavioral characteristics of the present day. If the rulers and ministers of Yue had really eaten, lived, and worked together with the peasantry, as some playwrights suggested, their behavior would have been no different from that of the revolutionary cadres of socialist China. This, according to Zhang, betrayed an unscientific reading of history and was most definitely not the way to make the past serve the present.[15]

The opera writer Fan Junhong, in a letter of September 1961 to Zhang Zhen in response to the latter's first letter, observed that he and his colleagues had also tried writing a drama on the *woxin changdan* theme and that he himself had either read or seen performances of a number of comparable efforts. Many of these were, in his view, hurried jobs, which left one with an unsatisfied feeling.[16] One problem with them—and in this respect he clearly agreed with Zhang Zhen—was that they made the past seem a dead ringer for the present. They idealized Goujian, even going so far in some cases as to refer to his spirit of "carrying the revolution through to the end" and adopting a theoretical standard of "uninterrupted revolution." They made demands on Goujian in accordance with modern standards of "justice" and "revolution," contrasting in an absolute way Goujian's "sense of justice" and "revolutionary spirit" with Fuchai's "lack of a sense of justice" and "reactionary nature"; they imbued the wars of the Spring and Autumn period with an anti-imperialist, anticolonialist flavor, sometimes even insinuating into them the guerrilla fighting of the Sino-Japanese War years; and when they depicted the hard work Goujian engaged in to make Yue strong it seemed little different from the efforts being undertaken under socialism to strengthen China. Such impositions of the present onto the past were, in Fan's view, highly problematic.[17]

Although in basic agreement with Zhang Zhen, Fan Junhong felt that in regard to a number of matters, in particular the nature of warfare during the Spring and Autumn era and relations between Wu and Yue, Zhang's discussion was inadequate. These issues, he felt, were more important, more serious, and more fundamental than Zhang acknowledged. They were important because every comrade who wrote on the *woxin changdan* theme encountered them from the outset and had to understand them; they were serious because virtually none of the *woxin changdan* dramas, even including the relatively successful ones, dealt with them properly; and they were fundamental in nature because the failure to handle them properly had a bearing on the way in which the characters of Goujian and Fuchai were portrayed, the nature of the struggle between Wu and Yue, and even the historical authenticity of the dramas and the question of how to understand correctly the role of historical drama in making the past serve the present. On the question of warfare during the Spring and Autumn period, Fan criticized as too vague Zhang's assertion (echoing a common view) that there were no just *(zhengyi)* wars at the time; he also took him to task for saying, on one hand, that there were no just wars but clearly implying, on the other, that Goujian's struggle against Wu was precisely such a war since it involved the resistance of an oppressed state against an oppressor state.[18]

Most of Fan's letter was devoted to the question of how relations between Wu and Yue should be treated; in the process he offered an illuminating account of the immense difficulties involved in writing historical dramas at this time. When he and his colleagues accepted the assignment of creating an opera on the *woxin changdan* theme, they were in broad agreement that to do so properly they must highlight the special qualities of Goujian's determined effort to make Yue strong. They further agreed that to accomplish this they must underscore, first, the Yue king's willingness to submit to any and all indignities as the price for achieving his goal, and, second, his desire to avenge the shame that had been inflicted on Yue. Since Yue was weak and Wu was strong, Yue had no choice but to submit to Wu. In these circumstances, if Goujian did not succumb to humiliation *(renru fuzhong)*, it would be impossible for him to lay the basis for Yue's future reconstruction *(fafen tuqiang)*. Similarly, the carrying out of ten years of economic growth *(shi nian shengju)* and ten years of military training *(shi nian jiaoxun)* was a long and arduous process, requiring unbending resolve on Goujian's part. But such resolve could be generated only if he was imbued with the desire to wipe out the humiliation previously inflicted on Yue and avenge himself against Wu.

On the basis of these ideas, Fan and his colleagues drafted an outline and then presented it to other comrades for discussion. Some of these were in basic agreement with the outline, suggesting only that in the course of describing Goujian's willingness to put up with humiliation, they should place more emphasis on his steadfastness and persistence in the face of adversity. Other comrades, however, did not approve of the outline. They pointed out that making the theme of "working hard to strengthen the country" *(fafen tuqiang)* dependent on the cycle of humiliation and revenge was out of keeping with the spirit of the present day and urged the authors to rethink the entire draft. The former reaction gave Fan and his cowriters much encouragement, but the latter troubled them greatly. After all, if they divorced Goujian from the specific setting on which his very existence depended, how could they write about his determination to strengthen his state? Faced with these conflicting responses, they were uncertain as to how to proceed.

At this point some comrades reminded them that in the country as a whole there were already some seventy to eighty troupes engaged in the production of operas on the *woxin changdan* theme, to the point where writing on this historical subject had become a central activity. Since it had become so central, they added, it was reasonable to suppose that the *woxin changdan* operas were consistent with government policy and, such being the case, that they necessarily embodied a contemporary spirit and were attentive to their impact on present-day society. In these circumstances, the only thing to do was to downplay or completely omit the theme of submission to humiliation, while highlighting the spirit of self-reliance and working hard to strengthen the country. As one of the comrades said to

Fan tellingly, "Everyone is doing this. It is necessary to take a position that is politically tenable. Otherwise it will be hard to avoid making mistakes. You must recognize that this is no ordinary topic!"

When Fan thought about this advice some time after, he felt that some of it rested on conjecture and some of it was fairly one-sided. But at the time it definitely had a big influence on him and his colleagues. So they decided to redo their outline. In the revised draft, fearful of committing errors, they were far more cautious in their depiction of the character of Goujian, the motif of submission to humiliation was weakened, the idea of revenge *(fuchou)* was eliminated entirely, any character shortcomings in Goujian were studiously avoided, behavior that did not embody a high degree of righteousness on his part was eliminated, and they were on the watch for anything that did not jibe with current policy. Operating in this fashion, they created a draft that was "elevated" in appearance but devoid of real meaning, the characters for the most part mimicking the thinking of modern people. They did not go so far as to shoehorn in such Great Leap political slogans as "the four togethernesses" *(sitong),* "make steel in a big way" *(dalian gangtie),* and "train militia in a big way" *(dalian minbing),*[19] which would only have invited audience ridicule. But having retreated fifty paces, Fan said he had no wish to mock those who had retreated a hundred. He added that even though many of the *woxin changdan* operas created at the time conveyed, in their handling of details, the sense of "letting a hundred flowers bloom," their spiritual substance was vapid and from a dramatic point of view they were total nonstarters.

It is clear from Fan Junhong's account that the process of putting together an opera on the *woxin changdan* theme at this point in time was a little like walking barefoot through a field of nettles. Fan tried to describe to Zhang Zhen what he had learned:

> You are a fan of "comedians' dialogues" *[xiangsheng]* and will recall that there is a traditional phase in comedians' dialogues that goes, "confused, clear, easy, hard." If I may be permitted to twist things a bit, when one is all mixed up about something, one often feels that it is easy; it is only after one has achieved a degree of clarity that one understands what is "difficult" about it. Whether I have truly attained clarity at this point is hard to say. But I've begun to sense what is "difficult." What is meant by difficult consists in having to write about working hard to strengthen the country, ensuring that what one has written is in accordance with historical truth, and incorporating into the final product a real sense of "theater" *[xi].*

If, Fan concluded in the final portion of his letter, one only took one part of the *woxin changdan* story and insisted on emphasizing it to the exclusion of all else, one could never resolve these competing demands. The *woxin changdan* story was an outstanding embodiment of the spirit of "working hard to strengthen the country." But it really couldn't be broken up in this way. Yue's taking ten years to build up its population and economy and another ten years to train its military was not the ultimate goal. The ultimate goal was to avenge itself, erase its humiliation at Wu's hands, raise itself up, and compete for the leadership of North China. At the same time, it had to be borne in mind that while Yue's eventual triumph clearly had to do with the determined efforts it went through over many years to strengthen itself, Wu's downfall did not result only from this; it was also brought on by its own failings. "A tree must first rot from within before insects can thrive on it." The profound lesson that Chinese had always derived from the *woxin changdan* story therefore was a double lesson, focused on the whole complex process by which Wu and Yue had traded places. If this lesson was to be meaningful for the present day, the positive teaching value embodied in Goujian's response to the humiliation of defeat had to be balanced by the negative teaching material personified in the character and behavior of Fuchai.[20]

MAO DUN'S ASSESSMENT OF THE *WOXIN CHANGDAN* DRAMAS

Some of the points raised in Fan Junhong's letter to Zhang Zhen were also highlighted in Mao Dun's book on the *woxin changdan* dramas, a phenomenon that had first whetted his interest after seeing a performance in Hangzhou in September 1960. Mao Dun stressed that the several dozen *woxin changdan* productions he eventually gained direct knowledge of were, with the single exception of Cao Yu's spoken drama, all "operas."* This circumstance is of the greatest importance and needs elaboration. In China, opera in its various regional manifestations had for some centuries been the quintessential form of popular entertainment.[21] "In the Ming and Qing

---

*There are important differences between Western and Chinese opera, leading some writers to use the term "drama" when referring to the latter, except when describing the most famous (and influential) regional form, Beijing (Peking) Opera. Prior to the twentieth century, Mackerras writes, "there was no such thing in China as a 'spoken play'—that is, a dramatic performance in which music, singing, and chanting find no place. Dramas consisted of sung verses, or 'arias,' interspersed with percussion-accompanied sections of stylized chanting in prose or, sometimes, spoken dialogue." *The Chinese Theatre in Modern Times*, 11.

dynasties," Barbara Ward tells us, "the overwhelming majority of opera performances took place in public (whether in such commercial establishments as the 'play gardens' or in connection with religious festivals), in front of unrestricted audiences as mixed as and very much larger than those of sixteenth-century England." She adds that, during this time, "for the great mass of the population . . . the entertainment media, especially the festival operas, were the most significant source of information about the believed-in historical past, the values and manners of the elite, attitudes and relationships between and among people of different status, and ideas of good (which usually triumphed in the end) and evil (which was usually routed)."[22] Indeed, so widely influential was opera as a font of cultural knowledge and moral values that one scholar has viewed it and its close kin "ritual" as the two "most important institutions of non-elite community life" in imperial times.[23]

This unique importance of opera in the Chinese world continued in the twentieth century. At the turn of the century, opera performances in the villages and towns of North China were a major shaping influence on the behavior and beliefs of young adherents of the Boxer movement.[24] Throughout the country, at least until the establishment of the People's Republic, sets of opera performances lasting several days regularly accompanied the large-scale religious festivals and temple fairs that were a routine feature of Chinese life. And, recognizing opera as "a powerful vehicle with which to mobilize the masses," the Chinese Communists during the anti-Japanese and civil wars of the 1930s and 1940s "organized thousands of village drama groups" to convey appropriate political messages to the populace.[25]

In the early 1950s, after the Communists gained national power, the use of drama for political mobilization became if anything even more pervasive. State and semiprivate troupes, under the auspices of the Ministry of Culture, were reported to have given forty-one thousand performances in 1953 alone, reaching over forty-five million viewers in the countryside, factories, mines, and armed forces; in 1954 these figures swelled to fifty-seven thousand performances and an audience of more than sixty-two million. By the end of the 1950s, according to Edgar Snow, every college, middle school, and state factory of any size had an amateur dramatic club and there were an average of seven performing groups in each of the twenty-four thousand communes then in existence. Beijing alone had half a dozen opera houses, and most provinces maintained at least one company that specialized in performing the opera style indigenous to its area.[26]

Many of the dramas performed during the Great Leap Forward dealt with contemporary themes and were heavily politicized, as befitted a period in which politics were overwhelmingly in command. But classical dramas on historical themes continued to be staged and became increasingly common in the early 1960s.[27] These dramas were by no means free of political constraints. But in the relatively relaxed atmosphere of the immediate post–Great Leap years there was, as we have seen, room for a good deal of disagreement over how historical subject matter in general, and the Goujian story in particular, should be handled. It was against this backdrop that Mao Dun's book was written. Although its main title—*On History and Historical Drama (Guanyu lishi he lishiju)*—signaled the key theoretical issue that Mao Dun wanted to weigh in on, the book's contents were, with the exception of one chapter, almost entirely devoted to the Goujian story, the *woxin changdan* operas, and Cao Yu's play.

Although Mao Dun said that he managed to collect and read some fifty different *woxin changdan* scripts in late 1960 and early 1961, a Ministry of Culture publication of 1961 took note of seventy-one such scripts and Mao Dun himself estimated the real number to be closer to one hundred. Yet, despite this proliferation of different versions of the opera and the great frequency with which it was performed all over China, because almost none of the *woxin changdan* librettos made it into newspapers and journals, they had not been given the attention in the press that Mao Dun felt their popularity merited. After reading through the scripts in his possession, he concluded that they were full of interest but that they also presented problems. So he decided to write a book examining the historical sources for the *woxin changdan* theme and, more broadly, the problems involved in writing literary works grounded in history.[28]

In the first half of the book, Mao Dun discussed the ancient sources for the Goujian story, noting which ones he thought were most reliable, which ones included fabricated material, and so forth. This was followed by an account of the pre-twentieth-century development of historical drama in China, including works that dealt with the Wu-Yue conflict, the most famous of which was *Huan sha ji* (Washing Silken Gauze) by the famous Ming playwright Liang Chenyu (ca. 1519–ca. 1591). This drama, which centered on Xi Shi and her part in weakening Wu, played an important role in the birth of the operatic form *kunqu*.[29] This, however, did not impress Mao Dun, who expressed the judgment that the *woxin changdan* operas of his own day were vastly superior to *Huan sha ji* and other Ming dramas dealing with the Goujian story.

Since so few of the *woxin changdan* librettos were ever published, the detail Mao Dun provided on them in the course of justifying this appraisal is of great value. The first respect in which the contemporary *woxin chang-dan* operas were superior, in his view, resided in the complete clarity of their central message: Goujian began in dire straits and ended in peace and happiness as a result of his ability to put up with all sorts of difficulties *(woxin changdan)* and his steadfast devotion to making Yue strong *(fafen tuqiang)*. While *Huan sha ji,* in accounting for Yue's ultimate triumph, put the main emphasis on the devious schemes *(yinmou)* implemented by Goujian and his ministers and had virtually nothing to say about their hard work, willingness to endure privation, and self-reliance, the *woxin changdan* scripts that Mao Dun read all, without exception, reversed these priorities entirely in their identification of the main impetus behind Yue's transformation from weakness to strength and its successful revenge against Wu. The *woxin changdan* operas of course did not incorporate the "beauty trap" *(meiren ji)* stratagem, which was a key theme in *Huan sha ji.* Some of them eliminated the character of Xi Shi entirely; others slotted her in but handled her in a completely different way, portraying her as having been forcibly seized by Wu soldiers rather than presented to Wu as tribute from Yue. There was no romantic relationship with Fan Li. Whatever Xi Shi did at the Wu court to secretly aid the Yue cause was done out of patriotic zeal, not as part of a previously devised spying operation.

A second strength of the *woxin changdan* dramas was that, in order to reinforce their central theme, they fabricated people and stories to serve as foils for such figures as Goujian, Fan Li, and Wen Zhong. Mao Dun freely acknowledged that the historical records did not contain references to the Yue people who failed to support Goujian's cause. But historical dramas were not the same as historical documents. They permitted, even required, invention, as long as the made-up persons and events did not go beyond what was possible in the historical conditions of the day and as long as they did not, in a counterhistorical way, superimpose the ideas of modern people on the ancients. In other words, just because the historical records failed to mention internal contradictions was no reason why people in the present couldn't imagine such contradictions as having existed and fabricate people and events embodying them. The main thing was that in doing so they must adhere scrupulously to the standpoint of historical materialism and not change the ancient to bring it in line with the modern or use history to make insinuations *(yingshe)* about the present.

The third virtue of the *woxin changdan* dramas of the early 1960s was the prominence they gave to portraying the power of the people. Mao Dun granted that this was not a theme that was openly articulated in the historical records. But given Yue's economic and military weakness at the outset, it was inconceivable, he felt, that its rulers could have built up its strength merely by undergoing self-imposed hardships *(woxin changdan)* and not by reliance on the energetic support of the people. Such support was depicted differently in the ancient sources than it would be in Mao Dun's day—the phrasing was not the same—but it was clearly implied; therefore it was entirely appropriate for the authors of the *woxin changdan* scripts to use their imaginations to describe how it manifested itself.

A final strength of the *woxin changdan* operas was the ingenuity and resourcefulness they demonstrated in working out details of plot development. In the fifty or so examples he read, Mao Dun said he encountered nine different ways of beginning the opera and three different ways of concluding it. He also praised the operas' treatment of the ways in which the strength of the people reinforced Goujian's resolve, how internal contradictions within the Yue ruling group emerged and were overcome, and other aspects of the story. Although he noted that in the handling of these two last issues, which were particularly thorny, not all of the scripts were above criticism, on the whole he felt that the operas were to be congratulated for their efforts to bring the Wu-Yue conflict to life and analyze it in accordance with the dictates of historical materialism.[30]

After reviewing the overall strengths of the *woxin changdan* texts, Mao Dun launched into a far more critical discussion of how they dealt with several of the more commonly discussed issues relating to historical drama: (1) how to make the past serve the present, (2) how to portray the historical role of the people, (3) the proper way to integrate historical truth and artistic invention, and (4) the appropriate use of language. Virtually all of the scripts incorporated the experience and even some of the slogans of the Great Leap, some giving less weight to this, others more. Mao Dun felt that a little of this was okay, as long as it did not involve insinuating into the minds of ancient people the consciousness of present-day cadres. It was true, for example, that there was a historical basis in Sima Qian's *Shiji* for asserting that Goujian engaged in farm labor and his wife in weaving. But at most it could be said that they did this temporarily to build up popular support; one couldn't go overboard and suggest that such behavior had become institutionalized or, worse still, that when Goujian acted in this way his thinking and consciousness were the same as the thinking and consciousness of people in the socialist present. Similarly, Mao Dun felt that while it was all right, even in the absence of historical evidence, for the *woxin changdan* librettos to include (as some did) vivid depictions of simulta-neously "constructing water conservancy projects in a big way" *(daxing shuili)* and "making steel in a big way" *(dalian gangtie)*, if such activities were fabricated with the realities of the Great Leap in mind, it was not appropriate. Other liberties taken in the *woxin changdan* scripts were, in his judgment, even less appropriate.

According to Mao Dun, roughly half of the librettos he read posited link-ages to present-day reality in their understanding of "making the past serve the present." This inevitably resulted in insinuations about the present and hence a slandering of contemporary socialist reality. At the same time, it trans-formed the past to bring it in line with the present and thus constituted a serious departure from the perspective of historical materialism. The authors of some of the other librettos, however, went to the opposite extreme: they were so fearful of committing presentist excesses that they became overcau-tious and, in their nervousness about doing more than the slightest amount of fabrication, ended up with scripts that were dry as dust and completely lacking in artistic appeal. Indeed, the only drama on the *woxin changdan* theme that, in Mao Dun's view, managed to steer successfully between the shoals of presentist distortion, on the one hand, and artistic insipidness, on the other, was Cao Yu's play, which he wrote after the *woxin changdan* op-eras and therefore had the benefit of learning from their shortcomings.[31]

Moving on, Mao Dun commended the *woxin changdan* operas for em-phasizing the historical role of the people. Although some did it better than others, all of them tried hard, in the absence of help from the historical sources, to visualize how this might have developed in the late Spring and Autumn period. During the long period when Yue was subordinate to Wu, a time when even its ruling stratum suffered from Wu's oppression, class contradictions within Yue moderated somewhat—a tendency that was re-inforced by Goujian's reliance on the efforts of the people in the rebuild-ing of his state. These circumstances provided a historical basis in the *woxin changdan* operas for the creation of characters representative of the strength of the people.

The authors did this in a variety of ways. Some of them credited the com-mon people with having initiated all the important proposals for Yue's eco-nomic development and military strengthening and even with having come up with such details as "tasting gall." In these circumstances, figures like Goujian, Wen Zhong, and Fan Li had no scope for their abilities and were in the position of only being able to accept the suggestions of the masses. Mao Dun felt that this was excessive in two respects: it overvalued the political awareness and intellectual-cultural level of the people of the time and it also overvalued the character of figures like Goujian by equating their behavior with that of cadres in his own day who, under the leadership of the Communist Party, followed the mass line and upheld a democratic work style. This way of portraying the strength of the people, Mao Dun concluded, was not very promising.

Other writers followed a second strategy in depicting the strength of the masses. They aspired not only to emphasize the power of the people but also to stake out a role for the members of the ruling class, with a resulting leadership style that resembled what people in Mao Dun's day called "from the masses, to the masses." This approach, in Mao Dun's opinion, was little different from the first one insofar as it made historical figures look just like modern people; its evaluation of Goujian, moreover, was even higher than the first strategy's.

A third solution, followed by some playwrights, instead of portraying the masses as directly initiating proposals, dealt with the role of the people in the promotion of Goujian's twenty-year plan for Yue's development more indirectly by writing about their strong determination to seek revenge, overturn foreign (Wu) rule, rely on their own efforts, and expand production. Mao Dun viewed this as a relatively effective strategy, in that it was easier to avoid errors and also had some basis in the historical record. He observed that Cao Yu's *The Gall and the Sword*, by combining the second and third solutions to the problem of depicting the strength of the people, seemed more believable and had greater artistic appeal, although mixed into the ideological stance of some of the play's characters were ideas that only modern people could possess.

In his discussion of the integration of historical truth and artistic invention, Mao Dun noted that his understanding of artistic invention was equivalent to what many of his contemporaries meant when they referred to artistic "truth." The *woxin changdan* scripts engaged in artistic invention in a number of ways. A dozen or so of the scripts he read did this by actually changing what happened historically. As a prime example, he noted their depiction of Yue and Wu as having engaged in only a single final battle, heedless of the fact that historically there were several final encounters between the two. Why, he asked, did they alter history in this way? And why did they change things around so that instead of Goujian rising in revolt to exact revenge against Wu, the Yue king attacked Wu only after Qi, Jin, and Chu requested his aid or after he had come under attack by Wu (in other words, in self-defense)? It was alleged, Mao Dun said, that the reason for having Goujian behave in this way was that the playwrights were intent upon avoiding the theme of "revenge" *(fuchou)* and also wanted to avoid putting Yue in the position of "being the first to fire" *(xian kai diyi qiang)*. They wanted to steer clear of the "revenge" motive because then the ostensible reason for Yue's going to war with Wu would not be just and honorable; similarly, they felt that if they portrayed Goujian as initiating hostilities, it would imply that Yue was the aggressor. The authors of the operas, in short, felt that by changing history in this fashion they would be conforming to the guiding principle that historical dramas should make the past serve the present. Mao Dun was unpersuaded by this reasoning. After all, Goujian, in his day, had no thought of avoiding revenge or of avoiding the initiation of hostilities. Contemporary playwrights, therefore, by imposing such ideas on him, were operating in a counterhistorical way. Mao Dun said that he was not demanding that history be followed slavishly in every last detail. He commended a Beijing opera rendering of the *woxin changdan* theme that, while omitting references to such taboos as "revenge" and "initiating hostilities," did so without substituting other motives or behaviors that would seriously alter what actually happened. Changing history and artistic fabrication, he insisted, were two different things. The latter was necessary; the former was not to be tolerated.[32]

Later in his book, Mao Dun returned to the matter of the failure of so many of the *woxin changdan* operas to deal candidly (if at all) with the place of the revenge motive in the Goujian story. Echoing Fan Junhong's critique of Zhang Zhen, he saw this omission as being related to the superficiality with which the operas in question treated the nature of the conflict between Wu and Yue. Why, he wondered, given the central importance of revenge in the conflict, didn't the authors of the dramas deal with it directly? Mao Dun said that, as far as he knew, no one had ventured to respond to this question publicly. His own view was that it had to do with the fact that just at this time surviving remnants of Hitlerism, in the service of American imperialism, had been using revanchism *(fuchouzhuyi)* to summon the people of West Germany to launch World War III—an aim shared by intransigent elements in Japan as well. In this environment, Chinese playwrights, fearful of being misunderstood, thought it best to skirt the revenge theme altogether. They had these scruples because they did not know their history very well. The fact was, although the Wu-Yue conflict for Goujian was all about revenge, for the people of Yue it was a war of liberation and was as different from West German revanchism as night from day. The banner of this sort of war of revenge therefore could be raised with dignity.[33]

Another form of artistic invention, one found in many of the *woxin changdan* operas and viewed by Mao Dun as inevitable, combined actual historical figures with fictitious events or episodes *(zhenren jiashi)*. Among the major individuals in the story, this was done most frequently in connection with Goujian and Fuchai, Goujian being portrayed as a distinctly positive figure, Fuchai as an entirely negative one, dissolute and muddle-headed, a laughable good-for-nothing. Mao Dun didn't object to some degree of embellishment of Goujian, although he disapproved of having him mouth such contemporary notions as "the mass line" *(qunzhong luxian)* and "tempering oneself through manual labor" *(laodong duanlian)*. However, the portrayal of Fuchai as the sort of fatuous and self-indulgent king *(hunjun)* commonly seen on the Chinese stage would clearly not do. First, it was too far removed from the historical Fuchai. Second, if Fuchai was really all that ineffectual, why would Goujian's success in avenging himself against him have been deemed so extraordinary that for two hundred years he was the toast of late Zhou feudal lords and thinkers? Third, Fuchai's going from victory to defeat, the nature of his quest, and the sources of his tragic life would, if depicted more truthfully, have immense educational value. But in using the method of caricature to portray the Wu king, their educational value was undermined. "To put it bluntly," Mao Dun wrote, "the sort of fabrication that superimposes all these things on the character of Fuchai is out of keeping with historical truth."[34]

The strategy of combining fictitious historical figures with actual historical episodes *(jiaren zhenshi)* was rarely encountered in the *woxin changdan* dramas, according to Mao Dun. Far more widespread and worthy of note was the practice of fictionalizing both people and events *(renshi liangjia)*. There were two parts of the Goujian story where this was commonly encountered: (1) concrete portrayals of people immersing themselves in hard work *(maitou kugan)* and relying on their own efforts *(zili gengsheng)* and (2) the resistance to Goujian's policies by conservatives, defeatists, and capitulationists within the Yue ruling group.

The problem, in both of these instances, was the lack of any grounding in the historical record. The issue was not whether it was okay or not to engage in historical invention, but on what foundation such invention should rest. It was perfectly legitimate to assume that in order to turn weakness into strength, Yue had to rely on its own efforts in the economic and military realms; it was also legitimate to assume that there were dissident elements within the Yue ruling group whose preference was for Goujian to let well enough alone and just focus on survival. It was reasonable therefore for the creators of the *woxin changdan* operas to engage in fabrication. But doing so was complicated. It was necessary, for instance, to be clear about what historical stage the Yue economy was in at the time and what level of development under these historical conditions it was plausible for Goujian and his people to strive for. It appeared, in Mao Dun's view, that the authors of the operas did in fact take these matters into account and that, although going too far in some instances, their hearts were in the right place.

What was particularly to be valued about the operas in these areas of artistic invention was their implementation of the policy of letting a hundred flowers bloom and a hundred schools of thought contend. This had resulted in the accumulation of a rich trove of experience; indeed, it was by absorbing the lessons gained from this experience that the last of the historical dramas on the Goujian story to see the light of day, *The Gall and the Sword*, was able to attain a new level of achievement. As an illustration of this, Mao Dun observed that the author of *The Gall and the Sword* didn't write about "making steel in a big way"; he simply wrote that Yue made iron plows. Moreover, he didn't naturalistically show iron plows being manufactured onstage, but instead pointed to this development by means of dialogue and by displaying an already manufactured iron plow. In this way Cao Yu's play avoided decking out the 2,400-year-old state of Yue like a Chinese village of 1958 with its little blast furnace towering skyward.[35]

The final topic Mao Dun took up was the appropriate use of language in historical dramas. There were two problems here. One was the use of classical allusions and terms (such as ancient place-names and official titles) that many modern Chinese would not understand. The other was using words and expressions that, however common in the present day, did not exist in the period being written about. The first problem, according to Mao Dun, was not ordinarily encountered in the *woxin changdan* dramas, as their authors made a strong effort to employ simple, unadorned language. The second problem, however, appeared with some regularity, as a result of which the period atmosphere of the dramas was substantially attenuated. Mao Dun recognized that this problem was harder to control in historical dramas than in the general run of operas or spoken dramas. But it was an issue that he felt had to be resolved.[36]

Some of the issues that Mao Dun and other writers raised in connection with the *woxin changdan* dramas were intellectual and artistic issues that any historian or literary critic might raise. The greater part by far, however, were reflections of the political constraints under which literary people labored at the time. These constraints were deeply embedded in what Perry Link has called the "socialist Chinese literary system" and tended to function with greater or lesser severity throughout the period from the establishment of the PRC in 1949 until around 1990.[37] Although the years of 1960 and 1961, which witnessed what Mao Dun called the "*woxin changdan* craze *[feng]*,"[38] were marked by a measure of relaxation, they were close enough in time to the intellectual devastation of the Anti-Rightist Campaign and the pressurized atmosphere of the Great Leap Forward to encourage a high level of political timidity among writers. There was no more blatant manifestation of this timidity than the suppression or soft-pedaling of the revenge theme in many of the *woxin changdan* operas, despite its laying at the very heart of the Goujian story. Although one might anticipate that a writer as prominent and popular as Cao Yu, with support at the very highest levels of the Chinese leadership (Zhou Enlai was an old friend), would be able to overcome such political unease, the reality proved more complicated.

CAO YU'S *THE GALL AND THE SWORD*

One reason for this was that Cao Yu himself was famously overcautious when it came to political matters. Genuinely concerned about the plight of the Chinese people and deeply patriotic, he had, like most other writers of his generation, chosen to remain in China in 1949. In the early years of the new regime, his pre-1949 plays were, after being revised, regularly performed and reprinted. He was admitted into the party on the eve of the Anti-Rightist Campaign and, during the campaign, wrote a number of articles and made speeches critical of rightists. Although he later claimed to regret this,[39] the fact is Cao Yu had complete faith in the party and, at a number of key junctures in his career (including the Tiananmen crackdown of June 1989), showed himself prepared to comply with its wishes.[40]

Cao Yu was overwhelmed by the tornado-like atmosphere of the Great Leap Forward. Unable to regain his bearings and adapt to what was going on around him, he became depressed and for a long time was unable to write anything. It was not until the period of extreme hardship created by the post-Leap food shortages and the deterioration of relations with the USSR—although culminating in the withdrawal of Soviet technical advisers along with their blueprints in July and August 1960, severe strains in the relationship had already begun to emerge in 1958 and 1959—that he finally

Figure 21. Cao Yu. Source: Cao Yu, *Cao Yu lun chuangzuo*
(Shanghai: Shanghai wenyi chubanshe, 1986).

snapped out of his funk and acceded to the urging of Luo Ruiqing (chief
of staff of the People's Liberation Army) and other leaders to write a play
on the *woxin changdan* story.[41] Prior to starting, Cao Yu read through the
relevant ancient sources and familiarized himself with many of the *woxin
changdan* operas of his own day. The latter, he felt, too often duplicated
each other; he was determined do something more original. Also, anxious
not to repeat his Korean War propaganda bust of the mid-1950s, described
by a Hong Kong critic as "an irredeemable bore,"[42] he threw himself into

the project, working closely with his two collaborators, the playwright-director Mei Qian and the actor Yu Shizhi. During the writing the three men lived in seclusion in the Western Hills area outside Beijing. After completing a first draft in August 1960, they circulated the play for comment among historians and literary critics; it was also the subject of seminars held in March 1961, one result of which was a change in the title from *Woxin changdan* to *Dan jian pian*. *The Gall and the Sword* was published in the summer of 1961 and greeted with enthusiasm when it opened in the capital in early October.[43]

One reason for the warm response of the theatergoing public was the reputation of the play's principal creator and the fact that it was Cao Yu's maiden attempt at historical drama; another was the central theme of the play—its implied promise that a country, by strenuous and unremitting effort, could overcome all difficulties and make itself strong—which was tailor-made for the economic and political crisis facing China in 1960 and 1961.[44]

The Gall and the Sword opens in front of the Yue ancestral shrine, where Goujian, following his humiliating defeat at the hands of Wu, is bidding farewell to his forebears. Outside the shrine, two petty officers of Wu, one a follower of Wu Zixu, the other a follower of Bo Pi, argue over what to do with Goujian, the former wanting to kill him immediately and the latter insisting that this would be a violation of orders. A senior Wu officer, one of Bo Pi's trusted commanders, comes out of the shrine, scolds the quarreling Wu officers, and tells them that the order to protect Goujian comes from the Wu king Fuchai. Wu Zixu himself now appears and wants to go into the shrine and kill Goujian. But Fan Li, appealing to his sense of honor, reminds him that after Goujian was taken captive, Yue presented Wu with much treasure in order to preserve Goujian's life, an arrangement to which Fuchai had consented. Wu Zixu, after extracting from Fan Li a promise that Yue will henceforth serve Wu loyally, backs off.

A middle-aged Yue subject and his young daughter rush in, wanting to report to Goujian the terrible things the Wu soldiers have done—they have killed the man's wife, stolen his grain, and set fire to his fields—and to ask him not to forget the desire of the Yue people for revenge. One of the Wu soldiers guarding the shrine promptly kills the man, who before dying gives his daughter some burnt rice to show Goujian as evidence of Wu's crimes. Fuchai and Bo Pi come onstage; Xi Shi also enters. The latter is only fifteen or sixteen years old and is a neighbor of the man whom the Wu soldiers have just killed; as one of the soldiers is on the point of killing the daughter as well, Xi Shi steps forward and invites him to kill her instead.

Fuchai eyes Xi Shi and is visibly captivated. Bo Pi, taking note of this, orders the soldier to put his sword away and Xi Shi is taken back to Wu.

Wu Zixu pleads with Fuchai to kill Goujian and destroy Yue. Bo Pi offers the opposite counsel. Fuchai, persuaded by Bo Pi, summons Goujian and tells him that he intends to treat him and the state of Yue with lenience, but that he and his wife must return with him to Wu. While everyone else thanks Fuchai for his kindness, Goujian undiplomatically berates the Wu king for the cruelty Wu has shown toward the subjects of Yue. The other Yue people finally prevail upon Goujian to simmer down. As he is departing for Wu by boat, he is given the burnt rice and urged not to forget the land and people of Yue.

The second act takes place three years later in Wu at the stone cottage in which Goujian, his wife, and Fan Li have been living. Goujian observes that a major reason Wu is so prosperous and Yue so poor is that the farmers of Yue still use wooden plows, while those of Wu use deeper-plowing iron ones. A Yue commoner's son, Wuba, who has accompanied Wen Zhong on a tribute mission to Wu, arrives at the cottage. He tells Goujian that the Yue people have suffered successive famine years and are faring poorly, but that no matter how great their hardship, they are determined to avenge the humiliating treatment suffered at the hands of Wu. Wuba has an iron plow with him and tells Goujian that Yue plans to start using such plows to increase its agricultural productivity. Fuchai's lead concubine, who, it turns out, is Xi Shi, now three years older, appears on the scene. No one at first recognizes her, but she reveals who she is and then proceeds to foil an effort on the part of Wu Zixu to have Goujian killed immediately, without authorization. Bo Pi comes onstage and announces that Goujian and his party are to be freed to return to Yue. Fan Li tells Wuba to report this to Wen Zhong; he also tells him to take the iron plow back to Yue with him so that artisans can cast iron plows for Yue farmers to use.

Act 3, which takes place six months later in an undeveloped rural area outside Kuaiji, opens with a conversation among some Yue farmers. They are suffering from severe famine, and on top of everything else the soldiers of Wu have forced some of them to take part in the construction of a hall for singing recitals, working them to the bone and giving them only moldy, rotten rice to eat. The farmers go off to the river to perform rain ceremonies. Goujian, Wen Zhong, and two bodyguards come onstage. They also kneel down and pray for rain. Goujian describes and bemoans the famine conditions, then turns to Wen Zhong, who has been in charge of Yue during his three-year absence, and complains about the sluggishness of Yue's development. A bodyguard offers Goujian a parasol to protect him from the sun; he refuses it, not wishing to enjoy such a luxury when his people must toil in the sun constantly.

The farmers who went to pray for rain, hearing that Goujian has come, return to greet him. Goujian expresses his empathy for the suffering they are enduring and tells them he has brought rice with him to allay their hunger. The commoners are overcome with gratitude. Some Wu soldiers appear and announce that they are going to fill in a well as punishment for the people's resistance to forced labor; they also tell the farmers that the rice Goujian has distributed has been furnished by Fuchai. On hearing this, some of the farmers throw the rice on the ground. At first Goujian is angered by this seeming ingratitude. But Wen Zhong admonishes him, telling him that the one thing of value that his people possess is their morale and spirit, the fact that they can't be bought off. Goujian eventually accepts this, especially after interrogating the leader of the common people, Kucheng, who earlier had accused the king of being spineless. Kucheng, after apologizing to Goujian for having behaved rudely toward him, explains that the farmers of Yue cannot depend on others, that they must rely entirely on their own efforts. What they want more than anything is to avenge the humiliation Wu has inflicted on Yue and for Goujian to take the lead in enriching and strengthening the country. Goujian acknowledges his error before the people. He asks Kucheng what the people will eat if they have no rice and what they will work the fields with if they have no draft animals or plows. Kucheng responds that they are accustomed to having nothing to eat but wild fruit and bitter greens and to plowing the fields with their bare hands. They show the king their bruised, scarred hands, so that he can see for himself. Goujian, greatly moved, joyfully proclaims that Yue henceforth will rely exclusively on its own exertions in the effort to become stronger and announces that with people like the common people of Yue he has nothing to worry about or to fear.

As if to formally confirm the change in his thinking, Goujian now announces that he has decided to establish the new capital of Yue right there in Kuaiji, near the border with Wu (and therefore more convenient for a future Yue attack against Wu), rather than further south. The local farmers, upon hearing this, are elated, and Wen Zhong, recognizing the change that has come over Goujian, congratulates him on his decision. Kucheng then presents to Goujian the "precious sword for the suppression of Yue" that Fuchai had earlier (in the first act) plunged into a rocky ledge by the Yue shrine as a symbol of Wu's future domination of Yue. Goujian speaks

Figure 22. A Cheng Shifa illustration for *The Gall and the Sword*. Cheng's illustrations were originally published in the Shanghai evening paper *Xinmin wanbao*. In the opening act of the play, Fan Li (right, wearing sword) restrains Wu Zixu (left) from entering the Yue ancestral shrine to kill Goujian. Source: Qiu Yang, Chen Changming, and Cheng Shifa, *Dan jian pian*.

Figure 23. A Cheng Shifa illustration for *The Gall and the Sword*. In act 3, when famine-stricken Yue commoners resist Wu's forced labor demands, Wu soldiers punish them by filling in a well with dirt and stones. Source: Qiu Yang, Chen Changming, and Cheng Shifa, *Dan jian pian*.

to the sword and tells it that in the future it will be of great use. Wen Zhong then points out to the king that Kucheng is the man who, three years before, as he was departing for Wu, gave him the burnt rice attesting to Wu's cruel oppression. Goujian asks Kucheng what the farmers lack. When told that they lack water buffaloes and plows, Wen Zhong says that buffaloes are being transported from Chu and that Wuba (who is one of Kucheng's sons) has already been charged with having plows fashioned. When Goujian asks what else they lack, all the farmers say "rain." A fierce wind arises and the sky darkens as storm clouds gather. Goujian prays to heaven for a substantial rain to relieve the farmers' distress. But as he prays the clouds disperse. He continues to pray. The scorching sun shines again overhead. Everyone stands in silence, and the act ends.

The fourth act takes place four years later on the outskirts of Kuaiji. The famine has lifted, agriculture prospers in Yue, and the fields are emerald green after an all-night rainfall. The humble bamboo structures that house Goujian when he plows the fields are visible; to the rear, Goujian's wife sits spinning hemp cloth. The lowing of water buffaloes is heard in the distance. But offsetting this bucolic backdrop, the oppressive demands of Wu (including its insistence that Fuchai's sword be returned) persist. The fierce, unyielding spirit of the people of Yue continues to be a source of guidance and inspiration for Goujian. Kucheng at one point presents the king with a gallbladder, telling him that the gallbladder will enable him to be clear-sighted and to understand the difference between the momentary strength that comes from physical might *(li)* and the enduring accomplishment that derives from acting in accordance with right (also *li,* but written differently). Goujian hangs the gallbladder from a stone ledge and repeats Kucheng's words to himself. That night, in a monologue, he details the oppressive actions of Wu, which have brought such misery to the people of Yue and humiliation to its ruler. He then compares himself disparagingly to his ancestor the Great Yu, who, dedicated to the welfare of his people, was so consumed with the task of taming the floodwaters that even when he passed the entrance to his home he did not go in. "As for me, when I ascended the throne, all I knew how to do was drink and hunt, enjoying myself to the hilt. When I became a little more knowledgeable, I was filled with arrogance and failed to understand the need to provide for the people. The name 'Kuaiji' became synonymous with dung and decay. Kuaiji, in my hands, turned into a thing of shame, unfit for human habitation." Depressed and frustrated by a state of affairs in which, although constantly humiliated, he is unable to be strong and strike back, Goujian also disparages himself in relation to his top ministers.

Goujian and his official advisers are concerned lest the Wu soldiers, in their search for Fuchai's sword, discover the secret cache of Yue weapons and undermine its plans for revenge. Kucheng, seeing what must be done to save the situation, goes to the King Yu shrine and announces to the Wu soldiers on guard that he is the one who took the sword, which he then consigned irretrievably to the bottom of a lake. He is promptly killed by the soldiers, thereby sacrificing his life for his country and terminating the sword search. When this brave act is announced to Goujian, he walks over to where the gallbladder is hanging and exclaims, "So that's why you presented me with this thing, this gallbladder!" He then launches into a long encomium in which he equates his deceased subject with the gallbladder and says that henceforth the gallbladder will serve as a symbolic reminder of Kucheng and all the fine qualities he possessed. Goujian's wife tells him that Wuba's wife has just given birth to twin boys and wants the king to name them. Goujian, significantly, names them Plow and Sword. The act ends when, for the third time, one of Goujian's bodyguards shouts out to him, "Goujian! Have you forgotten the shame of Kuaiji?" to which the king responds that he has not forgotten.

The play's final act takes place fifteen years later in front of the shrine to the Great Yu, situated by the river. The rocky ledge into which Fuchai plunged his sword has been turned into a memorial to Kucheng; Yue soldiers sharpen their swords on the stone annually in ritual demonstration of their spiritual bond to the martyred hero. Plow and Sword, Kucheng's grandsons, have joined the Yue army. The commoners who are gathered around talk animatedly of the impending Yue assault against Wu. The sounds of an approaching army are heard in the distance. It is Fuchai's army, paying an inspection visit prior to traveling north to the meeting where the Wu king hopes to be named overlord. Goujian and his top ministers decide that the best strategy in the circumstances is to feign subservience toward Wu, in the expectation that after Fuchai has gone north with his top forces, Yue can then launch a surprise attack on Gusu. Goujian and Wen Zhong therefore go to the riverbank to greet Fuchai.

As the Wu army nears Kuaiji, Wu Zixu and Bo Pi engage in their customary wrangling over how to deal with Yue. Wu Zixu says that Yue is on the verge of rising, Wu of perishing. "King," he exclaims, "you just don't understand! You aren't a boy, you're a man of over fifty years of age. You must see things clearly. . . . The court is filled with officials who dare not speak the truth." Wu Zixu predicts that before Fuchai has returned from his meeting, Goujian will already have attacked the Wu capital. He points out that Yue has become rich and powerful, while Wu, although strong on the outside, is rotten within. Fuchai, his patience with his prime minister's sniping exhausted, orders that a sword be given to him to kill himself. Wu, after requesting that his eyes be hung from the Gusu city wall so that he can witness the arrival of Yue's conquering army, makes one final speech, in which he praises Goujian for, among other things, his willingness to listen to the loyal remonstrance of his ministers and warns that if Fuchai does not kill the Yue king without delay, it will be the end for Wu. He then takes his life.

Fuchai, observing the numerous Yue warships lined up on the river, belatedly acknowledges the wisdom of Wu Zixu's recommendation and resolves to destroy Yue as soon as he returns from his meeting. To ensure Goujian's allegiance during his absence, he asks the Yue ruler to send his daughter to Wu to be betrothed to Fuchai's son. Goujian, overriding his wife's pleas, reluctantly agrees to sacrifice their daughter. Fuchai then says that he also wants to borrow Yue's warships to take north with him and will return them following the conference. Goujian adamantly rejects this request. Fuchai, infuriated at such defiance, issues an ultimatum that Yue must hand over both the princess and the warships by dawn the following day. If not, he will send his army in to kill Goujian and his ministers and destroy the Yue ancestral shrine.

Following this charged encounter, Fuchai, having no intention of waiting until the next morning, orders a surprise attack against Yue. His men set fire to three of Yue's warships, after which fighting breaks out between the two sides. The Yue forces, responding quickly and resourcefully, set fire to the warships of Wu, destroying half of them. A Yue soldier now comes onstage and reports to Goujian that Fuchai has abandoned his headquarters. At this critical juncture, Fan Li returns from a diplomatic mission and informs the king that Qi and Jin have both lined up against Wu. On hearing these tidings, Goujian announces a full-scale naval assault against Wu— this final stage of the fighting, only alluded to in the play, takes some three years to accomplish. At the end of this period, Fuchai is captured by Yue soldiers and escorted into their king's presence. Goujian orders a bodyguard to fetch Fuchai's "precious sword for the suppression of Yue." The bodyguard hands it to Goujian, who tells Wuba to give it back to Fuchai. Goujian then orders Fuchai to use the sword on himself. Fuchai, dumbfounded, takes the sword. The common people are jubilant and break into song. Goujian's countenance faces upward. A commoner suddenly points to the Kucheng rock and cries out. A gallbladder is suspended from the rock. Goujian, startled, looks at it. Wen Zhong asks him if he remembers the day when Kucheng gave him the gallbladder. Goujian says he has not forgotten and asks Wuba to give him the gallbladder. Holding it in his hand, he exclaims, "Lying on brushwood and tasting gall, striving constantly to become stronger. Goujian can never forget." The snow begins to come down heavily, filling the sky and blanketing the ground. The play ends.[45]

The Gall and the Sword, from a political standpoint, is something of an oddity. In certain respects, it seems clearly in tune with the spirit of the Great Leap Forward. Goujian recognizes the importance of Yue's introducing iron plows, as Wu had done, to improve its agricultural yields. There is repeated emphasis, as in the case of the *woxin changdan* operas, on the need for Yue to practice self-reliance and strive to build up the strength of the country, policies related not only to the Leap but also to the worsening relationship with the Soviet Union. Also in keeping with the operas, Cao Yu and his colleagues assign a major role to the people of Yue—above all, Kucheng—not just in supporting and encouraging Goujian, but even in instructing him and shaping his basic moral and political outlook. Indeed, one of the criticisms of the play commonly ventured in the early 1960s was that the character of Kucheng was too idealized, that of Goujian too passive, and that Kucheng came close to stealing the show from the Yue king.[46]

Where the play is politically ambiguous is in the emphasis it gives, first, to the protracted famine in Yue (which is referred to in act 2 and supplies the setting for the entirety of act 3) and, second, to the difficult relationship between Goujian and his top ministers, in particular Wen Zhong, and more broadly the recurrent theme of the importance of rulers heeding the loyal remonstrance of their officials. At the time that *Dan jian pian* was being written, a terrible famine was in progress in China. Natural calamities and labor shortages (resulting from a huge transfer of labor from rural to urban areas to promote industry) had depressed agricultural production, resulting in widespread starvation from 1959 through 1961. "Anywhere from 16.4 to 29.5 million extra people," according to MacFarquhar, "died during the leap, because of the leap."[47] The famine was, to a very considerable extent, a consequence of policies initiated by Mao himself with the support of allies in the upper echelons of the government, and once it became clear that mistakes had been made, it was Mao who (in autumn 1958 and again in spring 1959) called for adjustments. Mao was not, however, prepared to confess his errors publicly and take major corrective action, "probably because he did not want to acknowledge that Peng Dehuai," who had ventured serious criticisms of the Leap at the Lushan Conference in July 1959 and been ferociously attacked by the chairman as a result, "had been right." Quite to the contrary, in late 1959 and early 1960, in the context of the campaign against "right opportunism" that followed the attack on Peng, the Great Leap had been renewed, with Mao's encouragement, and mass starvation in the Chinese countryside ensued.[48]

It is worth noting that significant attention to famine in Yue is not a standard feature of twentieth-century renderings of the Goujian story. It is often omitted entirely or accorded only a line or two in passing;[49] in many instances where it is mentioned, moreover, it is not a real famine but a fabricated one, part of Yue's strategy for weakening Wu (which, it will be recalled, it does by asking Wu for a substantial loan of grain and then repaying it the following year after boiling the seed, thereby rendering the repaid grain barren).[50] The fact that in *The Gall and the Sword* so much notice is paid to the successive famine years suffered by the people of Yue is clearly an allusion to the famine then taking place in China. The question is, what are we to make of this? When I first read the play, I was confident that the account of the famine represented an implicit criticism of Mao Zedong. After all, where Mao during the Great Leap Forward distanced himself from the sufferings of China's farmers, Goujian is presented as a king in close touch with his people, sharing in their work on occasion, bemoaning the famine conditions under which they suffered, expressing empathy for them, even praying with them for rain. The contrast between the two rulers could not have been greater, and it did not make Mao look good.

Such a contrast could certainly have occurred to readers and viewers of *Dan jian pian*. But one must be extremely careful in assuming that it was consciously intended by Cao Yu and his colleagues. The famine in Yue, after all, was caused primarily by severe drought and secondarily by the oppressive actions of Wu (which can be interpreted here as a stand-in for the Soviet Union).[51] It certainly was not a consequence of misguided policies instituted by Goujian, who had been absent from Yue for three years and only returned six months prior to the opening of act 3 (at which point the famine was already in high gear); nor is there the slightest hint that it resulted from the policies of Wen Zhong, who had been in charge of the domestic affairs of Yue during his king's incarceration. While there can be little doubt, therefore, of a connection between the famine in *Dan jian pian* and the one occurring in China in the years 1959 through 1961, it would be a stretch to argue that the active response of Goujian to the Yue famine was intended as a veiled criticism of Mao's more complicated response to the famine of his day. This is especially so in light of Cao Yu's consistently demonstrated reluctance to stick his neck out politically.

The other feature of the play that, looked at in terms of contemporary developments, appears politically delicate and calls for scrutiny is Goujian's problematic relationship with his top ministers, in particular Wen Zhong. In the third act, the Yue king asks Wen Zhong why the enriching and strengthening of the country is so hard to accomplish, why everything moves forward at such a snail's pace. Wen Zhong denies that it is difficult and says that it just takes time. Goujian, not satisfied with this reply, tells Wen Zhong that with Fan Li he feels like a steed soaring through the heavens—everything is possible and results come quickly. But with him he feels earthbound, like an old cow, plodding along step by step. Wen Zhong confirms that, when one is on the ground, one must indeed proceed step by step.[52]

A little later in the same act, when Wen Zhong reproves Goujian for being annoyed by the Yue farmers' refusal of Wu's rice and the disrespectful behavior of Kucheng, he tells the king that he should be happy, not angry, at this reaction. An uneasy exchange follows. Goujian, still skeptical, asks Wen Zhong if this sort of impertinent conduct is to be regarded as indicative of popular spirit. Wen Zhong, genially, responds that, yes, it is in fact a healthy tendency. He adds that since Goujian's return from Wu the king has traveled all over Yue reassuring and pacifying the people, but he still does not comprehend the true feelings of the masses. "When a ruler is in the wrong," he says to Goujian, "his minister should remonstrate with him; but only when a ruler is truly wise is his minister able to speak bluntly." He tells Goujian that Kucheng is a learned commoner who has mastered the six arts and that he should call him over and talk to him.[53] While Wen Zhong goes to fetch Kucheng, Goujian, still somewhat vexed, soliloquizes:

> Wen Zhong's words are too severe, . . . not pleasing to the ear. People really are hard to use! The honest and capable ones are seldom tame and docile, [frowns] not tame and docile! But during periods of adversity, one must put up with such persons! [Turns things over in his mind, tries hard to convince himself, looks up.] Right, he's really right, his loyal admonition is reasonable enough. I should listen to what he says, should patiently heed the blunt talk of the common people. [Paces back and forth, blurts out:] But a commoner has had the impudence to say I have no backbone, that really is hard to take![54]

In the fourth act, in the long monologue in which Goujian pours scorn on himself in comparison to his ancestor the Great Yu, he again alludes to his difficulties with his top ministers: "In the presence of his officials," he asserts (referring to himself in the third person), "in the presence of such hard-to-control ministers as Fan Li and Wen Zhong, who cannot remain forever in a subordinate position, stands this king who doesn't amount to anything *[bu chengqi de junwang]*. What sort of man am I!"[55]

There are a number of themes in these passages that resonate tellingly with the figure of Mao Zedong. First, Goujian, like the PRC leader, shows himself to be impatient with the plodding, "step-by-step" approach to the achievement of prosperity and strength that Wen Zhong represents. "Gripped by the idea of instant, earthshaking progress"—these words, used by MacFarquhar to describe Mao, are equally applicable to the Yue king[56]— he prefers immediate results, of the sort identified in his mind with Fan Li. Second, Goujian's response to the fundamental principle of ministerial admonition, as enunciated by Wen Zhong, is, not unlike Mao's stance in regard to forthright criticism, inconsistent and conflicted.[57] One part of him clearly wants his top officials to be tame and docile, easily controlled. But another part acknowledges that honest and capable officials—the sort willing to tell a ruler when he is wrong—are seldom so acquiescent. In the upshot, although Goujian appears not to like Wen Zhong very much[58] and is clearly made nervous by his dependence on his dazzlingly talented top ministers, he is prepared, at least until Yue's immediate difficulties have been surmounted, to put up with their blunt counsel. In this respect, the Yue king seems to come off better than Mao, whose response to his critics at Lushan was rather less accommodating.

One remains, nevertheless, unconvinced of a fundamental difference between the two rulers. *Dan jian pian* concludes with Goujian's triumph over Fuchai. But many contemporary readers and viewers of the play will certainly have been familiar with other renderings of the Goujian story in which Wen Zhong, *after* Yue's conquest of Wu, runs afoul of the jealousy and suspicion of his king and is forced to commit suicide (an outcome prefigured in the play by the fate of another brusquely truth-telling minister, Wu Zixu). This poses an interesting conundrum. Like the hundreds of other stories that constitute such a vital part of China's cultural heritage, the Goujian story is on any given occasion encountered simultaneously in two ways, one narrowly exclusive, the other broadly inclusive. The former, as exemplified in *The Gall and the Sword*, is the realization of the story in a specific opera, spoken drama, schoolbook lesson, novel, newspaper article, or whatever. In this concrete rendering, character development, narrative (or plot) detail, the use of language, where and how the action begins and ends are all fixed by a contemporary creator, whose identity is generally indicated. But when Chinese readers and audiences encounter this rendering, they are also apt to have in their heads other possible versions of the story, greater or fewer in number depending on the vagaries of individual experience (age, educational level, and so on). Armed with this less-bounded, more broadly inclusive knowledge of the Goujian story, they instinctively pay close attention to how a particular character is handled, how the rendering begins and ends, what is omitted, invented, or emphasized, and like questions. (In the numerous contemporary reviews of *Dan jian pian* that I have seen, such questions are addressed repeatedly.) And, as a direct result of the raising of such questions, when readers and viewers see that the relationship between Goujian and Wen Zhong in *The Gall and the Sword* is fraught with tension, they are easily able to picture in their minds the tragic dénouement that, although not in the play, is very much a part of the Goujian story in its broader, more inclusive guise. Whether or not, carrying this line of reasoning a step further, contemporary readers and audiences might also be inclined to connect the dots between the responses of Goujian and Mao to criticism (especially criticism experienced as humiliation, which was a problem for both rulers) is a harder case to make, although it is a fact that during the Mao years Chinese habitually looked for political messages everywhere, regardless of whether they were in fact intended.

The last assertion bears further discussion. As in the matter of the famine, the point I wish to make is not that Cao Yu and his collaborators consciously sought, through their characterization of Goujian, to direct subtle barbs at Mao. Rather, it is to suggest that, by highlighting in the play such issues as the devastating famine in Yue and the prickly relationship between Goujian and his ministers, they in effect invited readers and viewers to consider the resonance between these issues and close analogues in the contemporary Chinese situation, of which everyone was aware. It is well to bear in mind that, during the relatively open years from 1959 to 1962—a period in which a certain amount of criticism of failed Leap policies was not only tolerated but even encouraged—Cao Yu and his colleagues were by no means alone among contemporary writers in calling attention to such sensitive matters.

The best-known instance of this was the historian and deputy mayor of Beijing Wu Han, whose writings on the intrepid Ming official Hai Rui (1513–1587) cut perilously close to the bone and eventually got Wu into deep trouble.[59] Hai Rui in late 1565 had submitted a memorial that was scathingly critical of the Jiajing emperor's personal conduct and disastrous neglect of public business over a twenty-year span—an action that resulted in this brave official's dismissal from office, imprisonment, and near death due to torture.[60] In June 1959 Wu Han published an article in the *People's Daily* vindicating Hai Rui ("Hai Rui Upbraids the Emperor"), and some time later followed it with an opera, *The Dismissal of Hai Rui*, which was first performed in Beijing in February 1961. The opera, although well received at the time, was severely criticized in November 1965 by Yao Wenyuan (later to become a member of the infamous Gang of Four) in an article that has often been regarded as the opening salvo of the Cultural Revolution. Yao, however, although charging Wu with having created a fictitious Hai Rui and written an antisocialist "poisonous weed," did not go so far as to introduce explicitly the parallel between Hai Rui and Peng Dehuai. This was left to Mao himself in a speech in Hangzhou in December, in which, after praising Yao's article, the chairman added: "Its defect is that it did not hit the crux of the matter. The crux of *Hai Rui Dismissed from Office* was the question of dismissal from office. The Jiajing emperor dismissed Hai Rui from office. In 1959 we dismissed Peng Dehuai from office. And Peng Dehuai is Hai Rui too."[61]

Up until around the mid-1970s, most Western scholars who discussed the Wu Han–Hai Rui affair assumed that the basic charges leveled by Yao Wenyuan and Mao at the onset of the Cultural Revolution—that Wu Han was essentially an anti-Maoist, whose opera embodied "criticism of Maoist policies in 1958–59, especially the treatment of Peng Dehuai and the commune programme of the Great Leap Forward"[62]—were on the whole accurate. Later treatments of the issue, however, have challenged this understanding for several reasons. First, Mao himself, at a work conference in Shanghai in March 1959 (that is, prior to the Lushan gathering), in the context of his broader effort to get party members to overcome their fear of criticizing and speaking out, had urged them to model themselves on Hai Rui (as well as another widely admired remonstrator, the early Tang official Wei Zheng). Second, Wu Han did not spontaneously decide to write on Hai Rui in response to Mao's suggestion; he was expressly encouraged to do so by a mysterious "leading comrade." Third, Wu Han's June 1959 article on Hai Rui preceded the criticisms leveled by Peng Dehuai at Lushan and therefore could not possibly have incorporated a veiled reference to them. Fourth, neither Wu Han nor any of the others who wrote on Hai

Rui in the late 1950s and early 1960s were punished at the time. For all of these reasons, MacFarquhar suggests that "at least in its origins the Hai Rui 'affair' was perfectly innocent and was seen as such by Mao."[63]

The years from 1959 to 1962 were a relaxed time only in a very limited sense. In line with Mao's periodic calls for blunt criticism and fearless truth-telling, highly placed party members urged people like Cao Yu and Wu Han to write about potentially sensitive political issues. But recent Chinese history (most dramatically the Anti-Rightist Campaign's entrapment of those intellectuals who had responded boldly to the Hundred Flowers summons) had amply demonstrated that engaging in such writing was perilous at best. The more one responded to the pressures to write, the more one exposed oneself to danger. And yet, these pressures, partly internal, partly external, were very real, and so people like Wu Han and Cao Yu, while taking whatever precautions they could, continued to write. When Wu Han, at the apparent instigation of the propaganda official Hu Qiaomu, published another piece on Hai Rui in September 1959, which was completed on the very day of Peng Dehuai's dismissal, he made sure to cover himself with "a disclaimer rejecting the pretensions of right opportunists" who might imagine themselves to be modern Hai Ruis.[64]

In Cao Yu's case, the political apprehensiveness expressed itself in a different way. Although *The Gall and the Sword* was generally well received, the reviews also pointed out certain shortcomings. One such, which a number of critics addressed, was the dramatic weakness of act 3. It is perhaps an indication of the sensitivity of the central subject matter of this act that most of those who criticized it either touched on the Yue famine only indirectly or made no reference to it at all.[65] Another shortcoming, noted earlier, was the weak portrayal of the central character Goujian in comparison with the commoner Kucheng. As Wu Han observed in his comment on the play, it went too far in depicting Goujian as an attentive listener to the voice of the people, resulting in a vulgarization of the notion that history was made by the masses.[66] Zhou Enlai, in a Beijing speech made to over one hundred playwrights in February 1962, although not venturing any specific criticisms of *The Gall and the Sword*, targeted it (and its chief author Cao Yu) as symptomatic of a more general political/ideological problem:

A new superstition hampers our thinking. As a result authors are afraid to write, many have had bad labels pinned on them, and little is produced. People only seek to avoid mistakes, they don't try to achieve something worthwhile. Comrade Cao Yu is a courageous author, a writer with self-confidence who is respected by all. Yet his writing in *The Gall and the Sword* is marked by anxiety. After he was admitted into the party, he should have become bolder, but instead he became more timid. Modesty is a good thing, but becoming more timid is not good. Joining the party should have been of benefit to him, his work reaching a higher level. But instead it has become more constrained . . . In the past, when I discussed matters with Comrade Cao Yu in Chongqing [during the Japanese war], he was much more at ease. Now it seems he has become more guarded. Fearful of making this mistake or that one, he has no ideas of his own, no self-assurance. This way one can't write good things.[67]

Although Zhou's criticism was seemingly well-intended, it was not in the last analysis terribly helpful. The "superstition" he said writers suffered from, after all, was an entirely rational response to the catch-22 environment they had been in for some years, and nothing Zhou said (or could have said) guaranteed that they would not be at risk if they now became bolder in their work. Such caveats do not seem to have concerned Cao Yu, however. On the contrary—and it is a sad commentary on the degree to which so many contemporary writers, despite everything they had been through, continued to invest an almost blind trust in the party and its top leaders[68]— he was overjoyed at Zhou's remarks. As he told his biographer in 1984:

When I heard the premier's criticism of me, it warmed my heart. I didn't feel at all on edge. It was as if I had been relieved of a heavy burden. I had indeed become timid and cautious. It wasn't that I had no ideas of my own; it was because I didn't exercise clear judgment. I hadn't been a target of criticism at that time. But the general principles he spoke of so cogently seemed correct to me. Now I understand the "left" deviation ideological trend, but at the time I didn't see it clearly. In my writing, too, I felt troubled; it was as if there was a wall around me that I couldn't see, that I might bump up against. The premier singled me out personally. But it was his hope that writers in general would throw off the millstones around their necks and free themselves from the "new superstition." I at least drew encouragement and inspiration from his words.[69]

The February meeting was preparatory to a much larger national conference of playwrights that was held in Guangzhou in March 1962. Cao Yu took even more encouragement from this meeting, at which Foreign Minister Chen Yi (who with Zhou Enlai had taken a leading role at the time in promoting greater liberalization in the intellectual realm) delivered a famously long speech in which, among other things, he advanced the comforting assertion that the great majority of China's intellectuals were supporters of the party and of socialism and therefore should be freed of the "bourgeois intellectual" stigma and treated henceforth as a part of the working people. Cao Yu's recollections of the importance of this conference to him were of a piece with his reactions to the earlier meeting:

> After liberation, like many other intellectuals I put a lot of effort into my work. Although in an organizational sense we were admitted to the party, the fact is we were still saddled with the "bourgeois intellectual" label, which in practice kept us from holding our heads high and breathing freely. With this label pressing down on us, how could we express ourselves without inhibition in our creative work in behalf of socialism? That time was also one in which our hearts were burdened by worries. Not only I, but many other comrades as well, experienced a deep fear that if we didn't do a good job, we would become "poisonous weeds who opposed the party and opposed socialism." The Guangzhou conference overnight liberated people's thinking and did away with the labels. Thirteen years after the founding of the People's Republic, that strange and confusing shadow, sometimes visible, sometimes hidden, finally vanished from our minds. How could this not cause people to express heartfelt gratitude toward the party? How could it not fill people with joy? Yet, this good time didn't last![70]

The good time, indeed, did not last. Cao Yu made an important and much praised speech at the Guangzhou conference and, after it was over, happily began work on a new play, *Wang Zhaojun,* that had been suggested to him by Zhou Enlai.[71] But when storm clouds once again appeared on the Chinese horizon in the latter months of 1962—the tenth plenum of the Central Committee held in September is generally seen as marking "a decisive turn to the left that would lead eventually to the Cultural Revolution"[72]— he interrupted the writing, and the play was left incomplete until after the Cultural Revolution years—years during which Cao Yu suffered severely.[73]

The Gall and the Sword, although certainly not one of Cao Yu's finest plays from an artistic point of view, was by general consensus the best of the *woxin changdan* dramas of the early 1960s and was enthusiastically received at the time of its appearance. Its importance in the context of this book rests in its use of the Goujian story to convey a specific set of political messages in socialist China, at the very moment that the same story was being used to convey a quite different set of political messages in the China of Chiang Kai-shek. The clearest and most positive of the play's messages was, of course, its central emphasis on working hard to enrich and strengthen the country *(fafen tuqiang)*—a major propaganda theme in the PRC of the early 1960s and one that was particularly compelling owing to the famine then ravaging China and the concurrent worsening of the relationship with the Soviet Union.

The other messages conveyed by the play were more ambiguous and, at least potentially, far less positive. One was the left deviation that Cao Yu acknowledged years later and that was perhaps best captured at the time by Wu Han in his criticism of the play's ahistorical democratization of class relations in late Zhou China. "If, in ancient times, kings listened as attentively [as Goujian] to the views of the common people," Wu observed, "peasant uprisings against the ruling class in history couldn't possibly have occurred."[74]

Other ambiguous political messages in *Dan jian pian* pertained to the impact of famine in Yue and the hard time Goujian had accepting advice from strong-willed advisers. My sense is that Cao Yu, who was genuinely and deeply distressed by the suffering taking place in rural China at the time *Dan jian pian* was being written, deliberately assigned a prominent place in the play to famine, not in order to take a dig at Mao, but as a means of reinforcing the play's overall contemporary relevance. The troubled relationship Goujian had with his top officials is more complicated. In light of Cao Yu's political timidity and abiding faith in the Communist Party, it seems extremely unlikely that he would engage in even the most indirect criticism of the party's paramount leader. We must distinguish clearly, however, between an author's intent and the range of possible meanings his or her language might assume in the minds of reading and viewing audiences, who have their own concerns, preoccupations, and distinct social biographies.[75] In the atmosphere of the early 1960s, marked as it was by widespread sentiment sympathetic to Peng Dehuai, it seems entirely plausible, as suggested earlier, that readers and viewers of *Dan jian pian,* most of whom would have also been acquainted with a broader, more-inclusive set of Goujian narratives, might equate Wen Zhong with the dismissed minister of defense, even though in the play itself Wen Zhong remained unpunished. They might, in short, on the basis of their wider experience of the Goujian story, fill in imagined blanks in the drama that Cao Yu had no intention of putting there.[76]

The identification of Wen Zhong with Peng Dehuai would, of course, have been all the more likely in a contemporary rendering of the Goujian story in which the Yue minister *was* punished. This was precisely the case in a version of the story written by a certain Yu Tianhua. Yu's book, entitled *King Goujian of Yue Avenges the Wrong Done to His Country (Yue wang Goujian xi guochou)*, is of special interest for a number of reasons. First, the original edition was published in November 1962 in Hong Kong, where Yu lived. Like all Hong Kong Chinese, Yu was greatly distressed by the tragic situation unfolding on the mainland, in response to which a mass exodus from Guangdong into the British colony had occurred in spring 1962.[77] The time and place of the book's publication are both important. In the "groundswell of pro–Peng Dehuai opinion" that prevailed within the party in the early 1960s,[78] it would have been entirely too risky to publish in the PRC a rendering of the Goujian story that included the Yue king's turning against his loyal minister; in none of the PRC versions that I have seen from these years is Wen Zhong's tragic fate so much as hinted at.* Hong Kong, however, was a safe venue for such publication (possibly the only one at the time within the greater Chinese world). Second, Yu draws special attention to the injustice done to Wen Zhong in an unusual elegiac tribute to the Yue minister in the book's appendix. The emphasis in the tribute is on Wen Zhong's loyalty and patriotism. Yu alludes to the proverbial wisdom that when an enemy state has been destroyed the triumphant ruler, having no further use for the ministers responsible for his success and nervous concerning the great merit they have accumulated, does away with them; this is the way, according to Yu, that the world has always worked and, even in the increasingly enlightened present, nothing much has changed. He goes on, however, to intimate that in such situations ministers have moral choices: they can, anticipating their ruler's behavior, abandon him and take flight (as Fan Li did) or, even knowing the risk, they can remain in service (Wen Zhong's choice).[79] Although it is highly probable, in my judgment, that Yu Tianhua had Peng Dehuai specifically in mind in singling Wen Zhong out

---

*Xiao Jun's historical novel, *A Story from the Annals of Wu and Yue,* does deal with the grizzly end of Wen Zhong, and the author did attempt unsuccessfully to get it published in the early 1960s. But, for reasons that will be made clear in the next chapter, it could not possibly have been understood as a criticism of Mao's treatment of Peng Dehuai.

in this fashion—Peng also was famously loyal and patriotic and at Lushan he also made a difficult moral choice—there is no way in which this can be known with certainty. The likelihood that readers of Yu's book would make such a connection is, nevertheless, great.

While the relationship of *The Gall and the Sword* to criticism of Mao and his policies must be viewed, in the final analysis, as ambiguous and uncertain, a persuasive case for such criticism can be made in regard to two other works centering on the Goujian story that appeared early in the post-Mao era. These were Xiao Jun's historical novel, *A Story from the Annals of Wu and Yue (Wu Yue chunqiu shihua)*, which although written in the 1950s was not published until 1980, and Bai Hua's play, *The Golden Spear of the King of Wu and the Sword of the King of Yue (Wu wang jin ge Yue wang jian)*, which was first performed before a sellout audience in Beijing in 1983. There were two main reasons for the greater political venturesomeness of these two works. One had to do with the personalities of their authors, which could not have been more different from Cao Yu's; the other pertained to the radically altered political environment within which Xiao Jun and Bai Hua's writings saw the light of day.

FIVE

Political Allegory in the 1980s
Xiao Jun and Bai Hua

ALTHOUGH THE GOUJIAN STORY DOES NOT appear to have had a significant impact during the Cultural Revolution decade, it never disappeared
entirely. Indeed, at a critical moment in the Qinghua University drama of
summer 1968, when worker-propaganda teams forced the warring student
factions on the elite Beijing campus to end their fighting and form an alliance, Kuai Dafu, the humiliated leader of the more radical student group,
made a long speech to his followers urging them to persevere, taking part
of his text directly from Goujian: "Sleep on a wooden plank, eat bile, gather
forces for ten years, review the bitter lessons for another ten years."[1] What
happened at Qinghua and on other major Chinese campuses signaled an
important turning point in the Cultural Revolution, sounding the death
knell to its Red Guard phase.[2] It was also Kuai Dafu's personal Mount
Kuaiji.[3] His speech, as William Hinton wrote in his account of the Qinghua
events, was an appeal "for organizational continuity, albeit underground,
until conditions were more favorable. . . . A plea for a comeback twenty
years later . . . when the time was ripe . . . to make another bid for power."[4]

Mao Zedong died in September 1976, bringing an end to two decades
of almost unrelieved havoc and misery in the lives of tens of millions of his
compatriots. After a brief period of transition, the political leadership of
China passed to a man, Deng Xiaoping, who along with his family had
suffered greatly during the Cultural Revolution. Deng was determined to

put China on a very different course, emphasizing order over chaos and modernization over revolution. Among the new policy directions that were adopted under Deng's leadership, beginning in the late 1970s, was a palpable (although frustratingly inconsistent) loosening of the political constraints on Chinese intellectual life. In these circumstances, criticism of the Mao years (and at least indirectly of Mao himself), although certainly not without its risks, became a live possibility.

XIAO JUN (1907–1988)

Few Chinese intellectuals perhaps had more reason to take advantage of this possibility than the writer Xiao Jun, who had been intermittently at war with the Communist Party ever since the early 1940s in Yan'an and, although by no means entirely unadmiring of Mao Zedong, bridled at the Chinese leader's arbitrary and dictatorial style of rule. Born in the northeastern province of Liaoning into a family of farmers and craftsmen, Xiao had little formal education and joined the army in his late teens. In the early 1930s, he began writing fiction in Harbin. Shortly after this, the provinces of northeastern China having come under Japanese control, he journeyed to Shanghai, where he became a disciple of Lu Xun. In 1935, with Lu Xun's help, he published his first novel, an anti-Japanese work entitled *Village in August (Bayue de xiangcun)*. After the outbreak of the Sino-Japanese War (1937–1945), Xiao Jun left Shanghai, eventually winding up in Yan'an, the wartime capital of the Communist movement. A free spirit, stubbornly defiant, and fearless in his criticism of Communist policies and actions that he considered unjust, inhumane, or senseless, Xiao repeatedly got into trouble with the party from the early 1940s on, though he was not effectively silenced until some years later.[5] "My 'interment,'" as he put it in his speech to the Fourth Congress of Writers and Artists in 1979, "began in 1949 and I have only recently managed to claw my way back out of the ground."[6]

During Xiao Jun's "thirty-year hibernation" (to use his own phrase),[7] he continued to write. Although much of his work dealt with contemporary themes, he was convinced that a greater understanding of the ideas and wisdom of the past might help people in the present and future to avoid repeating similar mistakes and to manage their affairs in a more sensible way. Xiao claimed to have a special fascination with three earlier turning points in Chinese history: the Shang-Zhou, the Spring and Autumn–Warring States, and the Ming-Qing.[8] Although he did not draw the analogy explicitly, each

Figure 24. Xiao Jun. Source: Zhang Yumao, *Xiao Jun zhuan.*

of these periods was well known for its turmoil, violent conflict, and despotic exercise of political power, thus serving as mirrors to the conditions prevailing in his own day. Xiao apparently never completed a work on the last of the three transitions, the Ming-Qing.[9] However, in 1944, while in Yan'an, he wrote a long Beijing opera on the Shang-Zhou transition, which, although not published until many years later, was performed over thirty-six days in early 1950 in Fushun (in Liaoning province), where the author was working at the time.[10]

In 1955 Xiao Jun, then living in Beijing, began work on *A Story from the Annals of Wu and Yue,* a fictional work dealing with the second of the three transitions, the Spring and Autumn period to the Warring States period. The novel was completed in the spring of 1957,[11] just prior to the launching of the Anti-Rightist Campaign (in which the writer came under severe attack). In 1960 Xiao sent it, along with his opera on the Shang-Zhou transition and another work, to the head of the Propaganda Department of the Beijing Municipal Party Committee, in an effort to get them approved for publication. While waiting for a response, he began work on a Beijing opera script entitled *The Annals of Wu and Yue (Wu Yue chunqiu),* which was a close adaptation of his similarly titled novel. Although not published until many years later, it was completed in 1962 in eight parts and over a hundred scenes.[12] When Xiao finally got word in 1961 that the three works he had sent out earlier had been rejected as not being in keeping with the needs of the times, he sent them to Mao Zedong himself, trying a gambit that had worked for him once before (discussed later). This time, however, he did not hear back from Mao. Instead, in April 1962 he learned that his manuscripts had been referred to a publishing house. Then, in June, the publishers sent the entire batch back to him, rejecting them with the usual excuses. Only now, we are told, did Xiao Jun become fully aware that he had been classified as an "undesirable" *(lingce de ren).* Or, as one of his biographers put it, "the real reason for the repeated rejections was that he was Xiao Jun!"[13]

Xiao Jun's *A Story from the Annals of Wu and Yue* was finally published in 1980. It had been more than two decades since any new work of his had been brought out on the mainland[14] and, although there were now plenty of competing historical novels in circulation, the large print run of two hundred thousand sold out quickly.[15] The novel follows in broadest terms the sequence of developments in the Eastern Han work *The Annals of Wu and Yue* (see chapter 1). The first of its two volumes thus deals not with Goujian and Yue, but with Wu Zixu's flight from his native Chu, his involvement in the bloody internal struggles within the Wu ruling group, the warring between Wu and Chu, and so forth. It is only at the very end of the first volume that Goujian enters the picture, in the fateful battle against Wu that resulted in the death of Helu and the accession of Fuchai to the Wu throne. In the second volume the novel's focus shifts to the conflict between Wu and Yue, Goujian's incarceration in Wu after his humiliating defeat at Mount Kuaiji, the multifaceted contrast between Fuchai and Goujian, Goujian's years of preparation for avenging himself against his longtime rival, and his ultimate triumph. What is of greatest significance about Xiao Jun's book for our purposes is that, unlike any of the prior PRC renderings of the Goujian story of which I am aware, it does not end with Yue's destruction of Wu but carries the narrative forward to describe the darker, more despotic Goujian who emerges in the aftermath of this climactic event. The novel thus affords its author an opportunity to shine a light with particular intensity on "the inherent nature of the tyrant" (*baojun de benxing*)[16] and, more broadly, the corruption attending the exercise of autocratic power, with which Xiao Jun was himself all too familiar.

Because of the relevance of his personal experience to the subject matter, especially of the last part of the novel, Xiao Jun's life in the years immediately preceding the writing needs to be described. After Japan's defeat in 1945, he had been sent back to his native Manchuria with the Red Army to help firm up the CCP's position in the area. In 1947, the party helped Xiao set up a journal, *Wenhuabao,* which, as chief editor, he was able to use to advance his views. Picturing himself as a revolutionary intellectual whose job was to wage battle constantly "in all places and at all times for what he considered right," Xiao took open issue with party policies and behavior in a number of key areas. He condemned the bloodshed accompanying the land-reform drive that was in full swing at the time. He disparaged the Soviet Union as imperialistic. Most significantly, he challenged the party's "right of autocratic rule," favoring a multiparty political system, conciliation with the Guomindang, and an end to the civil war then in progress. In late summer 1948, the party finally responded in a systematic way to Xiao's criticisms, making him the prime target of a major rectification campaign in Manchuria. Xiao, as was his habit, refused to acknowledge his errors, for which recalcitrance he was punished by being transferred to the Fushun coal mines in Liaoning.[17]

In 1951, after working at the mines for two years (mainly, it appears, in a lowly office job), Xiao Jun packed his belongings and, in defiance of the wishes of the local party bosses, left Fushun for Beijing, where his wife and children were residing. As an unregistered resident *(heiren)* of the capital, he was unable initially to earn a living and was forced to rely on the largesse of friends and relatives (as well as the intervention on his behalf of Beijing mayor Peng Zhen). Nevertheless, he managed over the next several years to write a number of books, including a novel drawing on his experience at the Fushun mines.[18] When, in late 1953, it became clear that publication of his writing was not going to be easy, he appealed directly to Mao, whose response, as reported years later by Xiao, was, "Publish Xiao Jun's works." Mao's directive made possible the publication of *Coal Mines in May* (*Wuyue de kuangshan;* 1954) and *The Past Generation* (*Guoqu de niandai;* 1957). Xiao Jun's comment on this episode, in his speech before the Fourth Congress of Writers and Artists in 1979, clearly echoed his antipathy to Maoist autocracy: "Unpublishable works were thus made publishable by a single sentence from Chairman Mao. What kind of a 'doctrine' is this? Is it a 'doctrine of publish by merit' or a 'doctrine of publish by fiat'?"[19]

Mao's authorization to "publish Xiao Jun's works," which reached the writer in June 1954, restored his confidence that he could make a living as a writer,[20] and it was not long after this that he began work on *A Story from the Annals of Wu and Yue.* In the novel, Xiao Jun placed much emphasis on the importance of the ruling class gaining the support of the general population and treating the people with compassion. The disparity between Fuchai and Goujian in this respect was sharply drawn. Fuchai, through his self-indulgence and arrogance, brought endless suffering to the people of Wu, his policies and actions engendering opposition both domestically and abroad. Goujian, in comparison, after his return from his confinement in Wu, won the sympathy and support of the Yue people, who joined together with him to save the state from destruction. An outstanding ruler, Goujian bore up under humiliations that others could not endure. He was also able temporarily to relinquish the pleasures and indulgences of a king and share the hard lives of the people, ingratiating himself with the latter, and breathing new life into his state when it seemed on the verge of extinction.

While thus giving Goujian his due and not disparaging him in order to play up the importance of the people in Yue's revival, Xiao Jun made no pretense of depicting the Yue ruler as a saint. Goujian's extreme ruthlessness in military settings was on display from beginning to end;[21] at one point he became infatuated with the Maiden of Yue (Yue nü), who had been engaged to teach swordsmanship to the Yue military, and only backed off after his wife intervened;[22] and, even prior to the conquest of Wu, Fan Li warned Wen Zhong that as a man Goujian was biased and narrow-minded, suspicious and jealous, sinister and cruel.[23] These character short-comings, nevertheless, were nothing compared to the behavior Goujian exhibited *following* the conquest of Wu. He now took actions that were of a qualitatively different sort, yielding to his worst impulses and behaving in ways that gave little or no thought to the feelings of those surrounding him or to the long-term welfare of Yue.

One instance of this occurred in the immediate aftermath of the Yue victory. Goujian, mindful of the great contribution Xi Shi had made to the weakening of Wu over time, planned to take her back to Yue. He met with her and asked her what she would like in the way of a reward. She replied that she had put up with the shame of serving Fuchai because of the humiliation Goujian himself had endured during his three-year incarceration and the hatred the people of Yue bore toward Wu. Now that Yue had vanquished Wu and these humiliations had been expunged, she wished no reward other than to be allowed to return to her village and resume her life of washing and weaving silk. Goujian was much moved by Xi Shi's response. He also took secret note of the fact that she was as beautiful as ever, having conceded little to the passage of time. The forced departure of the Maiden of Yue earlier, owing to the obstruction of his wife, was something he had had to tolerate since Yue's priority at that juncture was to avenge itself against Wu. But now things were different. It was time he got to enjoy some of the pleasures of being king, and so he resolved to make Xi Shi a royal concubine. With these thoughts in mind, he gave a noncommittal reply to Xi Shi's request and the two of them prepared for the journey back to Yue.

When Goujian's wife learned of their impending arrival in the capital, she decided to take precautionary measures against her husband's predatory instincts, and so sent a palace functionary to greet Goujian and convey the message that she wished to see Xi Shi and reward her personally. Goujian, not thinking anything amiss in this, was delighted and agreed to his queen's request. However, that night Fan Li, ever mindful of impending danger, sent someone to fetch Xi Shi. When she was brought into his presence, she saw that he had with him her childhood sweetheart, Tian He, to whom she had long ago been betrothed and who had for years faithfully awaited her return. Fan Li told Xi Shi that Goujian wished to bring her into the palace as a concubine, and that his wife, on account of her jealousy, intended to inflict harm on her. He therefore gave Tian He a bag of jewels to use for traveling expenses and told the two of them that they must flee the following day and go to Chu. They thanked Fan Li tearfully and left.[24]

Goujian's lack of gratitude toward those who had served him and Yue so well was evidenced in an even more painful way in his behavior toward his top official advisers. A few days after the flight of Xi Shi, at the victory banquet, Wen Zhong recited a congratulatory verse in which he alluded to the material rewards that everyone now anticipated. Goujian, however, wore a glum expression on his face the entire evening. After the banquet, Fan Li sought out Wen Zhong and tried to convince him that Goujian's only concern at this point was to acquire more territory and become overlord in Fuchai's place; he wasn't in a mood to distribute rewards to anybody. It was time, therefore, for the two of them to leave Yue and return to their native Chu. Wen Zhong couldn't bring himself to believe Fan Li's words. What good, in any case, would it be for them to return to Chu, where he had been a lowly county magistrate and Fan Li only a commoner? How could this be compared to the high status they enjoyed in Yue? He was sure that Goujian was going to treat them well and that he wasn't the sort of ingrate Fan Li represented him as being. Fan Li, with a cold smile, responded, "It is precisely because our merit is great that we will not be rewarded and that our lives are in danger."[25]

Fan Li knew that Wen Zhong was reluctant to pass up the opportunity to reap wealth and honor and that it was therefore of little use to press the matter further. Several days later he announced his resignation to Goujian and, after one final attempt to persuade Wen Zhong of the danger he was in, took his leave of Yue.[26]

After Goujian's incorporation of Wu and return to Yue, not only did he fail to bestow any special rewards, he also became increasingly cold and remote, no longer demonstrating humility in his dealings with his ministers and evincing little patience with their counsel. He also ceased to show concern for the hard lot of the common people and made the laws and punishments more severe, with the result that the people of Yue became more and more unhappy. Goujian now began to suspect everyone, so that his court officials, cowering in fear, distanced themselves from him and seldom went to the palace, one of them even pretending to go mad. Wen Zhong, observing these changes, began to understand Fan Li's warnings and, becoming more and more troubled, rarely appeared in court himself. Those who had long nursed feelings of envy toward Wen Zhong began to slander him in Goujian's presence, arousing the king's suspicions. When Goujian interrogated Wen Zhong, the latter defended himself as best he could, finally telling Goujian that he should have listened to Fan Li and gone back to Chu and intimating to the king that he was prepared to die. Goujian, unfeelingly, threw a sword at Wen Zhong's feet, ordered an attendant to give him a jar of poison, and turned around and left. Wen Zhong, with a bitter smile on his face, soliloquized: "I never would have guessed that a county magistrate from Chu would, as now, die at the hands of the king of Yue; I hope that later generations of loyal high officials will take my fate as a warning." He then returned home and took the poison.

Just as he had honored Fan Li after his departure by having a statue of him made and placed next to the throne, Goujian buried Wen Zhong with full honors in a hill west of the capital, which he named Zhong Hill (Zhong shan).

After eliminating his meritorious ministers one by one, Goujian followed up his victory over Wu with attacks against Chu and other states and eventually realized his ambition of being named overlord.[27]

In the many versions of the Goujian story that I have seen, after the defeat of Wu, Bo Pi, the perennial adversary of Wu Zixu at the Wu court and the man who, while indulging himself and winning Fuchai's confidence through flattery, consistently undermined Wu's position and contributed mightily to its eventual downfall, is almost invariably punished with death by Goujian as a fitting reward for his having betrayed his king and his state. In Xiao Jun's novel, however, the corrupt Wu minister meets up with a very different fate. As if serving as a foil to Goujian's lack of gratitude toward those who had served him and Yue most loyally, the deeply disloyal Bo Pi, instead of being killed, is awarded a position of prominence in the Yue government. Fan Li, in his last letter to Wen Zhong, took note of this and saw it as a clear indication that Goujian had designs on Chu (from which Bo Pi, like Fan Li and Wen Zhong, had originally hailed). Although at the time Wen Zhong resisted Fan Li's logic, in the context of his growing estrangement from Goujian, he soon arrived at the same conclusion.[28]

In weighing the political import of Xiao Jun's novel, in particular the final chapter (which includes the developments just recounted), the date of its completion (1957) must be kept in mind. Since the work was finished two years prior to the Lushan Conference, it obviously cannot have been intended as a critique of Mao's attack on Peng Dehuai. Even if Xiao's book had been written in the aftermath of Lushan, moreover, his portrayal of Wen Zhong would have precluded any easy identification with Mao's minister of defense. This portrayal was clearly very different from Yu Tianhua's, as discussed earlier. For Yu, Wen Zhong's remaining in the service of Goujian was a moral act, framed in terms of a minister's undying loyalty to his king and his willingness to risk his life in the process. Xiao Jun, instead, although giving Wen Zhong full credit for being an exceptional minister,

Figure 25. Wen Zhong's tragic fate. On the left side of this divided illustration stands a triumphant Goujian, while on the right Wen Zhong prepares to drink from the jar of poison received from the Yue king. Source: Xiao Jun, *Wu Yue chunqiu shihua*, 2:565.

depicts him as a man of petty official background who is motivated—one might almost say blinded—by the desire for material reward. The contrast with Fan Li is sharply drawn. Xiao Jun portrays Fan Li not as a member of the ruling class but as a man of the common people, who rose to his high position as a result of his great ability. His support of Goujian was clear-headed, and it was conditional on the attitude of the Yue king toward the people. Thus, when he saw that Goujian, after succeeding in his revenge against Wu, almost immediately began to display his savage and cruel side, he did not hesitate to forsake his official rank and salary and speedily re-join the common people.[29]

The political message embodied in *A Story from the Annals of Wu and Yue* is not, in my judgment, tied to a specific action on the part of Mao Ze-dong or any other of Xiao Jun's contemporaries. Xiao Jun certainly had plenty of "old scores" that, he assured his listeners in his speech to the Fourth Congress of Writers and Artists in 1979, he would not overlook when it came time for him to write his memoirs.[30] His novel, however, was less about settling old scores than about depicting the amoral world of a man for whom power and ruthless self-aggrandizement were everything and righteous ac-tion counted for little. Goujian's determination to make Xi Shi his concu-bine, his cruel and mean-spirited treatment of the officials most responsi-ble for his success against Wu, and his employment of the corrupt and traitorous Bo Pi in a high official capacity after the conquest were stun-ningly amoral acts that only a despot completely consumed with himself and utterly oblivious of the concerns and feelings of others could have com-mitted. As such, they were suggestive reminders of the kind of political world Xiao Jun himself inhabited in the 1950s, when the book was written, and could well have been read as such by Chinese readers in the early 1980s, after its publication.

In his 1979 speech at the Fourth Congress of Writers and Artists, Xiao Jun articulated four life goals that, he said, lay at the heart of everything he had ever said, done, or written. These goals were the Chinese nation's achievement of complete self-reliance, the liberation of the Chinese people, the emancipation of all people in China (most particularly the laboring classes), and a future that would "never again witness the appearance of a society in which exploitation or oppression of one's fellow man exists." "It is of no concern to me," he added, "whether these four goals . . . are real-ized in the name of socialism or of communism."[31] This last statement, with its clear intimation that the patriotic and humanistic aspirations Xiao held dear were severable from the guiding ideology of the contemporary

Chinese state, joined Xiao Jun at the hip to Bai Hua, a younger writer also willing to challenge the foundational faith of the regime.

BAI HUA (1930–)

Bai Hua, after a hard childhood, joined the Red Army during the civil war and was attached to a propaganda unit as a writer. He soon became a party member and was progressing smoothly in his career when he came under assault in the Anti-Rightist Campaign and was dismissed from both the party and the army. Although the "rightist" label was removed in 1961 and he was restored to his former positions in 1964, before long, like almost all writers, he fell victim to the Cultural Revolution. As a result, it was not until the late 1970s, after a hiatus of almost twenty years,[32] that Bai Hua resumed his activities as a writer. At this time he also repeatedly took strong public positions urging the new Deng regime to permit greater freedom within the cultural sphere and gained further notoriety as a consequence of his strong support for the short-lived democracy movement of 1979. "Comrade poets," he proclaimed at the time, "we would rather sing the praises of a brick in the democratic wall. Never should we again sing the praises of any savior."[33]

In 1979 Bai Hua published a film script entitled *Unrequited Love (Kulian)*.* It attracted little notice at the time, but two years later, after being made into a motion picture for wider public consumption, it came under sharp attack and was never released.[34] An important articulation of Chinese humanism, *Unrequited Love* told the story of a patriotic Chinese artist who returned from America to China in 1949 to help build up the country, but suffered repeated humiliation and persecution at the hands of small-minded bureaucrats and finally died as a hunted "criminal" during the Cultural Revolution. In the film script, the artist's daughter at one point says to her father provocatively, "Papa! You love this nation of ours. . . . But does this nation love you?" This was taken as a criticism of China's treatment of its intellectuals. Other parts of the film script were interpreted as attacks on Mao and on China's socialism. Bai Hua became the main target of a national campaign against bourgeois liberalism. The campaign was expressly authorized by Deng Xiaoping, who was especially critical of Bai Hua for his heretical view of patriotism as simple love of country, having no necessary

---

Kulian may also be (and sometimes is) translated more literally as *Bitter Love.*

Figure 26. Bai Hua. Source: Bai Hua, *Bai Hua xiaoshuo xuan* (Chengdu: Sichuan renmin chubanshe, 1982).

relationship to the Communist Party and socialism—a position not unlike that of Xiao Jun.[35] The campaign was, in a number of respects, appreciably more gentle than political campaigns of the Mao era and it failed to intimidate Chinese intellectuals to anywhere near the same degree. Nevertheless, Deng used it to signal clearly, among other things, that the brief period of relaxation that had marked the years of 1979 and 1980 was over and that criticism of Mao was now out of bounds.[36]

Bai Hua was forced to make a self-criticism in November 1981, but he said that he remained "perplexed by Comrade Mao Zedong's mistakes in his later years and the blind faith in him by the people, including myself."[37] Although he was censured by some colleagues for agreeing to make a self-criticism, by 1982 he was being publicly praised by others for the very qualities that had resulted in his difficulties the previous year. In the course of 1982, Bai Hua, writing at a feverish pace, completed four novelettes. However, he kept a low profile in general, and it was not until May 1983, when the Beijing People's Art Theater staged a major production of his new play on the Goujian story, that he returned to public view.[38]

Bai Hua's interest in Goujian had been sparked more than two decades earlier. In 1961–1962, while engaged in reform through labor in a Shanghai factory,[39] he had requested transfer to Shaoxing, so that he could research the environment in which the great writer Lu Xun, who was from Shaoxing, had been nurtured.[40] Bai Hua was assigned to a commune in the area in spring 1962 and years later said that this was a very important period in his development as a writer. In addition to reflecting on Lu Xun and several other topics, his thinking about a much earlier inhabitant of Shaoxing, King Goujian of Yue, also took shape at the time. What he basically concluded was that the ultimate goals of Yue's ruler and common people in their joint struggle to recover their country were different. The ruler wanted to recover his standing as ruler, while the common people were mainly concerned with recovering the national dignity they had enjoyed before becoming a conquered people. In the early stages of the struggle, the goals of the two were the same and it was easy for them to dedicate themselves to the same cause. But once the country was recovered, inevitably the interests of ruler and ruled diverged. Bai Hua's conclusions about the Goujian story were solidified during the enforced isolation of the Cultural Revolution years. Indeed, according to him, the things he wrote in the immediate post–Cultural Revolution period, including *Unrequited Love* and *The Golden Spear of the King of Wu and the Sword of the King of Yue*, were direct reflections of the thinking of those years.[41]

Although Bai Hua insisted that the depiction of Goujian in his play typified the behavior of kings in general, we may also view it as a character study of Goujian as an individual. The play begins with the Yue king's return from his captivity in Wu. As the royal party prepares to cross the river separating Wu and Yue, they see Wen Zhong coming to get them in a small fishing skiff. Goujian, piqued, questions the appropriateness of such a humble means of conveyance and wonders why the welcome for him is so understated. Wen Zhong explains that, during the king's three-year absence, Wu stripped Yue clean, that he had not had new warships built as this might arouse Wu's suspicions, and that he deliberately did not order the common people of Yue to come out en masse to welcome him back. Fan Li and Wen Zhong urge Goujian to change his attitude: his primary purpose now must be to gain the support of the Yue people by becoming one with them, so that the whole of Yue will be of one heart and mind. The king's wife seconds this, telling Goujian that he must not present himself to the population as a king who only knows how to enjoy himself and kill people. As the boat draws near to the Yue side, a crowd of welcomers appears after all, their cries becoming louder and louder. Wen Zhong impresses on Goujian how much better it is that the people have come out to greet him of their own accord rather than as a result of having been ordered to do so. Fan Li, agreeing, says that what the king is witnessing is the genuine, spontaneous enthusiasm of the Yue people. Goujian finally gets the message and, kneeling respectfully before Fan Li and Wen Zhong, thanks them for always serving as his good teachers and able helpers.[42]

A year later, in a Yue village, an old farmer named Gengmeng is engaged in conversation with Goujian, who has just arrived in a small boat. Goujian, as part of his effort to get closer to the people, is dressed in farmer's clothing, and the old man does not realize that he's talking to the king. He tells Goujian that normally Yue could count on at least three bumper harvests every ten years, but after its defeat by Wu, owing to the heavy taxes Wu imposed, there had been three years of starvation. But "our king," he continues, "spent three bitter years in Wu as a slave and finally gained some appreciation of the feelings of ordinary people. Our king is intelligent, he's become an understanding person. There aren't many understanding people, especially understanding kings." Goujian now identifies himself and tells Gengmeng, "I'm the same as you. I'm a person, a Yue person, with a Yue person's heart." The old man cannot believe that the man he is talking to is Goujian and, suspecting that it is a crazy person impersonating the king (a crime punishable by death), gruffly challenges him. A small crowd now gathers and Gengmeng's son, Bowu, who is a royal guard, confirms that it is indeed Goujian and urges his father to request the king's forgiveness for being so disrespectful. Goujian asks everyone to rise, telling them that the misunderstanding is not their fault but his. In the past, he says, he lived a sumptuous, extravagant life, full of ostentation and pomp, which made him, in the eyes of ordinary people, a strange and remote figure, so now that he has stepped down from his throne, it is small wonder no one recognizes him.[43]

Goujian makes a real effort to become one with the people of Yue. "If I don't plow the fields," he says to an awed Gengmeng, "how will I know the bitterness of those who farm? If the queen doesn't weave cloth, how will she know the grueling work of the young women who weave? If my son doesn't serve in the army, how will the queen and I know the frame of mind of the parents of soldiers all over the land who are thinking of their sons?"[44]

Occasionally, however, the king has lapses. One day he sees Fan Li training the fine-looking maidens who, following Wen Zhong's recommendation, are to be presented to Fuchai. Goujian is clearly taken with the beauty of Xi Shi. Fan Li, partly because he has previously formed a romantic attachment to Xi Shi, but more saliently because of the importance of the "beauty trap" in Yue's overall strategy for weakening Wu, senses trouble and tells Wen Zhong that he must escort Xi Shi to Wu without delay. When Goujian discovers this, he wonders how Fan Li can be so coldhearted and orders his fastest chariot to be made ready for him to engage in hot pursuit. Fan Li asks him how the people of Yue will view such inappropriate behavior on the part of their king. Goujian replies testily that he is the king and does not have to be bothered with what people think. He orders a guard to prepare his chariot. Fan Li cries out, "Wait a minute!" Goujian draws his sword. A shaken Fan Li exclaims, "Goujian! . . . Do you still remember the shame of our country's subjugation?" He repeats this twice more. Goujian haltingly says he dare not forget. Fan Li falls to his knees and asks the king to forgive his capital offense. As this exchange is occurring, Goujian's wife rushes onstage. Goujian, starting to regain control of himself, helps Fan Li up. He asks the queen and Fan Li whether he has acted improperly. Fan Li reassures him, but the queen chides Fan Li for humbling himself before Goujian in that way. He is not a mere subordinate official, she tells him, but a teacher of integrity and a friend who should be unafraid to give advice that is hard to hear. It's important that he speak bluntly. Goujian by this time has fully returned to his senses. The crisis over, the king and his minister go out together to drill Yue's three armies.[45]

In the fifth scene, which takes place four years after Goujian's return from

Wu, the king, his queen, Fan Li, and Wen Zhong reflect on the great advances Yue has made. Goujian praises his two top officials and tells them that after Yue has destroyed Wu, everything—treasure, territory, and beautiful women—will be divided equally among the three of them. Both ministers decline his generosity, saying that their only interest is in serving him and Yue faithfully. Some commoners enter, the same ones in the village scene discussed earlier. There is lighthearted bantering. Goujian announces to everyone that formerly he sinned before his ancestors and the gods of earth and grain, causing the people of Yue to be slaughtered and subjected to bullying and humiliation by the armies of Wu. But times have changed and the Wu of today is not the Wu of yore. The time is ripe, he says, to mount an attack against Wu.[46]

Three years later, Yue conquers Wu, and Fuchai, after a halfhearted attempt to kill himself with his golden spear, dies when a transfigured Xi Shi, instead of removing the spear at Fuchai's request, gives it a patriotic twist and plunges it deeper, until it pierces the Wu king's heart. Wen Zhong recovers the double-edged sword that Fuchai took from Goujian ten years earlier at Mount Kuaiji and suggests to Fan Li that they present it to their king as an eternal remembrance of everything they've been through. The two ministers have a thoughtful talk about their futures, now that the goal of destroying Wu has been achieved. Wen Zhong, while well aware of the dangers, has decided to serve Goujian to the end. Fan Li has other ideas. After he and Xi Shi meet and assure themselves that nothing has changed between them, and after Fan Li has endured one final, extremely uncomfortable conversation with Goujian, the two lovers take flight.

In the days following the victory over Wu, Goujian becomes a transformed person. Telling Wen Zhong that he wishes to appear as the king of a powerful state, he orders him to return to Yue ahead of schedule to supervise the construction of a new palace, no less grand than that of his longtime nemesis Fuchai, and to scour Wu and Yue for three hundred beautiful maidens to be brought to the palace to sing and dance for him. Wen Zhong, stupefied by Goujian's requests, so out of character with the king he has known, prostrates himself weeping at the king's feet. Goujian raises him up, tries to make the old minister understand why he has ordered him to do these things. But Wen Zhong, impervious to the king's explanations, prostrates himself again. Finally, after this happens a third time, Goujian loses patience and orders him to start on his journey.[47]

Several months later, at Mount Kuaiji, the old farmer Gengmeng, who is also a skilled craftsman and has been selected by Wen Zhong to take a principal part in the building of the new palace, is putting the finishing touches on his work in preparation for the imminent return of Goujian. He and Wen Zhong exchange greetings. When Wen Zhong says he is too old to attend the welcoming reception, Gengmeng encourages him to go, saying that he is to Yue what the main beam is to the new palace. He then presses Wen Zhong concerning all the odd things that have been taking place since the victory over Wu—Fan Li's sudden departure, the flurry of uncharacteristic demands from Goujian, and so on. The minister hurries him out as the king is about to arrive, telling him they will talk about it some other time.

Goujian enters with an honor guard and a troupe of beautiful women and orders the latter to dance for him. His wife, an unwilling participant in the occasion, kneels before him in the prisoner's garb she wore when they returned from their captivity years before. She expresses her concern about the changes that have come over him, observing that the things he has ordered done in recent months are the same as the stratagems Yue used in the past to weaken and destroy the king of Wu. The people of Yue, seeing this, have become alarmed. Goujian, annoyed by this devastating comparison, orders a subordinate to summon a doctor, saying that his wife has lost control of herself. When she accuses him of wanting to imprison her, he says to the others present, "Do you hear? Her words show that her illness is very serious. It really worries me." She tells him he is behaving hypocritically. He loses patience with her, says that she is sick, and orders soldiers to escort her to the seashore so that she can recover her sanity. Wen Zhong pleads with Goujian to be more forgiving of her, telling him that she speaks her mind freely only because she venerates him. But Goujian repeats his command to the soldiers, who now seize the queen. As they usher her out, she repeats again and again the question, "Goujian! Do you still remember the shame of our country's subjugation?" Goujian, callously, orders the beautiful women to dance and sing for him and invites Wen Zhong to watch with him.

Gengmeng and his family members, having made their way into the hall, now approach Goujian. But, inexplicably, he fails to recognize them, even when they remind him of the experiences they have shared together in the past. Becoming irritated, he brusquely tells them that if they have a problem a local official will help them and then has them forcibly removed from the palace. Wen Zhong, acutely pained by this, falls to his knees and accuses Goujian of having done wrong, which only prompts the king to retort that Wen Zhong must have caught the same sickness as his wife. Wen Zhong lectures Goujian on the importance of the people to everything he

Figure 27. Goujian's wife being led away by Yue soldiers. Source: Bai Hua, *Wu wang jinge Yue wang jian* (as reprinted in *Zuopin yu zhengming*).

has accomplished and expresses wonderment that the king can treat so shabbily those who have supported him, protected him, and sacrificed everything for him. Goujian responds that the ruler takes his mandate from Heaven and that his successes are determined by his own ability, wisdom, and tenacity. Wen Zhong, unable to believe his ears, warns Goujian that the only thing that is important is the hearts of the people and that if he loses them, like Fuchai, he will lose everything. At this Goujian flies into a rage and gives Wen Zhong his sword—the same one Fuchai earlier gave to Wu Zixu. The king fixes his eyes on Wen Zhong as the old minister slowly walks out of the hall, then abruptly turns around and, unleashing his full fury, sternly shouts, "Play music! Dance!" As the beautiful women enter and start singing and dancing, he says, "Dance! Sing! Bring on the wine, today King Goujian of Yue will drink to his heart's content to mark the victory of Yue!" He follows the dancing beauties into the inner recesses of the palace as the sound of the palace gates being shut and locked is heard. Everything turns quiet.

Gengmeng and a few others come onstage. Gengmeng is holding in his hands a bloodstained sword. He approaches Bowu, his son, who is on guard duty, and tells him that Wen Zhong has slit his throat. Bowu lowers his head, looks at the bloody sword, and, steadying himself with the handle of Fuchai's golden spear (which Goujian had given him after the victory over Wu to commemorate the heroic death of his younger brother, Zhonggeng), kneels down on the vermillion steps leading to the palace hall. Bowu takes the bloodstained sword, Gengmeng kneels by his side, the others also kneel. The light dims. All that can be seen finally is the reflection of the lamplight on Fuchai's golden spear and Goujian's precious sword, each held in one of Bowu's hands. The sound of weeping is heard, as the curtain slowly descends.[48]

The explosive combination of Bai Hua's recent notoriety and the potential for negative political commentary inherent in the Goujian story guaranteed that the opening of *The Golden Spear of the King of Wu and the Sword of the King of Yue* would be greeted with lively interest among Beijing theater aficionados.[49] They were not disappointed. Although published reviews were mixed, some lavishing praise on the play,[50] others criticizing it for such failings as its emphasis on subjective feeling and moral judgment rather than objective historical assessment,[51] the play was harshly condemned behind the scenes for its "use of the past to disparage the present" (*jie gu feng jin*)— a condemnation that before long resulted in its closure by the Beijing municipal government.[52]

Bai Hua responded to the attacks on a number of occasions. He was of course perfectly aware, he wrote later in 1983, that the play would arouse the suspicion that he was using the past to cast aspersions on the present. But without either acknowledging or denying this charge, he insisted that the main reason he had decided to write about this episode from the ancient past was his fascination with some of the main figures involved. The brilliance of their thinking—he especially admired Fan Li—possessed universal significance, transcending time and place—a notion, Bai Hua well knew, the more hidebound historical materialists of his day would find at best inexplicable and at worst reprehensible.[53]

Several years later, in a lecture at the Chinese University of Hong Kong, Bai Hua revisited the defense of his play, this time in a more systematic way:

> The concept advanced by the philosophers of Chinese history has been: observe the present in order to examine the past. There has been a general recognition that the study of history is for the purpose of deriving lessons for the present. There were many enlightened emperors who, willingly accepting satirical criticism, made use of the stories of the ancients to treat the ills of their own day. Even if the events of antiquity depicted in my play do bear some resemblance to events of the present time, mightn't

this be just the thing to induce us to become more vigilant in the mending of our flaws? Didn't Chairman Mao Zedong himself frequently advocate doing this? He praised Guo Moruo's *Qu Yuan,** and when we were faced with total victory in the 1940s he encouraged the writing and staging of dramas dealing with the rise and fall of Li Zicheng.† In my depiction of the story of Wu and Yue, all I did was add to the conventional rendering a chapter on the reemergence of Goujian's old behavior after the recovery of his state. This is what really happened in history. Moreover, the great Tang poet Li Bai long ago recognized the historical lesson involved. He wrote: "Yue king Goujian returned after his felling of Wu / The righteous officials and soldiers went back to their families resplendently clad in brocade / Harem women as numerous as flowers filled the living quarters of the palace / But now all one sees are partridges flying overhead."‡ All I did was recapitulate the sense of his poem. Today's China is not an empire. Why is there this insistence on the drawing of such exact parallels that people get all worked up over it?[54]

Although Bai Hua never to my knowledge came right out and acknowledged that the critical thrust of his play was directed at Mao Zedong—such acknowledgment by the creators of Chinese political allegory was extremely rare—it is widely accepted that such was the case.[55] Indeed, it is probably not too much of a stretch to see the play more broadly as a parable for Mao's entire career as a Chinese leader. The Guomindang's success in the extermination campaigns of the first half of the 1930s (paralleling Wu's early defeat of Yue) led to a period of years in the "wilderness" (the Long March and the primitive conditions in which Mao and other Com-

---

*Qu Yuan, said to have lived in the fourth and third centuries B.C.E., was one of Bai Hua's heroes. He committed suicide in protest when his remonstrations with the king of Chu were ignored and has been honored ever since as an example of "the politically engaged artist, willing to stand with patriotic integrity in isolated opposition to unjust policies." Kraus, "Bai Hua," 194–95; McDougall and Louie, *The Literature of China,* 299. Guo Moruo's play, a patriotic drama written and first performed in 1942, contained a barely concealed attack on Chiang Kai-shek, Madame Chiang, and the corrupt wartime politics of the Guomindang. See Kuo Mo-jo [Guo Moruo], *Chu Yuan.*

†Since at the time of the Ming-Qing transition Li Zicheng's initial success had quickly come to naught, the import of dramas about him was to caution people against overconfidence.

‡The partridge was used in the Tang as a metaphor for a bleak and desolate landscape. Li Bai's poem was entitled "Yue zhong langu" (Visiting the historical sites in Yue). A reminder that all material finery must come to an end and that nothing is permanent, it was written during a visit by the poet to the ancient Wu-Yue area. Zhang Cailiang, *Li Bai shi sibai shou,* 599–600.

munist leaders lived in Yan'an, close to the people), followed by the shift in the fortunes of the Guomindang and Communists during the Sino-Japanese War and the Communist victory in the subsequent civil war (paralleling Yue's eventual conquest of Wu). Then, after the triumph of the Communists at midcentury—a triumph that, like Yue's, seemed unimaginable during the early years and took over two decades to bring about—Mao, like Goujian, began more and more to behave like the Chinese emperors of yore: becoming remote from the people, out of touch with what was going on around the country, increasingly unwilling to listen to counsel displeasing to his ear, and, of course, in the climactic phase, like Goujian, turning against his most trusted and devoted advisers.

While the presence in the playwright's mind of such an extended analogy cannot of course be demonstrated, the evidence in support of Bai Hua's antipathy to Mao and Mao-style autocratic rule is overwhelming. In 1979, as we have seen, he proclaimed that "never should we again sing the praises of any savior." Later in the same year, he elaborated on this theme in his speech before the Fourth Congress of Writers and Artists: "Some true believers who pretend to go to every length in their devotion insist that there is such a thing as a savior in this world. They connect the concepts of savior and revolutionary leader, sometimes even equating the two in order to intimidate others. . . . It is time to ring down the curtain on the cruel farce of deifying one man in order to kill others!"[56] Further evidence of Bai Hua's feelings about Mao was provided by the screenplay *Unrequited Love,* which was manifestly an attack on the Chinese leader and, as Geremie Barmé observes, pointedly concluded with a symbolic setting sun.[57]

What was needed above all to confirm a meaningful link between Goujian and Mao was the recognition on Bai Hua's part that Mao, although affecting to be a revolutionary leader, was in fact no different from the feudal rulers of old. In his lecture at the Chinese University of Hong Kong (November 1987) Bai Hua had asserted that "today's China is not an empire." But, a year later, in a speech he gave at Columbia University, he argued in the most explicit fashion that the China of Mao Zedong was, in its core operating principles, a carbon copy of the imperial system of the past. Bai Hua's words are worth quoting at some length:

> I never foresaw that our generation of intellectuals, advancing wave
> upon wave in pursuit of the light of a new epoch, would once again
> end up in darkness. In the period of our youth, we risked our lives in
> the heroic fight for the completely new China of our dreams, thinking

that the revolution this time was different from all previous peasant uprisings and changes of dynasty (including the 1911 Revolution), that we were entering a new age. What awaited us was socialism; what awaited us was the utopian *[datong]* world of socialism, of communism. It wasn't until the period following the Cultural Revolution that we suddenly realized what had happened. China had changed a great deal, but it hadn't departed from the original mold. It still had a founding ancestor; it still operated according to the same old principles.

And what were the principles of operation of our founding ancestor? During the Cultural Revolution Mao Zedong deposed Liu Shaoqi and then deposed Lin Biao. These two people had both been appointed by Mao Zedong himself. In name they had been appointed by the party, but the party during the Mao Zedong era was Mao Zedong; it wasn't anyone in addition to Mao Zedong, nor was it the collective party membership. It was only after the dethroning of Lin Biao that I finally realized what was going on. Wasn't it the same thing as the emperor of any dynasty appointing or dethroning a crown prince? Many despots, in the appointment of an heir, after appointing someone deposed him, then after deposing him killed him, then after killing him appointed someone else, then deposed that person, then killed him. Even Xuanzong of the Tang, who ruled in a flourishing age, was like this.

During the Cultural Revolution it looked on the surface as if we had destroyed the old and implemented the new. But what old things did we destroy? Aside from the ravaging of a large quantity of cultural artifacts and places of historic interest and scenic beauty, in a spiritual sense what old things did we get rid of? On the contrary, what was put into effect during that time was the most outmoded thing of all: the idea of loyalty to the ruler—a loyalty that reached the most extreme and shameless degree. Every household put up a banner with "loyalty" written on it; every individual danced to the tune of "loyalty." Add to this Jiang Qing's time and again comparing herself to Wu Zetian and, at the time of Mao Zedong's death, Hua Guofeng's trumpeting the six character phrase [allegedly spoken by Mao as the end approached], "With you in charge my mind is at rest," to validate his succession to the orthodox line. Looking back over all of this once again, everything has finally become clear to me. The reason why the intellectuals, after being persecuted in campaign after campaign, found it so difficult to understand that they had been taken in was that they had viewed the Communist Party as a revolutionary party and Mao Zedong as a revolutionary leader; they had never pictured him— they dared not—as an emperor. And so, invariably, they failed to see the situation with clarity and always fell into the trap. The full recognition of this truth brings you to an awareness that the new generation, after exhausting itself in sacrifice and struggle, has come full circle, ending up in exactly the same place where it started.[58]

A sympathetic review of Bai Hua's play in the *People's Daily* observed that a clear distinction must be drawn between works that held history up as a mirror to the present *(yi shi wei jing)* and those that used the past to make veiled judgments about current realities *(yingshe xianshi)*. The two, the review insisted, were completely different. Just because the historical phenomena in a work bore a close resemblance in certain respects to the present day was no reason to put the label of "veiled criticism" on that work. The trouble was that during the Cultural Revolution, the practice of "attacking by innuendo" *(yingshe gongji)* had been so commonplace that it "had become virtually a synonym for historical drama." People therefore became extremely wary of it, and this exaggerated sensitivity had still not been entirely eradicated as of the early 1980s.[59]

The *People's Daily* review identifies, but fails to come squarely to grips with, a problem that had bedeviled historical writing all along in post-1949 China. Studying history for the purpose of deriving lessons for the present was good, but using history to cast aspersions on the present was bad. The difficulty arose when the historical lessons embodied in a work pointed to the negative consequences of a kind of behavior that also happened to be pervasive at the time of the work's creation. Bai Hua could thus defend himself by asserting that his play was constructive in intent, inasmuch as it was designed (using history as a mirror) to call attention to—and hopefully help correct—significant defects in contemporary Chinese life. Others, however, either because they knew that the defects Bai Hua had identified were precisely those that it was forbidden to criticize, or because they sensed that distancing themselves from a "troublemaker" like Bai Hua was the politically prudent thing to do, or simply because they disliked the playwright personally, could (with equal justification) attack *The Golden Spear of the King of Wu and the Sword of the King of Yue* for its use of the past to denigrate the present.

The bottom line, of course, was that in a political environment in which it was not possible to criticize openly the top leadership, such criticism could only be vented in vague and indirect ways. A time-honored device for accomplishing this in China was the ransacking of the past for narratives containing close parallels to the political behavior that the writer wanted to bring under critical scrutiny in his or her own day. It must never be acknowledged, however, that this was what was being done, for to acknowledge it would be to deprive oneself of the deniability essential to engaging in such forbidden political commentary in the first place.[60]

———————

The Goujian saga supplied both Bai Hua and Xiao Jun with a narrative that was made to order for the political criticism they wished to express, and the nature of the criticism was similar in the two cases. Bai Hua, however, was attacked while Xiao Jun was not. This may have been due, in some degree, to the greater attention-grabbing quality of a play as opposed to a work of fiction, and also to the fact that Xiao's novel was published in Harbin, while Bai Hua's play was published and staged in the Chinese capital. Surely, however, the most important reason by far was that Bai Hua in 1983 was in a highly exposed position, having only recently been the target of a major nationwide political campaign, while Xiao Jun had long been out of the public eye, his "thirty-year hibernation" finally having come to an end on the eve of his book's appearance. As Perry Link makes clear, contingent factors of this sort, rather than a work's substantive content, were often key in determining whether or not a writer would be attacked in any given instance.[61]

Link also observes that regardless of the reason for a writer's coming under attack, it could have a devastating effect on the near-term ability of that writer to publish anything of consequence.[62] Thus, despite the substantive similarities between Xiao Jun's and Bai Hua's treatments of Goujian, more than a dozen of Xiao Jun's works were published (or republished) in the years immediately following the appearance of his novel, while Bai Hua, for some time after the opening (and subsequent shutting down) of his play, found it difficult to publish or stage anything. As late as February 1987, according to the author, the Beijing municipal government forbade the staging of his drama on the great Song patriot Yue Fei, which was already in rehearsal at the Beijing People's Art Theater. Bai Hua claimed (with perhaps a touch of disingenuousness) not to be able to understand the reason for this action. When he had begun to write the play, he had taken the precaution of soliciting the opinions of a number of friends. They had said: "What problem does the play present? Who today could think of himself as a Song Gaozong or a Qin Gui? Is this a time in contemporary China when even Yue Fei cannot be openly praised, when one dare not denounce even Qin Gui?"* Bai Hua thought the problem might be that the Beijing municipal official in charge of the matter did not have a clear idea of what was and what was not bourgeois liberalization. He could not believe that the Central Committee itself could view the writing of a patriotic play on Yue Fei's resistance to the Jin as belonging to this reviled category. Bai Hua also, however, did not exclude the possibility that the reason for the ban was that "this was Bai Hua's play" and that even if it presented no ideological problem, at this time and place—the place being the capital—it was inopportune to stage a play by Bai Hua.[63]

The difficulties Bai Hua faced during the 1980s clearly indicate that the literary system within which he and other Chinese writers had worked for decades was still in place. In this system, the Goujian story could be used in different ways, depending on what was taking place in China at the moment. During the early 1960s, when severe economic problems and a deteriorating relationship with the Soviet Union converged to create a sense of major crisis, the story was used to motivate Chinese to rely on their own efforts and work harder to strengthen the nation. Twenty years later, in the aftermath of the Cultural Revolution and the death of Mao Zedong, it was used allegorically to identify serious problems in the way Chinese political life was organized and operated. By the end of the 1980s, and certainly in the 1990s, however, the grip of politics on important phases of Chinese life (including literature) weakened perceptibly. And as this happened, as we shall see in the following chapter, the ways in which the Goujian story was used once again underwent major changes, reflecting the transformations that were now beginning to reshape Chinese society.

---

*Yue Fei, as noted in chapter 2, was the general who led the Song resistance against the Jin dynasty in the twelfth century. As a result of treasonous charges trumped up by the then prime minister Qin Gui, he was recalled by Emperor Gaozong and executed.

SIX

The Goujian Story
in a Privatizing China

ON THE FIRST NIGHT OF THE LUNAR New Year of 2004 (January 22), Hu Xiaolong, a twenty-seven-year-old inhabitant of a village in the county-level city of Dujiangyan, some fifty kilometers northwest of the Sichuan capital, Chengdu, went on a murderous rampage, using a dagger and a cutter for chopping pig fodder to kill fellow villager Zhou Guohong and two other members of the Zhou household.

The motive was revenge. Twenty years earlier, when a large number of fish had died in a stream running through the village, Zhou Guohong's younger brother, Zhou Yuanfu, then just over ten years of age, and Hu Xiaolong's father had gone to the stream to collect the dead fish. There was a large fish that they both saw at the same instant and scrambled to get. Hu Xiaolong's father gave Zhou a shove, whereupon Zhou, not giving in, struck Hu on the head with a thin iron object. Ten years later, Zhou Yuanfu, as a result of an illness, committed suicide by hanging himself. A few years after this, Hu Xiaolong's father and mother both died in quick succession. To everyone's astonishment, in Hu Xiaolong's mind the deaths of his parents and the humiliation his father had suffered earlier at the hands of Zhou Yuanfu were connected. For years Hu practiced martial arts to build up his physical strength and took part in a number of martial arts competitions. According to the villagers, he was an eccentric man of few words and kept to himself. Although he had never picked a quarrel with the Zhou fam-

Figure 28. Reporter examining graffiti scrawled by Hu Xiaolong at his home.
Source: Lanjun, "Emo wei xue jiachi xiwu 20 nian," Jan. 28, 2004.

ily, he treated them as virtual strangers and nursed a deep hatred toward them.

Several days after the revenge killings, reporters were taken to Hu Xiaolong's home. The wall opposite the courtyard entrance was covered with crude graffiti, which Hu, apparently the night before the murders, had scrawled with a piece of charcoal: "King Goujian of Yue slept on brushwood and tasted gall, three thousand Yue soldiers at long last destroyed Wu." "To withdraw in order to avoid the enemy's spears isn't cowardice; rather, it is to wait patiently for the right moment to fight, to defeat the enemy by surprise and send him to his death." On another wall was written: "If this grievance is not avenged, I swear I am unworthy and my manhood will have been wasted." And also, "Kill, kill, kill," and "Blood will stain the enemy's door, blood will be splattered over the enemy's door." Hu seemed to incriminate himself, finally, with a scribble that read, "The rage of a bygone day leads twenty years later to the misfortune of an entire family's destruction."[1]

What is fascinating about Hu Xiaolong's allusions to the Goujian story, both direct and indirect, is that they are totally personalized, even to the point where he identifies with the Yue ruler and views the story as a prototype for his own behavior. In the republican era, in Chiang Kai-shek's Taiwan, and in the PRC in the early 1960s and early 1980s, the Goujian story had been used either to symbolize collective national aspirations or to lay bare some of the more poisonous aspects of Chinese political life. Now, at a time when politics had retreated and was no longer the omnipresent force in ordinary Chinese lives that it had been during the Mao years, there was a dramatic shift to a newly opened space centering on individual concerns and hopes.

This space began to open in the late 1970s, as the quarter-century-long experiment with collectivized agriculture ended and household farming was resumed, market incentives started to play a growing role in the domestic economy, China's economic involvement with the rest of the world rapidly expanded, intellectual and cultural life were rejuvenated, and the academic world emerged from the deep freeze in which it had long been buried. These changes were accompanied in time by a dramatic increase in personal freedoms. It became much easier for Chinese to travel abroad for higher education, tourism, or to visit relatives; to move from one part of the country to another; and to choose what they wanted to do with their lives. By the early years of the twenty-first century, more than two decades after the launching of the Deng Xiaoping reforms, a sizable middle class had emerged and millions of Chinese had better and more fulfilling lives than before.

PATRIOTIC EDUCATION

In these changed circumstances, the Goujian story began to be treated in very different ways, closely mirroring the transformations that were taking place in the country. The nationalistic side of the story, which had predominated in earlier periods, continued to be exploited, but the emphasis now was different. In the aftermath of the Tiananmen demonstrations and crackdown of 1989, there was a felt, if unstated, need on the part of the Chinese government to come up with a new legitimating ideology to burnish the rapidly dimming luster of the original Marxist-Leninist-Maoist vision, and in the eyes of Deng Xiaoping, Jiang Zemin, and other key leaders, nationalism, to be inculcated via a multifaceted program of patriotic education, was the logical choice.[2]

In the implementation of patriotic education, a variety of approaches were pursued, including exposing young people to historical and cultural relics. Students were taken on field trips to foster their sense of national pride and self-confidence, build up patriotic feeling, and stimulate their willingness to dedicate themselves to the service of the country. The celebrated sword of Goujian, which had been unearthed by archeologists in Hubei in 1965, was used to illustrate the value of direct contact with the material culture of the past: "From the radiant brilliance of the sword of King Goujian of Yue, people experience the inspiration of the spirit of sleeping on brushwood and tasting gall, of making unremitting efforts to strengthen the nation."[3]

While patriotic education ought clearly to be the focal point of junior middle school history classes, a Jiangxi teacher asserted, it should not just concentrate on the glorious aspects of the Chinese past. Even more crucial was to cultivate an awareness of the suffering and hardship endured as a result of past Chinese humiliations. When teachers got to the five overlords of the Spring and Autumn, therefore, they should emphasize how Goujian slept on brushwood and tasted gall, how he strove with all his might to strengthen Yue, and how he eventually succeeded in destroying Wu and becoming the dominant political figure in North China. It should be made clear to students that when, in the early part of his kingship, Goujian allowed his state to be subjugated, it was because he was content to lead a life of pleasure, whereas the reason for his later success was that he had become intensely aware of suffering and hardship and had dedicated himself to the goal of revenge.[4]

Other writers as well stressed the importance of "national humiliation education" *(guochi jiaoyu)* as a subset of patriotic education.[5] But the emphasis in many of the articles I have seen was far more positive, highlighting the heroic figures and glorious achievements of the past and insisting on the valuable part that familiarity with such individuals and events from Chinese history should play in patriotic education. As a member of the Henan Academy of Social Sciences observed: "Everyone knows the story of King Goujian of Yue, his lying on brushwood and tasting gall. The reason this story has been so widely admired generation after generation is the vivid expression it gives to the spirit of hard struggle and going all out to make the country strong."[6]

Goujian, of course, was not the only heroic figure from the Chinese past to be cited in the writing on patriotic education at the turn of the century. Others commonly encountered were Yue Fei, Qu Yuan, Wen Tianxiang, Fan Zhongyan, Gu Yanwu, and Qi Jiguang. There are a number of further points to be made about this writing. First, in contrast with the early 1960s, when people who used historical material had to be extremely careful about how they handled it (see chapter 4), the attitude toward the Chinese past was now far more relaxed and welcoming. Gone is the sense one had in the earlier period that writers were constantly looking back over their shoulders to see who was watching them and whether what they were saying was politically prudent.[7] Second, some teachers, in their promotion of patriotic education, made a special point of showing the connection between love of country and more localized objects of affection. As two teachers from Shaoxing put it: "Only after it has been combined with love of one's native place, love of one's school, love of oneself, and learning to have respect for an occupation and become a useful person can patriotic education have real content and finally be carried out in action. Love of one's school, of one's native place, and of oneself are not only the prerequisite and foundation for love of one's country, they are also its concrete embodiment."[8]

The same authors pointed to a third prominent characteristic of the discourse on patriotic education during these years: alongside nationalism, an important place was assigned to what might be called citizenship training,[9] in which (significantly) the morality and culture of the past were seen as taking a key part. In Shaoxing, a new course devoted to morality and behavior *(daode yu xingwei)* was introduced, which placed a strong emphasis on the inculcation of traditional Chinese moral precepts and the nourishing of civilized habits of behavior.[10] Another writer listed twelve traditional virtues of the Chinese nation that were worth promoting in the present, in each instance supplying historical examples. Among these virtues, practically all of which had also been touted earlier in the century by the Nationalists, were putting the nation before the family and public concerns ahead of private ones; a willingness to endure hardships and difficulties in the pursuit of important undertakings; the value of human relations *(renlun)*, the moral obligation to show filial respect toward one's parents, and support for the old and love of the young; an emphasis on the moral habits of propriety and courtesy; and so on.[11]

TEACHING COMMUNIST PARTY MEMBERS TO BEHAVE

The references to the Goujian story in writing on patriotic education suggest that, even in this realm, with its professed goal of stimulating nationalistic sentiment among the youth of China, there was a strong ancillary emphasis on the nurturing of individuals whose lives reflected the highest standards of personal morality. Other uses of the Goujian story that became rampant in the waning years of the twentieth century expanded on this emphasis in a variety of ways.

The story was often referred to, for example, in writings directed at reforming the attitudes and behavior of Communist Party members. According to a party secretary affiliated with the head office of the Changsha Railway, the majority of leading cadres, following in the footsteps of such past luminaries as Goujian, Du Fu, Yue Fei, and Fan Zhongyan, as well as exemplary figures from the history of the Communist Party itself, had the proper attitude toward their work. They took their responsibilities seriously and did what they were supposed to do. But there was also, unfortunately, no shortage of leading cadres who fell short of this standard, some even engaging in corrupt activities to benefit themselves.[12] Although this article was published in 2003, the problem it referred to was hardly new, writers having for years addressed themselves to the issue of corruption among leading party members.

Such writing experienced an upsurge in the aftermath of the dramatic death in early April 1995 of the deputy mayor of Beijing, Wang Baosen. Wang at the time was under investigation in connection with his involvement in a major corruption scandal within the city government. Although it was alleged officially that he had committed suicide, because he was a protégé of Mayor Chen Xitong, a top party official who in the past had been a political rival of President Jiang Zemin in Shanghai, it was whispered by some that political assassination may have been the true cause of Wang's demise. Such rumors were fanned by an allegorical piece on Qu Yuan in the *Beijing Daily* on April 10, which, in an obvious allusion to Wang Baosen (whose death still hadn't been announced publicly), mischievously posed the question whether the late Spring and Autumn poet martyr had really committed suicide or had been done in by his political adversaries.[13]

The political circumstances surrounding Wang Baosen's death are of less concern to me than the attention it drew to corruption in high places. Of particular interest are a number of writings that now appeared in which the issue of forgetfulness—of leading cadres forgetting their responsibilities to the people—was developed in conjunction with the story of Fuchai. One very brief piece, entitled "The Perils of Forgetfulness" ("Wangxing de weihai"), took special note of the change in Fuchai's behavior over time. When he first acceded to the throne, the Wu king had ordered his servants to shout out to him whenever he entered or left the palace, "Fuchai, have you forgotten that the king of Yue killed your father?" Fuchai heeded these reminders and before long launched a successful attack against Yue and took its king prisoner. After this triumph, however, he let things slide; he gave himself up to wine and women and became forgetful of his responsibilities as ruler. As a result, Wu became weaker and weaker. In the meantime Goujian, after his return to Yue, took the exact opposite path. He worked from early morning to late at night and tasted gall every day to remind himself of the need to erase the bitter humiliation to which he and his state had been subjected. This persistence and hard work ultimately paid off, as Goujian achieved a decisive victory over his longtime rival. "When the flourishing and decline of Wu are joined together with the remembering and forgetting of King Fuchai of Wu, it is apparent how very dangerous forgetfulness can be!"

Everyone naturally has a memory, the author reminds us, but not everyone uses it well. When memory is deficient, forgetfulness inevitably thrives. After citing the cases of several top Communist officials (including Wang Baosen) who, as a result of their forgetfulness, embezzled public funds, he concludes on a more positive note: Nowadays, when we talk about not forgetting, it doesn't take the form of the ancients' "ordering servants to shout out" or having to taste gall every day. It consists, rather, in constantly bearing in mind the lessons of history, the education we have received from the party, and the ideals of communism. Peng Dehuai and Chen Yi were two great Communists who understood this well. The latter in particular reminded himself every day not to forget his roots, by which he meant the fundamental purposes of the party, the responsibilities of party members, the true qualities of a public servant. These cautionary words should be inscribed in every Communist's heart.[14]

According to another commentator on the problem of corruption in high places, much enlightenment was to be derived from scrutinizing the reasons behind Fuchai's suicide. This action was the inevitable consequence of the Wu king's having given himself over to a life of pleasure seeking and self-gratification—a weakness that Goujian, with the prompting of Wen Zhong, was able to exploit to devastating effect. "If ordinary people have a few interests and desires," the author wrote, "this is no big deal. But when a man holds substantive power, his interests and desires make him susceptible to others indulging his tastes and exploiting him, in the end causing him to trip and fall, 'capsizing the boat.' The lesson to be derived from such past failings is clear. It is to be hoped that our leading cadres in their work and their lives will exercise self-restraint, examine their conduct carefully, show self-respect, and not, because of the satisfaction of some momentary craving, end up replicating the fate of King Fuchai of Wu."[15]

The core issue that all of these writers, directly or indirectly, addressed was the proper exercise of power. Already prior to the death of Wang Baosen, this was an issue that was much discussed. One particularly illuminating example was a piece by a Henan cadre, Zhang Yunnan, that was published in 1994. Zhang, like the others, saw deep meaning in the example of Fuchai. The reason Fuchai was named overlord was that, early in his career, he did not forget the injunction to avenge the killing of his father, he appointed officials on the basis of their ability and integrity, he followed the advice of Wu Zixu, and he was impartial and wise in his handling of affairs. As a result he received strong support from the people of Wu and made use of their power in a proper way. However, after achieving his success, Fuchai failed to bear firmly in mind the fundamental principles of "using power" *(jieli)* and "losing power" *(shili)*. He became arrogant and self-satisfied and sought a life of pleasure. Goujian, seeing his opportunity, deployed various stratagems to exploit the situation. He used (or "borrowed") Bo Pi's power to "kill" Wu Zixu and Xi Shi's power to "kill" Fuchai. "But the reality is that it was Fuchai who killed himself."

Clearly, Zhang does not refer here to the literal fact that Fuchai ended his own life, but rather to the part the Wu king took in bringing on the demise of Wu. Zhang uses the character *jie* in *jieli* in two ways: to make use of one's own power and to borrow someone else's power. In an environment dominated by market economy and reform (as in the midnineties), he contends, there are abundant opportunities for people with ulterior motives to exploit (borrow) the power of ranking officials for their own purposes. Some leaders, whose consciousness is not very high, who are not well-informed, or who are politically naïve, are sitting ducks when exposed to the flattery of others. The flatterers, for their part, are prepared to go to any length to establish close relations with such leaders, pandering to their likings and giving them things that bring them pleasure, until they are happy and satisfied. Once such a relationship has been established, their goal of "borrowing power" from such leaders has basically been attained. The "powerholders" in question start to serve them (instead of the people), saying or doing anything on their behalf, fulfilling all of their requests, completely ignoring party discipline and the law of the land. Such is the face of much of the corruption encountered at present in China.

The use of power, Zhang concludes, may be likened to a vegetable knife. A vegetable knife can be used to slice vegetables, but it can also be used to kill a person. Those in the position of socialist leaders, once they have a good grasp of the fundamental principles of "making use of power," are able in practice to prevent scheming and intriguing of the sort that involve using power to kill people and are proficient at using power to do the things that bring benefit to the development of production and the lives of the masses.[16]

Although the foregoing observers focused specifically on corruption, others in the 1990s worried about the closely related problem of the decline of what one of them called "the glorious tradition of hard struggle." One of the unfortunate consequences of the increase in material comforts during the period of reform was that some party cadres and members of the military had come to the view that hard struggle was no longer necessary. Many individuals in positions of influence had gone soft, living lives of extravagance and conspicuous display, engaging in nepotistic behavior, and forgetting their duties as servants of the people. The tradition of engaging in arduous struggle in order to accomplish important goals was a basic component of the national spirit of China. It had existed for thousands of years—witness Shennong's invention of Chinese agriculture and herbal medicine, the Great Yu's taming of the floodwaters, the building of the Great Wall, and the exertions of Goujian in the rejuvenation of Yue. This fine tradition, moreover, was manifested not only in such momentous activities as these; it was also reflected in the hardships individual scholars had endured throughout Chinese history in order to pursue their studies. And it had been promoted explicitly by such great thinkers as Confucius and Mencius. In the present day, China still faced difficult challenges, such as reducing the gap between rich and poor, eliminating exploitation, and liberating the productive forces of the economy. To address these challenges successfully, it was essential to preserve and develop the great tradition of hard struggle.[17]

INDIVIDUAL AND GROUP MOTIVATION: KEYS TO SUCCESS

The Goujian story, sometimes simply distilled into the proverb *woxin changdan*, was also appropriated in countless instances for the purpose of individual and collective motivation. Zhu Baoqin, a self-study student attached to a middle school in Xining, Qinghai, after failing an examination, concluded that this setback was owing to her insufficient grasp of the material, her not having been methodical in her studies, her lack of perseverance, and her underestimation of the difficulty of the test. After completely changing her thinking, she began her struggle anew; in the spirit of "sleeping on brushwood and tasting gall," she overcame innumerable obstacles, got good grades in all of her courses, and eventually earned her diploma.[18]

In April 1992, when Peng Sanyuan took up the post of director of the Lingling Region Textile Mill in Hunan, the textile industry was in a slump and the mill faced a daunting array of problems. As an indication of his determination to revive its fortunes and restore it to its former position, Peng had a sign put up at the mill entrance, which stated in part, "Three years of sleeping on brushwood and tasting gall, and in 1995 Lingling Textile will once again flourish." Peng instituted numerous changes in the management of the mill and enforced strict discipline among all people associated with it. Like Goujian, moreover, he subjected himself to the same constraints and deprivations that he imposed on everyone else. By 1995 Lingling Textile had once again become profitable and Peng's dream was fulfilled.[19]

Xi Qisheng was the party branch secretary in a village in Wuxi county, Jiangsu. When he started in this position in 1979 the village leadership was in a weakened state, industrial production was not prospering, and insecurity was widespread among the village's inhabitants—there were difficulties everywhere. Xi was weighed down by this. He felt that the entire village was watching him, looking to him for help. Finally, he decided that he would not rest until new life had been injected into the local economy and the villagers had been lifted out of their poverty. "I rallied the party branch members and urged them, in the spirit of King Goujian of Yue's sleeping on brushwood and tasting gall, to exert themselves to make the village prosperous and build up the economy through concerted effort. For years, working day and night, we threw ourselves vigorously into developing the economy. Finally, as a result of everyone's pooled efforts, our industrial production rounded the bend and in recent years we have achieved rapid advances." Given the widespread problem of tension and mistrust between local people and their resident party leaders, Xi proudly added that as the material conditions of the inhabitants of his village improved, they came to feel that "the village party branch was a leadership body that really could bring benefits to everyone, that it was an organization on which they could depend. As the party branch boosted the villagers' confidence in the leadership, many of them drew close to it and popular feeling was united, establishing a precondition for the development of our work in the future."[20]

The Goujian story occasionally cropped up in unexpected contexts. An important part of the learning process, in the view of Fu Boting and Feng Ruifang, involved nourishing the capacity of students to negate or deny. To avoid complacency among high achievers and poor self-esteem among low ones, students should be taught not to be guided entirely by their past performance. They should also be encouraged in certain situations to take issue with the views of others. Galileo challenged Aristotle's theory of falling bodies and established a new theory. Indeed, the whole history of science could be viewed as a history of negation. Finally, students should be urged not to indulge their weaknesses and to face up to their mistakes in order to avoid repeating them again and again. Here, Fu and Feng pointed to the example of Goujian, who "dared to negate his past, transformed himself, adapted to a new environment, and finally realized his dream of rejuvenating his state."[21]

The Goujian story even had something to say to the SARS crisis that was spawned in China and then spread around the world in the spring of 2003. As the crisis finally began to moderate, it was not uncommon for people to feel that some good might come out of it, that the crisis presented a learning opportunity that Chinese could put to constructive use in the future. There was nothing automatic about this, however. One commentator asked his readers to look again at the ancient story of King Goujian of Yue. Goujian's turning defeat into victory did not just happen. Before he was able to bring good fortune out of bad, he had to go through a period of profound self-examination and analysis of the factors that had resulted in Yue's humiliating defeat. This, along with his subjective awakening and the energetic initiatives he took on behalf of his state, constituted the prerequisite for Yue's turning its crisis into an opportunity. "Without this prerequisite, I'm afraid, we wouldn't have the story of 'sleeping on brushwood and tasting gall' that has been so widely admired down through the ages." Similarly, if China was to derive something positive from the SARS crisis, it too, like Goujian, must engage in painful reflection, expose its shortcomings (mainly in the area of information dissemination and coordination), and face up to its responsibilities.[22]

According to the advice of two individuals attached to a Jiangsu personnel department, first-time job hunters, especially those whose academic credentials were below par, must not expect to find the job of their dreams right off. Rather, they should lay the foundation for future success by first going through a period of sleeping on brushwood and tasting gall. "To sleep on brushwood" in this context meant to tolerate a low salary and rudimentary working conditions; "to taste gall" was to experience the hard knocks of starting out in a new position and to go through a demanding course of self-improvement. "Putting up with adversity in the short term," the authors counseled, "isn't really such a bad thing. As a twenty-first-century 'Goujian,' you'll become more self-confident and have a greater competitive edge."[23]

A sense of competitiveness was not only necessary for advancing in one's job. It was also important, a middle school history teacher argued in 1998, for just about everything else in contemporary life. Competition lay at the very heart of the new market economy that had come into existence in China. It was also a fundamental feature of the world in which young Chinese would be growing up in the twenty-first century. Students must be brought to understand the dialectical relationship between success and failure. Failure (defeat) was often the starting point of success (victory). This was what the story of King Goujian of Yue taught. Having a proper understanding of the temporary nature of success and failure and their capacity to change into one another was what enabled competitors to be good at contending and ultimately give full play to their capabilities. To meet the challenges of the new century, therefore, history instruction must enter a new phase characterized by elevating the quality of students, nurturing their competitive skills, developing their intelligence, and stimulating their creative powers.[24]

A parent, developing some of the same themes (including the need for young people to learn how to compete effectively) and also citing the example of Goujian, discussed the situation of her two sons. The older son, unable to deal with difficulties, was apathetic about competing, while the younger one wanted to "win" so badly that he was incapable of suffering defeat without getting extremely upset. The mother worried about what it was going to be like when the boys grew up and had to deal with real-life situations. Since each son's problem was different, to help them overcome their difficulties she adopted different strategies. But the aim in each instance was the same: to teach her sons that only by being able to tolerate failure or defeat was it possible to be successful in life—a dictum that in the conclusion to her brief account she extended to the youth of the country in general.[25]

The links between the foregoing examples and the Goujian story are clear. But in their specific subject matter they stray very far indeed from the original story. In his primary school Chinese class, the exemplary teacher Xue Fagen dealt with this issue frontally, unpacking for his students the different levels of meaning that a proverb like "sleeping on brushwood and tasting gall" might embrace. After ascertaining from the class the proverb's literal meanings, he pushed the students a step further: "If Goujian did nothing but sleep on firewood at night and taste gall before each meal, would that truly count as 'sleeping on brushwood and tasting gall'?" No, it would not, the students responded. Goujian also cultivated the soil to enrich his state, trained his soldiers to form a powerful army, and searched for people of ability to devise plans to make the country strong. Xue next asked whether, if Goujian only persevered for a few days or a few months, that would truly count as "sleeping on brushwood and tasting gall," to which the class again responded that, no, it would not, because Goujian "slept on brushwood and tasted gall" for a very long time, twenty or more years according to the text of the lesson.

After summarizing the different meanings of "sleeping on brushwood and tasting gall"—being prepared to put up with humiliation in the pursuit of an important goal *(renru fuzhong)*, working with a will to make the country strong *(fafen tuqiang)*, and persistence *(jianchi bu xie)*—Xue Fagen pushed the class an important step further:

TEACHER: Students, Goujian needed to sleep on brushwood and taste gall. Do we need to sleep on brushwood and taste gall?

STUDENTS: No.

TEACHER: Why?

STUDENTS: Because we don't need to take revenge.

TEACHER: If you have no grievances and no hatreds, then you don't need to sleep on brushwood and taste gall? Is that right?

STUDENTS: Our lives are very happy, we don't need to experience such hardship.

TEACHER: So if your lives are blessed, you can just sit back and enjoy! Students, please listen carefully to what I have to say: For China's space flight program, Chinese scientists slept on brushwood and tasted gall for several decades before finally sending a first person into space in a man-made earth satellite. Did Chinese scientists have grievances or hatreds? Did they sleep on firewood every day and before each meal have to taste a gallbladder?

STUDENT: Teacher, I do feel that we need to sleep on brushwood and taste gall. For instance, if the Chinese soccer team wants to become world champion, it must sleep on brushwood and taste gall.

TEACHER: What the Chinese soccer team needs is the spirit of sleeping on brushwood and tasting gall!

STUDENT: I too must sleep on brushwood and taste gall.

TEACHER: You also have no grievances or hatreds, why do you need to sleep on brushwood and taste gall?

STUDENT: If in the future I want to become a really rich person, now I must sleep on brushwood and taste gall and study very hard.

TEACHER: In order to realize your own lofty ambitions, you too must have the spirit of sleeping on brushwood and tasting gall!

STUDENT: Our school right now is in the process of setting up an experimental primary school. This also will require sleeping on brushwood and tasting gall.

TEACHER: If our school wants to develop, it too will need this spirit. The spirit of sleeping on brushwood and tasting gall is precisely the spirit of enduring humiliation in pursuit of an important undertaking, working with a will to make the country strong, and persisting![26]

Xue Fagen's teaching of *woxin changdan,* apart from exemplifying how young Chinese are still being introduced to widely known proverbs in the classroom, clearly demonstrated how the spirit of the Goujian story could be adapted metaphorically to contemporary Chinese life. One is reminded of Bruner's comment, in his discussion of the "power of story to shape everyday experience," that the remarkable thing about narrative templates is "that they are so particular, so local, so unique—yet have such reach."[27] Xue's reading of *woxin changdan* supplied a superb illustration of this insight. Like the other examples in this section, it pointed to a goal that, although perhaps implicit in the original story, was now restated in such broadened terms as to open up new interpretive ground. This goal, with its undeniably modern tinge, was to achieve success in a new Chinese environment marked by unprecedented competition.

The factors contributing to individual success, it was recognized, embraced a wide spectrum. A history teacher from Gansu, for example, drawing on such historical models as Goujian, Sima Qian, and Columbus, contended that nonintellectual qualities (motivation, interest, goals, emotions, determination, personality) were at least as important as intellectual ones (memory, imagination, judgment, thinking) for successful learning and therefore must be cultivated and developed in history classes.[28] The authors of another discussion placed special emphasis on the part taken by external and internal pressure. Among the examples from history they cited were Su Qin of the Warring States, who following a period of intense study— he pricked his thigh with an awl to stay awake late into the night—was appointed chief minister of the six-state alliance against Qin; Goujian, who was able to fulfill his goal of rejuvenating Yue only after sleeping on brushwood and tasting gall; Mao Zedong, who wrote his essays *On Contradiction* and *On Practice* while living in a cave in Yan'an with nothing more than an oil lamp for light; and Karl Marx, who endured political persecution and impoverishment while completing the writing of *Capital.* People, the authors concluded, must strive if they were to amount to anything. But to strive you had to have a sense of purpose; this sense of purpose or goal acted as an invisible form of pressure that could be of great help along the path to success.[29]

PREPARING THE LITTLE EMPERORS
AND EMPRESSES FOR REAL LIFE

A variation on many of the problems discussed in the preceding section was presented by the "little emperor" *(xiao huangdi)* syndrome, a by-product of the one-child policy that had been adopted early in the Deng Xiaoping era to slow China's population growth. The social costs of this policy, however justifiable the larger goal may have been, were substantial. There were forced abortions and heavy fines for violators, especially in the early stages of the policy's implementation. The combination of the long-standing Chinese preference for sons and the growing accessibility in the 1980s and 1990s of ultrasound machines enabled couples to choose their child's sex, resulting in hundreds of thousands, if not millions, of aborted female fetuses. This, in turn, gave rise to a ratio between male and female births that as of 2000 was shockingly high, standing (according to official Chinese census data) at an estimated 120 to 100.[30]

Additionally, the distortions of the one-child policy often resulted in problems for the children themselves, especially in urban areas. In some instances, the policy created intense pressure on the single child to be a high achiever and so fulfill his or her family's social expectations.[31] In other cases, it contributed to a situation in which the children were spoiled and overprotected at home, prompting worried educators to argue that unless the handling of difficulties and reverses were somehow incorporated into their education, these youngsters would be paralyzed in the face of the frustrations they would inevitably encounter in life. These, as well as other difficulties, led to the emergence in the 1980s and 1990s of a flourishing educational subfield devoted to teaching young people how to deal with, and even take advantage of, setbacks *(cuozhe jiaoyu);* predictably, in their contributions to this subfield, educators (and on occasion students themselves) touted the inspirational value of the story of Goujian.

"We are a generation of self-centered individuals who cannot tolerate difficulties." These words, written by a second-year middle school student in her weekly journal, were referred to by a professor of psychology as a "common flaw" in the psychological makeup of contemporary Chinese youth: they were unable to cope with serious reverses, they could not tolerate heavy pressure.[32] This defect was especially pronounced among the little empresses and emperors, who grew up in an environment of unprecedented abundance and affluence. When at home, according to one account, they did nothing but read, watch television, and play games. Their parents did everything for them: they took them to and from school every day, avoided giving them any household chores, and watched over them like hawks, lest they encounter difficulties of any sort.[33] In the land of "honey and sugar" in which the great majority of urban children lived, another writer asserted, there was no conception of hardship, suffering, or frustration. Young people were presented with a completely positive, optimistic outlook on everything, causing them to believe absolutely in the vision of a communist utopia just around the corner.[34]

Many observers alluded to the growing number of Chinese youth who, ill-equipped to deal with life's slings and arrows, suffered from depression, ran away from home, or even, with worrisome frequency, committed suicide.[35] But the main concern of those who wrote on *cuozhe* education was to prepare young people to achieve success in the fiercely competitive environment that China had become.[36] It was not uncommon to encounter the argument, drawn from Mencius, that it was the very process of dealing with hardship and deprivation that enabled people to succeed in life. As a researcher at a Guangzhou institute for the study of young people put it, "'The fragrance of plum blossoms emerges out of the bitter cold, the sharp edge of a fine sword comes from the grinding.' The reason the story of King Goujian of Yue's sleeping on brushwood and tasting gall has been universally acclaimed over the centuries and is recounted with such satisfaction is the personal appeal of a man who was undaunted in the face of adverse circumstances and setbacks, went all out to build up the strength of his state, and reasserted his authority and power."[37]

That this message got through to at least some of China's youth was suggested by the prizewinning essay of one Wang Lei, a middle school student from the southwestern province of Guizhou. "Some people liken setbacks to a miracle drug," Wang wrote, "a priceless asset. That's exactly right." Middle school students must understand that encountering setbacks was not the same as failing; true failure came when one lost one's confidence and abandoned one's conviction that with struggle success would come:

King Goujian of Yue suffered every kind of humiliation; then after returning to his state he slept on brushwood and tasted gall—only after going through all of these trials did he in one bold stroke wipe out the state of Wu. If Zhang Haidi,* who suffers from high paraplegia, had discontinued her studies after gaining a smattering of knowledge, how would she have become the richly learned person that she is? . . . Setbacks and success go hand in hand. People live and develop amid setbacks; only after experiencing all of life's flavors, the bitter as well as the sweet, can they achieve success.[38]

In discussions of *cuozhe* education, Japan was repeatedly cited as a nation that, because of its large population and dependence on the rest of the world for raw materials, had had to work very hard to attain success and from early on had made it a point to incorporate dealing with hardship into its educational system. China could learn much from the Japanese model.[39] Young Chinese could also benefit from familiarity with contemporary (as well as historical) exemplars, as the example of Zhang Haidi suggested— and from foreign as well as Chinese ones. The inclusion of such foreigners as the duke of Wellington, Nelson Mandela, Thomas Edison, Marie Curie, Alfred Nobel, and Franklin D. Roosevelt as models for emulation,[40] not to mention the national example of Japan, clearly suggested that, although overcoming great obstacles to achieve success might be a long-admired Chinese virtue, it was not something the Chinese had an exclusive patent on. The Goujian story, in this as in other respects, embodied values that other peoples around the world also found immensely appealing.

MARKETING THE GOUJIAN STORY
AT THE TURN OF THE TWENTY-FIRST CENTURY

Apart from widespread privatization of the Goujian story at the turn of the century in response to a rapidly expanding arena of individual concerns and aspirations, the story's dissemination was also profoundly shaped by a number of structural developments taking place in the China of these years. One

---

*Zhang Haidi was left paralyzed from the waist down at age five after undergoing a series of operations to remove tumors from her spine. Through determination and perseverance, she learned several foreign languages, translated a number of novels into Chinese, and has written best-selling books of her own. She has also achieved prominence as an advocate for the rights of the disabled in China.

such development was the proliferation of new print outlets accompanying the extraordinary growth of the country's tertiary educational sector in the post-Mao era—and, no less important, the availability of new research technologies for accessing these outlets. In writing this chapter, I have made extensive use of a Chinese database that enables full-text searches of more than seven thousand two hundred journals, magazines, newsletters, and other vehicles of periodic academic communication, representing a vast range of specialized interests and covering the years from 1994 to the present.[41] To give some idea of the power of such a database, as of January 13, 2007, a search for "Goujian" resulted in hits in 5,549 articles, and a search for "*woxin changdan,*" hits in 7,292 articles. Clearly, without such a search engine, the research on which much of this chapter is based would simply not have been possible.

A second development, one of enormous consequence, was the dramatic expansion of television from the early 1980s on. In 1978 there were 0.59 color television sets per one hundred urban Chinese families; this figure increased a hundred times in the course of the 1980s, the viewership in the country as a whole reaching an estimated 80 percent by 1994.[42] Unlike academic periodicals, which are consumed by limited numbers of highly specialized readers, television in China today reaches an immense mass audience. The implications of this for wide dissemination of the Goujian story (and, of course, many other ancient stories as well) have been huge. During the first half of the twentieth century, educated Chinese learned about the story mainly from ancient works, school primers, and opera performances, while individuals with little or no formal education came to know it primarily through opera and mass education materials (and possibly radio). By the end of the century, although regular viewing of live opera had declined in China, the audience for televised historical dramas, which occupied an important place in television programming overall, had increased exponentially.

An early instance of television's capacity to arouse interest in the Goujian story came in 1996 and 1997 with China Central Television's (CCTV) sixty-episode extravaganza on late Zhou history titled *The States of the Eastern Zhou (Dong Zhou lieguo)*. Based mainly on the famous Ming dynasty historical romance *A Chronicle of the States of the Eastern Zhou (Dong Zhou lieguo zhi),* the drama's Spring and Autumn portion (the first thirty episodes) concluded with six segments centering on the Goujian story.[43] Immediately afterward, a publishing house, responding to the "widespread and protracted" interest generated nationwide and judging the Goujian saga to be the most influential and dramatic tale of the late Zhou, rushed into print a long novel on the story (which, it turns out, although allegedly written by one Hong Bicheng, was in fact a plagiarized version of Xiao Jun's novel of 1980).[44] More recently still, in 2006–2007, the Goujian story was the subject of no fewer than three major multipart television productions, each featuring a star male actor in the role of Goujian: *King Goujian of Yue* (*Yue wang Goujian*; forty-one episodes), *Sleeping on Brushwood and Tasting Gall* (*Woxin changdan*; forty-one episodes), and *A Tale of the Struggle to Become Overlord* (*Zhengba chuanqi*; forty-two episodes).[45] And in June 2006, CCTV broadcast an innovative and highly praised Shaoxing opera on the story.[46] We thus face the paradox that, in the late twentieth and early twenty-first centuries, although China was not, as in earlier periods, experiencing a national crisis that resonated in an especially powerful way with the Goujian story, more Chinese in absolute terms were likely to be familiar with the story than ever before.

A third development that encouraged greater Chinese knowledge of the Goujian story at the turn of the century was the story's commodification in the context of a rapidly expanding domestic tourism industry, part of a wider phenomenon taking place all over the country. The dissemination of the story in long-running television dramas was, of course, guaranteed to be profitable for the television industry, quite apart from tourism. Advertising revenues were substantial. *A Tale of the Struggle to Become Overlord*, although a Hong Kong production (Television Broadcasts Limited, or TVB), was initially broadcast (beginning on June 6, 2006) by Zhejiang TV, which in a daring effort to compete for viewers with the 2006 World Cup (which was televised by CCTV and began on June 9), purchased exclusive first-broadcast rights for the sizable sum of 32 million yuan.[47] Even more impressive was the hype surrounding *King Goujian of Yue,* a joint production of CCTV, Shaoxing TV, and media companies in Beijing and Hangzhou. Although it did not show in China until the spring of 2007 (beginning on May 10), already in the previous spring it excited the interest of a number of countries after airing on TV Festival de Cannes (the film festival's official television network), and by late summer 2006 Japan had purchased foreign broadcast and adaptation rights to the film for a record sum.[48] Also, in September 2006, a two-volume novel, written by Zhang Jing with the same title as the television production, was published in Henan, on the premise that the novel and television drama would each fuel interest in the other.[49]

Heavily promoted dramatizations of the Goujian story such as the foregoing interacted synergistically with the growth of Chinese tourism. A precedent was set in the 1990s with the explosion of interest in Xi Shi. Operas dealing with the famous beauty enjoyed great popularity in a wide area embracing Zhejiang, Shanghai, Jiangsu, Anhui, Shanxi, and even Taiwan; two very long Xi Shi novels appeared in 1995; and the local government of Xi Shi's home place, Zhuji (now a city under the administrative jurisdiction of the prefecture-level city Shaoxing), after renovating the Xi Shi Temple and opening it to the public, embarked on the promotion of a tourist economy centered on this city's most famous daughter.[50] "Overnight, it seemed, from every side there was a sudden burst of interest in this beautiful woman who lived more than two thousand years ago."[51]

The development of a Xi Shi–centered tourist economy in Zhuji was only one facet of greater Shaoxing's aggressive labors in recent years to derive maximum economic benefit from the Goujian story. A key figure in this effort has been Wang Yongchang, who became the city's party committee secretary in 2004 and also served as mayor from March 2002 to March 2005. Wang is firmly convinced that, for a city as historically and culturally blessed as Shaoxing, economic development must go hand in hand with historical preservation.[52] Although the Shaoxing area is home (by birth, residence, historical affiliation, or legendary ascription) to a long line of luminaries including the Great Yu, the fourth-century calligrapher Wang Xizhi, the early twentieth-century female revolutionary Qiu Jin (1875–1907), the modern writer Lu Xun (1881–1936), and PRC premier Zhou Enlai,[53] when it comes to exploiting the present-day economic potential of the city's ancient heritage, it is Goujian who occupies center place.

Wang Yongchang, taking his cue from two of the most important symbols associated with the Goujian story, identifies the basic spirit of the people of Shaoxing as the "gall and sword spirit" (dan jian jingshen) and has repeatedly emphasized its critical part in the city's economic success.[54] In conjunction with the Shaoxing Planning Bureau, he has taken an active part in developing plans for a section of the city to be called "City of the King of Yue" (Yue wang cheng), designed to serve as a site for the display of ancient Yue culture, encourage cultural tourism, highlight the special nature of Shaoxing, and enhance the city's competitive strength.[55] Most interesting for our purposes is Wang Yongchang's determination to capitalize on the television drama King Goujian of Yue, portions of which were filmed in the Houshan Scenic Area in Shaoxing. In March 2006 Wang, along with Minister of Culture Sun Jiazheng and a professor of ancient Chinese literature, Li Hanqiu, took part in a CCTV roundtable discussion on the question of what cultural imagery might best represent China to the world. At one point the program's moderator observed that in the wake of the wildly enthusiastic reception given in China to the fifty-four-episode Korean television drama *Jewel in the Palace (Dae Jang Geum)*, Chinese interest in things Korean had extended to cuisine, fashion, and even tourism. He wondered whether Wang and the other political leaders of Shaoxing, in taking the filming of *King Goujian of Yue* so seriously—several of them, including Wang, had attended the ribbon-cutting ceremony marking the start of the shooting—were consciously emulating the Korean marketing strategy. After acknowledging that he and his colleagues had indeed been influenced to some extent by the Korean example, Wang amplified his thinking:

> Our Shaoxing is an ancient city of historical renown that has existed for several thousand years. . . . During the Spring and Autumn–Warring States phase of its development, there was a King Goujian of Yue, who by sleeping on brushwood and tasting gall was able to turn the initial defeat of his state into eventual victory. His psychological makeup included a profound idea, namely, that by setting one's mind on a goal, putting a lot of effort into an undertaking and struggling incessantly—by going through such a process—one could realize the goal. In the course of our modern construction today, we must build on this spirit, and so we propose to develop the gall and sword spirit for a new era. The television drama *King Goujian of Yue* embodies this spirit of sleeping on brushwood and tasting gall. . . . The form of historical serialization is a highly effective and excellent vehicle for conveying the spirit, permitting it to be absorbed by a much larger audience, extending even to the populace as a whole.[56]

Apart from conveying the spirit of Goujian to a large number of Chinese around the country, *King Goujian of Yue* also promised to generate considerable economic benefits for the city of Shaoxing. The fact of the drama's being partly filmed in the Houshan Scenic Area promoted the city nationally as a prime site for domestic tourism. In addition to this, the set that CCTV went to considerable expense to build at Houshan—it included reproductions of Goujian's palace, his ancestral shrine, the Zhongli forge for the manufacture of swords,[57] the stable, and other structures—was left in place after the filming was completed in late 2005. The Houshan authorities, seeing an opportunity to attract more visitors to the scenic area, suspended a large red banner over one of the entrances to the park that announced, "The set from *King Goujian of Yue* lends even greater enchantment to the scenery of Houshan." They also entered into agreements of

Figure 29. Billboard at the Houshan Scenic Area (Shaoxing) promoting the TV film *Yue wang Goujian*. Chen Baoguo, who plays Goujian in the film, is shown in the foreground; behind him is a scene from the film shot at Houshan. Photograph by author, Jan. 5, 2007.

touristic cooperation with numerous travel agencies, resulting in an infusion of new revenue into the Shaoxing area in general.[58]

I don't want to suggest that the marketing of popular historical narratives like the Goujian story is a completely new phenomenon in China. In one form or another, it has doubtless existed for a very long time. But the scale of the commodification that has taken place in recent years, owing partly to the advent of new communications technologies and partly to the unprecedented emergence of a substantial middle class of affluent Chinese, has clearly eclipsed anything that existed earlier.

———————

The use of the Goujian story to strengthen people's moral fiber and inspire them, to teach them not to be discouraged by setbacks and show them how, by hard work and persistence, they could accomplish their goals and better their individual and communal lives, was not an entirely new development at the turn of the twenty-first century. The eminent early Qing writer Pu Songling (1640–1715), after repeated failures at the civil service examinations, wrote a famous couplet in which, in emulation of Chu general Xiang Yu in his defeat of the far-more-powerful Qin army (late third century B.C.E.) and Goujian in his conquest of Wu after surmounting numerous difficulties, he evinced his determination to continue with his writing, undaunted by setbacks.[59] In the 1930s, as we have seen, the artist-writer Feng Zikai wrote a short story in which the notion of *woxin changdan* was transposed

Figure 30. Banner at the entrance to Houshan announcing the added attraction created by the set from the TV film *Yue wang Goujian*. Photograph by author, Jan. 5, 2007.

from the national-level political discourse of humiliation and revenge so pervasive at the time to a more intimate and personal terrain, where it was used allegorically to motivate young Chinese to bring greater fulfillment into their lives (see chapter 2). And, it will be recalled, Huang Dashou, in his 1957 lesson plan for retired servicemen on Taiwan, paid special attention to the value of the Goujian story for the bolstering of personal morale (see chapter 3).

Nevertheless, the frequency with which the Goujian story was deployed at the turn of the twenty-first century, the wide array of different contexts in which it cropped up, and the ease with which, in a rapidly developing economy, it was exploited for commercial purposes were quite unprecedented, reflecting stunning shifts that had taken place in the post-Mao years. These years did not constitute a "Goujian moment," as was the case in some of the earlier periods dealt with in this book. That is, there was no overriding national issue or set of concerns—the humiliating aggression of Japan in the first half of the twentieth century, the Nationalist commitment to recovery of the mainland in the post-1949 years, or the sense of crisis in the early 1960s owing to the post-Leap famine and growing tensions with the USSR—that Chinese consciously believed to be tailor-made for the story. The decades surrounding the turn of the century were a more "normal" time as far as appropriation of the Goujian narrative was concerned.

There was no more stunning evidence of this normalcy than the fact that the major fictional and large-scale television productions of the Goujian story during these years all, without exception (although in varying ways), incorporated the ruthlessly ambitious, hard-hearted side of the Yue king.[60] In the first eight decades of the twentieth century, the inclusion of this facet of Goujian's character was either avoided entirely or explicitly subordinated to the king's extraordinary achievements in rejuvenating

Yue,[61] and its reinstatement in the early 1980s in the works of Xiao Jun and Bai Hua was clearly intended as political censure. Now the darker, more brutal Goujian could be dealt with in the simple interest of producing a better story, with little or no fear that it would be misconstrued as politically motivated. The narrative appeal of this more multifaceted version of the Yue king was articulated nicely in the synopsis prefacing the plagiarized Goujian novel of 1996:

> King Goujian of Yue was the figure from the Spring and Autumn and Warring States eras who was richest in story-like qualities, who was the most tragic, and also the most controversial. He was not only the ruler of a conquered state whose army was defeated and who became a prisoner, he was also a master of forbearance who kept his murderous intent well hidden; he was a man of virtue who cherished benevolence and righteousness and also an ungrateful pupil who capriciously killed his meritorious ministers. On top of this, he was the first person in Chinese history to employ the "beauty trap" and successfully establish this terrible precedent. In order to save his life and recover his former position, Goujian didn't hesitate to surrender himself to Wu as a slave or to taste with his own mouth the stool of the Wu king. Ought we sing the praises of a man of such complex makeup or should we spurn him?[62]

I use the word "normal" to describe the turn of the twenty-first century mainly to call attention to the loosening of state control over society and the depoliticization of everyday life that marked these years. (The reader will recall that when a similar relaxation of political constraints took place in Taiwan in the course of the 1980s, a parallel change in the treatment of the Goujian story also occurred there.) In other respects, however, this time period in the PRC was distinctive in too many ways to be considered truly "normal." The specific issues that invited allusion to the Goujian story— the emphasis on patriotic education as a new form of validation for an ideologically impoverished Communist regime, corruption among high-ranking party cadres, education for success in a newly competitive societal and world environment, and so forth—were issues particular to this time in Chinese history. In another time, there would have been other issues. Also, the dramatic changes in communications technology and economic circumstances that characterized these years, by turning the story into a source not only of inspiration but also of profit, added an important new dimension to how it played out in the Chinese world. The fact that the

Goujian story continued to speak to Chinese in such diverse ways, even at a time that did not specifically call attention to it, underscores its remarkable adaptableness and durability. It also makes all the more striking the degree to which the story's appeal and influence over the past century have remained concealed from the eyes of scholars in the West, a conundrum I will comment on in the conclusion to this book.

Conclusion
Cross-Cultural Perspectives

ONE OF THE MOST REMARKABLE things about the Goujian story as it has operated in China from the late Qing to the present has been its versatility, its all-purpose character. When I first encountered the story, it was in connection with the humiliating experience of foreign imperialism; indeed, the more I read in materials from the late Qing and republican years, the clearer it seemed that this was one of China's premier nationalist narratives at the time.[1] It counseled hope when things were at their bleakest. It was an optimistic story that promised national success, so long as the Chinese people did not forget the humiliations of the past and worked tirelessly to build up the country so that it could exact revenge for the wrongs it had suffered.

When I looked at some of the nationalist myth-stories that have been influential in other societies, however, questions were raised in my mind about my initial supposition. One thing prompting these questions was the peculiarity of the Goujian story as a nationalist narrative. Compare, for example, Goujian's humiliation after his early defeat with the Serbian defeat at the hands of the Turks in the Battle of Kosovo in 1389. This was a calamitous defeat for the Serbs, marking the fall of an impressive Serbian independent state and, after a second defeat at Kosovo, the inception of a four-hundred-year-long condition of vassalship under the Ottomans, an alien society with an alien religion. More than six centuries later, the memory of this battle and the year in which it occurred remained so vivid among Serbs—it had been kept alive by the Serbian Orthodox Church—that it was possible for an ambitious Serbian political leader, Slobodan Milosevic, by making a cynical appeal to racial hatred, to exploit it to tragic effect.[2] Now turn the clock back two thousand five hundred years to Yue's defeat at the hands of Wu. This was not a case of a Chinese state being vanquished by a non-Chinese one. In fact, a lot of scholars do not regard either Yue or Wu in the fifth century B.C.E. as being unambiguously "Chinese."[3] When all is said and done, the emphasis in the Goujian story is, first, on the humiliation of defeat, pure and simple, and second, on the way in which Goujian responded to this humiliation. In other words, what was at issue at the time was not national pride but personal honor, although of course later tellings of the story blurred this distinction completely.

Another aspect of the Goujian story's oddness as a nationalist narrative is that far from being an exclusively *Chinese* cultural resource, it has also been influential in other parts of East Asia, including countries that at one point or another have engaged in wars with China. Thus, Vietnam, with a long tradition of resistance against its much larger northern neighbor, identified itself historically with Yue; and when the Ming occupation was brought to an end in 1428, the great scholar-patriot Nguyen Trai marked the occasion in his *Binh Ngo Dai Cao* (A Great Proclamation on the Pacification of Wu) by equating China with Wu.[4] The story was also alluded to in late Meiji Japan at times of national crisis, such as the Tripartite Intervention (1895) following the Sino-Japanese War of 1894 and again during the Russo-Japanese War (1904–1905); both were instances in which Japan (like the state of Yue) faced much larger adversaries.[5]

Literary references to the Goujian story also made regular appearances in the writings of East Asians with classical Chinese training. Thus, in the 1870s, when the influential Meiji intellectual Fukuzawa Yukichi (1835–1901) wanted to criticize his compatriots who were so smitten with the West that they copied even its faults, he compared them to Dong Shi, the famously unattractive Yue woman who knitted her brows in imitation of Xi Shi and in the process only made herself uglier. Fukuzawa, significantly, did not have to explain the Dong Shi proverb to readers, who at the time could be counted on instinctively to know what he was referring to.[6] The point, in brief, is that although the Goujian story was part of the Chinese cultural tradition, this tradition did not belong solely to China; intellectuals from elsewhere in East Asia were until quite recently also steeped in it, much as European elites were schooled in the classical learning of Greece and Rome.

My doubts about the appropriateness of treating the Goujian story as a simple nationalist narrative became even stronger after I got deeper into post-1949 Taiwan and mainland materials and discovered the multiplicity of ways in which the story was used in the second half of the twentieth century, some of which, as we've seen, dealt with personal motivational issues or internal political criticism—matters having little to do with Chinese nationalism.

What all of this suggests is that while the Goujian story can clearly be used as a nationalist narrative, it is much more than that. Goujian himself was a psychologically complex figure, and what I have referred to repeatedly as the "Goujian story" in actuality embraces a number of lesser stories from which diverse meanings can be harvested, depending on the particular circumstances to which it is applied. Indeed, one of the most extraordinary things about the Goujian story is precisely this adaptability, the wealth of different situations to which it spoke over the course of the past century. On a spectrum of Chinese cultural stories ranging from the simplest to the most multifaceted and complex, the story of Goujian clearly belongs among the latter.

In his book *Tell Me a Story*, the cognitive psychologist Roger C. Schank lists five different types of stories: official, invented, firsthand experiential, secondhand, and culturally common.[7] Although the boundaries separating these types are far from absolute and the same story can fall into more than one category, the Goujian story clearly belongs to the final type, the culturally common. That is, it is a story that is shared by vast numbers of people who inhabit the Chinese cultural world.

The same basic point can be made about any other cultural grouping. All cultures have shared stories, derived from religious traditions, legends and myths, celebrated historical figures, popular cultural activities, and so on. Some stories will be widely known throughout a culture, others will be known primarily within particular subgroups, while still others will in general be familiar only to the better-educated members of the culture.

Schank makes the further point concerning culturally common stories that it is not unusual for them to be "referred to rather than told."[8] They are commonly communicated, he asserts, in highly elliptical ways, often via proverbs, since in many contexts that is all that is necessary for them to be understood. Thus, in the case of the Goujian story, although elaborated renderings of the story have been common enough since the late Qing in school texts, mass education pamphlets, operas, spoken dramas, and in more recent decades film, radio, and television, the proverb *woxin chang-*

dan has, as we have seen, frequently been encountered standing alone, either as a four-character phrase or (less often) in pictorial form. This coded means of cultural communication typically bars—or at least substantially impedes—understanding by anyone who has not been socialized in the Chinese world. It does not, however, generally present a problem for Chinese, who in most instances know the story behind the proverb and also know, from the circumstances in which the proverb is encountered, what the metaphors "sleeping on brushwood" and "tasting gall" mean in those circumstances.

How do people become initiated into such cultural secrets? Over the past few years I have occasionally asked acquaintances of Chinese background if they remember how they first encountered the Goujian story. In a surprising number of instances, they do. A retired history professor now in his late eighties and living in Shanghai remembers hearing the story over and over again, beginning when he was "a very little boy" in the 1920s. The story, he recalls, had only one meaning at the time: to take revenge against Japan, and for him, in the early years of the twenty-first century, that is still its core meaning. Another acquaintance, a friend who has lived in Hong Kong all her life, says that she first encountered the story as a young girl in the form of a popular opera aria sung by the celebrated Cantonese opera and film star Xin Ma Shizeng (Sun Ma Sze-tsang) and titled "Woxin changdan."[9] In the aria, which aired regularly on Hong Kong radio in the mid-1950s (and was also frequently heard by my friend on a phonograph recording at home), the Yue king bemoaned the lot of his state and expressed his determination to avenge himself against Wu. The full implied meaning of the aria—it spoke directly to the anxiety and concern felt by many Hong Kong Chinese at the time over developments in their homeland—became clearer to my friend as she grew older. But, as an indication of the potency of the initial encounter with it, to this day, more than a half century later, she can still sing portions of the aria from memory.

Two other acquaintances both heard the story for the first time as children in Taiwan. One, a doctoral candidate at an American university, told me that his father, a retired member of the Nationalist armed forces, had the habit of reading Chinese stories to the family every Sunday. It was in this setting, at about age five, that he had his earliest encounter with the Goujian story and he claims to have vivid memories still of this first experiencing of the narrative. The other Taiwan-born acquaintance, who currently teaches Chinese history in the greater Boston area, was introduced to the story by her primary school teacher when she was around seven. She was quite moved by it at the time. In retrospect, she feels that her teacher's inclusion of Goujian's darker side that emerged after the conquest of Wu—something that was rare in published renderings of the story during the Chiang Kai-shek years—quite possibly reflected his (the primary school teacher's) sense of disenchantment with the policies of the Nationalist government in the 1970s.

Although the information derived from these recollections is admittedly anecdotal, it contains a number of noteworthy features. First, in each and every instance, the Goujian story was initially encountered at a very young age. Second, the first exposure to the story occurred in a setting that would likely have been experienced only by someone growing up in a Chinese (or Chinese-influenced) cultural setting. Third, in at least three of the four recollections, it is not only the story itself that is remembered (in some detail) but also the specific circumstances under which it was originally encountered. And fourth, the historical moment when the story was initially heard tended to have a bearing on what was believed, either then or later, to be the core meaning of the story. We are dealing here, in other words, not with a narrative that has embodied a fixed, inflexible set of meanings over time, regardless of changes in historical context, but rather with one that has spoken directly—and with great sensitivity and responsiveness—to some of the more important developments distinguishing Chinese history over the past century.[10]

It may be clearer at this point why a narrative like the Goujian story has remained terra incognita to so many American (and doubtless other Western) students of twentieth-century China, even if as adults they have lived in the country for a stretch of time, made a serious study of its recent history, and acquired competence in the Chinese language. These latter can, of course, look up the proverb *woxin changdan* in a good Chinese-English dictionary and discover that it means to "sleep on brushwood and taste gall—undergo self-imposed hardships (to strengthen one's resolve to wipe out a national humiliation or to accomplish some ambition)." They are unlikely, however, to encounter an explicit link to the story behind the proverb unless they consult a comprehensive Chinese-Chinese dictionary.[11] And if in their Chinese reading what they run into is not the proverb *woxin changdan* but simply the name "Goujian," they will be even more at sea, since Chinese-English dictionaries (and even many Chinese ones) don't typically incorporate proper names. The Goujian story is an example of what I call "insider cultural knowledge." It is not a form of knowledge that Chinese deliberately conceal from non-Chinese. It tends to be hidden, rather, mainly because the ways in which it is acquired—transmission within the family setting, early school lessons that are heavily story-centered, popular operatic arias heard on the radio, and the like—are not generally available to people who have not had the experience of growing up in a Chinese cultural milieu.

Insider cultural knowledge is by no means exclusive to China. On the contrary, it is found in all cultures, as well as in the different phases of a given culture's evolution through time. As an instance of the latter, Marina Warner observes that when Joan of Arc "reached for metaphors that . . . came . . . close to rendering what she felt about her voices," the three images she chose—Michael the Archangel, Catherine of Alexandria, and Margaret of Antioch—"were as well known to her contemporaries, both French and English, as a football player's or a tennis star's or a singer's are today."[12] These saintly images were learned in fifteenth-century France and England in the settings of home and church. The access to such images among twenty-first-century French and English people is far less prevalent.

The circumstances of the functioning of insider cultural knowledge and the degree of its hiddenness are likely to differ from case to case. Let me give two examples from the contemporary American cultural environment. On March 4, 2006, the *New York Times* sportswriter William C. Rhoden published an article entitled "Cinderella Is a Myth, and David Is a Lie." Although no one could tell from the heading alone what Rhoden's article was specifically about—in it he expressed the view that in the upcoming national collegiate basketball tournament only the largest and best-funded institutions really had a shot at the title—virtually all readers who had grown up in America (or probably anywhere else in the West) could be expected to know, from their familiarity with the Cinderella fairy tale and the biblical story of David and Goliath, that the author was being cynically dismissive of the notion that those who started out with serious disadvantages had much chance of overcoming them and achieving success.[13]

In March 2005, while driving back to Boston after visiting my son and his family, I was listening to "On the Media," a national weekly radio program devoted to media criticism and analysis. The guest on the program was Charles Lewis, the founder (and from 1989 until 2004, the director) of the Center for Public Integrity, a nonprofit, nonpartisan organization in Washington, D.C., that does investigative reporting and research on public policy issues. The program host, Bob Garfield, was discussing with Lewis the effectiveness of the center's work in bringing about constructive change. "Let me ask you something, Don Quixote," he quipped not very encouragingly, "what are your top three windmills that you've tilted at that you thought deserved far more public attention and media attention but somehow amounted to nothing?" Lewis, instantly comprehending the allusions to the Cervantes title character Don Quixote (an impractical dreamer whose repeated efforts to right the world's wrongs came to naught) and "tilting at windmills" (a metaphoric reference to the idealistic, impractical nature of Quixote's labors), proceeded to discuss a few of his least-successful endeavors. A few minutes later, Garfield asked Lewis how often his efforts resulted in real change taking place. Lewis conceded that it probably wasn't more than 10 percent of the time. "All right," Garfield interjected, "let me change mythic archetypes here. Never mind Don Quixote. [LAUGHTER] Let's talk about Sisyphus"—"Yeah," Lewis broke in, "that [LAUGHS] might be more accurate [LAUGHS]." Garfield then finished his interrupted sentence, describing Sisyphus's "pushing the boulder perpetually up the hill." But Lewis, it is clear, had understood the metaphor from the start and didn't need to have it decoded.[14]

It is evident from the foregoing that, like China, America has its own storehouse of culturally common stories, the sources in these two examples being a fairy tale, the Hebrew Bible, an early seventeenth-century Spanish novel, and Greek mythology. Again, as in the Chinese case, the stories are often well enough known that they can be "referred to rather than told." Like the name "Goujian" or the proverb *woxin changdan* in Chinese, the story tags—Cinderella, David, tilting at windmills, Don Quixote, Sisyphus—are quite literally part of the English language, meaning-bearing names or phrases that pop up in a thousand and one situations and do not in general require further elaboration, although the degree to which this is true will in any given instance vary, the stories of Cinderella and David and Goliath, for example, being better known among Americans than those of Don Quixote and Sisyphus.

What is the likelihood that Chinese will have a comparable familiarity with these stories? It is hard to say. I would be surprised if the Sisyphus and Don Quixote stories were widely known in China. On the other hand, there is a good chance that the minority of Chinese who are Christian will have some degree of acquaintance with the story of David and Goliath, and since a Chinese version of the Cinderella story ("Hui guniang") has long been in circulation, a greater number still are likely to be aware of it. As these last two items clearly suggest, Western (and especially American) insider cultural knowledge does not present a straightforward case in the Chinese context, owing to the profound impact that the culture of the West (including many of its stories) has had on China for well over a century.[15] A more convincing instance of the impenetrability of insider cultural knowledge by outsiders would be the culturally common stories of, say, Mexico or Iran, which in all likelihood are as unfamiliar to Chinese readers as many of the culturally common stories of China are to people in the West.

The similarities between China and America are important, but there are also significant differences, distinctive aspects of the roles stories often play in the Chinese cultural world that find at best weak parallels in America (and perhaps the West as a whole). Certainly this is so with respect to the Goujian story as it has circulated from the late Qing dynasty to the present.

Roger Schank at one point asks the following question: "What is the point of telling a story instead of just saying what we want to say directly?"[16] Although what he has in mind are the goals individuals have in conversation with other individuals, his question is equally pertinent to storytelling in a more collective setting. Again and again in this book—in the republican period during the 1920s and 1930s, in Chiang Kai-shek's post-1949 Taiwan, and in the PRC at a number of junctures from the early 1960s to the present—we have learned how important it is for Chinese to communicate through *stories* what they want their fellow Chinese to feel and think and how they want them to behave. But why? The simplest answer to this question—and although seemingly evasive, it may well be the best—is that this is the way it has been done in China for as long as anyone can remember. Presumably, a major reason for this is that historically stories have had a major mnemonic role to play, above all in oral traditions, which predominated in Chinese antiquity and, in a country that prior to the mid-twentieth century still had more illiterate than literate people, remained robust until recent times. If what you wanted to communicate had a point and you wanted the person or persons you were communicating with to remember it, perhaps even pass it on to other people, it was natural in these circumstances to incorporate the point in a story. This was why opera, the audience for which cut across all classes, was such an effective medium for the transmission of important cultural information in late imperial times.[17]

But while the role of storytelling as an aid to memory may have been a vital contributory factor at the outset, Chinese from very early times developed an ancillary set of justifications for the importance of conveying information via stories. A core assumption, widely shared, was the notion that history had a way of repeating itself—at least in an approximate way. This meant that if you knew how someone had dealt with a particular situation in the past and what the results of that action had been, you would, if faced with an analogous situation in the present, know how to act. Ministers, when trying to persuade their kings of the merits or demerits of a particular course of conduct, presented them with precedents in the form of stories. Children and young people had stories of exemplary historical figures drummed into them, in the belief that such narratives, when internalized, constituted a moral and spiritual resource to be used throughout their lives. The didactic element in such story transmission was key: stories could be (and often were) entertaining, but their primary goal was to instruct.

For modern historians the notion that history repeats itself, even in a vague, impressionistic way, is not generally acceptable. Whether or not we believe in "progress," we are convinced that new things are always happening: unprecedented developments such as (taking the past century as an example) extraordinary advances in medical knowledge and health care; sharply increased population numbers; revolutionary changes in the technologies of communication, transportation, and warfare; and, on a more mundane level, extensive modifications in what we eat, how we dress, and what we do for entertainment. Yet, when it comes to the human condition in a psychological or moral (as opposed to material) sense, many of us would, I think, agree that the changes have been far less clear and certain, even over much larger stretches of time than a single century. Thus the ancient story of Sisyphus becomes, in Jerome Bruner's language, a "root metaphor" of the human plight, no less meaningful as a symbol of "self-sustaining frustration" today than it was when it was first enunciated. "Many situations," Bruner suggests, "can be assimilated to the image of Sisyphus, even the tenant farmer perpetually in debt to the landlord and forever too poor to buy his plot of land."[18] It is this psychological-moral continuity through time, I would contend, that also enables the sense of "sympathetic vibration" Yerushalmi writes of in *Zakhor,* the possibility of a special resonance between stories even from the remote past and matters of contemporary communal concern.

Thus, far from feeling odd or forced, it seemed perfectly natural for Chinese at a number of "moments" in the twentieth century to draw emotional and moral support from a story that, in its origins, went back almost two thousand five hundred years. Highly charged moments of this sort have been experienced in other cultures as well, prompting similar efforts to seek nourishment in stories from the culture's past. One example, discussed earlier, was the inspiration late twentieth-century Serbs drew from a traumatic defeat that took place more than six hundred years before.[19] Another example, this one from Jewish history, is the strong sense of connection modern Jews have felt with the alleged mass suicide of the Zealot defenders of the mountaintop fortress of Masada in 73 C.E., one of the final acts in the Jewish revolt against Rome and an event that marked the beginning of the centuries-long period of dispersion of the Jews from their homeland.[20]

The meaning of the Masada story has been hotly contested, especially in recent decades. But during the period stretching roughly from the 1930s to the early 1970s, the story was widely understood as a positive national symbol of the "new Jew," hardworking, independent, closely connected to the land, and prepared if necessary to make the ultimate sacrifice to defend it. Describing his view of Masada, an Israeli Jew who grew up in Palestine in the prewar years wrote: "In Masada we saw a liberation war, a heroic war, a war of a few against many, . . . a war of loyalty to the nation."[21] During World War II and its immediate aftermath, Masada was commonly seen as "a model of active resistance to persecution," in contrast to the passive behavior of Jews in the Holocaust (and, in the minds of some, the entire period of Jewish exile).[22] In the years after the establishment of the state of Israel in 1948, when the fledgling Jewish state was surrounded by hostile Arab countries and a siege mentality prevailed, many Jews saw Masada as a political metaphor for unbending Israeli militancy vis-à-vis its neighbors. This perspective lasted into the 1960s and 1970s, when a moderating of negative Jewish attitudes toward the Holocaust and a new awareness (after the trauma of the Yom Kippur War of 1973) of their own vulnerability weakened (or at least complicated) the hold of Masada on the imagination of many Israelis.[23]

Manifestly, this period of several decades in Jewish history constituted a "Masada moment," in the sense of a strong, ongoing resonance between the Masada story as interpretively constructed in these years, on the one hand, and a combination, on the other, of the emergence of a new national spirit among the Jewish people and the continuously hazardous political and military situation in which the Jews found themselves, first in Palestine and then in Israel.

The Masada story's importance for the Jewish people is very different in both functional and substantive terms from that of the Goujian story for the Chinese. For one thing, although the story is not widely known among non-Jews with no Israel connection, it is a weaker instance of insider cultural knowledge: tourists who visit China are likely to return home without ever encountering the Goujian story, despite its continuing vitality among the Chinese people, while a visit to Masada has long been a standard part of the tourist itinerary in Israel. For another thing, a central meaning of the Masada story is its symbolic reconnection of the Jewish people with their ancestral land after some two millennia of separation; the Chinese people never experienced a comparable rupture in their relationship to the land of their forebears. One other difference—although the list could certainly be extended—is that despite the great importance of the Goujian story to Chinese at a number of critical points in the twentieth century, it never acquired the degree of mythic centrality among the people that the Masada story attained among the Jews.[24] One reason for this, surely, is that Masada, as a story, is much simpler than the Goujian story, with the result that its capacity to speak to diverse historical situations is greatly reduced and its focus on the solitary issue of survival-extinction greatly magnified. Another reason, possibly, is Palestine-Israel's minuscule size in comparison with China, making it easier for Masada to develop into something akin to a national cult among the Jews.[25] And finally, given the part taken by the state in both Israel and China in the promotion of these stories (to be discussed shortly), we should not forget that Israel, since its inception, has been governed by a unitary state, while in China, state power was fragmented through much of the first half of the twentieth century, creating obstacles to making any one story dominant nationwide.

There are also, of course, important similarities between the Goujian and Masada stories. One is very specific in nature. Both stories, for all their differences, are narratives about peoples threatened with defeat—and very possibly annihilation—at the hands of vastly more powerful adversaries. It is understandable, therefore, that they should exercise a strong appeal for modern states facing analogous situations (although the appeal in the case of Masada, because of the way in which the revolt ended, is less straightforward than that of the Goujian saga).

The core issue of survival also suggests a broader and deeper parallel in the functioning of the two stories. Whether one chooses to interpret Masada positively or negatively, its emotional salience for Jews after the middle of the twentieth century is incomprehensible without reference to the Holocaust. Although the Chinese never experienced an event comparable to the Holocaust, in the sense of a threat to their very existence as a people,[26] they did, in the nineteenth and twentieth centuries, live through a period of chronic turbulence, humiliation, physical privation, and cultural loss. The burden of much of this book, in fact, has been to show how the Goujian story, with its promise of eventual triumph over seemingly insurmountable difficulties, provided millions of Chinese with a measure of hope in such circumstances.

Another point of resemblance is that, as with the Goujian story in China, the state in Israel became seriously involved in the propagation of the Masada story to justify or muster support for national policies. It organized important ceremonial events at Masada, one of the most striking of which was the reburial in 1969 of twenty-seven skeletons excavated at the site (and presumed to belong to the last defenders) in an elaborate military funeral conducted on the top of the Masada cliff. In the early 1970s, Israeli prime minister Golda Meir acknowledged having a "Masada complex," which she is said to have identified with "the spirit of Israel, a spirit that would prefer death rather than surrender to the dark terrors of the Jewish past."[27] And as recently as 1999, years after many Israelis had arrived at a critical awareness of the negative implications of the story, the Israel Ministry of Foreign Affairs described Masada, in language right out of the 1930s, as "the symbol of the determination of a people to be free in its own land."[28]

A final similarity, much more general in character, has to do with the relationship between past story and present reality that in both China and Israel (as well as many other societies) has exerted such power. Why do cultures, especially those with richly storied pasts, take so seriously the activity of combing these pasts for the narratives that resonate most evocatively with their present historical circumstances? Why, to return once again to Yerushalmi's insight, do peoples, at certain moments in their collective lives, reach back into an often misty time to recover elements, perhaps long forgotten or neglected (more true of Masada than of the Goujian story), with which there is a sudden "sense of empathy, of recognition"?

There is no simple answer to these questions. One thing worth noting is that cultures don't engage in this sort of activity with equal intensity at all times. Very often—and certainly this was true in the case of the Goujian story in twentieth-century China—they are prompted to do so in unresolved crisis situations, where one outcome (victory or survival, for example) is vastly preferred over another (defeat or extinction). In such situations, the right story presents a model of the world that incorporates either the proper spirit to be embraced or the desired resolution of the crisis, or both. The Goujian story exemplifies both, inasmuch as Goujian, through his adoption of the *woxin changdan* spirit, was able to breathe new life into his state and triumph over his enemies. Masada, unlike the Goujian story, does not guarantee the desired outcome; its emphasis, instead, as the following interviewee comment (echoing Golda Meir) suggests, is on Jews embodying the right spirit: "Israelis are the continuation of Masada. Not in the sense of committing suicide, but in the sense of not giving up."[29]

A larger point to be made is that the connection between past story and present history serves as a powerful instrumentality for defining a culture's boundaries, both objectively and subjectively. The Israeli philosopher Avishai Margalit, in discussing his notion of a "community of memory," asserts that "human beings . . . lead collective existences based on symbols that encapsulate shared memories."[30] These shared memories—not the past itself, Ernest Renan long ago cautioned, but the stories we tell one another about the past—are what bind national communities together in the present.[31] Jerome Bruner and Mark Elvin have had similar things to say about the relationship between "common stories" and the human groups or communities in which they circulate.[32] What these individuals all appear to suggest is that some form of symbolic sharing (whether in the form of stories or memories) is absolutely key both to a culture's objective existence and to an individual's subjective sense of belonging to that culture. Objectively, as Elvin puts it, "shared stories . . . define the space" in which a particular human group operates, "its conceptualized physical landscape."[33] Subjectively, common stories and memories are the very stuff out of which the imagined communities Benedict Anderson describes are formed.[34] They constitute at all times a special cultural language for discussing matters of immediate concern; and, especially in time of peril, they supply a floor of reassurance that individual fears and worries about what is happening—or what may happen—are shared by other members of the community.

In both of these senses, the objective and the subjective, narratives like the Goujian story are terribly important. They are important because of what they tell us about the interior of the Chinese world at particular moments in time, how those inhabiting this world felt—and how they talked and wrote—about the predicaments facing them, individually and collectively. Such stories, and the root metaphors they embody, form an undercurrent of meaning flowing beneath the surface of conventionally recounted history. What is so remarkable, even baffling, is that, in spite of their importance, Western students of twentieth-century China (including myself) have in the past shown little awareness of their existence. My hope is that, in this book, by focusing on one such story and the manifold ways in which it functioned over the course of a century, I have been able to convey some sense of what we have missed.

NOTES

In quoted material using the Wade-Giles system of romanization for Chinese names and terms, I have taken the liberty of substituting *pinyin* for the sake of readability.

PREFACE

1. Miller, *Timebends,* 348.

2. For an account of the process by which stories became elaborated in early China and continued to grow and change thereafter, see Owen, *An Anthology of Chinese Literature,* 88. Owen singles out as an example Wu Zixu, who happens to figure in important ways in the Goujian story.

3. In Joan of Arc's case, again, there is no stable text, and so, Mary Gordon tells us, there are as many renderings of her story in fiction, film, drama, and television as there are storytellers. *Joan of Arc,* 148–65.

4. On Lin, see Wen, "Lun Lin Zexu liufang shi de yongdian yishu," 89. On Zeng, see Xue, "Zeng Guofan wenhua ren'ge lun," 55. On Chiang, see chapter 2. For references to the Goujian story in poems left by immigrants at Angel Island, see Him Mark Lai et al., *Island,* 56, 124–25, 139, 143, 158, 160. On the identification of Chinese immigrants in the Philippines with the Goujian story, see "Kan Huashi lishiju *Yue wang Goujian.*"

5. The source of the fable is the Daoist text *Liezi.* "Yu gong yi shan," in *Guomin xiaoxue guoyu,* 4 (lesson 23): 65–66, and "Zengwenxi shuiku," in ibid.,

12 (lesson 6): 17–19; "Yu gong yi shan," in *Guomin zhongxue guowenke jiaokeshu,* 3 (lesson 15): 67–70.

6. An early discussion of this contemporary application of the story is in Mao's concluding speech at the Seventh National Congress of the Communist Party of China, delivered on June 11, 1945. See his "The Foolish Old Man Who Removed the Mountains," 3:321–24. For later references, see "Carry Out the Cultural Revolution Thoroughly and Transform the Educational System Completely," in *Peking Review,* June 24, 1966, 15–17; Liang and Shapiro, *Son of the Revolution,* 78, 175.

7. "In the present day," a commentator on historical drama observed in the early 1960s, "when the party has called on us to engage in arduous struggle *[jianku fendou]* and to work hard to strengthen the nation *[fafen tuqiang],* the story of King Goujian of Yue's sleeping on brushwood and tasting gall has appeal for large numbers of viewers." Wang Jisi, "Duo xiexie zheyang de lishi gushi xi," 121–22.

8. Bruner, *Making Stories,* 7, 34–35, 60.

1. THE GOUJIAN STORY IN ANTIQUITY

1. The fullest modern account of the life of Goujian is Yang Shanqun, *Yuewang Goujian xin zhuan* (1988); twice reprinted in Taiwan, first as *Woxin changdan* (1991), and subsequently as *Goujian* (1993). I use the 1991 Taiwan edition here.

2. It is reasonable to assume that all of the ancient sources on Goujian have some degree of fictional content, either deliberate or inadvertent. David Schaberg argues, with respect to the *Guoyu* and *Zuozhuan,* that although they "most certainly include a good deal of accurate information about the Spring and Autumn period, . . . that information is mixed with interested fictions, and it will never be possible to determine precisely where the fiction ends." *A Patterned Past,* 329 n. 36. For a similar argument, see Chu Binjie and Wang Hengzhan, "Lun xian Qin lishi sanwen zhong de xiaoshuo yinsu," 42–48.

3. The texts I've used are as follows: For *Shiji:* Nienhauser, *The Grand Scribe's Records,* vol. 7; Ssu-ma Ch'ien [Sima Qian], *Records of the Grand Historian of China;* Ssu-ma Ch'ien [Sima Qian], *Records of the Historian;* Szuma Chien [Sima Qian], *Selections from Records of the Historian;* and Takigawa, *Shiki kaichū kōshō.* For *Zuozhuan: The Ch'un Ts'ew with the Tso Chuen,* in Legge, trans., *The Chinese Classics,* vol. 5. For *Guoyu:* Lai Kehong, *Guoyu zhijie.* For *Lüshi chunqiu:* Knoblock and Riegel, *The Annals of Lü Buwei.*

4. Zhao Ye's original work, in twelve *juan,* no longer exists. There seems to be some degree of scholarly consensus that all editions now extant derive from a ten-*juan* edition compiled by the Shaoxing scholar Xu Tiangu (Hsü T'ien-ku) in 1306. See Johnson, "The Wu Tzu-hsü *Pien-wen* and Its Sources: Part I," 152–56; Zhou Shengchun, *Wu Yue chunqiu jijiao huikao,* introduction *(xulun),* 9–10; Huang Rensheng, *Xin yi Wu Yue chunqiu* (hereafter cited as *XYWYCQ*), reader's intro-

duction *(daodu)*, 2–13. The relationship of *The Annals of Wu and Yue* to *Zuozhuan*, *Guoyu*, and other earlier works is gone over in detail in the introduction to Lagerwey, "A Translation of *The Annals of Wu and Yüe*," 1–25. The parts of *The Annals of Wu and Yue* that have most concerned me are the last four *juan* (7–10), which center on Goujian. The first five *juan* look at the Wu-Yue rivalry mainly from the perspective of the state of Wu, while the focus of the sixth *juan* is the earlier (that is, pre-Goujian) history of the state of Yue. *The Annals of Wu and Yue* is described as "a highly fictionalized account" in Nienhauser, *The Indiana Companion to Traditional Chinese Literature*, 1:908. Lagerwey views the work as "utterly without significance as original history" and its author Zhao Ye as "the Sima Qian of historical romance" ("A Translation of *The Annals of Wu and Yüe*," iv, 20). Huang Rensheng, agreeing that *The Annals of Wu and Yue* contains a sizable amount of fictional material, regards it as China's earliest extant historical novel. See the long introductory essay on the text *(daodu)* in his *XYWYCQ*, 14–59; also his article "Lun *Wu Yue chunqiu* shi wo guo xiancun zuizao de wenyan changpian lishi xiaoshuo," 81–85. Zhou Shengchun, while not denying the inclusion of fictional elements in the modern edition of *The Annals of Wu and Yue*, insists that it nevertheless contains much of historical value in regard, for example, to agriculture, crafts, urban construction, politics, thought, military matters, and social customs in the Wu-Yue region (*Wu Yue chunqiu jijiao huikao*, introduction, 22–26). I have generally used Huang's edition of the work here but have also consulted—and sometimes found more persuasive—alternate readings in Zhang Jue, *Wu Yue chunqiu quanyi* (hereafter cited as *WYCQQY*).

5. Johnson, "Epic and History in Early China," 259. (Although Johnson's specific focus in this article is on the celebrated Wu official Wu Zixu, his observation also holds true of the work as a whole.)

6. Huang Rensheng lists a dozen examples of works from the Tang through the Qing that were heavily indebted to *The Annals of Wu and Yue* (*XYWYCQ*, reader's introduction, 59). Its impact on twentieth-century renderings of the Goujian story has repeatedly been made clear to me from my own reading; Xiao Jun, whose long fictional account of the story is dealt with in chapter 5, asserts that *The Annals of Wu and Yue* was his chief source (*Wu Yue chunqiu shihua*, vol. 1, preface, 2). Another work, *Yue jue shu*, although contemporary with *The Annals of Wu and Yue* and dealing with similar subject matter, appears to have been far less important in shaping later accounts of the story, perhaps, as Johnson notes, because it tends to be "disjointed and anecdotal," as compared to the "coherent and unified" character of *The Annals of Wu and Yue* ("The Wu Tzu-hsü *Pien-wen* and Its Sources: Part I," 129 n. 115). Lagerwey, who discusses *Yue jue shu* at length, regards *The Annals of Wu and Yue* as "by far the more interesting of the two books" ("A Translation of *The Annals of Wu and Yüe*," 196–97).

7. Although best known in Chinese historical drama and fiction for his alleged romance with the famous beauty Xi Shi, Fan Li (ca. 520–460 B.C.E.) was

one of the most respected political strategists of the late Spring and Autumn period. His political thought, the most reliable source for which is in the Yue volume of *Guoyu*, is discussed in Chang and Feng, *The Four Political Treatises of the Yellow Emperor*. For recent scholarly interest in Fan, see Zhou Guozhong, "Fuchu lishi dibiao de Fan Li," 9.

8. *XYWYCQ*, 211.

9. Ibid., 212–27.

10. Wu Zixu, although originally from the state of Chu, had moved to Wu in 522 B.C.E. and was the man largely responsible for Wu's military successes and domestic political well-being in the late sixth and early fifth centuries B.C.E. Sima Qian's biography of him (*juan* 66, memoir 6) has been translated in Nienhauser, *The Grand Scribe's Records*, 7:49–62; Owen, *An Anthology of Chinese Literature*, 88–96; and Ssu-ma Ch'ien, *Records of the Historian*, 16–29. See also the following three articles by David Johnson: "The Wu Tzu-hsü *Pien-wen* and Its Sources: Part I," 93–156; "The Wu Tzu-hsü *Pien-wen* and Its Sources: Part II," 465–505; and "Epic and History in Early China," 255–71.

11. *XYWYCQ*, 230–32.

12. Ibid., 234–36.

13. Ibid., 236–40.

14. A much less well-known instance of a Chinese who engaged in stool tasting for prognostic purposes was Guo Ba of the Tang. Guo's efforts, unlike Goujian's, backfired and he became an object of derision at the court of Empress Wu. See Yiren, "Goujian, Guo Ba zhi chang shi," 198–201. I am grateful to Wang Xi for bringing this reference to my notice. A son tasting his ill father's stool for prognostic purposes is commonly included in filial piety manuals. See, for example, Wang Miansan, *Huitu ershisi xiao*, 31–32.

15. *XYWYCQ*, 241–43 (quotations from 241–42).

16. Ibid., 244–52 (quotation from 246).

17. Ibid., 254–62.

18. Ibid., 262–64. There are variant accounts of the hardships to which Goujian subjected himself. See, for example, Knoblock and Riegel, *The Annals of Lü Buwei*, 211; Takigawa, *Shiki kaichū kōshō*, vol. 5, *juan* 41 ("Yue wang Goujian shijia"), 7. On the evolution of the phrase *woxin changdan* and its eventual linking up with the Goujian story, see Lu Jingkang, "'Woxin changdan' yuyuan kao," 21–22.

19. *XYWYCQ*, 264–68.

20. Ibid., 268–76.

21. The text of *Wu Yue chunqiu* says "five" years (*XYWYCQ*, 278), when the actual number should be three. Huang Rensheng (*XYWYCQ*, 279 n. 4) suggests that the discrepancy may be accounted for if the return to Yue is dated not from the termination of Goujian's captivity but from its inception (the fifth month of the fifth year of the Yue king's reign), which would bring the total to roughly

five years. For an alternative interpretation, calling attention to the fact that in ancient China "three," "five," "seven," and "nine" were often used to indicate "unreliable numbers" *(xushu)*, see *WYCQQY*, 340 n. 1.

22. *XYWYCQ*, 277–80.

23. Ibid., 280–84 (quotations from 281). Jiran's appraisal of the respective skills of Fan Li and Wen Zhong is exactly the reverse of Fan Li's own appraisal, conveyed to Goujian on the eve of his period of servitude in Wu. Goujian had originally intended to take Wen Zhong with him to Wu, leaving Fan Li to manage affairs in Yue. Fan Li, however, told him that whereas in military matters he was more skilled than Wen Zhong, in matters of governance Wen Zhong was the stronger. See Takigawa, *Shiki kaichū kōshō*, vol. 5, *juan* 41, 8 (and the English translation in Szuma Chien, *Selections from Records of the Historian*, 49).

24. *XYWYCQ*, 284–91. An alternative name for Gusu Palace was Guxu Palace. See ibid., 289 n. 43.

25. Jiran is referred to in some sources as Fan Li's teacher, which would suggest that he was a good deal older than indicated in *Wu Yue chunqiu*. For another account of his economic advice and the part it played in enriching the state of Yue, see Ssu-ma Ch'ien [Sima Qian], *Records of the Grand Historian of China*, 2:479–81. According to Sima Qian, after Goujian had followed Jiran's advice for ten years, Yue became so prosperous that he was "able to give generous gifts to his fighting men," as a result of which "his soldiers were willing to rush into the face of the arrows and stones of the enemy as though they were thirsty men going to drink their fill" (ibid.).

26. In numerous Chinese operas and fictional accounts, it is Fan Li whom Goujian sends on the search for beautiful women. Fan Li and Xi Shi fall in love, she is presented to Fuchai to divert him from his kingly responsibilities (a task that she fulfills with consummate skill), and eventually, after the destruction of Wu, the two lovers are reunited.

27. *XYWYCQ*, 295–99 (quotation from p. 296).

28. Ibid., 299–305. For a quite different account of the famine conditions first in Yue and later in Wu, see Knoblock and Riegel, *The Annals of Lü Buwei*, 320–21.

29. *XYWYCQ*, 305–9; also *WYCQQY*, 366–70.

30. *XYWYCQ*, 309–16.

31. There are differing accounts of the exact manner of Wu Zixu's death. In *Guoyu*, for instance, he draws his sword and commits suicide without prompting from Fuchai (Nienhauser, *The Grand Scribe's Records*, vol. 7, 57 n. 64). In the Wu Zixu memoir in *Shiji*, Wu, before cutting his throat, tells his houseman to pluck out his eyes and hang them above the east gate of the Wu capital, "so that I can watch the Yue invaders enter [the city] to destroy Wu" (ibid., 58); but in *Lüshi chunqiu*, it is Fuchai who tears out Wu Zixu's eyes (Knoblock and Riegel, *The Annals of Lü Buwei*, 595). Even in the same source there are sometimes

conflicting versions. In the Yue Yi memoir in *Shiji*, Fuchai is said to have drowned Wu Zixu in a leather bag in the river (Nienhauser, *The Grand Scribe's Records*, vol. 7, 259), whereas in the Wu Zixu memoir, the Wu king, enraged after hearing of Wu Zixu's final request to his houseman (above), had Wu's corpse placed in a wineskin and deposited in the river (ibid., 58). See also *Chan-kuo ts'e [Zhanguoce]*, 498 (in which Fuchai is said to have drowned Wu Zixu).

32. Much of the content of Goujian's account of his efforts in this vein is drawn from the "Yue yu" (Discourses of Yue) section of *Guoyu;* see Lai Kehong, *Guoyu zhijie*, 890–96.

33. Although working from the same original text as Huang Rensheng, Zhang Jue's reading of this passage—he understands it to say that Goujian put aside his responsibilities as ruler for three years (or, in the case of younger sons, three months) to stand vigil by the deceased son's coffin—differs sharply from Huang's and is not, to my mind, persuasive. See *WYCQQY*, 386.

34. I have followed Zhang Jue here. Although the original text states that no land tax had been collected for "seven" years, he argues convincingly that this is an error for "ten." He also differs from Huang Rensheng on the matter of Goujian's having "grown" the grain he consumed, Huang stating that Goujian "cooked" the grain he ate. *WYCQQY*, 384, 387.

35. *XYWYCQ*, 318–25.

36. There is some confusion in the original text here, as Fan Li had originally recommended that Goujian wait until the following spring and the Yue ruler had seemingly agreed to this. Huang Rensheng and Zhang Jue, both relying on *Zuozhuan* (Ai Gong 13) and in Huang's case *Shiji* (the chapter on the hereditary house of Wu) as well, agree that Fuchai's departure for Huangchi and Yue's attack on Wu occurred in the same year (Goujian 15). See *XYWYCQ*, 327 n. 3; *WYCQQY*, 390 n. 1.

37. *XYWYCQ*, 326–27.

38. Ibid., 328–33.

39. Ibid., 334–37.

40. Zhang Jue interprets this passage differently in two respects. The original refers to either a parent or a brother falling ill or dying. He regards this as a conventional phrase (and therefore to be understood as referring to parents only), on the grounds that Goujian's announcement is directed expressly to troops who have parents but are brotherless. On this point, I follow Zhang. But he also maintains that the phrase *zai junkou zhi zhong* in the original refers to Yue soldiers falling into the hands of the enemy, whereas Huang Rensheng understands it to have the more general meaning of Yue soldiers engaging the enemy in battle. Here I follow Huang, on the grounds that Zhang's rendering identifies only one among several wartime contingencies in a situation in which it would make more sense, logically speaking, for the Yue king to have in mind a range of possibilities (including not only capture by the enemy but also being

killed or wounded). Whatever the case, Goujian's statement that, in such circumstances, he will act as if the ill or deceased parent were his own parent is clearly not meant to be taken literally. See *WYCQQY*, 404, translation and notes 3–4. According to Han Feizi, Goujian's compassionate treatment of his men was not without ulterior motive; see *Han Fei Tzu*, 86, where Han Feizi writes: "The charioteer Wang Liang was good to his horses, and Goujian, the king of Yue, was good to his men, the one so that they would run for him, the other so that they would fight for him."

41. *XYWYCQ*, 337–41.

42. Ibid., 341–45; for more on Wu Zixu's death and "afterlife," see note 31 of this chapter.

43. Although, according to *Wu Yue chunqiu*, the war lasted for only one year, this is in error. See *XYWYCQ*, 347 n. 1; also *WYCQQY*, 411 n. 1.

44. *XYWYCQ*, 345–48.

45. The original text used by Huang Rensheng (ibid., 348) makes no reference to Goujian's being proclaimed overlord. See *WYCQQY*, 413, and the explanatory note (6) on 414.

46. I follow Zhang Jue here; ibid., 415–17.

47. Fan Li is often referred to as having floated off on the "three rivers and five lakes" (see, for example, chapter 3). For an interesting discussion of the meaning of the "rivers and lakes" imagery, see Hanchao Lu, *Street Criers*, 13–14. According to an account in *Shiji*, Fan Li went to Tao, a major center of commerce, assumed another identity, and became a successful businessman, but he remained a man of virtue and compassion. "Three times," the account reads, "he accumulated fortunes of a thousand catties of gold, and twice he gave them away among his poor friends and distant relations. This is what is meant by a rich man who delights in practicing virtue." Ssu-ma Ch'ien [Sima Qian], *Records of the Grand Historian of China*, 2:481. Elsewhere, in *Shiji*, Sima Qian implies that Fan Li, like Wen Zhong (see below in text), was rewarded by Goujian with death. Ibid., 1:226. What exactly became of Fan Li after his departure from Yue is not clear. For a discussion of the various possibilities, see Yang Shanqun, *Woxin changdan*, 163–64. Yang claims that Fan Li left Yue around 470 B.C.E., not (as stated in *Wu Yue chunqiu*) in 473.

48. *XYWYCQ*, 348–57; also *WYCQQY*, 414–25.

49. *XYWYCQ*, 357–64.

50. This could not have actually happened, as Confucius had died in 479 B.C.E., seven years earlier.

51. *XYWYCQ*, 364–69. *Wu Yue chunqiu* states (ibid., 368) that Goujian died in the twenty-seventh year of his reign, which would be 470 B.C.E. Most sources give 465 B.C.E. as the correct date. See Ssu-ma Ch'ien [Sima Qian], *Records of the Grand Historian of China*, 2:479; Nienhauser, *The Grand Scribe's Records*, vol. 7, 55; Yang Shanqun, *Woxin changdan*, 167–68; *WYCQQY*, 437 n. 1.

52. *Mo Tzu,* 48. For other versions of the same story, see Chan, *A Source Book in Chinese Philosophy,* 215; Knoblock and Riegel, *The Annals of Lü Buwei,* 490.

53. This incident is recounted in both the "Yue wang Goujian shijia" chapter of *Shiji* (see Takigawa, *Shiki kaichū kōshō,* vol. 5, *juan* 41, 3), and the *Zuozhuan,* under "Lu Ding gong" (Duke Ding of Lu) fourteenth year (see *The Ch'un Ts'ew with the Tso Chuen,* 786). For a translation of the *Shiji* account, see Szuma Chien, *Selections from Records of the Historian,* 47.

54. Ssu-ma Ch'ien [Sima Qian], *Records of the Grand Historian of China,* 1:227.

55. In Lagerwey's view, revenge is the unifying theme of the two parts of *The Annals of Wu and Yue,* the revenge of a son (Wu Zixu) in the first part and that of a king (Goujian) in the second. "A Translation of *The Annals of Wu and Yüeh,*" 25.

56. Nienhauser, *The Grand Scribe's Records,* vol. 7, 54; an alternative version is noted in ibid., 54 n. 45. See also Knoblock and Riegel, *The Annals of Lü Buwei,* 312–13.

57. On the variety of motives driving revenge in Chinese history and literature, see Guan Wu, "*Liaozhai zhiyi* fuchou zhuti qianlun," 40–44; Shang and Zhao, "Juewangzhe de fankang shenhua," 58–62; Du Songbo, "*Shiji* zhong de fuchou gushi chulun," 41–46.

58. The Song writer-official Su Shi (Su Dongpo), in an essay on enduring or forbearing *(ren),* observed: "When Goujian was surrounded at Kuaiji, he went as a slave to Wu and toiled there for three years without ever tiring in his determination. Those who would avenge themselves upon others but who are unable to submit to others have only the resolve of ordinary fellows. . . . The causes of Gaozu [Liu Bang]'s eventual victory and of Xiang Yu's eventual defeat lie precisely in this difference between being able and being unable to forbear." Egan, *Word, Image, and Deed in the Life of Su Shi,* 23–24.

59. Ssu-ma Ch'ien [Sima Qian], *Records of the Grand Historian of China,* 1:209, 228.

60. "No other intellectual in Chinese history," Vera Schwarcz writes, "paid so great a price for his commitment to the transmission of collective memory." *Bridge across Broken Time,* 102.

61. The letter to Ren [Jen] An is excerpted in de Bary and Bloom, *Sources of Chinese Tradition,* 2nd ed., 371–72. A full translation of the letter (by J. R. Hightower) is in Birch, *Anthology of Chinese Literature,* 95–102.

62. Nienhauser, *The Grand Scribe's Records,* vol. 7, 50, 60.

63. Kai-yu Hsu, *Chou En-lai,* 68–69. Han Suyin, in her account of the same incident, suggests that when Zhou made his remarks to Liu Ning he may well have had in mind the story of Han Xin, which he knew well from childhood. See her *Eldest Son,* 88 (and, on Han Xin, 16–17). The sensitivity to crawling as a self-demeaning act occurs again in an incident recounted by Mao Zedong's personal physician Li Zhisui. At an early point in the Cultural Revolution, ac-

cording to Li, Zhou and Mao met to plan one of the gatherings of the Red Guards in Tiananmen Square. In order to explain his ideas for dealing with the problem of crowd control, Zhou spread a map on the floor and knelt on the carpet to show Mao the direction the motorcade would take. Li continues with his account: "Mao stood, smoking a cigarette, watching Zhou crawl on the floor. For Zhou to kneel before Mao seemed to me humiliating, and I was deeply embarrassed to see a man of Zhou's stature, the premier of China, behave that way." Mao, however, "seemed to take a sardonic pleasure watching Zhou crawl before him," and, ironically, "because Zhou was so subservient and loyal, Mao held the premier in contempt." This incident, trivial in itself, was emblematic of Zhou's willingness (at least in the eyes of Li Zhisui) to subordinate his own pride and dignity for the sake of preserving his relationship with Mao, which in turn was seen by him as an essential precondition to any benefit he might bring to China. Li, *The Private Life of Chairman Mao,* 509–10.

64. Goujian, Han Xin, Sima Qian, and Zhou Enlai all exemplified the worldly understanding of forbearance. The Buddhist understanding was quite different. For an interesting comparison of the two, see Gao, "Shisu renru guan yu Fojiao de renru guan," 8–14.

2. THE BURDEN OF NATIONAL HUMILIATION

1. National humiliation days were by no means the only anniversaries observed during this time. There were also holidays of a more celebratory nature (such as the anniversary of the 1911 Revolution), days of national mourning (notably the anniversary of the death of Sun Yat-sen), and so on. Twenty-five such days are covered in *Gezhong jinianri shilüe*. On the entire range of national anniversaries and the ways in which they were observed, see Harrison, *The Making of the Republican Citizen.*

2. A major example of such thinking was the reformer, pioneer journalist, and contemporary European affairs commentator Wang Tao. According to Wang, the late Zhou–contemporary Europe analogy was first used by Zhang Sigui in his preface (1864) to W. A. P. Martin's translation of Henry Wheaton's *Elements of International Law (Wanguo gongfa)*. Cohen, *Between Tradition and Modernity,* 93–94, 294–95 nn. 2, 5. The analogy was used by many other Chinese as well in the late Qing. See, for example, Guo Songtao, in Hamilton, "Kuo Sung-tao," 12; Yan Fu, in Schwartz, "The Chinese Perception of World Order," 278–79.

3. See, for example, the treaty of September 26, 1815, which set up the Holy Alliance and in which the signatories (the kings of Austria, Prussia, and Russia) refer to themselves as "members of one and the same Christian nation" called upon by Providence to govern "three branches of the One family." In Hertslet, *The Map of Europe by Treaty,* 1:318.

4. As Richard Walker put it: "The moral code of the former Zhou feudal age

had meaning only when it added to the power and prestige of the state which claimed to adhere to it. The ritual framework of the feudal tradition could at times serve as a code of conduct for the individual states, but this code carried little weight unless power considerations argued in favor of adherence." *The Multi-State System of Ancient China*, 99. For further insight into the parallels between the contemporary West and late Zhou—and the power realities implicit in all multistate systems—see Frodsham, *The First Chinese Embassy to the West*, xxiv–xxv.

5. Lei, "The Warring States (473–221 B.C.)." See also Chang and Feng, *The Four Political Treatises of the Yellow Emperor*, 16–17.

6. Fangshi, "Lun xue guochou yi xian li guochi," 65–67.

7. The leading late Qing official Zeng Guofan, citing Goujian as a model, adhered to something very close to this pattern. See Xue, "Zeng Guofan wenhua ren'ge lun," 55.

8. Guo Songtao had once expressed amazement at the palpable lack of indignation felt by his countrymen against the Western importation of opium. Xiao Gongquan [Hsiao Kung-ch'üan], *Zhongguo zhengzhi sixiang shi*, 5:684–85. The awakening of national shame was a frequent theme in *Ziqiang zhai baofu xingguo lun chubian*, compiled by Wang Tao shortly before his death in 1897. To Liang Qichao, at the beginning of the twentieth century, "it seemed as though the Chinese could look with equanimity on foreign invasion." Levenson, *Liang Ch'ich'ao and the Mind of Modern China*, 111.

9. Kexuan, "Guochi pian," 221–27.

10. Early sources for this account are reviewed in Shaughnessy, "Western Zhou History," 299–307. See also Takigawa, *Shiki kaichū kōshō*, vol. 1, *juan* 4 *(Zhou benji)*, 6–10; *Ciyuan*, 1:460.

11. Another late Qing instance of terse classical allusion to the Goujian story, emphasizing the themes of humiliation, long-term planning (there are multiple allusions to this, including the wise strategic advice Wen Zhong rendered "the king of Yue"), and revenge, is found in the text accompanying an anti-Christian poster circulated in the lower Yangzi region in the late 1880s and early 1890s. Titled "Qin pi changdan" (Resting on skins and tasting gall), it is no. 25 in a series of such posters titled *Jinzun shengyu bixie quantu*.

12. Although Kexuan clearly wasn't thinking in such terms, the dramatic reversal of fortune found in both the Taiwang and Goujian stories also resonates with the Daoist view of life as a process of unending and ineluctable change— and hence a source of assurance, in the bleakest of times, that things will eventually get better. The Western Han poet Jia Yi (201–169 B.C.E.), at a troubled moment in his own life, composed (in 174 or 173 B.C.E.) a famous *fu*, "The Owl," in which he expressed this point of view and in so doing alluded to the hopeful trajectory of the Goujian story:

Good luck must be followed by bad;
Bad in turn bow to good.
Sorrow and joy throng the gate;
Weal and woe in the same land.
Wu was powerful and great;
Under Fuchai it sank in defeat.
Yue was crushed at Kuaiji,
But Goujian made it an overlord.

The translation of "The Owl," here excerpted, is Burton Watson's, found in his *Early Chinese Literature*, 256–57. Another translation (by J. R. Hightower) is in Birch, *Anthology of Chinese Literature*, 138–40.

13. An editorial of April 25, 1895, in the Shanghai newspaper *Shenbao*, written a week after the signing of the Treaty of Shimonoseki and sharply critical of the territorial ambitions of Japan, cited the paired early examples of Taiwang and Goujian, both of whom had yielded to greater strength for a time before finally asserting themselves and triumphing. During the campaign against Russian designs on Manchuria in the first years of the twentieth century, there were periodic references in the Chinese press to the Goujian story, which was seen as embodying the spirit Chinese needed to resist Russian claims. See Yang Tianshi and Wang Xuezhuang, *Ju E yundong, 1901–1905*, 17 (*Zhong-wai ribao*, Aug. 26, 1901), 18 (*Zhong-wai ribao*, Mar. 27, 1901), 25 (*Zhong-wai ribao*, Mar. 30, 1901), 152 (*Da gong bao*, May 11–12, 1903), 296 (*Jiangsu*, June 25, 1903). My thanks to Matthias Zachmann for the *Shenbao* reference and to Anne Chao for the references relating to the anti-Russian campaign.

14. I have consulted the reprint edition of Li Liangcheng's *Rexue hen*, 1–225. Li's work, replete with the tales of marvelous feats characteristic of knight-errant fiction, pays special attention to Chen Yin, Wei Xi, and other commoner martial arts specialists, elaborating on the references to such persons found in *Wu Yue chunqiu* (see chapter 1).

15. Croizier, *Koxinga and Chinese Nationalism*, 50–52.

16. The revolutionary Zhang Binglin, for one, "singled out Yue Fei as deserving of emulation because he 'employed southern troops to defeat the barbarians.'" Feigon, *Chen Duxiu*, 78. The violence of the anti-Manchu rhetoric of late Qing revolutionaries is discussed in Zarrow, "Historical Trauma," 67–107. I have followed the translation of Yue Fei's poem found in Wilhelm, "From Myth to Myth," 156. On Yue Fei, see also Mote, *Imperial China 900–1800*, 299–307. Mote notes the questions that have been raised by scholars concerning the authenticity of Yue Fei's famous *ci* (ibid., 305, 997–98 n. 25).

17. The Yue wang hui was cofounded by Bo Wenwei. There is some information on the organization in Feigon, *Chen Duxiu*, 76–77, 79–81; Kuo, *Ch'en Tu-hsiu (1879–1942) and the Chinese Communist Movement*, 31–33, 36–37. The

phrase *Yue wang* (literally, "King Yue") refers to the deified Yue Fei. The cult of Yue Fei emerged during the Yuan dynasty, and state shrines to him flourished during the Ming, especially after the Mongol invasions of 1449 (Mote, *Imperial China,* 304–5). Yue was buried at a site known today as the Yue Fei Temple (Yue wang [or Yue Fei] miao). It is situated at the northwest edge of West Lake in Hangzhou and was made into a state-protected cultural site in 1961. The site's later history, during and after the Cultural Revolution, is recounted in Sun and Huang, "Yue Fei xushu," 97–98.

18. A biography of Zheng is in Hummel, *Eminent Chinese of the Ch'ing Period,* 1:108–10. For a 1930s children's story recounting Zheng's liberation of Taiwan from the Dutch, see "Zheng Chenggong," 7:40–41. A fuller five-part account of Zheng's heroic achievements is in the Beiping newspaper *Shibao* (The truth post), Mar. 17–22, 1934.

19. A biography of Ch'i Chi-kuang [Qi Jiguang] is in Goodrich and Fang, *Dictionary of Ming Biography, 1368–1644,* 1:220–24; there is an extended discussion of his career in Ray Huang, *1587, a Year of No Significance,* 156–88; for a children's story about Qi Jiguang's apotheosis as nationalist hero, see Jiafan, "Guang bing," 2–4.

20. Shi Kefa was transformed by late Qing revolutionaries into an exemplar of racial nationalism. Ko-wu Huang, "Remembering Shi Kefa." There is a biography of him (under Shih K'o-fa) in Hummel, *Eminent Chinese of the Ch'ing Period,* 2:651–52; for an appraisal of the heroism of Wen Tianxiang, see Mote, "Confucian Eremitism in the Yüan Period," 233–34.

21. Mote, *Imperial China,* 305; Ruhlmann, "Traditional Heroes in Chinese Popular Fiction," 154. For an overview of writings of the 1930s and 1940s portraying Yue Fei as a national hero, see Sun and Huang, "Yue Fei xushu," 91–92. On the promotion of Yue Fei as a patriotic symbol after the Mukden Incident, see Huang Donglan, "Yue Fei miao," 168, 172.

22. Mote, *Imperial China,* 305.

23. At the fourth national congress of the Guomindang in November 1931, Chiang made a point of urging those in attendance to emulate Yue Fei in his loyalty and devotion to the national cause. Sun and Huang, "Yue Fei xushu," 96.

24. This kind of identification, borrowed from Stalinist Russia, was widely practiced according to Wagner in the historical dramas of the late 1950s in China. My clear impression is that the linkage can be extended beyond written literary works to the functioning of stories in political society generally. See Wagner, "'In Guise of a Congratulation,'" 71.

25. For the locus classicus of *guochi* and a brief account of the difference between its ancient and modern meanings, see Dai Yi's preface in Zhuang, *Guochi shidian,* 1; see also Liang Yiqun's introduction in Liang Yiqun et al., *Yibaige guochi jinian ri,* 1–2.

26. In a frequently reprinted biography of Zheng Chenggong written by a

Chinese student in Japan at the turn of the twentieth century, the "constantly recurring theme," according to Croizier, is "patriotic inspiration and national shame." Echoing the complaints of Fangshi, Kexuan, and others, Croizier adds that in the writings of student nationalists at the time, Zheng's "heroic patriotic deeds and spirit are contrasted with the shameful inertness of contemporary Chinese." *Koxinga and Chinese Nationalism,* 51–53.

27. On the relationship of Chinese nationalism to the Twenty-One Demands, see Luo Zhitian, "National Humiliation and National Assertion," 297–319. The Japanese side of the Twenty-One Demands is dealt with in Jansen, *Japan and China,* 209–23; for Yuan Shikai's response, see Young, *The Presidency of Yuan Shikai,* 186–92.

28. "Yuan Shikai bei po jieshou Riben tichu de 'ershiyi tiao,'" vol. 2, May 1915.

29. See Rankin, "Nationalistic Contestation and Mobilization Politics," 315–61.

30. Chinese lack of staying power was also addressed in connection with the anti-American boycott of 1905. Initially, according to one writer, newspapers were filled with coverage of boycott activities, but the spirit of Chinese protest proved unsustainable *(buneng chijiu)* and by the summer of 1906 there was not a single reference to it in the press. See He Xin Shi Shou, "Neng shuo buneng xing," 8. I am grateful to Jing Tsu for furnishing me with a copy of this article.

31. For detailed accounts, see Luo Zhitian, "National Humiliation and National Assertion," 300–309; Gerth, "Consumption as Resistance," 132–42.

32. Although eventually a multiplicity of national humiliation days were recognized and observed in China, initially there was only one National Humiliation Day, sometimes identified as May 7, sometimes as May 9. For a full discussion of the confusion over the correct date, see Cohen, "Remembering and Forgetting National Humiliation," 26–27 n. 13.

33. Zhichishe, *Guochi,* 16 (*Wu yue jiu ri hou zhi quanguo yuqing*). See also Chow, *The May Fourth Movement,* 22; Tyau, *China Awakened,* 141.

34. Hou, "Guoxue guochi laoku san da zhuyi biao li," 23–26 *(zazuan).*

35. Hou, "Shu Jiangsu sheng xiaozhang huiyi zhi gailüe," 54 *(tebie jishi).*

36. Luo Zhitian, "National Humiliation and National Assertion," 311–12.

37. For a fuller account of contemporary anxiety in regard to the Chinese people's "precious 'ability to forget'" (to cite the memorable words of Lu Xun), see Cohen, "Remembering and Forgetting National Humiliation," 4–17.

38. As an example, a patriotic children's song of 1930, entitled simply "Do Not Forget" ("Buyao wangji") and written apparently by someone from Shandong, concludes with the following line: "Buoy up our spirits, Unite in a common effort, Sleeping on brushwood and tasting gall *[woxin changdan],* Let us vow to destroy our enemies!" "Buyao wangji," 6.

39. The situation was rather like that relating to the memory of the Boxers in the 1920s. When the *North-China Herald* and *North-China Daily News* described the anti-imperialist activities of 1925–1927 as "antiforeign," "xenophobic," "sav-

age," and "irrational," Jeffrey Wasserstrom has argued, they used these terms as code words that clearly invoked the phantom of the Boxers without having to refer to the Boxers directly. Wasserstrom, "The Boxers as Symbol," 20. See also Cohen, *History in Three Keys*, 252.

40. Quoted from *The Living Age* 326 (Sept. 1, 1925): 241, in Wasserstrom, "The Boxers as Symbol," 20.

41. See Cohen, *History in Three Keys*, 251–54.

42. *Woxin changdan*, 15a-b. Zhonghua shuju issued a fifth printing of this story in 1932.

43. *Shimin qianzi ke*, 20th ed. (Jan. 1929); in the front matter *(gaibian jiyao)* of vol. 1 of the 46th ed. of June 1929, in which the main changes in this edition are spelled out, the compilers state that more than 3 million copies of the original edition had been printed. I am grateful to Jeffrey Wasserstrom for bringing this item to my attention.

44. In another mass education movement primer, there is a lesson on Fan Li, which briefly summarizes the Goujian story but makes no reference to the issue of national humiliation in the twentieth century. See "Fan Dafu," in *Pingmin qianzi ke*, 3:4–5.

45. *Shimin qianzi ke*, 20th ed., 2:53.

46. *Shimin qianzi ke*, 46th ed., vol. 1, front matter.

47. *War and Popular Culture*, 51–2. On Xiong Foxi, see also Hayford, *To the People;* his biography (under the spelling Hsiung Fo-hsi) is in Boorman, *Biographical Dictionary of Republican China*, 2:106–8; Chen Duo et al., *Xiandai xijujia Xiong Foxi.*

48. An editorial of 1933 in a Beiping daily, for example, after comparing China's efforts over the previous eighteen years unfavorably with what Goujian had been able to achieve in ten, stated: "Do we still have the face today to continue talking about 'avenging humiliation'? From this point forward we must not hear any more empty calls for 'avenging humiliation' and loud shouts of '*woxin changdan.*' If we want to keep our country from being reduced to slavery, our only choice is to put our shoulders to the wheel and be prepared to make any and all sacrifices, going all out against the enemy regardless of the danger." "Jinian 'wujiu' guochi," *Shibao* (The truth post), May 9, 1933, 1.

49. See the biography of the movement's leader, Yen Yang-ch'u (Yan Yangchu), in Boorman, *Biographical Dictionary of Republican China*, 4:53.

50. Xiong Foxi, *Woxin changdan*, in *Foxi xiju*, Series 4, 185–88. Some of the same themes are repeated in a conversation Goujian has with Fan Li, shortly after the exchange with his wife. Where, in most renderings of the Goujian story, it is the Yue king who is impatient to take revenge on Wu and Fan Li who counsels him not to be in such a hurry, in Xiong's play these roles are reversed. "We should put more into strengthening ourselves," Goujian tells Fan Li, "and less into shouting about overthrowing *[dadao]* others" (ibid., 188–89).

51. In a clear departure from conventional renderings of the Goujian story, the other famous beauty, Xi Shi, does not appear in the play at all.

52. Xiong Foxi, *Woxin changdan*, 191–202 (quotes from 193, 196).

53. Ibid., 208.

54. "Xiazi," in *Shimin qianzi ke*, 46th ed., 1:5.

55. Chiang, *China's Destiny and Chinese Economic Theory*, 164. Many readers will note the similarity to Mao Zedong's famous characterization of the Chinese people as being like "a clean sheet of paper," on which "the newest and most beautiful words can be written . . . [and] the newest and most beautiful pictures . . . painted." Mao, "China Is Poor and Blank," Apr. 15, 1958, 253.

56. "Yue wang Goujian," in *Xiaoxuexiao chuji yong guoyu duben*, 7:42–43.

57. *Woxin changdan de Yue wang Goujian*, 23. I have also seen the third printing of this booklet, identical to the first, and published in July 1948.

58. Ibid., 12, 21, 33, 29, 23, 35 (in order of the references in the text).

59. David Schaberg has much of interest to say about this characteristic of early Chinese historiography. Focusing on the *Zuozhuan* and *Guoyu* in particular, he maintains that "the perspective dominating the anecdotes [in these works] is that not of rulers but of ministers." See his *A Patterned Past*, 7.

60. In all of the republican-era accounts of the Goujian story that I have seen, I have only encountered one or two exceptions to this pattern. One, to be discussed later in this chapter, is Wei Juxian's book of 1944, entitled *Goujian*. Another is a short piece by Zhiqing, published in 1934, and noted in chapter 6, n. 61. Significantly, in both of these instances, the author, while touching on the dark side of Goujian's character, explicitly subordinates this aspect of the story to the king's achievement in revitalizing Yue and consummating his revenge mission against Wu.

61. *Shenbao*, May 7, 1925, 12; May 8, 1925, 12; May 9, 1925, 12; May 10, 1925, 18; May 11, 1925, 17; May 9, 1926, 19. See also *Shibao* (The eastern times), May 7, 8, 9, 10, 11, and 12, 1925; *Shishi xinbao* (China times), May 8, 9, and 10, 1925; May 9, 1926.

62. Ping, "Jinri zhi ri," *Shibao* (The eastern times), May 11, 1915, 5.

63. Tang, "Quanguo sheng jiaoyuhui diyici lianhehui jilüe," 39–40 *(tebie jishi)*. Other examples of very brief allusions to the Goujian story are Liu Shisun, "Guochi guangshuo," *Dagongbao* (Changsha), May 7, 1925, special section on May 7 (*Wuqi zhuanhao*) (calls on his *woxin changdan* compatriots to realize the true meaning of national humiliation by marking it every day of the year, not just on May 7); Daguan, "Wu qi guochi hu wu jiu guochi hu?" *Shenbao*, May 7, 1926, 19 (notes that although there is a lack of consensus on the date for the marking of National Humiliation Day, proponents of both the May 7 and May 9 dates, in their commitment to not forgetting past humiliation, embody the same *woxin changdan* psychology); Li Dichen, "Xuechi," *Shenbao*, May 10, 1928, 17 (emulating various models from the Chinese past, including Goujian's *woxin*

changdan, Chinese must think about avenging themselves constantly and not limit their sense of shame to a single anniversary day); Fugong, "Fuxin chang-dan zhi jiuyiba," *Shijie ribao* (The world morning post), Sept. 18, 1932, 9 (compatriots must work tirelessly *[changdan woxin]* to correct China's defects, and so lay the basis for "the destruction of Wu" *[zhao Wu],* which here refers to Japan); Zhao Jingyuan, "Cong jiuyiba guonan shuodao yige hao bangyang," 1–4 (counsels young readers, in responding to the Mukden Incident, to immerse themselves in the hard work of "sleeping on brushwood and tasting gall" and "vowing to eradicate the national humiliation," as Germany has done in the wake of Versailles); *Shijie ribao,* Sept. 18, 1933, special number on anniversary of the Mukden Incident (references throughout to *woxin changdan*); "Wusan, wusi, wuwu, wuqi," *Dagongbao* (Tianjin), May 5, 1934, 2–3 (Chinese must take a sincere vow to "spend ten years building up the economy and ten years training the military" *[shi nian shengju shi nian jiaoxun]*); Xiong Mengfei, "Jiuyiba san zhounian," *Shijie ribao,* Sept. 18, 1934, 9 (refers in poem to *zhao Wu* [the destruction of Wu], here denoting Japan).

64. Jia Fengzhen, "Zhong-Ri jiaoshe hou zhi jiaoyuguan," 155–56.

65. "Xuesheng zonghui xuanyan," *Shishi xinbao,* May 10, 1924 (under "Ge xuexiao").

66. [Cheng] Shewo, "Ji'nan can'an guoren ying tong ding si tong," *Minsheng bao,* May 12, 1928, 1.

67. Liang Qichao, "Di shidu de 'Wuqi,'" *Shishi xinbao,* May 7, 1925.

68. Zuming, "Guochi jinianri ganyan," *Shenbao,* May 9, 1921, 18. For other complaints about the short-lived nature of Chinese enthusiasm or fervor in connection with the May 9 (or May 7) anniversary, see Cohen, "Remembering and Forgetting National Humiliation in Twentieth-Century China," 33 n. 45. Also *Shishi xinbao,* May 9, 1925, section 3, 4 (cartoon); Shu, "Wuyue jiuri," *Shishi xinbao,* May 9, 1925, Shanghai section; Yuan Erti, "'Wuqi' yu 'wuqi,'" *Dagongbao* (Tianjin), May 7, 1927, 8; Liu Chenlie, "Wusan Ri bing tusha ge," *Minsheng bao,* May 9, 1928, 4; Shangyi, "Guochi jinian shuo wusan," *Minsheng bao,* May 10, 1928, 4.

69. Liuquan, "Guochi dao," *Shenbao,* May 9, 1924, 18.

70. Zhou Wenqi, "Guochi jinianri jingguo zhi ganxiang," *Shenbao,* May 11, 1921, 16.

71. Bu Wenxun, "Guochi ri gai chi sucai de wo jian," *Shenbao,* May 8, 1922, 20.

72. Despite the English title "New Youth," this magazine is not to be confused with the famous New Culture Movement journal *Xin qingnian,* which was also known in English as "New Youth." *Xin shaonian* first appeared in January 1936. Edited by Ye Shengtao and Feng Zikai, it was published by the Kaiming shudian in Shanghai.

73. Feng Zikai, "Jiu yiba zhi ye," 62–65.

74. Hung, *War and Popular Culture,* 136.

75. According to Jiang Tiejun, the director of the Whampoa Military Academy Memorial, the city of Guangzhou sought, in its restoration, to achieve the greatest possible fidelity to the original building complex. Mitchell, "Chiang: The Patriot," 13.

76. There is a colored photograph of the restored entrance of the academy in Mitchell's "Chiang: The Patriot." For photographs of the original entrance, see Zhongguo geming bowuguan, *Huangpu junxiao shi tuce*, 59, 60, 78, 79.

77. News account in *Shenbao*, May 10, 1928, 6.

78. The Northern Expedition had resumed its northward advance in December 1927. Since its route passed through Shandong, the Japanese government, on the pretext of protecting Japanese nationals and interests in the province, sent in troops, and these initiated hostilities with the Chinese army in Ji'nan on May 3. This was not a confrontation sought by Chiang Kai-shek, and defying strong anti-Japanese sentiment within the party and military establishment (not to mention the Chinese public at large) he ordered the withdrawal of Chinese forces from Ji'nan. Coble, *Facing Japan*, 19–21.

79. *Shenbao*, May 9, 1929, 6.

80. Ibid., May 10, 1929, 7.

81. Ibid., May 9, 1931, 13.

82. The book's lead foldout consists of an excerpt from the fourth article of the National Government's *Outline for National Reconstruction (Jianguo dagang)*, accompanied by a portrait of Sun Yat-sen, *Guochi tu*.

83. This would not, of course, apply to the crown of thorns, which many Chinese at the time probably would not have been able to decipher. See the second foldout, entitled "Guochi zhonglei biao," *Guochi tu*.

84. Yang Tianshi, in a fine article that illuminates the Chiang-Goujian connection and is the basis for much of the ensuing discussion, notes that because Chiang was a Zhejiang native he knew the Goujian story well. My own sense, as earlier argued, is that the Goujian story was widely disseminated throughout China during the republican era (and before) and would likely have been well known to Chiang regardless of his personal geographical origins. Yang Tianshi, "Lugouqiao shibian qian Jiang Jieshi de dui-Ri moulüe," 8. This article is reprinted in Yang Tianshi, *Jiang shi midang yu Jiang Jieshi zhenxiang*, 377–403. See also Xiao Hua, "1927–1937 nian Jiang Jieshi kang-Ri sixiang de xingcheng ji qi tedian," 72–73, 76.

85. Chiang's attraction to and identification with Goujian are emphasized in a number of papers by Grace Huang, which she wrote when she was a doctoral candidate at the University of Chicago. See her "Laying on Brushwood and Tasting Gall" and "Avenging National Humiliation."

86. The operations of the Political Indoctrination Department, which was part of the Military Affairs Commission, are discussed in Wakeman, *Spymaster*, 113–16.

87. The version I have seen was the vernacular one: He Jinghuang, "Yue wang Goujian," 49–55. The Nanchang Field Headquarters' connection with the compilation is spelled out in an editorial note (ibid., 49). I am grateful to Robert Culp for bringing this publication to my notice.

88. Van de Ven, "New States of War," 366–71.

89. Yang Tianshi, "Lugouqiao shibian qian Jiang Jieshi de dui-Ri moulüe," 10. Chiang's manuscript diary is in the Number Two Historical Archives in Nanjing. It is suggestive of the versatility of the Goujian story that it also had a profound influence on General Yang Hucheng, who, unlike Chiang Kai-shek, favored resistance to Japan after the Mukden Incident and was a lead participant in the kidnapping of the Guomindang leader in Xi'an in December 1936. Wu Changyi, "Yang Hucheng yu Jiang Jieshi," 4–7; Cao Yongjin, "Yang Hucheng de aiguo jingshen ji qi shenghua," 58.

90. Shu Yin, "Zai wutaishang de rensheng *(shang)*," 56–57.

91. Entry dated Sept. 20, 1931, as cited in Yang Tianshi, "Lugouqiao shibian qian Jiang Jieshi de dui-Ri moulüe," 8. After meeting with a Japanese military officer on January 30, 1934, Chiang wrote in his diary: "His contemptuousness was plainly visible in his expression. If we don't forbear and put up with temporary difficulties *[woxin changdan]*, how are we to revive the nation?" Ibid.

92. Diary entry dated Sept. 28, 1931, as cited in Yang Tianshi, "Jiuyiba shibianhou de Jiang Jieshi," 352.

93. Diary entry dated Feb. 14, 1934, as cited in Yang, "Lugouqiao shibian qian Jiang Jieshi de dui-Ri moulüe," 8.

94. Diary entry dated Feb. 15–16, 1934, as cited in ibid., 9.

95. Ibid., 9–10.

96. Quoted in Chiang, *China's Destiny*, 123.

97. Jiang Jieshi [Chiang Kai-shek], *Zhongguo zhi mingyun*, 149. In subsequent years, Chiang regularly alluded to the Goujian story in his speeches. See, for example, "Nuli wancheng xunzheng daye" (May 17, 1931), 618–19; "Jiao yang wei" (Feb. 12, 1934), 804–5.

98. Chiang's talk was excerpted in Zeng Die, "Yue wang Goujian zuo feiji," 19.

99. Eastman, "Nationalist China during the Nanking Decade, 1927–1937," 160–62.

100. Eastman, *The Abortive Revolution*, 28.

101. Zou Lu, "Ning fu fei Goujian qie bu pei wei Qin Gui," 45–46.

102. Edited by a Communist, Cong Dezi, the paper was published every ten days under the auspices of the Xi'an army headquarters of Zhang Xueliang and Yang Hucheng, two Nationalist commanders who favored immediate resistance against Japan. In the wake of the Xi'an Incident of December 1936, in which both Zhang and Yang played key roles, the Nationalists shut the paper down. Zhao Jiabi, "Zufu: Guan Jigang."

103. Lin Guanghan, "Wo wei Goujian, ren fei Fuchai," 3–8. Two items written in response to Lin's article were an unsigned piece titled "Du 'Wo wei Goujian, ren fei Fuchai' yihou," 25–27, and Chen Fudan, "Du 'Wo wei Goujian, ren fei Fuchai' ganyan," 27–28. Although the interpretation of Goujian's achievement as being the result mainly of Fuchai's failings was not commonly encountered during the republican period, it was not unprecedented. As far back as 1915, Chen Yuhua, a student at a girls' normal school in Fengtian, argued that Goujian was neither a hero nor a man of exceptional ability, the real secret of his ultimate triumph consisting in the errors and failings of Fuchai. See her "Goujian zhao Wu lun," 14–15.

104. Yang Tianshi discusses Chiang's diplomatic démarches in the years immediately following the Mukden Incident in "Lugouqiao shibian qian Jiang Jieshi de dui-Ri moulüe," 12–17.

105. See Yang Tianshi's discussion in "Lugouqiao shibian qian Jiang Jieshi de dui-Ri moulüe," 23–26; the need for concealing military preparations against Japan is also noted in Chiang, *China's Destiny*, 128.

106. Yang, "Lugouqiao shibian qian Jiang Jieshi de dui-Ri moulüe," 26–27.

107. *China's Destiny*, 106.

108. *Shenbao*, May 9, 1938, 2; ibid., May 8, 1939, 9.

109. Maolie, "Rusu," *Shenbao*, May 9, 1939, 14. The author refers here (presumably) to the destruction of the second temple by the Romans in 70 C.E., which not only brought an end to the temple service but also marked the end of Jewish sovereignty and the beginning of the Exile *(galut)*. This event, which took place on the Ninth of Av (Ab), was commemorated annually by fasting.

110. *Shenbao*, May 9, 1940, 7 (news notice headed "Wuwang wujiu guochi"); May 10, 1940, 7 (news account).

111. "Cong 'ershiyi tiao' dao 'Dong Ya xin zhixu,'" *Shenbao*, May 9, 1939, 4.

112. Quoted in an editorial entitled "Feizhi wujiu jinian de yiyi," *Shenbao*, May 8, 1940, 4.

113. Zhang Weiqi, *Woxin changdan*.

114. Written by Zhu Shuangyun and Gong Xiaolan, the opera's full title was *Woxin changdan: Guoju juben*.

115. Xi Zhengyong, *Goujian xuechi* (quotation on 22).

116. See "main aims of compilation" *(bianji dayi)*, in front matter of Chen Heqin and Zhu Zefu, *Woxin changdan* (vol. 6 in series titled *Zhongguo lishi gushi congkan*).

117. Ibid., 4–5.

118. Ibid., 6, 9, 13–14.

119. Ibid., 15–16.

120. *Shaoxing geming wenhua shiliao huibian*, 4 *(zongshu)*. I'm grateful to Keith Schoppa for bringing this publication to my attention.

121. See, for example, ibid., 490, 500, 519, 522.

122. Written by Zhu Xiang and originally published in *Shaoxing qianxian* 11 (June 20, 1938), reproduced in *Shaoxing geming wenhua shiliao huibian,* 443.

123. Shen Tao (lyrics), Hong Liang (melody), "Women yibai ershiwan ren," originally published in *Shaoxing qianxian* 11 (July 1938), reproduced in *Shaoxing geming wenhua shiliao huibian,* 497–98.

124. Ibid., 573.

125. Wang Biao, "Zhou Enlai 1939 nian Shaoxing zhi xing yu kang Ri minzu tongyi zhanxian," 16–18; see also He Yangming, "Shi shu kangzhan shiqi de *Dongnan ribao,*" 158.

126. Mei Qian, "Yici teshu de yanchu," 62–66. The reference to the Carleton Theater is in "Kang-Ri xiju huodong." As far as I know, Mei Qian's play was never published. The dialogue translated in the text is taken from Mei's "Yici teshu de yanchu"; although Mei doesn't specifically identify the events referred to in the opening lines of Qiu Jin's part, they seem clearly to describe the circumstances attending the foreign relief expedition's entry into Beijing in summer 1900.

127. Sanmu, "Huashuo kaoguxuejia he lishixuejia Wei Juxian," 8–13.

128. Wei, *Goujian,* 106; the title of chapter 7 includes the term *kangzhan* (see 55).

129. Pan, "Zhongguo lidai mingxian gushi ji bianji zhiqu," *Goujian,* 1–8.

130. Yang's exact words: "As a Zhejiang man, Chiang Kai-shek knew well the story of the Yue king Goujian who, by lying on brushwood and tasting gall and working hard to make his state strong, eventually destroyed the state of Wu." "Lugouqiao shibian qian Jiang Jieshi de dui-Ri moulüe," 8.

131. "For Who Hath Despised the Day of Small Things?" 595.

132. Kantor, "A Candidate, His Minister and the Search for Faith," *New York Times,* Apr. 30, 2007; also Obama, *Dreams from My Father,* 294.

133. Spiegel, "Memory and History," 149–62 (quotation from abstract on 149).

134. Elvin, *Changing Stories in the Chinese World,* 9; Bruner, *Making Stories,* 9 (also 7).

135. Yerushalmi, *Zakhor,* 113.

3. THE PLIGHT OF CHIANG KAI-SHEK'S TAIWAN

1. See, for example, Liu Zhen, *Guochi shigang,* 313, 330–31. In his message of October 10, 1963, marking the anniversary of the Wuchang uprising of 1911, Chiang Kai-shek stated: "Our war of resistance lasted for 14 years. Now it has been another 14 years since the fall of the mainland. Thus it can be truthfully said that our righteous war against aggression and slavery has been going on for 32 years." In Hsiung et al., *Contemporary Republic of China,* 400.

2. Tucker, *Patterns in the Dust,* 198. See also Clough, *Island China,* 96–98.

Although Chiang Kai-shek, in his speeches of 1950, regularly referred (as he had in earlier years) to the precedent of Goujian's coming back after sustaining a serious defeat, the tone was noticeably more optimistic after the outbreak of the Korean War than before. See, for example, the following two speeches: "Fuzhi de shiming yu mudi" (Mar. 13, 1950), 1959; "Guomin gemingjun jiangshi xuechi fuchou zhi dao" (Nov. 1950), 2078.

3. Chiang Kai-shek repeatedly admonished his compatriots to examine the reasons for the humiliating loss of the mainland and, mindful of their past mistakes, to strive to atone for them and make amends. See, for example, the summary of his remarks in 1952 on the occasion of the annual observance of the anniversary of the launching of the 1911 Revolution (Double Ten), in an editorial entitled "Dang guo de zhongxing" in the Guomindang party newspaper, *Zhongyang ribao,* Oct. 10, 1952.

4. Clough, "United States China Policy," 311.

5. For much of the information in this paragraph I have relied on Clough, "Taiwan under Nationalist Rule, 1949–1982," 815–40.

6. A Japanese student of Taiwan cinema says that on his first visit to Taiwan around 1980 huge signs were still in place at the station and other such locations containing messages like "Launch a counterattack against the mainland" *(fangong dalu)* and "Oppose communism, resist Russia" *(fangong kang E).* Kawase, *Taiwan dianying xiangyan,* 87.

7. Reprinted in Hsiung et al., *Contemporary Republic of China,* 399–402. Similar themes are broached in an editorial titled "Jiwang kailai, fangong fuguo" in *Zhongyang ribao,* Oct. 11, 1957; and in another editorial in the same paper, "Ji quan dang quan min liliang wancheng fangong fuguo daye," Nov. 24, 1974. See also the editorials from *Lianhebao* (United daily news) in *Fangong, minzhu, tuanjie, jinbu,* 1:53–69, 123–53; 2:1–44. On the core policy of reconquering the mainland, see Tsang, "Chiang Kai-shek and the Kuomintang's Policy to Reconquer the Chinese Mainland, 1949–1958," 48–72; Zhang Shuya, "Taihai weiji yu Meiguo dui 'fangong dalu' zhengce de zhuanbian," 232–97.

8. From a comparative analysis of Taiwan and mainland primary school texts, Roberta Martin concluded that, while the Communist authorities encouraged a break with Confucian values, the Nationalists promoted a "revitalization of the traditional Confucian system of social behaviour and personal mores." The Taiwan primers she used were published in 1970. See her "The Socialization of Children in China and on Taiwan," 260.

9. "Zhonghua wenhua fuxing yundong zhi tuixing," *Zhongyang ribao,* July 29, 1967. See also Chiang Kai-shek's statement that "traditional ethics are our sole spiritual weapon for launching a counterattack and recovering the nation" in the explanatory notes *(tijie)* introducing Sun Wen [Sun Yat-sen], "Huifu Zhongguo guyou daode," 1.

10. See, for example, Tan Zhijun's spoken drama, *Goujian fuguo;* Zhang

Daxia's opera, *Goujian fuguo;* and Li Hanxiang's film *Xi Shi* (1965), which was divided into two parts, the second of which was entitled "Goujian fuguo" (Leilei, "Fang Li Hanxiang tan *Xi Shi* de weida chu," 46). I have been unable to consult another example (most likely an opera): Qi Rushan, *Goujian fuguo,* published in Taibei in 1952.

11. Chen Wenquan, *Goujian yu Xi Shi.* Chen sometimes went by the name Wen Quan, the first character of his given name being treated as a surname. A partial listing of his spoken dramas, film scripts, and other writings is found in the front matter of *Goujian yu Xi Shi.*

12. Yu Youmin (Yu Keyu), "Yu xu," in Chen Wenquan, *Goujian yu Xi Shi,* 1.

13. Chen Wenquan, "Zixu" (author's preface), in *Goujian yu Xi Shi,* 2–3. Chen was by no means the first writer to portray Xi Shi as a moral paragon as well as a patriot. He was doubtless familiar with the romance *Xi Shi yanshi yanyi* (The Romance of Xi Shi), which was frequently reprinted in the twentieth century both on the mainland and in Taiwan. Although the authorship of this work was until recently unknown, it has now been identified as having come from the hand of the late Ming literary figure Mei Dingzuo (alt. Mei Yujin) (1549–1615) and has been reprinted in Zhou Xinhui, *Zhonghua shanben zhencang wenku.* Mei made it clear in the very first chapter that, in his view, Xi Shi was not just a woman of stunning beauty but also a great heroine and a woman of highest principle. Toward the end of the account, when Xi Shi finds out that Fuchai is already dead, she breaks into tears, lamenting the fact that while she had sacrificed her life to achieve Yue's revenge and erase the humiliations imposed on her country, she hadn't yet repaid the kindness shown her by the Wu king. Fidelity to one's husband, moreover, was a woman's duty. Although mindful of the love shown her by Fan Li, she could not in self-respect remain any longer in this world, forgetful of Fuchai's generosity and oblivious to the demands of righteousness. Thereupon, she raised her sleeves, covered her face, and threw herself into the river. The edition of *Xi Shi yanshi yanyi* used here is in *Si da meiren* (see especially 1–3, 57).

14. Chen Wenquan, *Goujian yu Xi Shi,* 22–31.

15. Ibid., 72, 75.

16. See, for example, ibid., 29, 40, 71. The parallel is least convincing, of course, in the implied characterization of the mainland in 1958 as prosperous.

17. Ibid., 8.

18. Ibid., 8–19 (quote on 18–19).

19. Ibid., 80–82.

20. Ibid., 97–104 (quote on 104).

21. Ibid., 104–5.

22. Ibid., 106.

23. Ibid., 106–9.

24. Ibid., 109–12.

25. Ibid., 65–66.

26. Tan's play appeared in *Zhonghua xiju ji*, a ten-volume collection of plays, all of which were written after the central government's move to Taiwan (1949). According to the biographical note on him, which appears at the end of the third volume (681–82), *Goujian fuguo*, his maiden effort at spoken drama, was followed by several other plays completed prior to the volume's publication date of 1971.

27. Hsu, "Cultural Values and Cultural Continuity," 24. One of Tan's radio plays was entitled *Xi Shi*.

28. See the biographical note in *Zhonghua xiju ji*, 3:681–82.

29. Tan Zhijun, *Goujian fuguo*, 13.

30. Ibid., 15–16.

31. Ibid., 48–50.

32. Ibid., 77, 83.

33. See Harrison, *The Making of the Republican Citizen*; Culp, *Articulating Citizenship*. Although Chiang Kai-shek was emphatic about the importance of the inculcation of such fundamental Confucian virtues as loyalty and filial piety, he tended to place them in a national salvation context, in which the concerns of state and society invariably took precedence over individual concerns. See, for example, his statement in *China's Destiny*, first published in March 1943: "To fulfill the principle of complete loyalty to the state and of filial piety toward the nation; to be altruistic and not seek personal advantage; to place the interests of the state ahead of those of the family; such is the highest standard of loyalty and filial piety." Chiang, *China's Destiny*, 165.

34. Tan Zhijun, *Goujian fuguo*, 127–28.

35. Although emphasis on a Confucian-based ideology as part of its offensive against communism was a distinctive part of the post-1950 policy of the Nationalists, it also characterized the ideology of the New Life Movement, launched by the Nationalists in 1934. One of the main targets of the New Life Movement consisted of those Chinese, in particular in Jiangxi province, who for some years prior to the Long March (which began in October 1934) had lived under Communist rule and were seen as being in need of a reinfusion of "traditional Chinese values." Eastman, *The Abortive Revolution*, 72–73; Wakeman, *Spymaster*, 112; van de Ven, "New States of War," 366–71.

36. Zhang Daxia, *Goujian fuguo*, 59 *(xiubian shuoming)*.

37. Tan Zhijun, *Goujian fuguo*, 147–48.

38. Zhang Daxia, *Goujian fuguo*, 59.

39. Ibid., 10–16, 56–57.

40. Nan'gong Bo was an immensely popular novelist, whose fictional works typically dealt with women, paying special attention to their private lives, feelings, and everything else that made them interesting and distinctive as human beings. His *Xi Shi* first appeared in 1962 and thereafter went through frequent reprintings, attesting to its great popularity. Wang Chengpin's *Xi Shi* is very different from the other treatments I have seen. Written in a very colloquial style, with

a lot of southern Chinese usages (including characters not found in most dictionaries), it is extremely bawdy. In comparison with other renderings of the story, it is also fairly bizarre. Goujian plays almost no part in the novel, Wu Zixu is alluded to only briefly, Wen Zhong is depicted as an envious official who tries to do Fan Li in, Xi Shi herself is represented as anything but a village innocent (when Fan Li first encounters her she is cavorting naked in a stream), and Bo Pi, on the long carriage ride with Xi Shi from Yue to Wu, reveals to his female companion his predilection for kinky sex by pulling down his trousers and urging her, with squeals of delight, to flay his bare buttocks harder and harder, much like a coachman whipping his horse, until the skin has been rendered completely raw. Although an alternate title, "Xi Shi zhao Wu" (Xi Shi destroys Wu), appears on the novel's first page, Xi Shi's part in the destruction of Yue's rival is not developed at all convincingly. Indeed, she doesn't even arrive in Wu until three-quarters of the way into the work (250). As far as I know, Wang Chengpin wrote nothing else besides *Xi Shi* and the book was printed only once.

41. *Xi Shi* won Best Film, Best Director, Best Male Lead, Best Color Photography, and Best Color Artistic Design at Taiwan's fourth annual (1965) Golden Horse (Jinma) awards. It was also judged the best Mandarin film of 1965 by the Chinese Film Critics Association of Taiwan (Taiwan Zhongguo yingpingren xiehui). Chen Feibao, "Li Hanxiang de daoyan yishu," 48; *Zhongguo dianying da cidian,* 1066. The film was commended for the convincing way in which it transformed Xi Shi from an ordinary beauty into a great patriot, and for the contemporary relevance for the Nationalist recovery of China *(fuguo)* of Goujian's dual policy of building up the economic and military strength of Yue. "Goujian de fuguo daji," 8–9; "Tantan Xi Shi zheige ren," 13; "*Xi Shi* you paishandaohai de zhanzheng changmian," 41. To view *Xi Shi,* I used the video recording *Hsi Shih* in two cassettes produced by the Mingfeng yingshi qiyeshe in Taizhong.

42. Nan'gong Bo's novel is one of the very few works dealing with the Goujian story during the Chiang Kai-shek years that presents the harsher side of the Yue king's character. For example, when the maiden from the southern forests of Yue *(nanlin chuzi),* who has been training the Yue army in swordsmanship for years (see chapter 1), expresses skepticism that Yue is strong enough to vanquish Wu, Goujian, fearing the danger of such pessimistic assessments being spread among the Yue soldiers (a fear shared by Wen Zhong), orders that she be poisoned to death—an action Fan Li considers excessively cruel. See Nan'gong Bo, *Xi Shi,* chapter 12. During the Chiang Kai-shek era, renderings of the Goujian story that, like Nan'gong Bo's book, were primarily centered on Xi Shi clearly afforded greater psychological—and political—scope for variant treatments of Goujian. Another Xi Shi–centered work that incorporates the unattractive side of Goujian is Mei Dingzuo's *Xi Shi yanshi yanyi,* which, although written well before the twentieth century (see n. 13 earlier), was reprinted in Taiwan a number of times, initially in 1971 (see especially *Xi Shi yanshi yanyi,* 58–60).

43. Tan Zhijun, *Goujian fuguo*, 152; Chen Wenquan, *Goujian yu Xi Shi*, 112.

44. Except, as noted in n. 42 earlier, in renderings of the story in which the central figure was Xi Shi. According to the film director Liao Xiangxiong, prior to the lifting of martial law the mass media in Taiwan operated under tight restriction and had become little more than stage props for the government's political propaganda. Under the circumstances, it was easier to get past the censors with films on historical subjects. Kawase, *Taiwan dianying xiangyan*, 87–88. During the early decades of Guomindang rule on Taiwan, the effects of the police state were pervasive. Israel, "Politics on Formosa," 3–11.

45. Although this hope was of course felt most intensely by recent refugees from the mainland, it was conveyed to all Chinese on Taiwan. There were, for example, lessons articulating it in the Chinese *(guoyu)* primers of grade school pupils. See the following lessons in *Guomin xiaoxue guoyu:* "Women de jia zai dalu shang," 6:99–100 (third-grade level); "Guangfu ge," 7:69–70 (fourth-grade level).

46. The adulation of Chiang was ubiquitous in post-1950 Taiwan, and it began early in life, primary school pupils being exposed to it year after year in their Chinese *(guoyu)* primers. See the following lessons in *Guomin xiaoxue guoyu:* "Jiang zongtong xiao de shihou," 3:31–32 (second-grade level); "Aiguo de Jiang zongtong," 5:27–28 (third-grade level); "Jiang zongtong de jiashu," 8:5–6 (fourth-grade level); "Ziqiang buxi de Jiang zongtong," 9:21–22 (fifth-grade level).

47. Li Fugen, "Chongxie Zhonghua gushi," 49.

48. Huang's fullest account of his extensive activities promoting the Goujian story is in "Goujian," in his *Zhonghua weiren gushi*, 56 n. 7. See also the introduction to his *Zhongxing shihua*, 3 (front matter). "Goujian mie Wu" is the first of the seven items in *Zhongxing shihua*, 1–30.

49. Stories of weaker states defeating more powerful ones and recovering lost territory were a favorite theme in grade school primers as well. See the following lessons in *Guomin xiaoxue guoyu:* "Aiguo de shaonian," 5:31–32 (third-grade level); "Shaokang zhongxing," 10:59–61 (fifth-grade level); "Shuangcheng fuguo," 10:65–67 (fifth-grade level); "Kunyang zhi zhan," 12:86–101 (sixth-grade level).

50. "Cheng Tianfang xiansheng xu," in *Zhongxing shihua*, 2 (front matter).

51. "Fuyin qianji," in *Zhongxing shihua*, 3 (front matter).

52. Huang Dashou, "Goujian mie Wu," 30.

53. Ibid., 29–30.

54. See Zanasi's "Globalizing *Hanjian*." There is good evidence, as Charles D. Musgrove shows, that this politically prescribed dichotomization did not necessarily reflect people's actual sentiments; see his "Cheering the Traitor," 3–27.

55. Taylor, *The Generalissimo's Son*, 248.

56. Ibid., 248–49; Clough, *Island China*, 103.

57. The lessons, which apparently weren't published at the time, were included as an appendix to Huang's *Zhonghua weiren gushi*, 341–86 (the aim and methodology of the lessons are explained on 341–42).

58. Huang Dashou, "Di yi ke," 343–50.

59. Huang Dashou, *Zhonghua weiren gushi*, 341–42.

60. The question of the legitimacy of revenge as a motive was a potentially sensitive one during the past century of Chinese history. It was, of course, widely accepted as an appropriate expression of patriotism in the run-up to the war with Japan. Then, in the *woxin changdan* operas of the early 1960s, according to Mao Dun, it was implicitly questioned, mainly for political/ideological reasons (see chapter 4). Although, in most of the century, revenge does not appear to have been readily challenged on *moral* grounds, this began to change by the turn of the twenty-first century. (See, for example, the following essay by a Zhejiang upper–middle school student: Chen Ling, "Yingxiong zhi chi," 62.) Also, at this time, numbers of scholars in the international relations field, concerned over the ease with which a China rapidly growing in wealth and power could give rise to a narrow popular nationalism bent on avenging the country's past humiliations, came out strongly in support of Beijing's taking a more constructive and temperate part in world affairs. Some of these scholars supported continued reliance on the "hide our capacities and bide our time" (*taoguang-yanghui*) strategy enunciated by Deng Xiaoping in late 1989 and late 1990, maintaining that China's strategic situation had not changed fundamentally in the intervening years and that Deng's assertions had been tempered by the injunctions that China act cautiously in international affairs, not take the lead, and not seek domination. Other scholars argued that this strategy was no longer appropriate, partly because in their view China's situation *had* changed greatly since Deng's day; partly because it was illogical, if China really intended to conceal something from the world, to announce such a policy publicly; and partly because *taoguang-yanghui* was too easily misconstrued by foreign governments as implying a long-term Chinese threat to world peace. Predictably, on both sides of the *taoguang-yanghui* debate, scholars regularly alluded to the Goujian story, although generally insisting that "concealing one's capacities and biding one's time" had a very different meaning for the state of Yue in the fifth century B.C.E. than for China in the early twenty-first century. For an illuminating analysis, see Xing Yue and Zhang Jibing, "*Taoguang-yanghui* zhanlüe zai sikao," 13–19 (the discussion of the Goujian story is on 15–16).

61. I base this statement partly on personal knowledge, having lived in Taiwan for sixteen months in the early 1960s; see also Taylor, *The Generalissimo's Son*, 248.

62. Huang Dashou, *Zhonghua weiren gushi*, 379–80.

63. Ibid., 341.

64. Huang Dashou, "Goujian," in *Zhonghua weiren gushi*, 56 n. 7.

65. Compare Huang's "Goujian mie Wu," 10–11, 12, 16–21, 24, 25, and his "Goujian," in Shen Gangbo et al., *Minzu yingxiong ji geming xianlie zhuanji*, 1:37–39, 53.

66. As of 1966, 97 percent of school-age children were in school. Hsiung et al., *Contemporary Republic of China*, 79.

67. Lu wrote widely on the history of the Chinese language, Chinese poetry, and the classics.

68. Lu Yuanjun, epilogue *(bayu)*, in Shen Gangbo et al., *Minzu yingxiong ji geming xianlie zhuanji* 2:1–3 (back matter).

69. Ibid., 2:4–5 (back matter).

70. There were many other books as well that emphasized the role of outstanding figures from the past as motivating forces in the present. *Minzu yingxiong* (1974), for example, contained fifty-eight brief accounts of past heroes, arranged by categories. The account of Goujian was placed in the category of those who wiped out a past humiliation (see 121–24). An earlier series, *Zhongguo weiren xiaozhuan*, specifically targeted younger children. Each biographical account in the series was published as a separate volume of around thirty pages. The one on Goujian, titled *Goujian*, was written by Zhao Longzhi.

71. Quoted by permission from David Der-wei Wang, "1905, 1955, 2005," unpublished paper (1906).

72. Huang Dashou, introduction, in his *Zhonghua weiren gushi*, 1–2.

73. Chen's book was first published in wartime Shanghai. The reprint included the preface to the 1940 edition unchanged, the publisher apparently viewing the situations of Taiwan in 1953 and Shanghai in 1940 (neither of which is specifically referred to in the preface) as sharing much in common.

74. Chen Enhui, *Xi Shi*, 58.

75. Ibid., 101.

76. Ibid., preface, 1–2.

77. Chen Enhui, *Xi Shi*, 47.

78. Ibid., 52; the same story is told in like circumstances in chapter 8 of *Xi Shi yanshi yanyi*.

79. Huang Jilu and Cheng Tianfang, both of whom had held high positions in the Nationalist government, wrote prefaces to *Zhongxing shihua*. Wang Yunwu, who wrote a preface to *Minzu yingxiong ji geming xianlie zhuanji*, served in numerous important posts first on the mainland and later in Taiwan.

80. Tien, *The Great Transition*, 195–97, 211–12.

81. It was equally explicit in a biography of Goujian *(Goujian zhuan)*, which I haven't been able to examine, that was compiled and published by the General Political Department of the Ministry of National Defense in 1952.

82. Lan Hong, *Woxin changdan*. See the book's rear outer cover for particulars. The National Editorial and Translation Office was the publisher, among other things, of the textbooks used in the national school system and was therefore in a key position to determine what reading material the youth of Taiwan should be exposed to.

83. Ibid., 56; for another example, see ibid., 49.

84. Ibid., 56–57.

85. Ibid., 57, 60.

86. Ibid., 64.

87. Su and Wen, *Woxin changdan,* 9.

88. Hsü, *The Rise of Modern China* (6th ed.), 911; also Clough, *Island China,* 61–62.

89. Chu, "Social Protests and Political Democratization in Taiwan," 99–100.

90. *The Rise of Modern China* (6th ed.), 919–20.

91. See "Cross-Strait Trade up 22 Percent in First Eight Months," *China Daily.*

92. Hsü, *The Rise of Modern China* (6th ed.), 922.

93. I hasten to add that I am not concerned here with the numerous publications that continued to appear dealing primarily with Xi Shi. Xi Shi's story, although an important part of the larger story of Goujian, also embraces its own distinctive themes that have no particular bearing on the Taiwan situation but have been of enduring fascination to Chinese readers. Indeed, there was something of a Xi Shi craze *(re)* on the mainland in the 1980s and 1990s (see chapter 6), and a goodly number of the Xi Shi books published on Taiwan from the mid-1980s on were reprints of PRC publications. My search for post-1985 titles with a primary focus on the Goujian story has been conducted mainly by means of the global online search engine WorldCat. Doubtless there were additional items relating to the story published after the 1980s in magazines and journals. But, for reasons shortly to be noted in the text, I would expect the story's coverage in such publications to follow the same trends—both quantitative and qualitative—as found in book-length literature. This reasoning applies equally to publicity given the story in nonprint media.

94. In Bai Hua, *Yuangu de zhong sheng yu jinri de huixiang* (1990). Bai Hua's play, which premiered in Beijing in early 1983, is discussed in chapter 5.

95. The two Taiwan reprints were *Woxin changdan* (1991) and *Goujian* (1993).

96. Wang Pizhen, *Goujian yu Fuchai* (1995); Li Cheng, *Goujian yu Fuchai* (1997).

97. Itō Michiharu et al., *Bazhe zhi dao.* I have not been able to examine this work. Since a work of the same title appeared a few years earlier in Japan and had only Japanese as authors, my guess is that the Taiwan publication is a Chinese translation (or possibly adaptation) of the original Japanese study.

98. According to the front matter of the novel, Wang, although trained in animal husbandry and veterinary medicine and for many years on the faculty of an agricultural school in Yunnan, wrote over eighty historical novels after his retirement in 1982.

99. The emergence of the not-very-nice postconquest Goujian is detailed in Wang Pizhen, *Goujian yu Fuchai,* 217–27.

100. For details concerning the postconquest Goujian, see Li Cheng, *Goujian yu Fuchai,* 347–51.

101. Yang Shanqun, preface to first Taiwan edition *(Woxin changdan)*, 1–2.

102. There is an abundant literature on the subject. See, for example, "Zhonghua minzu wenming shi ke zhuisu dao wannian yiqian," 24 *(wenzhai)*; Amin and Peiyu, "Zhonghua wenming shi ke zhuisu dao wannian qian," 43; Shi Shi and Huang Dashou, "Chongxie Zhonghua gushi jianyishu," 76–78; Shi Shi and Huang Dashou, *Taiwan xian zhumin shi;* Shi Shi, "Taiwan xian zhumin de lishi jieshao," 50–51; Zhang Qizhi and Zhang Le, "Zhuanjia xin kaozheng," 42–43; Yang Hongjie, "Houtu wenhua yu Zhonghua wenming shi," 31–37; Lin Zhibo, "Fang zhuming shixuejia Shi Shi."

103. For an example of the latter, see He Youji, "Taiwan Gaoshan zu tongbao de gen zai Zhejiang Shaoxing," 36–38.

104. Neither "Taiwan" nor "China" of course existed six thousand years ago in any meaningful sense. One of the critical features of the mythified past in nationalist historiography is the premise of great antiquity, the idea that nations, as Benedict Anderson has put it, "loom out of an immemorial past." There is nothing, Anderson cautions, inherent or natural about this idea. But with the emergence of the concept of linear, continuous time in the latter part of the eighteenth century, nationalism began to be "read" genealogically, "as the expression of an historical tradition of serial continuity." And over the next two centuries, no game was more avidly engaged in by nationalist historians than that of determining how far back into the past a nation's roots could be extended. *Imagined Communities,* 11, 195; see also ibid., xiv, 5, 193–205. The glee with which participants in the *Zhonghua minzu shi* project have heralded the evidence that Chinese civilization is ten thousand, rather than (as had previously been believed) five thousand, years old is illustrative of this aspect of nationalist historiography.

105. See the review by Tantai Huimin, 42–43.

106. Li Fugen, "Chongxie Zhonghua gushi," 49.

4. CRISIS AND RESPONSE

1. A partial exception was Xiao Jun's novel *Wu Yue chunqiu shihua,* which was completed in 1957; it was not published, however, until 1980. It is dealt with in the following chapter.

2. According to the critic Zhu Zhai, writing in early 1963, "the story of the warfare between Wu and Yue during the Spring and Autumn period is the subject matter that has been selected and used with greatest frequency, the main plot in all instances being drawn from the *woxin changdan* story." "Zai tan guanyu lishiju wenti de zhenglun," 65. See also Liu Youkuan, "Man tan *Dan jian pian*," 4.

3. Wu Han, "Woxin changdan de gushi," *Guangming ribao,* Jan. 11, 1961. Other examples are Wang Sidi, *Woxin changdan de gushi* (1962), and Shi Mang, "Fafen tuqiang," 95–104 (according to the postscript to Shi's *Wu Yue fengyun,* in

which "Fafen tuqiang" appeared as an appendix, the article was originally published in fall 1961 in the magazine *Qiu shi*).

4. Mao Dun, *Guanyu lishi he lishiju*, 1. The book originally appeared in the form of two long articles in *Wenxue pinglun*, 5 (1961): 37–65, 6 (1961): 1–57. The articles as well as the main body of the book were dated Dec. 2, 1961, the postface to the book July 1, 1962.

5. *Dan jian pian (wu mu huaju)* (1962). There are other editions of the play. The one I have used, which has occasional minor changes in wording, is *Dan jian pian (wu mu lishiju)* (1979). Like most plays from this time, *The Gall and the Sword* was a collective undertaking. Cao Yu was listed on the title page as the member of the group who "held the pen" (i.e., was responsible for doing the writing); the other two key persons, whose names also appeared on the title page, were the playwright-director Mei Qian and the actor Yu Shizhi. The play was directed by Jiao Juyin for the Beijing People's Art Theater. It was first published in a combined issue of *Renmin wenxue* 7–8 (July 1961): 129–64. According to McDougall and Louie, during the early 1960s Cao Yu's best-known plays were often performed to full houses in the capital. *The Literature of China*, 306–7.

6. Tung, "Introduction," 16–17. See also Wagner, *The Contemporary Chinese Historical Drama*, 83; and his "'In Guise of a Congratulation,'" 55–56. For brief summations of the Hundred Flowers and Anti-Rightist movements, see Teiwes, "The Establishment and Consolidation of the New Regime, 1949–57," 77–85.

7. For summations of the issues, see Lu Mei, "Guanyu lishiju wenti de zhengming," 36–41 (reprinted in *Lishiju lunji*, 353–66); Zhao Cong, *Zhongguo dalu de xiqu gaige*; Tung and Mackerras, *Drama in the People's Republic of China*, 29–91; Unger, *Using the Past to Serve the Present*, 9–103.

8. Wang Jisi, "Duo xiexie zheyang de lishi gushi xi," 121–22. See also Ma Shaobo, "Tan lishiju de 'gu wei jin yong,'" 10, 12; Qi Yanming, "Lishiju he lishi zhenshixing," 49; Zhang Zhen, "Gu wei jin yong ji qita," 63 (reprinted in *Lishiju lunji*, 216). On the importance of getting a good match between a dramatized episode from the past and what was going on at present, see Wagner, "'In Guise of a Congratulation,'" 54.

9. Zhang Zhen, "Gu wei jin yong ji qita," 62 (also in *Lishiju lunji*, 216).

10. Mao's sensitivity to China's multifaceted dependence on the USSR, starting already in the 1950s, is discussed in Meisner, *Mao's China and After*, 223–24; see also Lieberthal, "The Great Leap Forward," 97–101. Years later, with the Soviet Union clearly in mind, the Chinese leader identified 1958 as a time of important policy shifts: "From 1958, we decided to make self-reliance our major policy and striving for foreign aid a secondary aim." Quoted in Whiting, "The Sino-Soviet Split," 484; also 491, 501, 517–18.

11. McDougall and Louie, *The Literature of China*, 307; Fisher, "'The Play's the Thing,'" 40; Zhao Cong, *Zhongguo dalu de xiqu gaige*, 159–60; Zhang Yaojie, "Cao Yu yu Zhou Enlai," section 3.

12. In later years, after China and the USSR had become open antagonists, this of course changed. See the bitter criticism of the Soviets in the postscript (dated Aug. 1979) to Shi Mang, *Wu Yue fengyun*, 105–6. See also Zhang Yaojie, "Cao Yu yu Zhou Enlai," section 3 (Zhang, in addition to noting the break with the Soviet Union in 1960, also cited the contemporaneous amplification of Chiang Kai-shek's calls for launching an attack against the mainland).

13. The views of Qi Hong, Qian Yingyu, Fu Jun, and others, originally published in late 1960 or early 1961 in *Shanghai xiju* (Shanghai drama), are summarized in Lu Mei, "Guanyu lishiju wenti de zhengming," 39–41 (also in *Lishiju lunji*, 359–62).

14. Zhang Zhen, "Gu wei jin yong ji qita," 65–67 (also in *Lishiju lunji*, 222–24).

15. Zhang Zhen, "Lun lishi de jutixing," 145–49.

16. A *Xijubao* editor ventured a similar criticism of one of the *woxin chang-dan* scripts he had read in manuscript form. Qu Liuyi, "Chuangzuo ye yao you woxin changdan jingshen," 42.

17. Fan Junhong, "Guanyu 'woxin changdan,'" 83, 85–86 (reprinted in *Lishiju lunji*, 229–30, 235).

18. Fan Junhong, "Guanyu 'woxin changdan,'" 83–85 (also in *Lishiju lunji*, 231–36); Zhang Zhen, "Gu wei jin yong ji qita," 67 (also in *Lishiju lunji*, 224–26).

19. "The four togethernesses" were eat together, live together, labor together, and take counsel together. The term was first used in print in *Renmin ribao* on July 23, 1960. See Hsia, *Metaphor, Myth, Ritual and the People's Commune*, 28–29; Hsia, *A Terminological Study of the* Hsia-fang *Movement*, 34–35. The other two slogans refer to the Great Leap promotion of "backyard" steel production and a large-scale militia force, both of which reflected deliberate departures from Soviet-style practices. Lieberthal, "The Great Leap Forward," 97–98, 101.

20. Fan Junhong, "Guanyu 'woxin changdan,'" 87–89 (also in *Lishiju lunji*, 239–45).

21. For an overview of the various types of regional theater active in China prior to 1949, see Mackerras, *The Chinese Theatre in Modern Times*, part 2.

22. Ward, "Regional Operas and Their Audiences," 172, 186–87.

23. Johnson, "Actions Speak Louder Than Words," 31. The close connection between opera and ritual, according to Johnson, rested in the fact that for both performance was fundamental.

24. Cohen, *History in Three Keys*, 106–7, 228.

25. MacFarquhar, *The Origins of the Cultural Revolution*, 3:110; see also Hung, *War and Popular Culture*, 221–69.

26. MacFarquhar, *The Origins of the Cultural Revolution*, 3:110; for more detailed figures, see Tung, "Introduction," 4–5.

27. This did not last very long. Things began to tighten up in the literary

sphere in 1962. Mao Zedong returned to active involvement in the party leadership in this year and devoted a good deal of his critical attention to the field of art and literature. By 1963 and 1964, pressure was building from Mao, Jiang Qing, and others to reform opera so that it more closely reflected contemporary life. In 1965 Mao accused writers of only wanting to write about "emperors, kings, generals, and ministers" and launched an attack on the Ministry of Culture and traditional theater. Mao Dun, who although not a party member had headed the ministry since the establishment of the PRC in 1949, was replaced early in the same year. McDougall, "Writers and Performers," 277–78; Goldman, *China's Intellectuals*, 74–88.

28. *Guanyu lishi he lishiju*, 1–2. For further discussion of the circumstances surrounding the creation of Mao Dun's book, see Qin Chuan, "Mao Dun lun Guo Moruo de *Nüshen* ji qita," 35–36.

29. Hu, "Ming Dynasty Drama," 70–72; biography of Liang Chenyu (Ch'enyü) in Goodrich and Fang, *Dictionary of Ming Biography*, 1:893–94 (also 2:1463).

30. Mao Dun, *Guanyu lishi he lishiju*, 114–18.

31. Ibid., 118–23.

32. Ibid., 124–29.

33. Ibid., 139–40.

34. Ibid., 129–32 (quotation on 130). Mao Dun supplied additional examples on these pages of real people combined with fabricated events. Also, he contended that Bo Pi, like Fuchai, was portrayed in the operas with excessive caricature.

35. Ibid., 132–34.

36. Ibid., 137–39.

37. Link, *The Uses of Literature*.

38. *Guanyu lishi he lishiju*, 134. Cao Yu's biographer Tian Benxiang also referred to the *woxin changdan* craze or fad (he used the term *re*) in operatic performances of the early 1960s; see his *Cao Yu zhuan*, 403, and also the article Tian coauthored with Liu Yijun, "Xiju dashi Cao Yu" *(xia)*, 12.

39. Tian Benxiang, *Cao Yu zhuan*, 398–99.

40. During the campaign against spiritual pollution in autumn 1983, Cao Yu (like Wang Meng) chose to denounce spiritual pollution when, according to Link, he "could have avoided it." Link, *The Uses of Literature*, 99. Cao Yu, as his actions in 1983 suggest, was a strong backer of the Deng regime. In 1989 he was one of a minority of intellectuals who not only didn't support the Tiananmen demonstrations but actually spoke out in favor of the use of force to crush them in June. McDougall and Louie, *The Literature of China*, 307; Barmé and Minford, *Seeds of Fire*, 464.

41. The identification of Luo is in Zhang Yaojie, "Cao Yu yu Zhou Enlai," section 3.

42. Lau, *Ts'ao Yü*, 77. For a PRC critique, see Zhao Huiping, *Cao Yu xiju xinshang*, 14–17. The play was called *Bright Skies (Minglang de tian)*. Initially writ-

ten in 1954 in four acts, later changed to three, it charged the Americans with germ warfare in Korea. McDougall and Louie, *The Literature of China*, 306; Zhao Huiping, *Cao Yu xiju xinshang*, 182–83.

43. A detailed account of the writing process is in Tian Benxiang, *Cao Yu zhuan*, 403–8.

44. Ibid., 408; Zhao Huiping, *Cao Yu xiju xinshang*, 184; Pan Keming, *Cao Yu yanjiu wushi nian*, 154; Qiu Yang, epilogue *(houji)*, in Qiu Yang et al., *Dan jian pian*.

45. I have based this summation of *The Gall and the Sword* on the 1979 edition (the quoted lines of Goujian in act 4 are on 97 and 100; those of Wu Zixu and Goujian in act 5 are on 115 and 134). The decisive part taken by a naval confrontation in the climactic scene of *Dan jian pian* differs from other renderings of the Goujian story of which I am aware (the story more typically ends with Yue's storming of the Wu capital, which is barely alluded to in Cao Yu's play). Fuchai's demand that Goujian lend him his warships, along with Goujian's adamant refusal, very possibly allude to a serious dispute that took place between Khrushchev and Mao in the summer of 1958 over Moscow's proposal for a joint submarine flotilla. Mao, like Goujian extremely sensitive to issues of state sovereignty, was convinced (despite Khrushchev's protestations to the contrary) that the Soviet Union wanted to control China militarily and refused to accede to the proposal. I am grateful to Rudolf Wagner for drawing my attention to this suggestive parallel. On the tension over this and other matters between Khrushchev and Mao, see Chen Jian and Yang Kuisong, "Chinese Politics and the Collapse of the Sino-Soviet Alliance," 268–70.

46. Liu Youkuan, "Man tan *Dan jian pian*," 8; Zhang Guangnian, "*Dan jian pian* zhi tan," 6–7 (reprinted in *Lishiju lunji*, 196–97); Wu Han, "Lishiju shi yishu ye shi lishi," 41; Zhang Geng, "*Dan jian pian* sui xiang," 175–76; Zhang Guangnian, "*Dan jian pian* de sixiangxing," 180–81, 183; Li Xifan, "*Dan jian pian* he lishiju," 211–12 (reprinted from *Renmin ribao*, Sept. 6, 1961).

47. MacFarquhar, *The Origins of the Cultural Revolution*, 2:328–30 (quotation on 330).

48. Ibid., 335; Lieberthal, "The Great Leap Forward," 104–13.

49. See, for example, the secondary school primer *Woxin changdan de Yue wang Goujian*, 36–37.

50. For an example, see Yu Tianhua, *Yue wang Goujian xi guochou*, 65–68. In this rendering, Yue's borrowing of grain for "famine relief" takes place at a time when the people of the state are in fact prospering; it is specifically described as a "pretext" (65) to gauge the true circumstances of Wu. When the loan is repaid the following year (after being rendered infertile), it results in an unprecedented famine in Wu (68).

51. This is suggested in McDougall and Louie, *The Literature of China*, 307.

52. Cao Yu, *Dan jian pian* (1979 ed.), 60.

53. Although in the ancient sources, Kucheng is one of the top ministers of Yue, Cao Yu and his collaborators have transformed him into a commoner.

54. Cao Yu, *Dan jian pian* (1979 ed.), 65–66.

55. Ibid., 98.

56. MacFarquhar, *The Origins of the Cultural Revolution*, 2:335.

57. The same Mao who was intolerant of personal criticism often condemned "the harmful work-style of fearing to speak the truth." Ibid., 207.

58. The point is emphasized in Yan, "Tan *Dan jian pian* de yishu chengjiu," 79, 86.

59. The ensuing discussion of the Wu Han/Hai Rui affair is based mainly on MacFarquhar, *The Origins of the Cultural Revolution*, 2:207–12, and Fisher, "'The Play's the Thing.'"

60. See the biography of Hai Rui [Jui] in Goodrich and Fang, *Dictionary of Ming Biography*, 1:474–9.

61. Stuart Schram, *Chairman Mao Talks to the People*, 237.

62. Fisher, "'The Play's the Thing,'" 11.

63. The quotation is in MacFarquhar, *The Origins of the Cultural Revolution*, 2:212. Fisher identifies the high-ranking propaganda official Hu Qiaomu as the person who personally encouraged Wu Han to take on Hai Rui ("'The Play's the Thing,'" 33). MacFarquhar, however, questioning the reliability of the source for this, is not convinced (*The Origins of the Cultural Revolution*, 2:402 n. 135). Fisher (41) notes that, prior to the staging of Wu Han's *Dismissal of Hai Rui*, several other Hai Rui dramas were performed. One of these, Zhou Xinfang's *Hai Rui Submits His Memorial*, is the subject of Wagner, "'In Guise of a Congratulation.'"

64. MacFarquhar, *The Origins of the Cultural Revolution*, 2:211.

65. See, for example, Yan, "Tan *Dan jian pian* de yishu chengjiu," 85; Zhang Guangnian, "*Dan jian pian* zhi tan," 6–7 (in *Lishiju lunji* reprint, 194–96); Zhang Guangnian, "*Dan jian pian* de sixiangxing," 183; Li Xifan, "*Dan jian pian* he lishi," 204, 207. Zhang Guangnian's first article, above, is one piece that did refer to the Yue famine in explicit terms.

66. Wu Han, "Lishiju shi yishu ye shi lishi," 41.

67. Quoted in Tian Benxiang, *Cao Yu zhuan*, 410; also in Zhang Yaojie, "Cao Yu yu Zhou Enlai," section 3. After the Maoist period, Chinese critics were much more forthcoming in identifying the problems with Cao Yu's post-1949 plays. Zhao Huiping, for example, attributing these problems directly to the ideological and political constraints of the Mao years, wrote: "Cao Yu's loss of his artistic individuality after liberation constitutes a profound lesson. During the past twenty or thirty years [Zhao was writing in the late 1980s], if our various policies relating to literature and art had been able to value and conform to the laws of the arts, Cao Yu would surely have created more and better works." *Cao Yu xiju xinshang*, 17. See also Pan Keming, *Cao Yu yanjiu wushi nian*, 263–66; Tian Benxiang, *Cao Yu zhuan*, 409.

68. For an insightful reflection on this phenomenon, see Link, *Evening Chats in Beijing*, 142–44.

69. Tian Benxiang, *Cao Yu zhuan*, 411.

70. Ibid., 411–12. Cao Yu was not the only intellectual to respond with great enthusiasm to Chen Yi's speech. The excitement generated by it radiated throughout the Chinese intellectual community. Hiestand, "Chen Yi and the Revival of the Hundred Flowers Campaign, 1961–1963," 80–83.

71. The speech, under the title "Man tan juzuo," was published in *Zhongguo xiju* 6 (1962): 1–4. Zhou's request that he write a play on the Han beauty Wang Zhaojun is discussed by Cao Yu in his *Cao Yu zizhuan*, 160–64.

72. MacFarquhar, *The Origins of the Cultural Revolution*, 3:286.

73. For a brief account of his Cultural Revolution troubles, which almost drove him to suicide, see Cao Yu, *Cao Yu zizhuan*, 165–68.

74. Wu Han, "Lishiju shi yishu ye shi lishi," 41.

75. See Fisher, "'The Play's the Thing,'" 12. The notion of a reader's (or viewer's) social biography helping to shape a work's meaning is a key feature of reader-reception theory in the field of literary criticism.

76. Compare to Wagner's partly parallel argument, in his analysis of Zhou Xinfang's Hai Rui drama, that "literary PRC texts do not only interact with social reality, but that at times the readers' own immediate experience and concerns become an essential part of the text without which the text remains incomplete." "'In Guise of a Congratulation,'" 93.

77. Yu Tianhua took explicit note of his unhappiness over the crisis on the mainland in the preface to his 1961 work *Su Qin zhuan*. According to MacFarquhar, during three weeks of "uncontrolled emigration" in May 1962 almost one hundred thousand people crossed into Hong Kong, and the "Hong Kong fever" spread from Guangdong to other southern provinces. *The Origins of the Cultural Revolution*, 3:206.

78. MacFarquhar, *The Origins of the Cultural Revolution*, 2:212.

79. Yu Tianhua, "Ji Yue guo da chen Wen Zhong," 99–100. Yu's book was reissued without changes in 1965 under the title *Woxin changdan*.

5 · POLITICAL ALLEGORY IN THE 1980S

1. I haven't seen the original text of Kuai's speech; the rough translation here is in Hinton, *Hundred Day War*, 235. The speech is briefly referred to in Yang Jian, "Hongweibing jituan xiang zhiqing jituan de lishixing guodu," 27. I am grateful to Weili Ye for alerting me to the prevalence in Beijing at this time of allusions to the Goujian story.

2. Harding, "The Chinese State in Crisis, 1966–9," 219–20.

3. One of Kuai Dafu's rival student leaders, Shen Ruhuai, in a recent memoir, notes that the events here alluded to marked the withering away of Kuai's

Red Guard regime. He adds that during the climactic period from late July to mid-August 1968, "the working class of the capital nailed Kuai Dafu permanently to history's pillar of shame." *Qinghua daxue wenge jishi,* 428–29.

4. Hinton, *Hundred Day War,* 235 (also 244). One reason the Goujian story's political impact during the Cultural Revolution appears to have been weaker than in the immediately preceding decades is that the themes of humiliation and revenge, as manifested at the time, were more reflective of personal than of national goals. The case of Kuai Dafu certainly suggests this. It may also be significant that one of the most sought-after underground manuscripts in the latter years of the Cultural Revolution was a translation of Dumas's *The Count of Monte Cristo,* the core theme of which was the lead character's quest for *personal* revenge. I'm grateful to Perry Link for bringing the Dumas book's popularity to my attention. See also MacFarquhar and Schoenhals, *Mao's Last Revolution,* 349–50.

5. Merle Goldman supplies much interesting detail on Xiao Jun's ongoing battle with the party, especially in the early 1940s in Yan'an and in the late 1940s in Manchuria. *Literary Dissent in Communist China,* xii, 27–29, 37, 45, 67–68, 70–86. See also Hsia, *A History of Modern Chinese Fiction,* 273–80.

6. Xiao Jun, "A Personal Statement," 133–34.

7. Ibid., 134.

8. Preface to Xiao Jun, *Wu Yue chunqiu shihua,* 1:1.

9. Ibid.

10. It was entitled *Wu wang fa Zhou* (King Wu [of the Zhou dynasty] vanquishes Zhou [the name of the tyrannical last king of the Shang]). Wang Ke and Xu Sai, *Xiao Jun pingzhuan,* 233.

11. Such at least is what Xiao Jun claims in both the preface and postscript to the novel. *Wu Yue chunqiu shihua,* 1:3, 2:570. The date of April 12, 1956, given at the end of the text (ibid., 2:569) may refer to the completion of the first draft, as asserted by Zhang Yumao in his *Xiao Jun zhuan,* 283–84.

12. The opera was published in 1984. The differences between the opera and novel are discussed in Wang Ke and Xu Sai, *Xiao Jun pingzhuan,* 239–41; Xiao Jun also discussed them in "Lishi xiaoshuo 'Wu Yue chunqiu shihua' he jingju 'Wu Yue chun qiu' de chengyin yu guocheng," dated Sept. 5, 1980, 2:287–94.

13. See the postscript in *Wu Yue chunqiu shihua,* 2:570; Wang Ke and Xu Sai, *Xiao Jun pingzhuan,* 239–40; Zhang Yumao, *Xiao Jun zhuan,* 276; Wang Defen, *Wo he Xiao Jun fengyu 50 nian,* 255–59.

14. Between 1957, when *The Past Generation (Guoqu de niandai)* appeared, and 1980, a few of Xiao Jun's earlier works were reprinted in Hong Kong. Apart from this, a collection of short stories jointly written with Xiao Hong and first published in 1933 was reissued in Harbin in 1979.

15. Wang Ke and Xu Sai, *Xiao Jun pingzhuan,* 258.

16. Wang Ke and Xu Sai use this phrase to characterize Xiao Jun's depiction of the postconquest Goujian (ibid., 241).

17. Goldman, *Literary Dissent in Communist China*, 70–86. The quoted phrases are on 72, 75. See also Wang Ke and Xu Sai, *Xiao Jun pingzhuan*, 215–23, 230–33.

18. The circumstances of Xiao Jun's departure from Fushun and his life in Beijing are described in Huang Yue, *Yan'an si guai*, 223–25; Wang Ke and Xu Sai, *Xiao Jun pingzhuan*, 234–38.

19. Xiao Jun, "A Personal Statement," 134–35; in this speech Xiao confused the successful appeal to Mao of the early 1950s with the unsuccessful one of a decade later. The earlier one is noted in Wang Ke and Xu Sai, *Xiao Jun pingzhuan*, 236–37; Huang Yue, *Yan'an si guai*, 224.

20. Huang Yue, *Yan'an si guai*, 224–25.

21. Xiao Jun, *Wu Yue chunqiu shihua*, 1:308–9, 2:545–47.

22. Much of the first chapter of part 4 of the book deals with this episode. See ibid., 2:445–83.

23. Ibid., 2:552.

24. Ibid., 2:557–59.

25. Ibid., 2:559–62.

26. Ibid., 2:562–63.

27. Ibid., 2:564–69.

28. Ibid., 2:563–64. Bo Pi, who in the latter stages of Fuchai's reign was running the Wu government almost single-handedly, had been given private assurances by Yue that if it conquered Wu he would be awarded a high official position in Yue or, if he preferred, allowed to return to Chu and hold office there (ibid., 2:538). This, of course, given the nature of past dealings between Yue and Bo Pi, was not a promise that Goujian would have felt obliged to honor.

29. See the analysis of Zhang Yumao, *Xiao Jun zhuan*, 288–90.

30. Xiao Jun, "A Personal Statement," 136. One of these old scores was with Zhou Yang, who as a powerful figure in the literary establishment had caused Xiao no end of suffering over the years. Xiao's public attack on Zhou's report at the 1979 congress (ibid.) was devastating.

31. Ibid., 132.

32. Bai Hua, in a recent interview, described his enforced separation from the world of literature as having, "strictly speaking," lasted from his being branded a rightist in 1958 until the end of the Cultural Revolution. Zhu Jianguo, "Bai Hua Zhuhai shuo gudu," 80.

33. Quoted in Kraus, "Bai Hua," 190; see also Bai Hua, "No Breakthrough, No Literature," 61.

34. In the PRC, that is. A film was made from the screenplay and distributed in Taiwan. Kraus, "Bai Hua," 192 n. 17.

35. Michael Duke summarizes the standard Dengist position: "The highest expression of patriotism in the PRC today, according to the leadership, is to love the Communist Party. Criticism of the party per se . . . is automatically regarded

as unpatriotic and possibly treasonous, depending on the need for conformity felt by the leadership at any particular time." *Blooming and Contending,* 141.

36. Detailed discussions of the campaign against Bai Hua are in Kraus, "Bai Hua," 185–93; Goldman, *Sowing the Seeds of Democracy in China,* 88–112; and Duke, *Blooming and Contending,* 20–24, 123–48. Duke also supplies extensive literary analysis of *Unrequited Love.* For an interesting retrospective discussion by Bai Hua himself of the campaign against him, see the writer's lecture (Sept. 17, 1988) "Cong dalu xianzhuang kan Zhongguo qianjing," 11–12.

37. Goldman, *Sowing the Seeds of Democracy in China,* 98. See Perry Link's perceptive observations on the problem of blind faith in the regime in his *Evening Chats in Beijing,* 142–44.

38. Goldman, *Sowing the Seeds of Democracy in China,* 98–103; Kraus, "Bai Hua," 193.

39. The factory, according to Kraus ("Bai Hua," 187), was the "August First" Movie Equipment Factory.

40. According to what he told an interviewer in 2003, Bai Hua's first choice had been to return to Yunnan, where he had earlier spent time in the army. This, however, alarmed the Shanghai municipal authorities, who suspected him of wanting to go to Yunnan to establish secret contacts with foreign countries. The request was therefore rejected. Zhu Jianguo, "Bai Hua Zhuhai shuo gudu," 81–82. Not long prior to this, Bai Hua asserted that Shaoxing had been his first choice after all. See Bai Hua, *Ru meng suiyue,* 183.

41. Zhu Jianguo, "Bai Hua Zhuhai shuo gudu," 82, 85. Bai Hua's reflections on the Goujian story during the Shaoxing years are also discussed in his *Ru meng suiyue,* 188–89.

42. Bai Hua, *Wu wang jin ge Yue wang jian, Shiyue,* 68–70. *Shiyue,* a literary bimonthly, was the first journal to publish Bai Hua's play; it is the edition used here. The play was reprinted several times.

43. Bai Hua, *Wu wang jin ge Yue wang jian,* 70–72.

44. Ibid., 72.

45. This episode forms the main content of scene 4, in ibid., 80–83.

46. Ibid., 83–86.

47. Ibid., 86–91.

48. Ibid., 91–95, 64.

49. The anticipation was so great, according to Zhu Hong, who was living in Beijing at the time, that people were prepared to spend a month's salary to obtain a ticket (personal communication, May 6, 2004).

50. See, for example, Zhu Ying, "Jing han yu nei shen jian yu wai," 50–51, 80; Sun Zejun, "Qian tan *Wu wang jin ge Yue wang jian* de wumei sheji," 33; Fang Jie, "Huaju *Wu wang jin ge Yue wang jian* guan hou," 48–49 (Fang Jie's review was originally published in *Renmin ribao,* May 10, 1983).

51. See in particular Lin Kehuan, "Lishi yishi yu daode pipan," 34–35; Ding Yi, "Buyao weile guannian wangle lishi," 46–47.

52. Bai Hua, "Zhongguo dangdai wenxue de shiluo yu fugui" (lecture, Nov. 26, 1987), 141; Bai Hua, preface, *Yuangu de zhongsheng yu jinri de huixiang*, 2. Bai Hua said that the public announcement of the closing failed to elaborate on the reasons. As a result of this action, he claims to have lost a year's freedom of writing and movement.

53. Bai Hua, "*Wu wang jin ge Yue wang jian* chuangzuo duanxiang," 33; reprinted in Bai Hua, *Yuangu de zhongsheng yu jinri de huixiang*, 302. Bai Hua's universal humanism—his insistence on the ability of some individuals to transcend the limitations of time and place—was also applied to Qu Yuan. See his "Zhongguo zuojia" (lecture, Mar. 1988), 147. For criticism of this notion, see the reviews of Lin Kehuan and Ding Yi, cited in n. 51 earlier.

54. Bai Hua, "Zhongguo dangdai wenxue de shiluo yu fugui," 141–42.

55. Some have suggested that Deng Xiaoping may also have been a target. See Goldman, *Sowing the Seeds of Democracy in China*, 130; Barmé, "History for the Masses," 267; Kraus, *Bai Hua*, 193–94.

56. Bai Hua, "No Breakthrough, No Literature," 61.

57. Barmé, "History for the Masses," 267. The symbolism referred to the ubiquitous use of "the red sun in our hearts" as a metaphor for Mao, particularly during the Cultural Revolution.

58. Bai Hua, "Zhongguo de bei'ai" (lecture, Nov. 5, 1988), 25–26.

59. Fang Jie, "Huaju *Wu wang jin ge Yue wang jian* guan hou," 49.

60. On the importance of deniability in buffering a writer's criticism of China's leadership, see Link, *The Uses of Literature*, 59, 91.

61. Link points out that the selection of Bai Hua as the target of the 1981 campaign was something of a puzzle, since *Unrequited Love* "did not stand out as an especially provocative piece during 1979." The purpose of the campaign, he concludes, "was not to punish Bai Hua personally but to use him as an example through which to oppose 'bourgeois liberalism' generally." Ibid., 29 n. 55.

62. Ibid., 92. This was, of course, precisely what had happened to Xiao Jun earlier.

63. Bai Hua, "Zhongguo dangdai wenxue de shiluo yu fugui," 142. The play, titled *Huaihua qu*, was published in Bai Hua, *Yuangu de zhongsheng yu jinri de huixiang*, 121–208. In Bai Hua's preface to this collection, he advances a number of other reasons why the play may have been banned (ibid., 3).

6. THE GOUJIAN STORY IN A PRIVATIZING CHINA

1. Lanjun (pseud.), "Emo wei xue jiachi xiwu 20 nian." I am grateful to Dan Shao for bringing this episode to my attention.

2. For a brief introduction, see Wang, "Teaching Patriotism in China," 13–17.

3. Wu Xiaocong, "Wenwu zai aiguozhuyi jiaoyu zhong de zhongyao zuoyong," 84–86 (quotation from 85). Goujian's sword is on display at the Hubei Provincial Museum. It was still in remarkable condition when it came out of the ground and is viewed as an important example of the bronze metallurgical skill of the day. See the exhibition catalogue: Li Wen, *Yue wang Goujian jian yu Wu wang Fuchai mao.*

4. Song, "Chuzhong lishi jiaoxue ying zhongshi youhuan yishi de peiyang," 45.

5. See, for example, Liu Jimian, "Aiguozhuyi jiaoyu zhong buke hulüe guochi jiaoyu," 30–31.

6. Yang Bing'an, "Lüe lun zhenfen minzu jingshen," 5. See also Tai, "Zhongshi lishi renwu zai aiguozhuyi jiaoyu zhong de jiaohua zuoyong," 51–55; Zhang Jiugen, "Zai lishike jiaoxue zhong jinxing aiguozhuyi jiaoyu de changshi," 78.

7. One writer, in arguing for greater emphasis in China's schools on the cultural traditions of the past, contended that the main spirit of these traditions was none other than patriotic education. Ruan Lixuan, "Wenhua chuantong jiaoyu chuyi," 72–75. Others assigned a major place to China's cultural traditions as a source of inspiration in the present. Yang Bing'an, "Lüe lun zhenfen minzu jingshen"; Zhou Yongzhao, "Tan Zhongguo chuantong daode yu peiyang 'si you' xinren," 29–30.

8. He Yunwei and An Hua, "Wo xiao aiguozhuyi jiaoyu de shijian yu sikao," 84–88 (quotation on 87). For another piece that puts a local spin on patriotic education (in this instance focusing on Shanghai) and argues that such education must begin in early childhood, see Gu Yifan, "Aiguozhuyi jiaoyu yao cong wawa zhuaqi," 60.

9. See especially Culp, *Articulating Citizenship.*

10. He Yunwei and An Hua, "Wo xiao aiguozhuyi jiaoyu de shijian yu sikao," especially 85–86.

11. Liu Yi, "Zhonghua minzu chuantong meide de jiben neihan," 30–33.

12. Teng, "Qiantan dang de lingdao ganbu de shiyeguan," 26–27.

13. Tyler, "Beijing Suicide (or Was It Murder?) Spurs Politics by Allegory."

14. Yang Kunquan, "Wangxing de weihai," 46. Yang states that it was Fuchai's grandfather who was killed by Yue; since most sources say that it was his father I've changed the text. Another piece that focuses on the themes of "forgetting" and "not forgetting" in the Fuchai story is Ji Dacheng, "Tan 'wang,'" 39.

15. Zhang Wenhui, "Yue mie Wu de qishi," 30.

16. "Cong 'Wu wang Fuchai de beiju' tan jieli yu shili," 45–46. Zhang Yunnan has a fuller discussion of issues pertaining to corruption and how to handle it in "Lun quanli fubai ji qi duice," 43–46.

17. Zhao Jingyun, "Jianku chuangye jingshen shi shehuizhuyi benzhi de keguan yaoqiu," 14–17 (the reference to Goujian is on 14); Du Xin, "Baochi he

fayang jianku fendou de guangrong chuantong," 54–62 (the reference to Gou-jian is on 56).

18. Zhu Baoqin, "Ganshou chenggong," 25.

19. Ou Xianting, "Woxin changdan xie chunqiu," 24–25.

20. Xi Qisheng, "Nuli suzao hao ziji de xingxiang," 29–30.

21. Fu Boting and Feng Ruifang, "Peiyang xuesheng shuli 'fouding guan,'" 19.

22. A Liang, "Buneng wangque monan," 1.

23. Wang Zhi and Tang Feng, "Ye tan woxin changdan," 53. For a somewhat different take on the value of "sleeping on brushwood and tasting gall" as a strategy for dealing with rejection in one's search for the ideal job, see Sun Hongming, "Qiuzhi zhong de 'woxin changdan,'" 21.

24. Hu Caiwen, "Qiantan lishike de jingzheng yishi jiaoyu," 75.

25. Xu, "Erzi buzai shubuqi," 33–34.

26. Yu Yueming, "Jiaoshi—'fuyou gexing de duzhe,'" 73–74; see also Wang Lan, "Chongman zhihui de yuwen ke," 30 (the excerpt in this article is very similar to that in the previous one and appears to be from Xue Fagen's class, although it is not identified as such).

27. Bruner, *Making Stories,* 7, 35. Two recent examples of the power of story to shape people's reading of their own history, the first focusing on stories from English-language literature, the second on stories from the Hebrew Bible, are Azar Nafisi's remarkable book *Reading Lolita in Tehran* and Daniel Mendelsohn's deeply absorbing memoir *The Lost.*

28. Li Yongjun, "Peiyang feizhili yinsu, tigao lishi ketang jiaoxue shixiao," 54–55.

29. Lan Shenghong and Li Yuyin, "Ren wu yali nan chengcai," 47.

30. Riley, "China's Population," 17.

31. See, for example, French, "In China."

32. Yang Yue, "Xinhua shuping."

33. Chen Jijing, "Cuozhe jiaoyu zongheng tan," 20–21; see also Xiao Lihua, "Cuozhe jiaoyu," 75. A very different view of the home life of affluent Chinese children is presented in Kristof, "Chinese Medicine for American Schools."

34. Huang Shihong, "Youhuan yishi," 13.

35. See, for example, Xiao Lihua, "Cuozhe jiaoyu," 74–75; Fu Xuangang, "Xiang weiren xuexi," 4–5.

36. "There is little question," writes Howard French, "that the driving force for most parents is the challenge of succeeding in an increasingly competitive society." "In China," *New York Times.*

37. Chen Jijing, "Cuozhe jiaoyu zongheng tan," 21.

38. Wang Lei, "Miandui cuozhe," 36.

39. Chen Jijing, "Cuozhe jiaoyu zongheng tan," 20; Huang Shihong, "Youhuan yishi," 13; Xiao Lihua, "Cuozhe jiaoyu," 77; Guan Hongyu, "'Yi wu busao, heyi sao tianxia?'" 33.

40. See, for example, Fu Xuangang, "Xiang weiren xuexi," 5; Xiao Lihua, "Cuozhe jiaoyu," 78; Fu Rong, "Daxuesheng cuozhe xinli de tiaoshi yu jiaozheng," 100; Zhuge, "Xiao dui nashi de tongku," 53.

41. It is called *China Academic Journals* (Beijing: Tsinghua Tongfang Optical Disc Co.) and is distributed in the United States by East View Publications in Minneapolis. The publisher has recently introduced a much more limited database titled *Century Journals Project.* It consists of a selection of "the most important academic journals" published in China prior to 1994; these have been digitized from 1950 through 1993.

42. This information is taken from the website of the Museum of Broadcast Communications: China.

43. *Dong Zhou lieguo zhi* was originally written by the Ming author Yu Shaoyu; it was subsequently revised by another Ming writer, Feng Menglong. The edition I have consulted was further revised in the Qing by Cai Yuanfang. It contains 108 chapters, with chapters 71 through 83 dealing with the Goujian story. Synopses of each episode of the Spring and Autumn portion of the television drama are found in "*Dong Zhou lieguo chunqiu pian* juqing fenji jieshao." For a review of this part, see Liu Bo, "Hui-yu canban hua Chunqiu," 27.

44. The title and formatting of the contents differ. But there is nothing subtle about the plagiarism. With the exception of the first chapter, a small portion of the second, and the ending of the final chapter, the rest of Hong's book is an almost exact character-for-character reproduction of Xiao Jun's novel. The publisher's note *(chuban shuoming)* referring to the stimulus of the TV serialization is in Hong, *Yue wang Goujian,* 1 (front matter).

45. The actors playing the part of Goujian were Chen Baoguo *(Yue wang Goujian),* Chen Daoming *(Woxin changdan),* and Liu Songren *(Zhengba chuanqi). Woxin changdan* (official English title: "The Great Revival"), produced by CCTV, began broadcasting in the PRC on January 10, 2007. The other two productions are discussed below in the text. Some television reporters complained that the overload of dramas on the Goujian story reflected a lack of imagination and resourcefulness on the part of the Chinese television industry. See, for example, Li Junna, "Liangge 'Goujian' sange 'mingbu' yingshiju chuangzuo pinpin 'zhuiwei,'"; also Li Yan and Xiao Yang, "Liu Songren tiyan 'woxin changdan.'"

46. It was titled *Yue wang Goujian* (King Goujian of Yue). See the review by Ji Guoping, "Kangkai beiliang qu cong gu chang dao jin," 20–21.

47. The drama didn't begin airing in Hong Kong until December 18, 2006. Most provincial-level television stations chose not to compete with the World Cup. Zhejiang TV's maverick strategy is outlined in "He dali shen 'si ke' Zhejiang weishi *Zhengba chuanqi* kaibo."

48. "*Yue wang Goujian* rexiao haiwai"; "*Yue wang Goujian* guowai maichu tianjia"; "Guangbo hui luomu."

49. See "Changpian lishi xiaoshuo *Yue wang Goujian* liangjian wentan."

50. Even though, like the Great Yu (see text), the historicity of Xi Shi has not gone unchallenged. See, for example, Gu Xijia, "Xi Shi de chuanshuo," 33; Shen Zu'an, "Dadan de tupo," 8; Gong, "Lishishang zhen you Xi Shi ma?"

51. Gu Xijia, "Xi Shi de chuanshuo," 33. For other sources that took note of the "Xi Shi craze" *(re),* see Ruan Xun, "Nuli suzao laobaixing xin zhong de Xi Shi xingxiang," 9; Dong Fang, "Nongyu de xiangqing," 26. Among the Xi Shi operas widely discussed at the time were the Shaoxing opera *Xi Shi duanlan,* written by Ruan Xun in collaboration with Chen Weilong and first performed in 1995, and the Beijing opera *Xi Shi gui Yue,* written by Luo Huaizhen in 1988. The two novels were Chen Weijun, *Xi Shi,* and Yang Peijin, *Huan sha wanghou.*

52. See the Xinhua News Agency article "Wang Yongchang daibiao."

53. Sites relating to these people have for some time formed part of the Shaoxing tourist's itinerary and have been refurbished in recent years. See the guidebook *Gucheng Shaoxing,* 1–108.

54. Hu Ruifang et al., "Bu yi paiming lun yingxiong"; Gu Chun and Ding Jianping, "'Danjian' jingshen."

55. "Wang Yongchang diaoyan Yue wang cheng guihua jianshe." A similar project involves developing the site of the mountaintop fortifications erected by Goujian in a part of ancient Yue now known as Xiaoshan (north of Shaoxing and currently under the jurisdiction of Hangzhou). For a detailed description of these plans, see the Xiaoshan county website.

56. "Hexie Zhongguo de wenhua mingpian (3 yue 14 ri)." The shaping influence of Goujian—and the Great Yu—on the spirit of Shaoxing was acknowledged (and applauded) by Lu Xun, who in the view of some writers embodied the spirit himself. See Tan Yuliang, "Lun Lu Xun sixiang zhibian jianjinshi wancheng de fazhan xiansuo," 134; Wu Guoqun, "Mao Dun yu Lu Xun chuantong wenhua yuanyuan yu wenhua xingge zhi yitong," 17, 20; Zhang Wanyi, "Lu Xun yu Wu-Yue wenhua," 139–40.

57. Zhongli, a fictional master sword maker of Yue, was the title character in the early 1960s opera *Zhongli jian* (The swords of Zhongli). In the opera, he passes on his craft to his granddaughter, whose skillfully fashioned swords—she made eight thousand of them—are an important factor in enabling Goujian to vanquish Wu. See Zhao Cong, *Zhongguo dalu de xiqu gaige,* 159–60; Liu Naichong, "Kan pingju *Zhongli jian* hou manbi," 22–25.

58. "Houshan." See also "TV Series Titled *Goujian, King of Yue.*"

59. Hu Pu, "Weiren, mingren yu yinglian," 57; Kang Lin, "Yiwei shenchang de quanlian," 48; Zhou Hongjun, "Mingren yu zimianlian," 39; Zhang Lili, "Rang zhengzhi ke daoyu chongman meili," 41.

60. See the synopsis of the final episode of *Dong Zhou lieguo* (the television drama) in "*Dong Zhou lieguo chunqiu pian* juqing fenji jieshao"; the epilogue of Hong Bicheng's plagiarized novel, 462–71; the novel (1996) of Tongchuan et al.,

Dong Zhou lieguo, 1:468–69; the novel (2003) of Li Jie, *Wu Yue chunqiu,* 2:490–98; the summary of the final episode (number 42) of the television drama *Zhengba chuanqi;* and the synopsis of the television drama *Woxin changdan* in "Daxing lishiju *Woxin changdan* gushi genggai." The television drama *Yue wang Goujian* and the novel of the same title, both written by Zhang Jing and following near-identical story lines, develop the callously ambitious side of Goujian's character in a way that differs markedly from other renderings. On the eve of Goujian's return to Yue, Goujian's teenaged son, who had joined his parents in Wu some months before, devises a plan to assassinate Fuchai at a banquet given by Wu Zixu celebrating Fuchai's recovery from his illness. Goujian, who knows of his son's scheme, informs Fuchai in advance in order to demonstrate in the strongest possible way his loyalty to the Wu king; this of course results in the son's being killed at the banquet. See Zhang Jing, *Yue wang Goujian,* 2:398–411; see also Huang Jianzhong preface, in ibid., 1:4. Goujian's brutality is also put on full display in the novel's epilogue (2:597–605).

61. As an instance of the latter, a commentator in 1934, after noting Goujian's harsh side (including his responsibility for the forced suicide of Wen Zhong), asks his readers to bear in mind "how the king erased the humiliation Yue had experienced, how he built up the strength of the state, and how in one leap he went from being the ruler of a vanquished state to the chief of all the lords. If we conceive of the matter in this vein, despite the shivers Goujian sends down our spines, we will immediately be filled with admiration for this extraordinary man . . . [and] treat Goujian as our teacher." Zhiqing, "Buwang guochi de Goujian," 18–19. See also Wei Juxian's treatment of Goujian (discussed at the end of chapter 2).

62. Hong, *Yue wang Goujian,* 2 (front matter).

CONCLUSION

1. Another, of course, was the story of Yue Fei. The Yue Fei story, however, was rarely referred to in discussions of national humiliation, which was Goujian territory.

2. Kaplan, *Balkan Ghosts,* 35–40. Avishai Margalit has an interesting discussion of why 1389 carries such emotional power for the Serbs while 1066, the year of the Battle of Hastings, is all but forgotten by the British. See his *The Ethics of Memory,* 96–98.

3. See, for example, Yang Chengjian, "Wu Yue wenhua de fenye," 8–16.

4. I thank Hue-Tam Ho Tai for calling Nguyen Trai's proclamation to my attention. Professor Tai, who is a historian of Vietnam and was born in that country, informs me that the Goujian story was part of her early cultural training.

5. I am grateful to Matthias Zachmann for furnishing me with the first two parts of an editorial on the Tripartite Intervention by the famous journalist

Miyake Setsurei; it was entitled "Shōtan-gashin" and appeared in *Nihon*, first part, Meiji 28/5/15 (May 15, 1895), second part, Meiji 28/5/27 (May 27, 1895); my thanks also to Matsuzawa Hiroaki for informing me of the frequent reference to *woxin changdan* in Japanese writing at the time of the Russo-Japanese War.

6. Albert Craig took note of this in the second of his three lectures on "Fukuzawa Yukichi: Interpreting History," delivered at Harvard University on April 22, 2004. Fukuzawa's reference to the proverb *Dong Shi xiao pin* appears in his book *An Encouragement of Learning (Gakumon no susume)*.

7. Schank, *Tell Me a Story*, 30.

8. Ibid., 38.

9. Xin Ma Shizeng also starred in a film entitled *Woxin changdan*, which was released in 1955.

10. Some readers will recognize a degree of similarity between what I'm driving at here and Mark Elvin's intriguing notion of "inner history," which he describes as the stories that people live in and that constitute part of their social inheritance. See the introduction to his *Changing Stories in the Chinese World*, especially 5–10.

11. The definition of *woxin changdan* provided in the text is taken from *Han-Ying cidian (xiuding ban)*, 1061. Even dictionaries of Chinese proverbs do not necessarily supply a linkage to the Goujian story. See, for example, Xiong Guangyi, *Zhongguo chengyu da cidian*, 246. A full account of the proverb's roots in the Goujian story is found in *Ciyuan*, rev. ed., 3:2578.

12. Warner, *Joan of Arc*, 131–32.

13. "Cinderella Is a Myth," *New York Times*, Mar. 4, 2006.

14. "On the Media" is produced by WNYC in New York City. The website of "On the Media" contains the full transcript of the Charles Lewis interview, titled "The Digging Life."

15. Cohen, "The Asymmetry in Intellectual Relations between China and the West in the Twentieth Century," 1:61–93.

16. Schank, *Tell Me a Story*, 40. Compare this to Jerome Bruner's question (and warning): "Why do we use story as the form for telling about what happens in life and in our own lives? Why not images, or lists of dates and places and the names and qualities of our friends and enemies? Why this seemingly innate addiction to story? Beware an easy answer!" *Making Stories*, 27.

17. Ward, "Regional Operas and Their Audiences," 172, 186–87.

18. Bruner, *Making Stories*, 60.

19. The Serbs didn't have to wait until the late twentieth century to reconnect emotionally with the defeat of 1389. Already during World War I, John Reed reported from the front, "Every [Serbian] peasant soldier knows what he is fighting for . . . When he was a baby, his mother greeted him, 'Hail, little avenger of Kossovo!'" Kaplan, *Balkan Ghosts*, 38.

20. Although its reliability has often been questioned, the account of this

event that has most heavily influenced modern Jewish understanding is that of the Jewish historian Josephus, who was a contemporary of the Jewish revolts. Josephus's work *Wars of the Jews* first became available in modern Hebrew translation in 1923. Zerubavel, *Recovered Roots*, 60–63.

21. As quoted in Zerubavel, "The Death of Memory and the Memory of Death," 76.

22. Zerubavel, *Recovered Roots*, 70.

23. "For the better part of two generations," Dan Williams has written (for the Jerusalem Post Service), "the Masada myth was a symbol of the fledgling Zionist enterprise; it now threatens to slip back into obscurity." "Masada—Symbol of Resistance or Overblown Myth?" The diminished salience of the Masada myth-story over time may also be seen from another perspective: at the height of its impact (the decades from the 1930s into the 1970s), it was Israel that played David to the Arab world's Goliath; but after the 1967 and 1973 wars these perceptions were gradually reversed, as Israel, with the most powerful military in the region, assumed the mantle of Goliath and the Arab world became the new David. According to this symbolic logic, Israel, in the fighting that took place in the summer of 2006, could eliminate 90 percent of Hezbollah's fighting capacity, but Hezbollah could "still declare victory," claiming "that it fought the mighty Israeli Army to a draw." See Erlanger, "The Long-Term Battle."

24. A detailed study of the Masada story as myth is Ben-Yehuda, *The Masada Myth*.

25. "The Masada commemoration," Bernard Lewis writes, "was adopted by the Israeli state and made the center of something verging on a national cult." *History*, 4–5.

26. Although some have drawn a strained analogy between the Holocaust and the traumas of the Cultural Revolution, the differences between these two events far outweigh any similarities. For an insightful analysis of the changing relationship between Masada and the Holocaust as historical metaphors, see Zerubavel, "The Death of Memory and the Memory of Death."

27. Zerubavel, *Recovered Roots*, 64–65, 129–31, 135, 209–10 (quotation on 209).

28. Israel Ministry of Foreign Affairs, "Masada—Symbol of Jewish Freedom."

29. Quoted in Zerubavel, *Recovered Roots*, 70. Another of the people Zerubavel interviewed made essentially the same point: "The whole country is like Masada . . . We have to fight until the very end, not to yield and not to give up." Ibid.

30. Margalit, *The Ethics of Memory*, 95.

31. Renan's ideas, developed in his famous essay "What Is a Nation?" are discussed by Kwame Anthony Appiah in his review of Margalit's book, *New York Review of Books*, Mar. 13, 2003, 35–37. J. M. Coetzee, suggestively, has Susan Barton, a character in his novel *Foe*, ask at one point: "Is that the secret meaning of the word story, do you think: a storing place of memories?" 59.

32. Bruner states that "the sharing of common stories creates an interpretive

community," which, he adds, is critically important "for promoting cultural co-hesion." *Making Stories,* 25. On Elvin, see below in text.

33. Elvin, *Changing Stories in the Chinese World,* 5.

34. Although Anderson uses "imagined communities" to refer primarily to nations (a particular kind of political community), the concept is easily trans-ferable to other communal realms: religious, cultural, and so on. A nation, ac-cording to the author, is "imagined" "because the members of even the smallest nation will never know most of their fellow-members, meet them, or even hear of them, yet in the minds of each lives the image of their communion." A na-tion is imagined as a "community" because, despite the differences prevailing within it, it "is always conceived as a deep, horizontal comradeship." Anderson, *Imagined Communities,* 5–7.

CHARACTER LIST

Characters for authors and titles cited in the text and notes are included here only if not found in the bibliography.

aiguo 愛國
aimei 曖昧
aimin 愛民
An Lushan 安祿山

ba 霸
Ban Chao 班超
baojun de benxing 暴君的本性
Baosi 褒姒
Baowei Shaoxing ge 保衛紹興歌
Bayue de xiangcun 八月的鄉村
bei qinlüezhe 被侵略者
Bin 豳
Bo Pi 伯嚭
Bowu 伯武
Boyikao 伯邑攷
bu chengqi de junwang 不成器的君王

Cai Gongshi　蔡公時

Cao Cao　曹操

Cao Mo (Gui)　曹沫 (劌)

Chen Baoguo　陳寶國

Chen Dabei　陳大悲

Chen Daoming　陳道明

Chen Duxiu　陳獨秀

Chen Gongbo　陳公博

Chen Shui-bian　陳水扁

Chen Xitong　陳希同

Chen Yi　陳毅

Chen Yin　陳音

Cheng Tianfang　程天放

"Chenggong zhi lu"　成功之路

chi　恥

Chi bi　赤壁

Chiang Ching-kuo (Jiang Jingguo)　蔣經國

Chu　楚

Chuang wang ru jing　闖王入京

Cong Dezi　叢德滋

cuozhe jiaoyu　挫折教育

dadao　打倒

dadao diguozhuyi　打倒帝國主義

dadao Wu guo　打倒吳國

Daji　妲己

dalian gangtie　大煉鋼鐵

dalian minbing　大練民兵

dan (female operatic role)　旦

dan (grain measure)　石

dan jian jingshen　膽劍精神

Dangren hun　黨人魂

daode yu xingwei　道德與行爲

datong　大同

daxing shuili　大興水利

Deng Xiaoping　鄧小平

di　狄

dingwei　丁未

Dingxian　定縣

Dong Shi　東施

Dong Shi xiao pin　東施效顰

Dong Zhou lieguo　東周列國

Dong Zhou lieguo zhi　東周列國志

Du Fu　杜甫

Duke Ai of Lu　魯哀公

Duke Huan of Qi　齊桓公

Duke Mu of Qin　秦穆公

Duke Wen of Jin　晉文公

(Earlier) Qin　前秦

Eastern Jin (317–420)　東晉

Emperor Wu of Han　漢武帝

fafen tuqiang　發憤圖強

Fan Li　范蠡

Fan Zhongyan　范仲淹

fangong　反共

Fangong dahechang　反攻大合唱

fangong dalu　反攻大陸

fangong fuguo　反攻復國

fangong kang E　反共抗俄

fangong xuechi　反攻雪恥

Fei River　淝水

feng　風

Fengqiu　封丘

Fu Jun　傅駿

Fuchai　夫差

fuchou　復仇

fuchouzhuyi　復仇主義

fuguo　復國

fuguo xuechi 復國雪恥

Fujiao 夫椒

Fukuzawa Yukichi 福澤諭吉

furen 夫人

fuxing minzu 復興民族

Gaoshan 高山

Gaozong 高宗

ge 葛

gebu 葛布

Gengmeng 更孟

Goujian fuguo 勾踐復國

"Goujian mie Wu" 勾踐滅吳

Goujianzhuyi 勾踐主義

Gu Gong Danfu 古公亶父

gu wei jin yong 古爲今用

Gu Yanwu 顧炎武

Guanwa Palace 館娃宮

guangfu dalu 光復大陸

Guo Moruo 郭沫若

Guo Songtao 郭嵩燾

Guo Ziyi 郭子儀

guochi 國恥

guochi ge 國恥歌

guochi jiaoyu 國恥教育

guochi ri 國恥日

guojia xingwang renren you ze 國家興亡人人有責

Guoli bianyi guan 國立編譯館

guomin 國民

guonan 國難

Guoqu de niandai 過去的年代

guowen 國文

guoyin zimu 國音字母

Guoyu 國語

Guoyu duben   國語讀本

Gusu (alt. xu) Palace   姑蘇(胥)臺

Hai Rui   海瑞

Han Xin   韓信

Hangu Pass   函谷關

heiren   黑人

Helu   闔廬

Houshan Scenic Area   吼山風景區

Hu Qiaomu   胡喬木

Hu Xiaolong   胡小龍

Hua Guofeng   華國鋒

Huan sha ji   浣紗記

Huang Chao   黃巢

Huang Di   黃帝

Huang Jilu   黃季陸

Huangchi   黃池

Huangpu junxiao   黃埔軍校

"Hui guniang"   灰姑娘

huijia shunan   毀家紓難

hundan   混蛋

hunjun   昏君

Jia Yi   賈誼

Jiajing   嘉靖

jianchi buxie   堅持不懈

Jiang Qing   江青

Jiang xiang he   將相和

Jiang Zemin   江澤民

jianku fendou   艱苦奮鬥

Jiao Juyin   焦菊隱

jiaotu   焦土

jiaoxun shi nian   教訓十年

jiaren zhenshi   假人真事

Jiaxing　嘉興

Jie　桀

jie gu feng jin　借古諷今

jieli　借力

Jimo　即墨

Jin dynasty (1115–1234)　金

Jin (Eastern Zhou state)　晉

jingkang　靖康

jinianpin　紀念品

jinzhong baoguo　盡忠報國

Jiran　計然

jisi　己巳

juben　劇本

Junshi weiyuanhui weiyuanzhang　軍事委員會委員長

Ka'erdeng daxiyuan　卡爾登大戲院

kangzhan　抗戰

ketou　磕頭

Kexuan　可軒

King Jie of Xia　夏桀王

King Ping of Chu　楚平王

King Tang of Shang　商湯王

King Wen of Zhou　周文王

King Zhou of Shang　商紂王

koutou　叩頭

Kuai Dafu　蒯大富

Kuaiji　會稽

Kucheng　苦成

Kulian　苦戀

Langye　瑯琊

laodong duanlian　勞動鍛煉

laosheng　老生

Laozi　老子

Lee Teng-hui (Li Denghui)　李登輝

Lei Haizong　雷海宗

li (might)　力

li (right)　理

Li Bai　李白

Li Hanqiu　李漢秋

Li Ling　李陵

Li Zicheng　李自成

Lian Po　廉頗

Liang Chenyu　梁辰魚

Liao Xiangxiong　廖祥雄

lienü　烈女

Liezi　列子

lijing tuzhi　勵精圖治

Lin Biao　林彪

Lin Xiangru　藺相如

Lin Zexu　林則徐

Ling Tower　靈臺

lingce de ren　另冊的人

Liu Bang (Gaozu)　劉邦 (高祖)

Liu Bei　劉備

Liu Ning　柳寧

Liu Shaoqi　劉少奇

Liu Songren　劉松仁

Liu Xiu　劉秀

Lu　魯

Lu Tower　鹿臺

Lu Xun　魯迅

Lushan Conference　廬山會議

Lü Buwei　呂不韋

Lüshi chunqiu　呂氏春秋

Luo Ruiqing　羅瑞卿

maiguo xingwei　賣國行爲

maitou kugan　埋頭苦幹

"Man jiang hong"　滿江紅

Mao Zedong　毛澤東

meinü　美女

meiren ji　美人計

ming chi　明恥

Minzhong shudian　民衆書店

Mount Guxu (alt. su, yu)　姑胥(蘇,餘)山

Mount Kuaiji　會稽山

Mount Lingyan　靈岩山

Mount Muke　木客山

Mount Qi　岐山

Mount Tai　泰山

Moxi　妺喜

Mozi　墨子

nanlin chuzi　南林處子

nian nian zhao Wu　廿年沼吳

Ningluo　苧蘿

Nongmin kangzhan congshu　農民抗戰叢書

Peng Dehuai　彭德懷

Peng Sanyuan　彭叁元

Peng Zhen　彭真

Pu Songling　蒲松齡

Qi　齊

Qi Hong　齊虹

Qi Jiguang　戚繼光

Qian Gate　前門

Qian Yingyu　錢英郁

Qiantang　錢塘

Qin　秦

Qin Gui　秦檜

Qingshan Opera Company　青山越劇團

qinlüezhe　侵略者

qinzhan　侵佔

Qiu Jin　秋瑾

Qiu Jin yu Xu Xilin　秋瑾與徐錫麟

Qu Yuan　屈原

qunzhong luxian　群眾路綫

re　熱

ren　忍

Ren An　任安

renlun　人倫

renru fuzhong　忍辱負重

renshen　壬申

renshi liangjia　人事兩假

rong　戎

Shang　商

Shangwu　商務

shangyou guren　尚友古人

Shaokang　少康

Shaoxing　紹興

Shaoxing Yue wang hun　紹興越王魂

shengju jiaoxun　生聚教訓

shengju shi nian　生聚十年

Shennong　神農

Shi Kefa　史可法

shi nian jiaoxun　十年教訓

shi nian shengju　十年生聚

Shiji　史記

shili　失力

Sima Qian　司馬遷

sitong　四同

Song　宋

Songling　松陵

Su Nü　素女

Su Qin　蘇秦

Su Shi (alt. Dongpo)　蘇軾 (東坡)

Sun Jiazheng　孫家正
Sun Quan　孫權
Sun Yat-sen (Sun Yixian)　孫逸仙
Suzhou　蘇州

Taiwang　太王
taizai　太宰
taoguang-yanghui　韜光養晦
Teng　滕
Tian Dan　田單
Tian Han　田漢
Tian He　田和
touxiang　投降

wang　王
Wang Baosen　王寶森
Wang Mang　王莽
Wang Meng　王蒙
Wang Shouren (alt. Yangming)　王守仁 (陽明)
Wang Xizhi　王羲之
Wang Yongchang　王永昌
Wang Yunwu　王雲五
Wang Zhaojun　王昭君
wangguo zhi wu　亡國之物
wei guo wang jia　為國忘家
Wei Xi　衛茜
Wei Zheng　魏徵
Weida de lingxiu　偉大的領袖
Weida de Zhonghua　偉大的中華
Wen Tianxiang　文天祥
Wen Tower　文臺
Wen Zhong　文種
Wenhuabao　文化報
Wu　吳
wu fenzhong zhi redu　五分鐘之熱度

Wu Sangui　吳三桂
Wu She　伍奢
Wu Zetian　武則天
Wu Zixu　伍子胥
Wuba　無霸
wutiaojian touxiang　無條件投降
wuwang guochi　勿忘國恥
wuwang qian chi　無忘前恥

xi　戲
Xi Shi　西施
Xia　夏
xian kai diyi qiang　先開第一槍
xiandaihua　現代化
Xiang Yu　項羽
xiangsheng　相聲
xiao huangdi　小皇帝
Xiao xiaoshuo　小小說
Xibo　西伯
xin guojia　新國家
Xin Ma Shizeng (Sun Ma Sze-tsang)　新馬師曾
Xin qingnian　新青年
xinli jianshe　心理建設
Xiongnu　匈奴
Xu Gate　胥門
Xu Xilin　徐錫麟
xuanzhan　宣戰
Xuanzong　玄宗
Xue Fagen　薛法根
xuechi　雪恥
xuechi fuchou　雪恥復仇
xuechi fuguo　雪恥復國
xuechi ri　雪恥日
Xuzhou　徐州

Yan 燕

Yan Di 炎帝

yang 陽

Yang Hucheng 楊虎城

Yao Wenyuan 姚文元

Yen Chia-kan (Yan Jiagan) 嚴家淦

yi shi wei jing 以史為鏡

yin 陰

Yin 殷

yingshe 影射

yingshe gongji 影射攻擊

yingshe xianshi 影射現實

yinmou 陰謀

Yongdong 甬東

you wei xue 猶未雪

Youli 羑里

Yu 禹

Yu Shizhi 于是之

Yuan Shikai 袁世凱

Yuanchang (alt. Yunchang) 元常(允常)

Yue 越

Yue Fei 岳飛

Yue jue shu 越絕書

Yue nü 越女

Yue wang cheng 越王城

Yue wang hui 岳王會

Yue wang hun bibao 越王魂壁報

Yue wang hun shiri tongxun 越王魂十日通訊

zai junkou zhi zhong 在軍寇之中

Zeng Guofan 曾國藩

Zengwenxi 曾文溪

zhandou wenyi 戰鬥文藝

Zhang Binglin 章炳麟

Zhang Haidi 張海迪

Zhang Xueliang　張學良

Zhao　趙

zhao Wu　沼吳

Zhao Ye　趙曄

Zhe　浙

zhen aiguo de ren　真愛國的人

Zheng Chenggong　鄭成功

Zheng Dan　鄭旦

zhengyi　正義

zhenren jiashi　真人假事

Zhong shan　種山

zhong xiao jie yi　忠孝節義

Zhonggeng　仲耕

Zhonghua　中華

Zhonghua minzu shi　中華民族史

Zhongli　鍾離

Zhou　紂

Zhou Enlai　周恩來

Zhou Guohong　周國洪

Zhou Xinfang　周信芳

Zhou Yang　周揚

Zhou Yuanfu　周元福

Zhoushan　舟山

Zhuan Yi　專毅

Zhuji　諸暨

zili gengsheng　自力更生

zong dongyuan　總動員

Zuili　檇李

Zuozhuan　左傳

BIBLIOGRAPHY

A Liang 阿良. "Buneng wangque monan" 不能忘卻磨難 [We can't forget the ordeal]. *Xinxihua jianshe* 信息化建設 6 (2003): 1.

"Aiguo de Jiang zongtong" 愛國的蔣總統 [President Chiang's patriotic nature]. In *Guomin xiaoxue guoyu* 5:27–28.

"Aiguo de shaonian" 愛國的少年 [The patriotic youth]. In *Guomin xiaoxue guoyu* 5:31–32.

Amin 阿敏 and Peiyu 培玉. "Zhonghua wenming shi ke zhuisu dao wannian qian: Haixia liang an shixuejia gong ti xin guandian" 中華文明史可追溯到萬年前：海峽兩岸史學家共提新觀點 [The history of Chinese civilization can be traced back ten thousand years: New viewpoints jointly advanced by historians from both sides of the strait]. *Taisheng zazhi* 臺聲雜誌 3 (1998): 43.

Anderson, Benedict. *Imagined Communities: Reflections on the Origin and Spread of Nationalism,* rev. ed. London: Verso, 1991.

Appiah, Kwame Anthony. Review of A. Margalit, *The Ethics of Memory. New York Review of Books,* Mar. 13, 2003, 35–37.

Bai Hua 白樺. *Bai Hua liuxue de xin* 白樺流血的心 [The grieving heart of Bai Hua]. Xianggang: Mingbao chubanshe, 1989.

———. "Cong dalu xianzhuang kan Zhongguo qianjing" 從大陸現狀看中國前景 [Looking at China's prospects from the point of view of the current situation on the mainland], lecture, Iowa, Sept. 17, 1988. In Bai Hua, *Bai Hua liuxue de xin,* 2–23.

———. *Huaihua qu* 槐花曲 [The scholar tree-flower song]. In Bai Hua, *Yuangu de zhong sheng yu jinri de huixiang,* 121–208.

———. "No Breakthrough, No Literature," trans. Denis C. Mair. In Goldblatt, ed., *Chinese Literature for the 1980s,* 56–67.

———. *Ru meng suiyue* 如夢歲月 [Time's passage as in a dream]. Shanghai: Xuelin chubanshe, 2002.

———. *Wu wang jin ge Yue wang jian* 吳王金戈越王劍 [The golden spear of the king of Wu and the sword of the king of Yue]. *Shiyue* 十月 2 (1983): 65–95, 64. Reprinted in Bai Hua, *Yuangu de zhong sheng yu jinri de huixiang,* 1–119.

———. "*Wu wang jin ge Yue wang jian* chuangzuo duanxiang" 《吳王金戈越王劍》創作斷想 [Stray thoughts on the writing of *The Golden Spear of the King of Wu and the Sword of the King of Yue*]. *Xijubao* 戲劇報 9 (1983): 33–35.

———. *Yuangu de zhong sheng yu jinri de huixiang* 遠古的鐘聲與今日的廻響 [The tolling of the bells of remote antiquity and the echoes of today]. Taibei: Sanmin shuju, 1990.

———. "Zhongguo dangdai wenxue de shiluo yu fugui" 中國當代文學的失落與復歸 [The decline and recovery of contemporary Chinese literature], lecture, Chinese University of Hong Kong, Nov. 26, 1987. In Bai Hua, *Bai Hua liuxue de xin,* 110–45.

———. "Zhongguo de bei'ai" 中國的悲哀 [China's sorrow], lecture, Columbia University, Nov. 5, 1988. In Bai Hua, *Bai Hua liuxue de xin,* 24–30.

———. "Zhongguo zuojia" 中國作家 [Chinese writers], lecture, West Germany, Mar. 1988. In Bai Hua, *Bai Hua liuxue de xin,* 146–55.

Barmé, Geremie. "History for the Masses." In Unger, ed., *Using the Past to Serve the Present,* 260–86.

Barmé, Geremie, and John Minford, eds. *Seeds of Fire: Chinese Voices of Conscience.* New York: Noonday Press, 1989.

Ben-Yehuda, Nachman. *The Masada Myth: Collective Memory and Mythmaking in Israel.* Madison: University of Wisconsin Press, 1995.

Birch, Cyril, ed. *Anthology of Chinese Literature: From Early Times to the Fourteenth Century.* New York: Grove Press, 1965.

Boorman, Howard L., ed. *Biographical Dictionary of Republican China,* 4 vols. New York: Columbia University Press, 1967–1971.

Bruner, Jerome. *Making Stories: Law, Literature, Life.* Cambridge, MA: Harvard University Press, 2002.

Bu Wenxun 卜聞勛. "Guochi ri gai chi sucai de wo jian" 國恥日改吃素菜的我見 [My view that on National Humiliation Day we should switch to eating vegetarian food]. *Shenbao,* May 8, 1922.

"Buyao wangji" 不要忘記 [Do not forget]. *Ertong shijie* 兒童世界 25, no. 13 (Mar. 29, 1930): 6.

Cao Yongjin 曹勇進. "Yang Hucheng de aiguo jingshen ji qi shenghua" 楊虎城的愛國精神及其升華 [Yang Hucheng's patriotic spirit and its elevation to a higher level]. *Tanqiu* 探求 5 (1994): 56–58.

Cao Yu 曹禺. *Cao Yu zizhuan* 曹禺自傳 [Autobiography of Cao Yu]. Nanjing: Jiangsu wenyi chubanshe, 1996.

———. *Dan jian pian (wu mu huaju)* 膽劍篇（五幕話劇）[The gall and the sword: A spoken drama in five acts]. Beijing: Zhongguo xiju chubanshe, 1962. Originally appeared in *Renmin wenxue* 人民文學 7–8 (July 1961): 129–64.

———. *Dan jian pian (wu mu lishiju)* 膽劍篇（五幕歷史劇）[The gall and the sword: A historical drama in five acts]. Chengdu: Sichuan renmin chubanshe, 1979.

———. "Man tan juzuo" 漫談劇作 [An informal discussion of drama]. *Zhongguo xiju* 中國戲劇 6 (1962): 1–4.

"Carry Out the Cultural Revolution Thoroughly and Transform the Educational System Completely." *Peking Review,* June 24, 1966, 15–17 (originally in *People's Daily,* June 18, 1966).

Chan, Wing-tsit, trans. and comp. *A Source Book in Chinese Philosophy.* Princeton: Princeton University Press, 1963.

Chan-kuo ts'e [Zhanguoce]. J. I. Crump, trans., rev. ed. Ann Arbor: Center for Chinese Studies, University of Michigan, 1996.

Chang, Leo S., and Yu Feng. *The Four Political Treatises of the Yellow Emperor.* Honolulu: University of Hawaii Press, 1998.

"Changpian lishi xiaoshuo *Yue wang Goujian* liangjian wentan" 長篇歷史小説《越王勾踐》亮劍文壇 [Historical novel titled *King Goujian of Yue* presented to literary world], Oct. 30, 2006. http://hb.people.com.cn/croot/01/0137/content.asp?id = 96216%20&cn = 0137 (accessed Dec. 25, 2006).

Chen Duo 陳多 et al., comps. *Xiandai xijujia Xiong Foxi* 現代戲劇家熊佛西 [The modern playwright Xiong Foxi]. Beijing: Zhongguo xiju chubanshe, 1985.

Chen Enhui 陳恩惠. *Xi Shi* 西施. Tainan: Dafang shuju, 1953 (orig. ed.: Shanghai, 1940).

Chen Feibao 陳飛寶. "Li Hanxiang de daoyan yishu" 李翰祥的導演藝術 [Li Hanxiang's directorial art]. *Dianying yishu* 電影藝術 4 (1997): 41–48.

Chen Fudan 陳復旦. "Du 'Wo wei Goujian, ren fei Fuchai' ganyan" 讀 "我為勾踐，人非夫差" 感言 [Reactions after reading "We are Goujian, but the other side isn't Fuchai"]. *Xibei xiangdao* 西北嚮導 12 (1936): 27–28.

Chen Heqin 陳鶴琴 and Zhu Zefu 朱澤甫, comps. *Woxin changdan* 臥薪嘗膽. Shanghai: Minzhong shudian, 1938.

Chen Jian and Yang Kuisong. "Chinese Politics and the Collapse of the Sino-Soviet Alliance." In Odd Arne Westad, ed., *Brothers in Arms: The Rise and Fall of the Sino-Soviet Alliance, 1945–1963,* 246–94. Washington, D.C.: Woodrow Wilson Center Press/Stanford: Stanford University Press, 1998.

Chen Jijing 陳冀京. "Cuozhe jiaoyu zongheng tan" 挫折教育縱橫談 [A wide-ranging discussion of education for coping with setbacks]. *Dangdai qingnian yanjiu* 當代青年研究 6 (1995): 20–21.

Chen Ling 陳淩. "Yingxiong zhi chi: Goujian zhi wojian" 英雄之恥：勾踐之我見

[The shame of the hero: My view of Goujian]. *Youxiu zuowen xuanping (gaozhong ban)* 優秀作文選評（高中版）Z1 (2006): 62.

Chen Weijun 陳瑋君. *Xi Shi* 西施. Hangzhou: Zhejiang wenyi, 1995.

Chen Wenquan 陳文泉. *Goujian yu Xi Shi* 勾踐與西施 [Goujian and Xi Shi]. Taibei: Xin shiji juyi she, 1959.

Chen Yuhua 陳玉華. "Goujian zhao Wu lun" 勾踐沼吳論 [A discussion of Goujian's destruction of Wu]. *Funü zazhi* 婦女雜誌 1, no. 5 (May 5, 1915): 14–15.

[Cheng] Shewo 成舍我. "Ji'nan can'an guoren ying tong ding si tong" 濟南慘案國人應痛定思痛 [Chinese should learn a lesson from the painful experience of the Ji'nan massacre]. *Minsheng bao* 民生報, May 12, 1928.

Chiang Kai-shek. *China's Destiny and Chinese Economic Theory,* with notes and commentary by Philip Jaffe. London: Dennis Dobson, 1947.

Chow Tse-tsung. *The May Fourth Movement: Intellectual Revolution in Modern China.* Cambridge, MA: Harvard University Press, 1960.

Chu Binjie 褚斌傑 and Wang Hengzhan 王恆展. "Lun xian Qin lishi sanwen zhong de xiaoshuo yinsu" 論先秦歷史散文中的小説因素 [A discussion of fictional elements in pre-Qin historical prose]. *Tianzhong xuekan* 天中學刊 10, no. 2 (May 1995): 42–48.

Chu, Yun-han. "Social Protests and Political Democratization in Taiwan." In Murray A. Rubinstein, ed., *The Other Taiwan: 1945 to the Present,* 99–113. Armonk, NY: M. E. Sharpe, 1994.

Ch'un Ts'ew with the Tso Chuen, The, trans. James Legge. In *The Chinese Classics,* vol. 5. Hong Kong: Hong Kong University Press, 1960.

Ciyuan 辭源 [The roots of words], rev. ed., 4 vols. Hong Kong: Shangwu yinshuguan, 1979–84.

Clough, Ralph N. *Island China.* Cambridge, MA: Harvard University Press, 1978.

———. "Taiwan under Nationalist Rule, 1949–1982." In Roderick MacFarquhar and John K. Fairbank, eds., *The Cambridge History of China,* vol. 15: *The People's Republic,* part 2: *Revolutions within the Chinese Revolution, 1966–1982,* 815–40. Cambridge: Cambridge University Press, 1991.

———. "United States China Policy." Reprinted in Franz Schurmann and Orville Schell, eds., *The China Reader: Communist China,* 306–18. New York: Vintage, 1967.

Coble, Parks M. *Facing Japan: Chinese Politics and Japanese Imperialism, 1931–1937.* Cambridge, MA: Council on East Asian Studies, Harvard University, 1991.

Coetzee, J. M. *Foe.* New York: Penguin, 1987.

Cohen, Paul A. "The Asymmetry in Intellectual Relations between China and the West in the Twentieth Century." In Zhang Qixiong 張啓雄, ed., "*Ershi shiji de Zhongguo yu shijie" lunwen xuanji* "二十世紀的中國與世界" 論文選集 ["China and the world in the twentieth century": Selected essays], 1:61–93. Taibei: Zhongyang yanjiuyuan jindaishi yanjiusuo, 2001.

————. *Between Tradition and Modernity: Wang T'ao and Reform in Late Ch'ing China.* Cambridge, MA: Harvard University Press, 1974.

————. *History in Three Keys: The Boxers as Event, Experience, and Myth.* New York: Columbia University Press, 1997.

————. "Remembering and Forgetting National Humiliation in Twentieth-Century China." *Twentieth-Century China* 27, no. 2 (Apr. 2002): 1–39.

"Cong 'ershiyi tiao' dao 'Dong Ya xin zhixu'" 從 "二十一條" 到 "東亞新秩序" [From the "Twenty-One Demands" to the "New Order in East Asia"]. *Shenbao,* May 9, 1939.

Craig, Albert. "Fukuzawa Yukichi: Interpreting History," lecture, Harvard University, Apr. 22, 2004.

Croizier, Ralph C. *Koxinga and Chinese Nationalism: History, Myth, and the Hero.* Cambridge, MA: East Asian Research Center, Harvard University, 1977.

"Cross-Strait Trade up 22 Percent in First Eight Months." http://www.chinadaily.com.cn/china/2006–09/17/content_690644.htm (accessed Feb. 4, 2007).

Culp, Robert. *Articulating Citizenship: Civic Education and Student Politics in Southeastern China, 1912–1940.* Cambridge, MA: Harvard University Asia Center, 2007.

Daguan 達觀 [pseud.]. "Wu qi guochi hu wu jiu guochi hu?" 五七國恥乎五九國恥乎 [May 7 national humiliation or May 9 national humiliation?]. *Shenbao,* May 7, 1926.

"Dang guo de zhongxing" 黨國的中興 [Resurgence of the party and nation]. *Zhongyang ribao,* Oct. 10, 1952 (reprinted in *Zhongyang ribao: Wushinianlai shelun xuanji,* 95).

"Daxing lishiju *Woxin changdan* gushi genggai" 大型歷史劇《臥薪嘗膽》故事梗概 [The gist of the story in the full-length historical drama *Sleeping on brushwood and tasting gall*]. http://yule.sohu.com/20060420/n242909587.shtml (accessed Dec. 24, 2006).

de Bary, Wm. Theodore, and Irene Bloom, comps. *Sources of Chinese Tradition,* 2nd ed. New York: Columbia University Press, 1999.

"Digging Life, The," Mar. 14, 2005. http://www.onthemedia.org/transcripts/transcripts_030405_digging.html (accessed June 4, 2006).

Ding Yi 丁毅. "Buyao weile guannian wangle lishi: Ye ping *Wu wang jin ge Yue wang jian*" 不要爲了觀念忘了歷史：也評《吳王金戈越王劍》 [We mustn't neglect history for the sake of an idea: A further critique of *The Golden Spear of the King of Wu and the Sword of the King of Yue*]. *Zuopin yu zhengming* 作品與爭鳴 10 (Oct. 1983): 46–47.

Dong Fang 東方. "Nongyu de xiangqing: Ji juzuojia, minjian wenyi jia Ruan Xun" 濃郁的鄉情：記劇作家民間文藝家阮遜 [The strong flavor of the countryside: A note on Ruan Xun, playwright and writer on folk literature and art]. *Xi wen* 戲文 4 (1996): 26–27.

"*Dong Zhou lieguo chunqiu pian* juqing fenji jieshao"《東周列國春秋篇》劇

情分集介紹 [Introducing the different episodes in the story of *The States of the Eastern Zhou, Spring and Autumn part*]. http://www.tvpad.cn/guzhuang/h0468a.html (accessed Dec. 26, 2006).

Du Songbo 杜松柏. "*Shiji* zhong de fuchou gushi chulun" 《史記》中的復仇故事芻論 [A tentative discussion of revenge stories in *Records of the Historian*]. *Sichuan shifan xueyuan xuebao (zhexue shehui kexue ban)* 四川師範學院學報（哲學社會科學版）1 (Jan. 2002): 41–46.

"Du 'Wo wei Goujian, ren fei Fuchai' yihou" 讀 "我為勾踐, 人非夫差" 以後 [After reading "We are Goujian, but the other side isn't Fuchai"]. *Xibei xiangdao* 西北嚮導 10 (1936): 25–27.

Du Xin 杜辛. "Baochi he fayang jianku fendou de guangrong chuantong" 保持和發揚艱苦奮鬥的光榮傳統 [Uphold and develop the glorious tradition of hard struggle]. *Dangdai sichao* 當代思潮 5 (1995): 54–62.

Duke, Michael. *Blooming and Contending: Chinese Literature in the Post-Mao Era.* Bloomington: Indiana University Press, 1985.

Eastman, Lloyd E. *The Abortive Revolution: China under Nationalist Rule, 1927–1937.* Cambridge, MA: Harvard University Press, 1974.

———. "Nationalist China during the Nanking Decade, 1927–1937." In John K. Fairbank and Albert Feuerwerker, eds., *The Cambridge History of China,* vol. 13: *Republican China, 1912–1949,* part 2, 116–67. Cambridge: Cambridge University Press, 1986.

Egan, Ronald C. *Word, Image, and Deed in the Life of Su Shi.* Cambridge, MA: Council on East Asian Studies, Harvard University, and the Harvard-Yenching Institute, 1994.

Elvin, Mark. *Changing Stories in the Chinese World.* Stanford: Stanford University Press, 1997.

Erlanger, Steven. "The Long-Term Battle: Defining 'Victory' before the World." *New York Times,* Aug. 3, 2006.

"Fan Dafu" 范大夫 [Minister Fan]. In *Pingmin qianzi ke* 平民千字課 [Textbook of one thousand characters for the common people], 4 *ce,* 86th rev. ed., 3:4–5. Shanghai: Pingmin jiaoyu cujin hui, 1925.

Fan Junhong 范鈞宏. "Guanyu 'woxin changdan': Zhi Zhang Zhen tongzhi" 關於 "臥薪嘗膽": 致張真同志 [On "*woxin changdan*": A letter to Comrade Zhang Zhen]. *Juben* 劇本 9 (Sept. 1961): 83–89. Reprinted in *Lishiju lunji,* 229–45.

Fang Jie 方杰. "Huaju *Wu wang jin ge Yue wang jian* guan hou" 話劇《吳王金戈越王劍》觀後 [After seeing the spoken drama *The Golden Spear of the King of Wu and the Sword of the King of Yue*]. *Zuopin yu zhengming* 作品與爭鳴 10 (Oct. 1983): 48–49. Originally published in *Renmin ribao,* May 10, 1983.

Fangong, minzhu, tuanjie, jinbu: Ben bao chuangkan ershinianlai yixilie shelun zongji 反共, 民主, 團結, 進步： 本報創刊二十年來一系列社論總集 [Anti-communism, democracy, unity, progress: A general collection of editorials pub-

lished in this paper in the twenty years since its founding], 2 vols. Taibei: Lianhebao 聯合報, 1971.

Fangshi 放士 [pseud.]. "Lun xue guochou yi xian li guochi" 論雪國讎宜先勵
國恥 [To avenge ourselves against our national enemies we must first foster a
sense of national shame]. *Dongfang zazhi* 東方雜誌 1, no. 4, Guangxu 30/4/25
(June 8, 1904): 65–67.

Feigon, Lee. *Chen Duxiu: Founder of the Chinese Communist Party.* Princeton:
Princeton University Press, 1983.

"Feizhi wujiu jinian de yiyi" 廢止五九紀念的意義 [The meaning of the aboli-
tion of the May 9 anniversary]. *Shenbao*, May 8, 1940.

Feng Zikai 豐子愷. "Jiu yiba zhi ye" 九一八之夜 [The night of September 18].
Xin shaonian 新少年 2, no. 6 (Sept. 1936): 62–65.

Fisher, Tom. "'The Play's the Thing': Wu Han and Hai Rui Revisited." In Unger,
ed., *Using the Past to Serve the Present*, 9–45.

French, Howard W. "In China, Children of the Rich Learn Class, Minus the
Struggle." *New York Times*, Sept. 22, 2006.

Frodsham, J. D., trans. and annot. *The First Chinese Embassy to the West: The
Journals of Kuo Sung-t'ao, Liu Hsi-hung, and Chang Te-yi.* Oxford: Clarendon
Press, 1974.

Fu Boting 富伯亭 and Feng Ruifang 馮瑞芳. "Peiyang xuesheng shuli 'fouding
guan'" 培養學生樹立 "否定觀" [Train students to acquire a "capacity to
deny"]. *Shanxi jiaoyu* 山西教育 11 (1994): 19.

Fu Rong 付蓉. "Daxuesheng cuozhe xinli de tiaoshi yu jiaozheng" 大學生挫
折心理的調適與矯正 [Making adjustments and corrections in the attitude of
university students toward setbacks]. *Anqing shifan xueyuan xuebao (shehui
kexue ban)* 安慶師範學院學報（社會科學版）21, no. 1 (Jan. 2002): 99–101.

Fu Xuangang 付選剛. "Xiang weiren xuexi" 向偉人學習 [Emulating great
people]. *Yulin gaodeng zhuanke xuexiao xuebao* 榆林高等專科學校學報 2
(1995): 4–7.

Fugong 凫公 [pseud.]. "Fuxin changdan zhi jiuyiba" 腐心嘗膽之九一八 [Hate-
ful and bitter September 18]. *Shijie ribao*, Sept. 18, 1932.

Gao Ming 高銘. "Shisu renru guan yu Fojiao de renru guan" 世俗忍辱觀與佛
教的忍辱觀 [The worldly view of forbearance and the Buddhist view of for-
bearance]. *Fayin luntan* 法音論壇 4 (1994): 8–14.

Gerth, Karl G. "Consumption as Resistance: The National Products Movement
and Anti-Japanese Boycotts in Modern China." In Harald Fuess, ed., *The Japanese Empire in East Asia and Its Postwar Legacy*, 119–42. Munich: Iudicium Ver-
lag, 1998.

Gezhong jinianri shilüe 各種紀念日史略 [A concise history of the various commemoration days], compiled and printed by Guomin zhengfu junshi weiyuanhui weiyuanzhang Nanchang xingying zhengzhi xunlian chu 國民政府軍
事委員會委員長南昌行營政治訓練處 [Political training department of the

Nanchang field headquarters of the head of the military affairs commission of the national government]. Ca. 1932.

Goldblatt, Howard, ed. *Chinese Literature for the 1980s: The Fourth Congress of Writers and Artists*. Armonk, NY: M. E. Sharpe, 1982.

Goldman, Merle. *China's Intellectuals: Advise and Dissent*. Cambridge, MA: Harvard University Press, 1981.

———. *Literary Dissent in Communist China*. Cambridge, MA: Harvard University Press, 1967.

———. *Sowing the Seeds of Democracy in China: Political Reform in the Deng Xiaoping Era*. Cambridge, MA: Harvard University Press, 1994.

Gong Weiying 龔維英. "Lishishang zhen you Xi Shi ma?" 歷史上真有西施嗎 [Did history really have a Xi Shi?]. *Anhui shixue* 安徽史學 6 (1986): 61–62.

Goodrich, L. Carrington, and Chaoying Fang, eds. *Dictionary of Ming Biography, 1368–1644,* 2 vols. New York: Columbia University Press, 1976.

Gordon, Mary. *Joan of Arc*. New York: Lipper / Viking, 2000.

"Goujian de fuguo daji" 勾踐的復國大計 [Goujian's great program for national recovery]. *Guoji dianying* 國際電影 114 (May 1965): 8–9.

Goujian zhuan 勾踐傳 [Biography of Goujian]. Comp. and published by the Guofang bu zong zhengzhi bu [General Political Department of the Ministry of National Defense]. Taibei, 1952.

Gu Chun 顧春 and Ding Jianping 丁建萍. "'Danjian' jingshen: Meili Shaoxing de chengshi zhi hun" "膽劍" 精神：魅力紹興的城市之魂 [The spirit of the gall and the sword: The soul of the enchanting city of Shaoxing]. http://zjnews .zjol.com.cn/05zjnews/system/2005/09/20/006309218.shtml (accessed Sept. 23, 2005).

Gu Xijia 顧希賈. "Xi Shi de chuanshuo, shishi ji qita" 西施的傳說, 史實及其他 [Legend, historical fact, and other matters pertaining to Xi Shi]. *Minjian wenxue luntan* 民間文學論壇 1 (1998): 33–39.

Gu Yifan 顧一凡. "Aiguozhuyi jiaoyu yao cong wawa zhuaqi" 愛國主義教育要從娃娃抓起 [Patriotic education must be stressed beginning with childhood]. *Lishi jiaoxue wenti* 歷史教學問題 3 (1998): 60.

Guan Hongyu 關鴻羽. "'Yi wu busao, heyi sao tianxia?'—Tan 'zili, ziqiang jiaoyu' de jizhong zuofa" "一屋不掃, 何以掃天下?"—談 "自理, 自強教育" 的幾種做法 [If you can't keep your house in order, how can you keep the world in order?—A discussion of several ways of "teaching people to fend for themselves and improve themselves"]. *Beijing jiaoyu* 北京教育 Z2 (1995): 33.

Guan Wu 關兀. "*Liaozhai zhiyi* fuchou zhuti qianlun"《聊齋志異》復仇主題淺論 [An introduction to the subject of revenge in *Liaozhai zhiyi*]. *Shiyan daxue xuebao* 十堰大學學報 4 (1996): 27–31; 2 (1997): 40–44.

"Guangbo hui luomu, Chen Baoguo *Yue wang Goujian* jinjun Riben shichang" 廣播會落幕, 陳寶國《越王勾踐》進軍日本市場 [Curtain falls on gathering of broadcasters, Chen Baoguo and *King Goujian of Yue* take Japanese market by storm]. http://www.cctv.com/performance/20060828/100788.shtml (accessed Dec. 25, 2006).

"Guangfu ge" 光復歌 [A paean to recovery of the mainland]. In *Guomin xiaoxue guoyu* 7:69–70.

Gucheng Shaoxing 古城紹興 [The ancient city of Shaoxing]. Hangzhou: Zhejiang renmin chubanshe, 1984.

Guochi tu 國恥圖 [National humiliation illustrated]. Shanghai: Shangwu yinshuguan, 1931 or 1932.

Guomin xiaoxue guoyu 國民小學國語 [National primary school Chinese], comp. Guoli bianyi guan [National institute for compilation and translation], 13 vols. Taibei, 1974.

Guomin zhongxue guowenke jiaokeshu 國民中學國文科教科書 [National middle school Chinese textbook], comp. Guoli bianyi guan, 6 vols. Taibei, 1974.

Hamilton, David. "Kuo Sung-tao: A Maverick Confucian." *Papers on China* 15 (1961): 1–29.

Han Fei Tzu: Basic Writings, trans. Burton Watson. New York: Columbia University Press, 1964.

Han Suyin. *Eldest Son: Zhou Enlai and the Making of Modern China, 1898–1976.* New York: Hill and Wang, 1994.

Han-Ying cidian (xiuding ban) 漢英詞典（修訂版）[A Chinese-English dictionary (revised edition)]. Beijing: Waiyu jiaoxue yu yanjiu chubanshe, 2001.

Harding, Harry. "The Chinese State in Crisis, 1966–9." In MacFarquhar, ed., *The Politics of China,* 148–247.

Harrison, Henrietta. *The Making of the Republican Citizen: Political Ceremonies and Symbols in China, 1911–1929.* Oxford: Oxford University Press, 2000.

Hayford, Charles W. *To the People: James Yen and Village China.* New York: Columbia University Press, 1990.

"He dali shen 'si ke' Zhejiang weishi *Zhengba chuanqi* kaibo" 和大力神 "死磕" 浙江衛視《爭霸傳奇》開播 [In "stiff challenge" to Titan, Zhejiang TV begins broadcasting *A Tale of the Struggle to Become Overlord*]. http://big5.xinhuanet .com/gate/big5/news.xinhuanet.com/ent/2006- 06/07/content_4656782.htm (accessed Jan. 17, 2007).

He Jinghuang 何敬煌. "Yue wang Goujian" 越王勾踐 [King Goujian of Yue]. *Zhejiang qingnian* 浙江青年 1, no. 4 (Feb. 1935): 49–55.

He Xin Shi Shou 和欣氏壽 [pseud.]. "Neng shuo buneng xing" 能說不能行 [We can talk but we're unable to act]. *Fubao* 復報 3 (July 16, 1906): 5–9.

He Yangming 何揚鳴. "Shi shu kangzhan shiqi de *Dongnan ribao*" 試述抗戰時期的《東南日報》[A preliminary discussion of the *Southeast daily* during the anti-Japanese war period]. *Kang Ri zhanzheng yanjiu* 抗日戰爭研究 2 (2003): 147–60.

He Youji 何有基. "Taiwan Gaoshan zu tongbao de gen zai Zhejiang Shaoxing"

臺灣高山族同胞的根在浙江紹興 [Taiwan's Gaoshan compatriots hailed originally from Shaoxing, Zhejiang]. *Taisheng zazhi* 臺聲雜誌 5 (2000): 36–38.

He Yunwei 何云偉 and An Hua 安化. "Wo xiao aiguozhuyi jiaoyu de shijian yu sikao" 我校愛國主義教育的實踐與思考 [The practice and thought behind patriotic education in our school]. *Shaoxing shizhuan xuebao* 紹興師專學報 15, no. 2 (1995): 84–88.

Hertslet, Edward, ed. *The Map of Europe by Treaty,* 4 vols. London: Butterworths, 1875–91.

"Hexie Zhongguo de wenhua mingpian (3 yue 14 ri)" 和諧中國的文化名片（3月 14日） [The harmonious China culture card (March 14)]. http://www.cctv .com/news/china/20060315/100698.shtml (accessed May 10, 2006).

Hiestand, Kristen A. "Chen Yi and the Revival of the Hundred Flowers Campaign, 1961–1963." Senior Honors Thesis, Harvard College, April 2002.

Hinton, William. *Hundred Day War: The Cultural Revolution at Tsinghua University.* New York: Monthly Review Press, 1972.

Hong Bicheng 洪畢誠. *Yue wang Goujian:* Dong Zhou lieguo *chunqiu wuba zhengxiong ji* 越王勾踐：《東周列國》春秋五霸爭雄記 [King Goujian of Yue: The account in *The States of the Eastern Zhou* of the struggle for supremacy among the five overlords in the Spring and Autumn era]. Chengdu: Chengdu chubanshe, 1996.

Hou Hongjian 侯鴻鑑. "Guoxue guochi laoku san da zhuyi biao li" 國學國恥 勞苦三大主義表例 [Illustrative charts displaying the three great principles: Chinese learning, national humiliation, and hard work]. *Jiaoyu zazhi* 教育雜誌 7, no. 7 (July 1915): 23–26 *(zazuan).*

———. "Shu Jiangsu sheng xiaozhang huiyi zhi gailüe" 述江蘇省校長會議之 概略 [A brief account of the meeting of the principals of Jiangsu province]. *Jiaoyu zazhi* 教育雜誌 7, no. 8 (Aug. 1915): 54 *(tebie jishi).*

"Houshan: Qiao jie waili hao fazhan" 吼山：巧借外力好發展 [Houshan: Taking opportune advantage of outside forces to benefit development], Sept. 12, 2005. http://www.gaobu.gov.cn/new_show.asp?id = 7869 (accessed May 13, 2006).

Hsi Shih [Xi Shi] 西施. Video recording. Taizhong: Mingfeng yingshi qiyeshe, n.d.

Hsia, C. T. *A History of Modern Chinese Fiction,* 3rd ed. Bloomington: Indiana University Press, 1999.

Hsia, T. A. *Metaphor, Myth, Ritual and the People's Commune.* Studies in Chinese Communist Terminology, no. 7. Berkeley: Center for Chinese Studies, Institute of International Studies, University of California, 1961.

———. *A Terminological Study of the* Hsia-fang *Movement.* Studies in Chinese Communist Terminology, no. 10. Berkeley: Center for Chinese Studies, Institute of International Studies, University of California, 1963.

Hsiung, James C., et al., eds. *Contemporary Republic of China: The Taiwan Experience, 1950–1980.* New York: Praeger, 1981.

Hsu, Cho-yun. "Cultural Values and Cultural Continuity." In Hsiung et al., eds., *Contemporary Republic of China*, 21–28.

Hsü, Immanuel C. Y. *The Rise of Modern China*, 6th ed. New York: Oxford University Press, 2000.

Hsu, Kai-yu. *Chou En-lai: China's Gray Eminence*. Garden City, NY: Doubleday, 1968.

Hu Caiwen 胡才文. "Qiantan lishike de jingzheng yishi jiaoyu" 淺談歷史課的競爭意識教育 [A brief discussion of the teaching of competitive consciousness in history classes]. *Wanxi xueyuan xuebao* 皖西學院學報 2 (1998): 75.

Hu, John. "Ming Dynasty Drama." In Colin Mackerras, ed., *Chinese Theater from Its Origins to the Present Day*, 60–91. Honolulu: University of Hawaii Press, 1983.

Hu Pu 胡樸. "Weiren, mingren yu yinglian" 偉人, 名人與楹聯 [Great men, famous men, and couplets]. *Lishui shizhuan xuebao (shehui kexue ban)* 麗水師專學報（社會科學版）6 (1996): 55–58.

Hu Ruifang 胡叡芳 et al. "Bu yi paiming lun yingxiong, Zhejiang chengshi jingzhengli zhi Shaoxing" 不以 排名論英雄, 浙江城市競爭力之紹興 [Shaoxing, a competitive Zhejiang city, doesn't define its success in terms of its ranking]. http://www.zj.xinhuanet.com/zhejiang/2004-09/27/content_2944898.htm (accessed May 10, 2006).

Huang Dashou 黃大受. "Di yi ke: Woxin changdan de Yue wang Goujian" 第一課：臥薪嘗膽的越王勾踐 [Lesson one: The self-imposed hardships undergone by King Goujian of Yue]. In Huang Dashou, *Zhonghua weiren gushi*, 343–50.

———. "Goujian" 勾踐. In Huang Dashou, *Zhonghua weiren gushi*, 17–56.

———. "Goujian" 勾踐. In Shen Gangbo et al., eds., *Minzu yingxiong ji geming xianlie zhuanji*, 1:14–54.

———. "Goujian mie Wu" 勾踐滅吳 [Goujian destroys Wu]. In Huang Dashou, *Zhongxing shihua*, 1–30.

———. *Zhonghua weiren gushi* 中華偉人故事 [Stories of great Chinese]. Taibei: Huanqiu shuju, 1975.

———. *Zhongxing shihua* 中興史話 [Historical accounts of national resurgence]. Taibei: Shijie shuju, 1955.

Huang Donglan 黃東蘭. "Yue Fei miao: Chuangzao gonggong jiyi de 'chang'" 岳飛廟：創造公共記憶的 "場" [The Yue Fei temple: The creation of a public commemoration "site"]. In Sun Jiang 孫江, comp., *Shijian, jiyi, xushu* 事件, 記憶, 敘述 [Event, memory, narrative], 158–77. Hangzhou: Zhejiang renmin chubanshe, 2004.

Huang, Grace. "Avenging National Humiliation: Chiang Kaishek's Response to the Japanese Occupation of Manchuria." Paper presented at the annual meeting of the American Political Science Association, Sept. 3, 2004.

———. "Laying on Brushwood and Tasting Gall: Jiang Jieshi's (Chiang Kai-shek's) Response to the May 3rd Tragedy." Paper presented at the New England regional meeting of the Association for Asian Studies, Cambridge, MA, Oct. 25, 2003.

Huang, Ko-wu. "Remembering Shi Kefa: Changing Images of a Hero in Late Imperial and Early Republican China." Paper presented at the annual meeting of the Association for Asian Studies, Boston, Mar. 23, 2007.

Huang, Ray. *1587, a Year of No Significance: The Ming Dynasty in Decline*. New Haven: Yale University Press, 1981.

Huang Rensheng 黃仁生. "Lun *Wu Yue chunqiu* shi wo guo xiancun zuizao de wenyan changpian lishi xiaoshuo" 論《吳越春秋》是我國現存最早的文言長篇歷史小說 [*The Annals of Wu and Yue* is China's earliest extant historical novel in the literary style]. *Hunan shifan daxue shehui kexue xuebao* 湖南師範大學社會科學學報 3 (1994): 81–85.

———, comp. *Xin yi Wu Yue chunqiu* 新譯吳越春秋 [A new interpretation of *The Annals of Wu and Yue*]. Taibei: Sanmin shuju, 1996.

Huang Shihong 黃士洪. "Youhuan yishi: Bei hulüele de deyu keti" 憂患意識：被忽略了的德育課題 [Awareness of hardship: An overlooked topic in moral education]. *Sichuan jiaoyu* 四川教育 10 (1996): 13.

Huang Yue 黃樾 [Huang Changyong 黃昌勇]. *Yan'an si guai* 延安四怪 [The four devils of Yan'an]. Beijing: Zhongguo qingnian chubanshe, 1998.

Hummel, Arthur W., ed. *Eminent Chinese of the Ch'ing Period (1644–1912)*, 2 vols. Washington, DC: United States Government Printing Office, 1943–1944.

Hung, Chang-tai. *War and Popular Culture: Resistance in Modern China, 1937–1945*. Berkeley: University of California Press, 1994.

Israel, John. "Politics on Formosa." *China Quarterly* 15 (July–Sept. 1963): 3–11.

Israel Ministry of Foreign Affairs. "Masada—Symbol of Jewish Freedom," Aug. 17, 1999. http://www.mfa.gov.il/MFA/MFAArchive/1990_1999/1999/8/Masada+-+Symbol+of+Jewish+Freedom.htm (accessed Feb. 9, 2007).

Itō Michiharu 伊藤道治 et al. *Bazhe zhi dao: Jin Wen gong, Wu wang Fuchai, Yue wang Goujian, Qin Shihuang Ying Zheng* 霸者之道：晉文公，吳王夫差，越王勾踐，秦始皇嬴政 [The way of the overlords: Duke Wen of Jin, King Fuchai of Wu, King Goujian of Yue, and the first emperor of Qin Ying Zheng]. Banqiao, Taibei county: Pei zhen wenhua qiye youxian gongsi, 2001.

Jansen, Marius B. *Japan and China: From War to Peace, 1894–1972*. Chicago: Rand McNally, 1975.

Ji Dacheng 冀大成. "Tan 'wang'" 談 "忘" [A discussion of "forgetting"]. *Zhongguo jianyan jianyi* 中國檢驗檢疫 6 (1996): 39.

Ji Guoping 季國平. "Kangkai beiliang qu cong gu chang dao jin: Guan xin bian yueju *Yue wang Goujian*" 慷慨悲涼曲從古唱到今：觀新編越劇《越王勾踐》[A fervently forlorn verse sung from ancient times to the present: Viewing the newly composed Shaoxing opera *King Goujian of Yue*]. *Zhongguo xiju* 中國戲劇 7 (2006): 20–21.

"Ji quan dang quan min liliang wancheng fangong fuguo daye" 集全黨全民力量完成反攻復國大業 [Amass the strength of the entire party and the entire people to carry out the great undertaking of launching a counterattack and recovering the nation]. *Zhongyang ribao*, Nov. 24, 1974 (reprinted in *Zhongyang ribao: Wushinianlai shelun xuanji*, 234–37).

Jia Fengzhen 賈豐臻. "Zhong-Ri jiaoshe hou zhi jiaoyuguan" 中日交涉後之教育觀 [Views on education after the Sino-Japanese negotiations]. *Jiaoyu zazhi* 教育雜誌 7, no. 8 (Aug. 1915): 155–62.

Jia Yi. "The Owl." In Burton Watson, trans., *Early Chinese Literature*, 256–57. New York: Columbia University Press, 1962.

Jiafan 家範 [pseud.]. "Guang bing" 光餅 [Qi Jiguang cakes]. *Ertong shijie* 兒童世界 22, no. 18 (Nov. 3, 1928): 2–4.

Jiang Jieshi 蔣介石. "Fuzhi de shiming yu mudi" 復職的使命與目的 [My mission and goals on being reinstated in my post]. Speech of Mar. 13, 1950. In Zhang Qiyun, comp., *Xian zongtong Jiang gong quanji*, 2:1955–60.

———. "Guomin gemingjun jiangshi xuechi fuchou zhi dao" 國民革命軍將士雪恥復仇之道 [The path to erasing humiliation and taking revenge followed by the officers and men of the national revolutionary army]. Speech of Nov. 1950. In Zhang Qiyun, comp., *Xian zongtong Jiang gong quanji*, 2:2077–78.

———. "Jiao yang wei" 教養衛 [Moral instruction, material support, strict discipline]. Speech of Feb. 12, 1934. In Zhang Qiyun, comp., *Xian zongtong Jiang gong quanji*, 1:803–7.

———. "Nuli wancheng xunzheng daye" 努力完成訓政大業 [Work hard to bring to fruition the great cause of political tutelage]. Speech of May 17, 1931. In Zhang Qiyun, comp., *Xian zongtong Jiang gong quanji*, 1:618–20.

———. *Zhongguo zhi mingyun* 中國之命運 [China's destiny]. In Zhang Qiyun, comp., *Xian zongtong Jiang gong quanji*, 1:126–82.

"Jiang zongtong de jiashu" 蔣總統的家書 [President Chiang's family correspondence]. In *Guomin xiaoxue guoyu* 8:5–6.

"Jiang zongtong xiao de shihou" 蔣總統小的時候 [When President Chiang was young]. In *Guomin xiaoxue guoyu* 3:31–32.

"Jinian 'wujiu' guochi" 紀念 "五九" 國恥 [Commemorating the "May 9" national humiliation]. *Shibao* [The truth post], May 9, 1933.

"Jiwang kailai, fangong fuguo" 繼往開來，反攻復國 [Carry on the heritage of the past and pave the way for future generations, launch a counterattack and recover the nation]. *Zhongyang ribao*, Oct. 11, 1957 (reprinted in *Zhongyang ribao: Wushinianlai shelun xuanji*, 106–9).

Johnson, David. "Actions Speak Louder Than Words: The Cultural Significance of Chinese Ritual Opera." In Johnson, ed., *Ritual Opera, Operatic Ritual: "Mulien Rescues His Mother" in Chinese Popular Culture*, 1–45. Berkeley: Chinese Popular Culture Project, University of California, 1989.

————. "Epic and History in Early China: The Matter of Wu Tzu-hsü." *Journal of Asian Studies* 40, no. 2 (Feb. 1981): 255–71.

————. "The Wu Tzu-hsü *Pien-wen* and Its Sources: Part I." *Harvard Journal of Asiatic Studies* 40, no. 1 (June 1980): 93–156.

————. "The Wu Tzu-hsü *Pien-wen* and Its Sources: Part II." *Harvard Journal of Asiatic Studies* 40, no. 2 (Dec. 1980): 465–505.

"Kan Huashi lishiju *Yue wang Goujian*" 看華視歷史劇《越王勾踐》[Viewing the Chinese Television System's (Taiwan) airing of the historical drama *King Goujian of Yue*]. http://www.siongpo.com/20070323/forum1.htm (accessed May 5, 2007).

Kang Lin 康林. "Yiwei shenchang de quanlian" 意味深長的勸聯 [Exhortatory couplets of profound meaning]. *Nanfang guotu ziyuan* 南方國土資源 7 (2003): 48.

"Kang-Ri xiju huodong" 抗日戲劇活動 [Theater activities during the Japanese war]. http://www.shtong.gov.cn/node2/node4/node2249/huangpu/node35504/node35515/node35517/userobject1ai20450.html (accessed Feb. 5, 2007).

Kantor, Jodi. "A Candidate, His Minister, and the Search for Faith." *New York Times,* Apr. 30, 2007.

Kaplan, Robert D. *Balkan Ghosts: A Journey through History.* New York: Picador, 2005.

Kawase Ken'ichi 川瀨健一. *Taiwan dianying xiangyan: Bainian dao lan* 台灣電影饗宴：百年導覽 [The offerings of Taiwan cinema: An overview of a century of directing], trans. Li Changchuan 李常傳. Taibei: Nantian shuju, 2002.

Kexuan 可選 [pseud.]. "Guochi pian" 國恥篇 [Essay on national humiliation]. *Dongfang zazhi* 東方雜誌 1, no. 10, Guangxu 30/10/25 (Dec. 1, 1904): 221–27.

Knoblock, John, and Jeffrey Riegel. *The Annals of Lü Buwei: A Complete Translation and Study.* Stanford: Stanford University Press, 2000.

Kraus, Richard. "Bai Hua: The Political Authority of a Writer." In Carol Lee Hamrin and Timothy Cheek, eds., *China's Establishment Intellectuals,* 185–211. Armonk, NY: M. E. Sharpe, 1986.

Kristof, Nicholas D. "Chinese Medicine for American Schools." *New York Times,* June 27, 2006.

"Kunyang zhi zhan" 昆陽之戰 [The battle of Kunyang]. In *Guomin xiaoxue guoyu* 12:86–101.

Kuo Mo-jo [Guo Moruo]. *Chu Yuan: A Play in Five Acts,* trans. Yang Xianyi and Gladys Yang. Beijing: Foreign Languages Press, 1953.

Kuo, Thomas C. *Ch'en Tu-hsiu (1879–1942) and the Chinese Communist Movement.* South Orange, NJ: Seton Hall University Press, 1975.

Lagerwey, John. "A Translation of *The Annals of Wu and Yüe,* Part I, with a Study of Its Sources." Ph.D. diss., Harvard University, 1975.

Lai, Him Mark, Genny Lim, and Judy Yung. *Island: Poetry and History of Chinese Immigrants on Angel Island, 1910–1940.* San Francisco: Hoc Doi, 1980.

Lai Kehong 來可泓, ed. *Guoyu zhijie* 國語直解 [Discourses of the states: A straightforward interpretation]. Shanghai: Fudan daxue chubanshe, 2000.

Lan Hong 藍虹. *Woxin changdan* 臥薪嘗膽. Taibei: Dongguang chubanshe, 1976.

Lan Shenghong 蘭勝宏 and Li Yuyin 李玉銀. "Ren wu yali nan chengcai" 人無壓力難成才 [It is hard for people to amount to something in the absence of pressure]. *Xinwen yu chengcai* 新聞與成才 8 (1997): 47.

Lanjun 蘭俊 [pseud.]. "Emo wei xue jiachi xiwu 20 nian, chuyi ye tidao xue jian choumen" 惡魔為雪家恥習武 20 年, 初一夜提刀血濺仇門 [Villain in order to avenge private grievance practices martial arts for twenty years, on first night of new lunar year wielding knife spills blood of enemy family]. http://news.sina.com.cn/s/2004–01–28/15492710673.shtml (accessed Feb. 23, 2006).

Lau, Joseph S. M. *Ts'ao Yü, the Reluctant Disciple of Chekhov and O'Neill: A Study in Literary Influence.* Hong Kong: Hong Kong University Press, 1970.

Lei Haizong. "The Warring States (473–221 B.C.): The Modern Period in Ancient China." http://www.cic.sfu.ca/nacc/articles/leihaizong/leihaizong.html (accessed Aug. 23, 2006).

Leilei 雷雷 [pseud.]. "Fang Li Hanxiang tan *Xi Shi* de weida chu" 訪李翰祥談《西施》的偉大處 [A conversation with Li Hanxiang about the great aspects of *Xi Shi*]. *Guoji dianying* 國際電影 120 (Nov. 1965): 44–47.

Levenson, Joseph R. *Liang Ch'i-ch'ao and the Mind of Modern China.* Cambridge, MA: Harvard University Press, 1965.

Lewis, Bernard. *History: Remembered, Recovered, Invented.* New York: Simon and Schuster, 1987.

Li Cheng 李誠. *Goujian yu Fuchai: Guanwa gong zhong yan chunqiu* 勾踐與夫差：館娃宮中演春秋 [Goujian and Fuchai: The spring and autumn period as played out in the Guanwa palace]. Sanxia zhen, Taibei county: San feng chubanshe, 1997.

Li Dichen 李滌塵. "Xuechi" 雪恥 [Wiping away humiliation]. *Shenbao,* May 10, 1928.

Li Fugen 李富根. "Chongxie Zhonghua gushi: Fang Shi Shi jiaoshou he tade Taiwan hezuozhe Huang Dashou jiaoshou" 重寫中華古史：訪史式教授和他的臺灣合作者黃大受教授 [Rewriting ancient Chinese history: An interview with Professor Shi Shi and his Taiwan collaborator Professor Huang Dashou]. *Jinri Zhongguo* 今日中國 1 (2000): 47–49.

"Li Hanxiang ouxin wei *Xi Shi*" 李翰祥嘔心為《西施》 [The great effort put into *Xi Shi* by Li Hanxiang]. *Dianying shijie* 電影世界 66 (March 1965): 36–37.

Li Jie 李劼. *Wu Yue chunqiu* 吳越春秋 [The annals of Wu and Yue], 2 vols. Beijing: Zhishi chubanshe, 2003.

Li Junna 李君娜. "Liangge 'Goujian' sange 'mingbu' yingshiju chuangzuo pinpin 'zhuiwei'" 兩個"勾踐"三個"名捕"影視劇創作頻頻"追尾" [Television dramas with two "Goujians" and three "famous police officers" keep "chasing each

other's tails"], Sept. 2, 2005. http://media.people.com.cn/GB/40606/3662895
.html (accessed Feb. 9, 2007).

Li Liangcheng 李亮丞. *Rexue hen* 熱血痕 [Traces of righteous ardor]. Beijing:
Huaxia chubanshe, 1995.

Li Wen 李文, ed. *Yue wang Goujian jian yu Wu wang Fuchai mao* 越王勾
踐劍與吳王夫差矛 [The sword of King Goujian of Yue and the spear of King
Fuchai of Wu]. Hong Kong: The Museum of Chinese Historical Relics, 1984.

Li Xifan 李希凡. "*Dan jian pian* he lishiju: Man tan *Dan jian pian* de yishu chuli
he xingxiang chuangzao"《膽劍篇》和歷史劇：漫談《膽劍篇》的藝術處理
和形象創造 [*The Gall and the Sword* and historical drama: An informal discussion of artistic treatment and image creation in *The Gall and the Sword*].
In *Lishi lunji*, 199–214. Reprinted from *Renmin ribao*, Sept. 6, 1961.

Li Yan 李彦 and Xiao Yang 蕭揚. "Liu Songren tiyan 'woxin changdan,' san wei
Goujian 'da zhuangche'" 劉松仁體驗 "臥薪嘗膽," 三位勾踐 "大撞車" [Liu
Songren learns about "sleeping on brushwood and tasting gall," three Goujians in "big collision"], Sept. 15, 2005. http://www.hebei.com.cn/node2/node
27/node1104/userobject1ai367826.html (accessed Sept. 22, 2005).

Li Yongjun 李永軍. "Peiyang feizhili yinsu, tigao lishi ketang jiaoxue shixiao"
培養非智力因素, 提高歷史課堂教學實效 [Cultivate nonintellectual factors,
enhance the substantive results of teaching in history classes]. *Gansu jiaoyu*
甘肅教育 1–2 (2003): 54–55.

Li Zhisui. *The Private Life of Chairman Mao: The Memoirs of Mao's Personal Physician*, trans. Tai Hung-chao, with editorial assistance of Anne Thurston. New
York: Random House, 1994.

Liang Heng and Judith Shapiro. *Son of the Revolution*. New York: Vintage Books,
1984.

Liang Qichao 梁啟超. "Di shidu de 'Wuqi'" 第十度的 "五七" [The tenth "May
7"]. *Shishi xinbao*, May 7, 1925.

Liang Yiqun 梁義群 et al., eds. *Yibaige guochi jinian ri* 一百個國恥紀念日 [One
hundred national humiliation commemoration days]. Beijing: Zhongguo
qingnian chubanshe, 1995.

Lieberthal, Kenneth. "The Great Leap Forward and the Split in the Yan'an Leadership, 1958–65." In MacFarquhar, ed., *The Politics of China*, 87–147.

Lin Guanghan 林光漢. "Wo wei Goujian, ren fei Fuchai" 我為勾踐, 人非夫差
[We are Goujian, but the other side isn't Fuchai]. *Xibei xiangdao* 西北嚮導 9
(1936): 3–8.

Lin Kehuan 林克歡. "Lishi yishi yu daode pipan: Ping *Wu wang jin ge Yue wang
jian* de zhongda buzu" 歷史意識與道德批判：評《吳王金戈越王劍》的重大
不足 [Historical consciousness and moral criticism: A critique of the major
inadequacies of *The Golden Spear of the King of Wu and the Sword of the King
of Yue*]. *Xijubao* 戲劇報 6 (1983): 34–35.

Lin Zhibo 林治波. "Fang zhuming shixuejia Shi Shi: Chongxin renshi Zhonghua wenhua" 訪著名史學家史式：重新認識中華文化 [Interview with the historian Shi Shi: A fresh understanding of Chinese culture], Mar. 31, 2006. http://culture.people.com.cn/GB/27296/4260312.html (accessed Jan. 7, 2008).

Link, Perry. *Evening Chats in Beijing: Probing China's Predicament*. New York: W. W. Norton, 1992.

———. *The Uses of Literature: Life in the Socialist Chinese Literary System*. Princeton: Princeton University Press, 2000.

Lishiju lunji 歷史劇論集 [Essays on historical drama], comp., *Xijubao* bianjibu《戲劇報》編輯部 [*Xijubao* editorial department]. Shanghai: Shanghai wenyi chubanshe, 1962.

Liu Bo 劉波. "Hui-yu canban hua Chunqiu: Dianshiju *Dong Zhou lieguo chunqiu pian* de de yu shi" 謴譽 參半話春秋：《東周列國春秋篇》的得與失 [Mixed reception for the Spring and Autumn: The strengths and weaknesses of the TV drama *The States of the Eastern Zhou—Spring and Autumn part*]. *Dianying pingjie* 電影評介 5 (1997): 27.

Liu Chenlie 劉陳列. "Wusan Ri bing tusha ge" 五三日兵屠殺歌 [A song about the Japanese military's May 3 massacre]. *Minsheng bao,* May 9, 1928.

Liu Jimian 劉繼綿. "Aiguozhuyi jiaoyu zhong buke hulüe guochi jiaoyu" 愛國主義教育中不可忽略國恥教育 [Patriotic education must not neglect national humiliation education]. *Sixiang zhengzhi ke jiaoxue* 思想政治課教學 3 (1995): 30–31.

Liu Naichong 劉乃崇. "Kan pingju *Zhongli jian* hou manbi" 看評劇《鍾離劍》後漫筆 [Notes jotted down after viewing the northern opera *The Swords of Zhongli*]. *Zhongguo xiju* 中國戲劇 14 (1961): 22–25.

Liu Shisun 劉石孫. "Guochi guangshuo" 國恥廣說 [A general discussion of national humiliation]. *Dagongbao* 大公報 (Changsha), May 7, 1925.

Liu Yi 劉義. "Zhonghua minzu chuantong meide de jiben neihan" 中華民族傳統美德的基本内涵 [The basic meaning of the traditional virtues of the Chinese nation]. *Lanzhou xuekan* 蘭州學刊 3 (1996): 30–33.

Liu Youkuan 劉有寬. "Man tan *Dan jian pian*" 漫談《膽劍篇》 [An informal discussion of *The Gall and the Sword*]. *Xijubao* 戲劇報 21–22 (Nov. 1961): 4–10.

Liu Zhen 劉珍. *Guochi shigang* 國恥史綱 [An outline history of national humiliation]. Taibei: Zhengzhong shuju, 1974.

Liuquan 六泉 [pseud.]. "Guochi dao" 國恥道 [The way of national humiliation]. *Shenbao,* May 9, 1924.

Lu, Hanchao. *Street Criers: A Cultural History of Chinese Beggars*. Stanford: Stanford University Press, 2005.

Lu Jingkang 陸精康. "'Woxin changdan' yuyuan kao" "臥薪嘗膽" 語源考 [An examination of the origins of the proverb "woxin changdan"]. *Yuwen jianshe* 語文建設 2 (2002): 21–22.

Lu Mei 魯煤. "Guanyu lishiju wenti de zhengming: Zonghe baodao" 關於歷史劇問題的爭鳴：綜合報道 [The controversy over questions pertaining to his-

torical drama: A comprehensive report]. *Xijubao* 戲劇報 7–8 (Apr. 1961): 36–
41. Reprinted in *Lishiju lunji*, 353–66.

Lu Yuanjun 盧元駿. Epilogue *(bayu)*. In Shen Gangbo et al., eds., *Minzu yingxiong ji geming xianlie zhuanji*, 2:1–5 (back matter).

Luo Huaizhen 羅懷臻. *Xi Shi gui Yue* 西施歸越 [Xi Shi returns to Yue]. *Juben*
劇本 6 (1995): 39–50.

Luo, Zhitian. "National Humiliation and National Assertion: The Chinese Response to the Twenty-One Demands." *Modern Asian Studies* 27, no. 2 (1993):
297–319.

Ma Shaobo 馬少波. "Tan lishiju de 'gu wei jin yong'" 談歷史劇的 "古爲今用"
[A discussion of "making the past serve the present" in historical dramas]. *Beijing xiju* 北京戲劇 1 (Apr. 1960): 9–13.

MacFarquhar, Roderick. *The Origins of the Cultural Revolution, 2: The Great Leap
Forward, 1958–1960.* New York: Columbia University Press, 1983.

———. *The Origins of the Cultural Revolution, 3: The Coming of the Cataclysm,
1961–1966.* New York: Columbia University Press, 1997.

———, ed. *The Politics of China: The Eras of Mao and Deng,* 2nd ed. Cambridge:
Cambridge University Press, 1997.

MacFarquhar, Roderick, and Michael Schoenhals. *Mao's Last Revolution.* Cambridge, MA: Harvard University Press, 2006.

Mackerras, Colin. *The Chinese Theatre in Modern Times: From 1840 to the Present
Day.* London: Thames and Hudson, 1975.

Mao Dun 茅盾. *Guanyu lishi he lishiju: Cong* "woxin changdan" *de xuduo bu-
tong juben shuoqi* 關於歷史和歷史劇：從 "臥薪嘗膽" 的許多不同劇本說起
[On history and historical drama: With special reference to the numerous different librettos on the *woxin changdan* theme]. Beijing: Zuojia chubanshe, 1962.
Originally appeared as an article in *Wenxue pinglun* 文學評論 5 (1961): 37–65;
6 (1961): 1–57.

Mao Zedong. "China Is Poor and Blank" (Apr. 15, 1958). Excerpted in Stuart R.
Schram, ed., *The Political Thought of Mao Tse-tung*, 252–53. New York: Praeger,
1963.

———. "The Foolish Old Man Who Removed the Mountains." In *Selected
Works of Mao Tse-tung*, 3:321–24. Beijing: Foreign Languages Press, 1965.

Maolie 茂烈 [pseud.]. "Rusu" 茹素 [Practicing vegetarianism]. *Shenbao,* May 9,
1939.

Margalit, Avishai. *The Ethics of Memory.* Cambridge, MA: Harvard University
Press, 2002.

Martin, Roberta. "The Socialization of Children in China and on Taiwan: An
Analysis of Elementary School Textbooks." *China Quarterly* 62 (June 1975):
242–62.

McDougall, Bonnie S., and Kam Louie. *The Literature of China in the Twentieth
Century.* New York: Columbia University Press, 1997.

———. "Writers and Performers, Their Works, and Their Audiences in the First Three Decades." In McDougall, ed., *Popular Chinese Literature and Performing Arts in the People's Republic of China, 1949–1979*, 269–304. Berkeley: University of California Press, 1984.

Mei Dingzuo 梅鼎祚. *Xi Shi yanshi yanyi* 西施豔史演義 [The romance of Xi Shi]. Reprinted in Zhou Xinhui 周心慧, comp., *Zhonghua shanben zhencang wenku* 中華善本珍藏文庫 [A library of fine Chinese works], vol. 3, *shangjuan* 上卷, 33–65. Beijing: Zhongguo zhigong chubanshe, 2001.

Mei Qian 梅阡. "Yici teshu de yanchu" 一次特殊的演出 [A special performance]. In Ke Wenhui 柯文輝, comp., *Mei Qian* 梅阡, 62–66. Beijing: Beijing shiyue wenyi chubanshe, 1995.

Meisner, Maurice. *Mao's China and After: A History of the People's Republic.* New York: Free Press, 1986.

Mendelsohn, Daniel. *The Lost: A Search for Six of Six Million.* New York: HarperCollins, 2006.

Miller, Arthur. *Timebends: A Life.* New York: Grove Press, 1987.

Minsheng bao 民生報 [People's livelihood news].

Minzu yingxiong 民族英雄 [National heroes]. Taibei: Shixin chubanshe, 1974.

Mitchell, Tom. "Chiang: The Patriot." *South China Morning Post,* Jan. 3, 2001.

Miyake Setsurei 三宅雪嶺. "Shōtan-gashin" 嘗膽臥薪 [Tasting gall and sleeping on brushwood]. *Nihon* 日本, first part, Meiji 28/5/15 (May 15, 1895), second part, Meiji 28/5/27 (May 27, 1895).

Mo Tzu: Basic Writings, trans. Burton Watson. New York: Columbia University Press, 1963.

Mote, Frederick W. "Confucian Eremitism in the Yüan Period." In Arthur F. Wright, ed., *The Confucian Persuasion*, 202–40. Stanford: Stanford University Press, 1960.

———. *Imperial China 900–1800.* Cambridge, MA: Harvard University Press, 1999.

Museum of Broadcast Communications: China. http://www.museum.tv/archives/etv/C/htmlC/china/china.htm (accessed Feb. 9, 2007).

Musgrove, Charles D. "Cheering the Traitor: The Post-War Trial of Chen Bijun, April 1946." *Twentieth-Century China* 30, no. 2 (Apr. 2005): 3–27.

Nafisi, Azar. *Reading Lolita in Tehran: A Memoir in Books.* London: Fourth Estate, 2004.

Nan'gong Bo 南宮搏. *Xi Shi* 西施. Taibei: Zhongguo shibao, 1967.

Nienhauser, William H., Jr., ed. *The Grand Scribe's Records,* vol. 7, *The Memoirs of Pre-Han China by Sima Qian,* trans. Tsai-fa Cheng, Zongli Lu, William H. Nienhauser, Jr., and Robert Reynolds. Bloomington: Indiana University Press, 1994.

———, ed. and comp. *The Indiana Companion to Traditional Chinese Literature,* 2 vols. Bloomington: Indiana University Press, 1986, 1998.

Obama, Barack. *Dreams from My Father: A Story of Race and Inheritance.* Rev. ed. New York: Three Rivers Press, 2004.

Ou Xianting 歐顯庭. "Woxin changdan xie chunqiu: Ji quanguo laomo Lingling diqu fangzhichang changzhang Peng Sanyuan" 臥薪嘗膽寫春秋：記全國勞模零陵地區紡織廠廠長彭叁元 [Writing history by means of perseverance: An account of Peng Sanyuan, national model worker and director of the Lingling region textile mill]. *Jing mao daokan* 經貿導刊 7 (1995): 24–25.

Owen, Stephen, ed. and trans. *An Anthology of Chinese Literature: Beginnings to 1911.* New York: W. W. Norton, 1996.

Pan Gongzhan 潘公展. "Zhongguo lidai mingxian gushi ji bianji zhiqu" 中國歷代名賢故事集編輯旨趣 [Reasons for compiling the collection of stories of famous Chinese worthies through the ages]. In Wei Juxian, *Goujian,* 1–8.

Pan Keming 潘克明, comp. *Cao Yu yanjiu wushi nian* 曹禺研究五十年 [Fifty years of research on Cao Yu]. Tianjin: Tianjin jiaoyu chubanshe, 1987.

Peel, J. D. Y. "For Who Hath Despised the Day of Small Things? Missionary Narratives and Historical Anthropology." *Comparative Studies in Society and History* 37, no. 3 (July 1995): 581–607.

Ping 萍 [pseud.]. "Jinri zhi ri" 今日之日 [The present time]. *Shibao* [The eastern times], May 11, 1915.

Qi Rushan 齊如山. *Goujian fuguo* 勾踐復國 [Goujian recovers his country]. Taibei: Wenyi chuangzuo chubanshe, 1952.

Qi Yanming 齊燕銘. "Lishiju he lishi zhenshixing" 歷史劇和歷史真實性 [Historical drama and historical truthfulness]. *Juben* 劇本 12 (Dec. 1960): 49–50.

Qin Chuan 秦川. "Mao Dun lun Guo Moruo de *Nüshen* ji qita" 茅盾論郭沫若的《女神》及其他 [Mao Dun's discussion of Guo Moruo's *Goddesses* and other matters]. *Guo Moruo xuekan* 郭沫若學刊 3 (1996): 33–38.

"Qin pi changdan" 寢皮嘗膽 [Resting on skins and tasting gall]. *Jinzun shengyu bixie quantu* 謹遵聖諭辟邪全圖 [Heresy exposed in respectful obedience to the Sacred Edict: A complete picture gallery], poster no. 25. In *The Cause of the Riots in the Yangtse Valley: A "Complete Picture Gallery."* Hankou, 1891.

Qiu Yang 邱楊, Chen Changming 陳長明, and Cheng Shifa 程十髮. *Dan jian pian: Genju Cao Yu deng chuangzuo juben gaibian* 膽劍篇：根據曹禺等創作劇本改編 [The gall and the sword: An adaptation of the playscript written by Cao Yu and others]. Beijing: Renmin meishu chubanshe, 1963.

Qu Liuyi 曲六乙. "Chuangzuo ye yao you woxin changdan jingshen" 創作也要有臥薪嘗膽精神 [The spirit of *woxin changdan* must also be applied in creative work]. *Xijubao* 戲劇報 7–8 (Apr. 1961): 42–43.

Rankin, Mary Backus. "Nationalistic Contestation and Mobilization Politics: Practice and Rhetoric of Railway-Rights Recovery at the End of the Qing." *Modern China* 28, no. 3 (July 2002): 315–61.

Renmin ribao 人民日報 [People's daily].

Rhoden, William C. "Cinderella Is a Myth, and David Is a Lie." *New York Times,* Mar. 4, 2006.

Riley, Nancy E. "China's Population: New Trends and Challenges." *Population Bulletin* 59, no. 2 (June 2004): 3–36.

Ruan Lixuan 阮麗璿. "Wenhua chuantong jiaoyu chuyi" 文化傳統教育芻議 [Tentative suggestions for teaching our cultural traditions]. *Zhangzhou shiyuan xuebao* 漳州師院學報 3 (1996): 72–75.

Ruan Xun 阮遜. "Nuli suzao laobaixing xin zhong de Xi Shi xingxiang" 努力塑造老百姓心中的西施形象 [Trying to portray the image of Xi Shi in the hearts of ordinary people]. *Xi wen* 戲文 4 (1996): 9–10.

Ruan Xun 阮遜 and Chen Weilong 陳偉龍. *Xi Shi duanlan* 西施斷纜 [Xi Shi casts off]. *Xi wen* 戲文 4 (1996): 38–49.

Ruhlmann, Robert. "Traditional Heroes in Chinese Popular Fiction." In Arthur F. Wright, ed., *The Confucian Persuasion,* 141–76. Stanford: Stanford University Press, 1960.

Sanmu 散木 [pseud.]. "Huashuo kaoguxuejia he lishixuejia Wei Juxian" 話説考古學家和歷史學家衞聚賢 [An account of the archeologist and historian Wei Juxian]. *Wenshi zazhi* 文史雜誌 3 (2004): 8–13.

Schaberg, David. *A Patterned Past: Form and Thought in Early Chinese Historiography.* Cambridge, MA: Harvard University Asia Center, 2001.

Schank, Roger C. *Tell Me a Story: Narrative and Intelligence.* Evanston, IL: Northwestern University Press, 1995.

Schram, Stuart, ed. *Chairman Mao Talks to the People: Talks and Letters, 1956–1971.* New York: Pantheon, 1974.

Schwarcz, Vera. *Bridge across Broken Time: Chinese and Jewish Cultural Memory.* New Haven: Yale University Press, 1998.

Schwartz, Benjamin I. "The Chinese Perception of World Order, Past and Present." In John King Fairbank, ed., *The Chinese World Order: Traditional China's Foreign Relations,* 276–88. Cambridge, MA: Harvard University Press, 1968.

Shang Xiancheng 尚顯成 and Zhao Liming 趙黎明. "Juewangzhe de fankang shenhua: *Shiji* fuchou xingxiang de yuanxing fenxi" 絕望者的反抗神話：《史記》復仇形象的原型分析 [The rebellion mythology of the despairing: An analysis of prototypical revenge images in *Records of the Historian*]. *Xiangfan xueyuan xuebao* 襄樊學院學報 23, no. 3 (May 2002): 58–62.

Shangyi 商一 [pseud.]. "Guochi jinian shuo wusan" 國恥紀念說五三 [Marking national humiliation by talking about May 3]. *Minsheng bao,* May 10, 1928.

"Shaokang zhongxing" 少康中興 [Shaokang's restoration]. In *Guomin xiaoxue guoyu* 10:59–61.

Shaoxing geming wenhua shiliao huibian 紹興革命文化史料匯編 [A collection of materials on the revolutionary culture of Shaoxing]. Beijing: Tuanjie chubanshe, 1992.

Shaughnessy, Edward L. "Western Zhou History." In Michael Loewe and Edward L. Shaughnessy, eds., *The Cambridge History of Ancient China: From the Origins of Civilization to 221 B.C.*, 292–351. Cambridge: Cambridge University Press, 1999.

Shen Gangbo 沈剛伯 et al., eds., *Minzu yingxiong ji geming xianlie zhuanji* 民族英雄及革命先烈傳記 [Biographies of national heroes and revolutionary martyrs], 2 vols. Taibei: Zhengzhong shuju, 1966.

Shen Ruhuai 沈如槐. *Qinghua daxue wenge jishi: Yige hongweibing lingxiu de zishu* 清華大學文革紀 事：一個紅衛兵領袖的自述 [A record of events in the Cultural Revolution at Qinghua University: The personal account of a Red Guard leader]. Hong Kong: Shidai yishu chubanshe, 2004.

Shen Tao 沈濤 and Hong Liang 鴻梁. "Women yibai ershiwan ren" 我們一百二十萬人 [We one million two hundred thousand people]. In *Shaoxing geming wenhua shiliao huibian*, 497–98.

Shen Zu'an 沈祖安. "Dadan de tupo, kegui de tansuo: Zan Zhuji shi Yuejutuan xin xi *Xi Shi*" 大膽的突破,可貴的 探索：贊諸暨市越劇團新戲《西施》 [Bold breakthrough, commendable probing: In praise of the Zhuji Shaoxing opera troupe's new production of *Xi Shi*]. *Xi wen* 戲文 4 (1996): 8.

Shenbao 申報.

Shi Mang 史莽. "Fafen tuqiang" 發憤圖強 [Working hard to strengthen the country]. In Shi Mang, *Wu Yue fengyun*, 95–104.

———. *Wu Yue fengyun* 吳越風雲 [The stormy history of Wu and Yue]. Hangzhou: Zhejiang renmin chubanshe, 1980.

Shi Shi 史式. "Taiwan xian zhumin de lishi jieshao" 臺灣先住民的歷史介紹 [Introducing the history of the first inhabitants of Taiwan]. *Lishi jiaoxue* 歷史教學 1 (2000): 50–51.

Shi Shi 史式 and Huang Dashou 黃大受. "Chongxie Zhonghua gushi jianyishu" 重寫中華古史建議書 [Proposal to rewrite the ancient history of China]. *Wen shi zazhi* 文史雜誌 2 (1999): 76–78.

———. *Taiwan xian zhumin shi* 臺灣先住民史 [A history of the first inhabitants of Taiwan]. Beijing: Jiuzhou tushu chubanshe, 1999.

Shibao 時報 [The eastern times].

Shibao 實報 [The truth post].

Shijie ribao 世界日報 [The world morning post].

Shimin qianzi ke 市民千字課 [Textbook of one thousand characters for townspeople]. Shanghai: Shangwu yinshuguan, Jan. 1929 (20th ed.); June 1929 (46th ed.).

Shishi xinbao 時事新報 [China times].

Shu 漱 [pseud.]. "Wuyue jiuri" 五月九日 [May 9]. *Shishi xinbao*, May 9, 1925, Shanghai section.

Shu Yin 舒湮. "Zai wutaishang de rensheng *(shang)*: Wo de juzuo he yanxi shenghuo" 在舞臺上的人生 (上)：我的劇作和演戲生活 [A career on the stage (part 1): My life in drama and acting]. *Xin wenxue shiliao* 新文學史料 4 (1996): 50–59, 45.

"Shuangcheng fuguo" 雙城復國 [A pair of cities recover the country]. In *Guomin xiaoxue guoyu* 10:65–67.

Song Jun 宋軍. "Chuzhong lishi jiaoxue ying zhongshi youhuan yishi de peiyang" 初中歷史教學應重視憂患意識的培養 [Junior middle school history teaching should pay special attention to nourishing an awareness of suffering and adversity]. *Jiangxi jiaoyu* 江西教育 4 (1996): 45.

Spiegel, Gabrielle M. "Memory and History: Liturgical Time and Historical Time." *History and Theory* 41 (May 2002): 149–62.

Ssu-ma Ch'ien [Sima Qian]. *Records of the Grand Historian of China,* trans. Burton Watson, 2 vols. New York: Columbia University Press, 1961.

———. *Records of the Historian: Chapters from the* Shih chi *of Ssu-ma Ch'ien,* trans. Burton Watson. New York: Columbia University Press, 1969.

Su Shangyao 蘇尚耀 and Wen Kai 文愷. *Woxin changdan: Goujian.* 臥薪嘗膽：勾踐. In vol. 5 of Su Shangyao and Wen Kai, *Yibaige lishi mingren gushi* 一百個歷史名人故事 [One hundred tales of famous historical figures], 6 vols. Taibei: Wenhua tushu gongsi, 1978.

Sun Hongming 孫洪明. "Qiuzhi zhong de 'woxin changdan'" 求職中的 "臥薪嘗膽" ["Sleeping on brushwood and tasting gall" in job-hunting]. *Siwei yu zhihui* 思維與智慧 11 (2001): 21.

Sun Jiang 孫江 and Huang Donglan 黃東蘭. "Yue Fei xushu, gonggong jiyi yu guozu rentong" 岳飛敍述, 公共記憶與國族認同 [Narratives of Yue Fei, public memory, and national identity]. *Ershiyi shiji* 二十一世紀 86 (Dec. 2004): 88–100.

Sun Wen [Sun Yat-sen] 孫文. "Huifu Zhongguo guyou daode" 恢復中國固有道德 [Restoring China's traditional ethics], parts 1–2. In *Guomin zhongxue guowenke jiaokeshu* 4:1–13.

Sun Zejun 孫澤鈞. "Qian tan *Wu wang jin ge Yue wang jian* de wumei sheji" 淺談《吳王金戈越王劍》的舞美設計 [A brief discussion of the artistic stage design of *The Golden Spear of the King of Wu and the Sword of the King of Yue*]. *Xijubao* 戲劇報 6 (1983): 33.

Szuma Chien [Sima Qian]. *Selections from Records of the Historian,* trans. Yang Hsien-yi and Gladys Yang. Beijing: Foreign Languages Press, 1979.

Tai Junwen 太俊文. "Zhongshi lishi renwu zai aiguozhuyi jiaoyu zhong de jiaohua zuoyong" 重視歷史人物在愛國主義教育中的教化作用 [Take seriously the educational function of historical figures in patriotic education]. *Qujing shizhuan xuebao* 曲靖師專學報 15, no. 4 (1996): 51–55.

Takigawa Kametarō 瀧川龜太郎. *Shiki kaichū kōshō (Shiji huizhu kaozheng)* 史記會注考證 [Critical annotated edition of *Records of the Historian*], 10 vols. Taibei: Yiwen yinshuguan, n.d. (original ed. 1932–34).

Tan Yuliang 譚玉良. "Lun Lu Xun sixiang zhibian jianjinshi wancheng de fazhan xiansuo" 論魯迅思想質 變漸進式完成的發展綫索 [A discussion of the evolving thread of the realization of incremental qualitative change in the thought of Lu Xun]. *Shehui kexue yanjiu* 社會科學研究 3 (1995): 130–34.

Tan Zhijun 譚崝軍. *Goujian fuguo* 勾踐復國 [Goujian recovers his country]. In *Zhonghua xiju ji* 中華戲劇集 [Collection of Chinese plays], 10 vols., 3: 1–153. Taibei: Zhongguo xiju yishu zhongxin chubanbu, 1970–71.

Tang Hualong 湯化龍. "Quanguo sheng jiaoyuhui diyici lianhehui jilüe" 全國省教育會第一次聯合會記 略 [Summary account of the first joint meeting of the provincial educational associations of China]. *Jiaoyu zazhi* 教育雜誌 7, no. 6 (June 1915): 39–40.

Tantai Huimin 澹台惠敏. Review of Shi Shi and Huang Dashou, *Taiwan xian zhumin shi. Taisheng zazhi* 臺聲雜誌 1 (2000): 42–43.

"Tantan Xi Shi zheige ren" 談談西施這個人 [A discussion of the person of Xi Shi]. *Guoji dianying* 國際電影 114 (May 1965): 13.

Taylor, Jay. *The Generalissimo's Son: Chiang Ching-kuo and the Revolutions in China and Taiwan.* Cambridge, MA: Harvard University Press, 2000.

Teiwes, Frederick C. "The Establishment and Consolidation of the New Regime, 1949–57." In MacFarquhar, ed., *The Politics of China,* 5–86.

Teng Libin 滕立斌. "Qiantan dang de lingdao ganbu de shiyeguan" 淺談黨的領導幹部的事業觀 [A brief discussion of the work attitude of leading cadres in the party]. *Lilun xuexi yu tansuo* 理論學習與探索 4 (2003): 26–27.

Tian Benxiang 田本相. *Cao Yu zhuan* 曹禺傳 [Biography of Cao Yu]. Beijing: Beijing shi yue wenyi chubanshe, 1988.

Tian Benxiang 田本相 and Liu Yijun 劉一軍. "Xiju dashi Cao Yu" *(xia)* 戲劇大師曹禺（下）[The master playwright Cao Yu (part 2)]. *Xin wenhua shiliao* 新文化史料 6 (1997): 8–15.

Tien, Hung-mao. *The Great Transition: Political and Social Change in the Republic of China.* Stanford: Hoover Institution Press, 1989.

Tongchuan 桐川 et al. *Dong Zhou lieguo* 東周列國 [The states of the eastern Zhou], 2 vols. Beijing: Zongjiao wenhua chubanshe, 1996.

Tsang, Steve. "Chiang Kai-shek and the Kuomintang's Policy to Reconquer the Chinese Mainland, 1949–1958." In Steve Tsang, ed., *In the Shadow of China: Political Developments in Taiwan since 1949,* 48–72. Honolulu: University of Hawaii Press, 1993.

Tucker, Nancy Bernkopf. *Patterns in the Dust: Chinese-American Relations and the Recognition Controversy, 1949–1950.* New York: Columbia University Press, 1983.

Tung, Constantine. "Introduction: Tradition and Experience of the Drama of the People's Republic of China." In Constantine Tung and Colin Mackerras, eds., *Drama in the People's Republic of China,* 1–27. Albany: State University of New York Press, 1987.

"TV Series Titled *Goujian, King of Yue,* Advertising Houshan Mountain,"

Sept. 6, 2005. http://old.sx.gov.cn/english/newdisplay.asp?id=8562&lb=enxw (accessed Sept. 22, 2005).

Tyau, Min-ch'ien T. Z. *China Awakened.* New York: Macmillan, 1922.

Tyler, Patrick E. "Beijing Suicide (or Was It Murder?) Spurs Politics by Allegory." *New York Times,* Apr. 24, 1995.

Unger, Jonathan, ed. *Using the Past to Serve the Present: Historiography and Politics in Contemporary China.* Armonk, NY: M. E. Sharpe, 1993.

van de Ven, Hans. "New States of War: Communist and Nationalist Warfare and State Building (1928- 1934)." In Hans van de Ven, ed., *Warfare in Chinese History,* 321–97. Leiden: Brill, 2000.

Wagner, Rudolf G. *The Contemporary Chinese Historical Drama: Four Studies.* Berkeley: University of California Press, 1990.

———. "'In Guise of a Congratulation': Political Symbolism in Zhou Xinfang's Play *Hai Rui Submits His Memorial.*" In Unger, ed., *Using the Past to Serve the Present,* 46–103.

Wakeman, Frederic, Jr. *Spymaster: Dai Li and the Chinese Secret Service.* Berkeley: University of California Press, 2003.

Walker, Richard. *The Multi-State System of Ancient China.* Hamden, CT: Shoe String Press, 1953.

Wang Biao 王彪. "Zhou Enlai 1939 nian Shaoxing zhi xing yu kang Ri minzu tongyi zhanxian" 周恩來 1939 年紹興之行與抗日民族統一戰綫 [Zhou Enlai's 1939 visit to Shaoxing and the national united front against Japan]. *Zhejiang xuekan* 浙江學刊 2 (1998): 16–18.

Wang Chengpin 王成品. *Xi Shi* 西施. Taizhong: Zeng wen chubanshe, 1974.

Wang, David Der-wei. "1905, 1955, 2005: Three Moments of Modern Chinese Literature," unpublished paper (2006).

Wang Defen 王德芬. *Wo he Xiao Jun fengyu 50 nian* 我和蕭軍風雨五十年 [The trials and hardships of my fifty years with Xiao Jun]. Beijing: Zhongguo gongren chubanshe, 2004.

Wang Jisi 王季思. "Duo xiexie zheyang de lishi gushi xi" 多謝謝這樣的歷史故事戲 [Many thanks to these dramas dealing with historical stories]. *Juben* 劇本 2–3 (Feb.–Mar. 1961): 120–25.

Wang Ke 王科 and Xu Sai 徐塞. *Xiao Jun pingzhuan* 蕭軍評傳 [A critical biography of Xiao Jun]. Chongqing: Chongqing chubanshe, 1993.

Wang Lan 王蘭. "Chongman zhihui de yuwen ke: 'Woxin changdan' jiaoxue pianduan ji pingxi" 充滿智慧的語文課：「臥薪嘗膽」教學片斷及評析 [A Chinese class brimming with wisdom: An excerpt from the teaching of "sleeping on brushwood and tasting gall," along with an assessment]. *Xiaoxue jiaoxue sheji* 小學教學設計 10 (2005): 30.

Wang Lei 王蕾. "Miandui cuozhe" 面對挫折 [Facing setbacks]. *Yuwen shijie* 語文世界 8 (1996): 36.

Wang Miansan 王勉三, ed. *Huitu ershisi xiao* 繪圖二十四孝 [Twenty-four acts of filial piety illustrated], 3rd ed. Shanghai: Shijie shuju, 1935.

Wang Pizhen 王丕震. *Goujian yu Fuchai* 勾踐與夫差 [Goujian and Fuchai]. Taibei: Qiuhaitang chuban youxian gongsi, 1995.

Wang, Samuel. "Teaching Patriotism in China." *China Strategic Review* 1, no. 4 (July 5, 1996): 13–17.

Wang Sidi 王斯諦. *Woxin changdan de gushi* 臥薪嘗膽的故事 [The *woxin chang-dan* story]. Beijing: Zhonghua shuju, 1962.

Wang Tao 王韜, comp. *Ziqiang zhai baofu xingguo lun chubian* 自強齋保富興國論初編 [Essays from the Self-Strengthening Studio on the safeguarding of China's wealth and the revival of the nation: First collection]. Shanghai, 1897.

"Wang Yongchang daibiao: Fazhan jingji tongshi wuwang gucheng wenhua baohu" 王永昌代表: 發展經濟同時勿忘古城文化保護 [Representative Wang Yongchang: While developing the economy, don't forget to preserve the culture of the ancient city]. http://www.gov.cn/ztzl/2006-03/09/content_223264 .htm (accessed May 10, 2006).

"Wang Yongchang diaoyan Yue wang cheng guihua jianshe, qiangdiao zhanshi gucheng wenhua" 王永昌調研越王城規劃建設, 強調展示古越文化 [Wang Yongchang surveys plans for the construction of the city of the king of Yue, emphasizes that it will put on display the culture of ancient Yue]. http://zjnews .zjol.com.cn/05zjnews/system/2006/04/28/006595873.shtml (accessed May 10, 2006).

Wang Zhi 王智 and Tang Feng 唐鋒. "Ye tan woxin changdan" 也談臥薪嘗膽 [More on sleeping on brushwood and tasting gall]. *Dangjian yu rencai* 黨建與人才 10–11 (2002): 53.

Ward, Barbara E. "Regional Operas and Their Audiences: Evidence from Hong Kong." In David Johnson, Andrew J. Nathan, and Evelyn S. Rawski, eds., *Popular Culture in Late Imperial China*, 161–87. Berkeley: University of California Press, 1985.

Warner, Marina. *Joan of Arc: The Image of Female Heroism*. New York: Knopf, 1981.

Wasserstrom, Jeffrey. "The Boxers as Symbol: The Use and Abuse of the Yi He Tuan." Unpublished paper, 1984.

Wei Juxian 衛聚賢. *Goujian* 勾踐 [Goujian]. Chongqing: Shengli chubanshe, 1944.

Wen Zhou 文舟. "Lun Lin Zexu liufang shi de yongdian yishu" 論林則徐流放詩的用典藝術 [The art of using allusions in Lin Zexu's exile poetry]. *Xinjiang daxue xuebao (zhexue shehui kexue ban)* 新疆大學學報（哲學社會科學版）24, no. 3 (1996): 89–95.

Whiting, Allen. "The Sino-Soviet Split." In Roderick MacFarquhar and John K. Fairbank, eds., *The Cambridge History of China*: vol. 14: *The People's Republic*, part 1: *The Emergence of Revolutionary China, 1949–1965*, 478–538. Cambridge: Cambridge University Press, 1987.

Wilhelm, Helmut. "From Myth to Myth: The Case of Yüeh Fei's Biography." In Arthur F. Wright and Denis Twitchett, eds., *Confucian Personalities,* 146–61. Stanford: Stanford University Press, 1962.

Williams, Dan. "Masada—Symbol of Resistance or Overblown Myth?" July 27, 2001. http://www.jewishsf.com/content/2-0-/module/displaystory/story_id/16528/format/html/edition_id/324/displaystory.html (accessed Feb. 9, 2007).

"Women de jia zai dalu shang" 我們的家在大陸上 [Our home is on the mainland]. In *Guomin xiaoxue guoyu* 6:99–100.

Woxin changdan 臥薪嘗膽 [Sleeping on brushwood and tasting gall], vol. 36 of series entitled *Xiao xiaoshuo* 小小説 [Short works of fiction]. Shanghai: Zhonghua shuju, 1921.

Woxin changdan de Yue wang Goujian 臥薪嘗膽的越王勾踐 [The forbearance and persistence of King Goujian of Yue]. Shanghai: Da dong shuju, 1947.

Wu Changyi 吳長翼. "Yang Hucheng yu Jiang Jieshi" 楊虎城與蔣介石 [Yang Hucheng and Chiang Kai-shek]. *Wenshi chunqiu* 文史春秋 4 (1994): 4–7.

Wu Guoqun 吳國群. "Mao Dun yu Lu Xun chuantong wenhua yuanyuan yu wenhua xingge zhi yitong" 茅盾與魯迅傳統文化淵源與文化性格之異同 [Similarities and differences in traditional cultural origins and cultural temperament between Mao Dun and Lu Xun]. *Zhejiang xuekan* 浙江學刊 4 (1996): 16–20.

Wu Han 吳晗. "Lishiju shi yishu ye shi lishi" 歷史劇是藝術也是歷史 [Historical dramas are both art and history]. *Xijubao* 戲劇報 6 (June 1962): 38–42.

———. "Woxin changdan de gushi." 臥薪嘗膽的故事. *Guangming ribao* 光明日報 [Enlightenment daily], Jan. 11, 1961. Reprinted in Wu Han, *Wu Han wenji* 吳晗文集 [Wu Han's collected essays], 4 vols., 4:202–5. Beijing: Beijing chubanshe, 1988.

Wu Xiaocong 吳曉叢. "Wenwu zai aiguozhuyi jiaoyu zhong de zhongyao zuoyong" 文物在愛國主義教育中的重要作用 [The important function of cultural relics in patriotic education]. *Wen bo* 文博 4 (1995): 84–86.

"Wusan, wusi, wuwu, wuqi" 五三、五四、五五、五七 [May 3, May 4, May 5, May 7]. *Dagongbao* 大公報 (Tianjin), May 5, 1934.

Xi Qisheng 奚其生. "Nuli suzao hao ziji de xingxiang: Tantan wo dang cun zhishu de jidian tihui" 努力塑造好自己的形象：談談我當村支書的幾點體會 [Working hard to create a good image of ourselves: A discussion of some of the things I have learned as village party branch secretary]. *Jiangnan luntan* 江南論壇 59, no. 1 (Feb. 1995): 29–30.

"*Xi Shi* de weida zhi chu!" 《西施》的偉大之處! [The great aspects of *Xi Shi*]. *Guoji dianying* 國際電影 114 (May 1965): 10–11.

"*Xi Shi* kongqian weida de waijing changmian" 《西施》空前偉大的外景場面 [The unprecedented scale of the outdoor scenes in *Xi Shi*]. *Guoji dianying* 國際電影 117 (Aug. 1965): 44–46.

Xi Shi yanshi yanyi 西施豔史演義 [The romance of Xi Shi]. In *Si da meiren* 四大美人 [Four great beauties]. Taibei: Wenhai chubanshe, 1971.

"*Xi Shi* you paishan-daohai de zhanzheng changmian" 《西施》有排山倒海的戰爭場面 [The immense power of the battle scenes in *Xi Shi*]. *Guoji dianying* 國際電影 119 (Oct. 1965): 39–41.

Xi Zhengyong 席徵庸. *Goujian xuechi* 勾踐雪恥 [Goujian avenges past humiliations]. Changsha: Zhonghua pingmin jiaoyu cujin hui, Nov. 1937.

Xiao Gongquan [Hsiao Kung-ch'üan] 蕭公權. *Zhongguo zhengzhi sixiang shi* 中國政治思想史 [A history of Chinese political thought], 6 vols. Taibei: Zhonghua wenhua chuban shiye weiyuanhui, 1961.

Xiao Hua 蕭華. "1927–1937 nian Jiang Jieshi kang-Ri sixiang de xingcheng ji qi tedian" 1927–1937 年蔣介石抗日思想的形成及其特點 [The formation of Chiang Kai-shek's thinking about resisting Japan during the 1927–1937 period and its distinguishing features]. *Minguo dang'an* 民國檔案 2 (1996): 71–78.

Xiao Jun. "Lishi xiaoshuo 'Wu Yue chunqiu shihua' he jingju 'Wu Yue chun qiu' de chengyin yu guocheng" 歷史小説《吳越春秋史話》和京劇《吳越春秋》的成因與過程 [Factors contributing to and the process of creating the historical novel *A Story from the Annals of Wu and Yue* and the Beijing opera *The Annals of Wu and Yue*]. In Xiao Jun, *Xiao Jun xiju ji*, 2:287–94.

———. "A Personal Statement," trans. Howard Goldblatt. In Goldblatt, ed., *Chinese Literature for the 1980s*, 132–36.

———. *Wu wang fa Zhou* 武王伐紂 [King Wu vanquishes Zhou]. In Xiao Jun, *Xiao Jun xiju ji*, vol. 1.

———. *Wu Yue chunqiu* 吳越春秋 [The annals of Wu and Yue]. In Xiao Jun, *Xiao Jun xiju ji*, vol. 2.

———. *Wu Yue chunqiu shihua* 吳越春秋史話 [A story from the annals of Wu and Yue]. 2 vols. Harbin: Heilongjiang renmin chubanshe, 1980.

———. *Xiao Jun xiju ji* 蕭軍戲劇集 [The operas of Xiao Jun], 2 vols. Harbin: Heilongjiang renmin chubanshe, 1984.

Xiao Lihua 蕭力華. "Cuozhe jiaoyu: Jiating jiaoyu burong hushi de wenti" 挫折教育：家庭教育不容忽視的問題 [Education for dealing with setbacks: Problems in home education that must not be neglected]. *Huizhou daxue xuebao (shehui kexue ban)* 惠州大學學報（社會科學版）1 (1997): 74–78.

Xiaoshan 蕭山 county website. http://www.xsnet.cn/gb/content/2006–02/11/content_625195.htm (accessed Jan. 31, 2007).

Xiaoxuexiao chuji yong guoyu duben 小學校初級用國語讀本 [Chinese primer for lower primary students], 8 vols. Taiyuan, 1936.

"Xiazi" 瞎子 [Blind people]. In *Shimin qianzi ke*, 46th ed., 1:5.

Xing Yue 邢悦 and Zhang Jibing 張冀兵. "*Taoguang-yanghui* zhanlüe zai sikao—Jian lun ruhe shuli Zhongguo de guoji xingxiang" "韜光養晦" 戰略再思考——兼論如何樹立中國的國際形象 [Further reflection on the strategy of "hiding one's capacities and biding one's time"—Along with a discussion of how to establish China's international image]. *Guoji guancha* 國際觀察 6 (2006): 13–19.

Xiong Foxi 熊佛西. *Woxin changdan* 臥薪嘗膽. In *Foxi xiju* 佛西戲劇 [The plays of Xiong Foxi], series 4. Shanghai: Shangwu yinshuguan, 1933.

Xiong Guangyi 熊光義, comp. *Zhongguo chengyu da cidian* 中國成語大辭典 [Dictionary of Chinese proverbs]. Taibei: Yuandong tushu gongsi, 1983.

Xiong Mengfei 熊夢飛. "Jiuyiba san zhounian" 九一八三周年 [The third anniversary of September 18]. *Shijie ribao*, Sept. 18, 1934.

Xu Rong 許蓉. "Erzi buzai shubuqi" 兒子不再輸不起 [Our sons are no longer afraid to suffer defeat]. *Shaonian ertong yanjiu* 少年兒童研究 4 (1998): 33–34.

Xue Qilin 薛麒麟. "Zeng Guofan wenhua ren'ge lun" 曾國藩文化人格論 [Zeng Guofan's cultural personality]. *Loudi shizhuan xuebao* 婁底師專學報 1 (1995): 52–57.

"Xuesheng zonghui xuanyan" 學生總會宣言 [Manifesto at general meeting of students]. *Shishi xinbao*, May 10, 1924.

Yan Zhenfen 顔振奮. "Tan *Dan jian pian* de yishu chengjiu" 談《膽劍篇》的藝術成就 [The artistic achievement of *The Gall and the Sword*]. *Juben* 劇本 10 (Oct. 1961): 78–87.

Yang Bing'an 楊丙安. "Lüe lun zhenfen minzu jingshen" 略論振奮民族精神 [A brief discussion of stimulating the national spirit]. *Daode yu wenming* 道德與文明 6 (1997): 4–6.

Yang Chengjian 楊成鑒. "Wu Yue wenhua de fenye" 吳越文化的分野 [The dividing line between the cultures of Wu and Yue]. *Ningbo daxue xuebao (renwen kexue ban)* 寧波大學學報（人文科學版）4 (1995): 8–16.

Yang Hongjie 楊洪傑. "Houtu wenhua yu Zhonghua wenming shi" 后土文化與中華文明史 [Earth culture and the history of Chinese civilization]. *Yuncheng xueyuan xuebao* 運城學院學報 22, no. 6 (Dec. 2004): 31–37.

Yang Jian 楊健. "Hongweibing jituan xiang zhiqing jituan de lishixing guodu (1968 nian qiu—1971 nian qiu)" 紅衛兵集團向知青集團的歷史性過渡 (1968 年秋—1971 年秋) [The historic transition from red guard group to educated youth group (fall 1968—fall 1971)]. *Zhongguo qingnian yanjiu* 中國青年研究 2 (1996): 24–28.

Yang Kunquan 楊坤權. "Wangxing de weihai" 忘性的危害 [The perils of forgetfulness]. *Dang jian* 黨建 9 (1995): 46.

Yang Peijin 楊佩瑾. *Huan sha wanghou* 浣紗王后 [The queen who washed silken gauze]. Beijing: Zhongguo qingnian, 1995.

Yang Shanqun 楊善群. *Goujian* 勾踐. Taibei: Zhi shufang, 1993.

———. *Woxin changdan: Yuewang Goujian xin zhuan* 臥薪嘗膽：越王勾踐新傳 [Lying on brushwood and tasting gall: A new biography of King Goujian of Yue]. Taibei: Yunlong chubanshe, 1991.

———. *Yuewang Goujian xin zhuan* 越王勾踐新傳 [A new biography of King Goujian of Yue]. Shanghai: Shanghai renmin chubanshe, 1988.

Yang Tianshi 楊天石. "Jiuyiba shibianhou de Jiang Jieshi" 九一八事變後的蔣

介石 [Chiang Kai-shek after the September 18 incident]. In Yang Tianshi, *Jiang shi midang yu Jiang Jieshi zhenxiang* 蔣氏秘檔與蔣介石真相 [The secret files of Mr. Chiang and the truth about Chiang Kai-shek], 350–69. Beijing: Shehui kexue wenxian chubanshe, 2002.

———. "Lugouqiao shibian qian Jiang Jieshi de dui-Ri moulüe: Yi Jiang shi riji wei zhongxin suo zuo de kaocha" 盧溝橋事變前蔣介石的對日謀略：以蔣氏日記為中心所作的考察 [Chiang Kai-shek's Japan strategy prior to the Marco Polo Bridge incident: An examination mainly based on Mr. Chiang's diary]. *Jindaishi yanjiu* 近代史研究 2 (2001): 1–27; reprinted in Yang Tianshi, *Jiang shi midang yu Jiang Jieshi zhenxiang*, 377–403.

Yang Tianshi and Wang Xuezhuang 王學莊, eds. *Ju E yundong, 1901–1905* 拒俄運動 1901–1905 [The anti-Russian movement, 1901–1905]. Beijing: Zhongguo shehui kexue chubanshe, 1979.

Yang Yue 楊越. "Xinhua shuping: You biyao jinxing 'cuozhe yu monan' jiaoyu" 新華述評：有必要進行 "挫折與磨難" 教育 [New China commentary: The need to teach people how to deal with "setbacks and hardships"]. http://news .xinhuanet.com/zonghe/2002–07/17/content_485851.htm (accessed Feb. 8, 2007).

Yerushalmi, Yosef Hayim. *Zakhor: Jewish History and Jewish Memory.* Seattle: University of Washington Press, 2002.

Yiren 伊人 [pseud.]. "Goujian, Guo Ba zhi chang shi" 勾踐, 郭霸之嘗矢 [The stool-tasting of Goujian and Guo Ba]. In Zhu Dajian 朱大建, comp., *Shanghai zuojia sanwen bai pian* 上海作家散文百 篇 [One hundred items of prose by Shanghai authors], 198–201. Shanghai: Wenhui chubanshe, 2002.

Young, Ernest P. *The Presidency of Yuan Shih-k'ai: Liberalism and Dictatorship in Early Republican China.* Ann Arbor: University of Michigan Press, 1977.

"Yu gong yi shan" 愚公移山 [The foolish old man who removed the mountains]. In *Guomin xiaoxue guoyu* 4 (lesson 23): 65–66.

"Yu gong yi shan" 愚公移山. In *Guomin zhongxue guowenke jiaokeshu* 3 (lesson 15): 67–70.

Yu Shaoyu 余邵魚, Feng Menglong 馮夢龍, and Cai Yuanfang 蔡元放. *Dong Zhou lieguo zhi* 東周列國志 [A chronicle of the states of the eastern Zhou]. Taibei: Shijie shuju, 1962.

Yu Tianhua 余天華. "Ji Yue guo da chen Wen Zhong" 祭越國大臣文種 [An elegiac tribute to Yue minister Wen Zhong]. In Yu Tianhua, *Yue wang Goujian xi guochou*, 99–100.

———. *Su Qin zhuan* 蘇秦傳 [Biography of Su Qin]. Hong Kong: Jing gong yinshuju, 1961.

———. *Yue wang Goujian xi guochou* 越王勾踐洗國仇 [King Goujian of Yue avenges the wrong done to his country]. Hong Kong: Jing gong yinshuju, 1962.

Yu Yueming 虞岳明. "Jiaoshi—'fuyou gexing de duzhe'—Teji jiaoshi Xue Fagen 'woxin changdan' jiaoxue pianduan ji fenxi" 教師—"富有個性的讀者"—特級教師薛法根 "臥薪嘗膽" 教學片段及分析 [Schoolteacher—"a reader full of individuality"—An excerpt from special grade teacher Xue Fagen's teaching of "sleeping on brushwood and tasting gall," along with an analysis]. *Jiaoyu keyan luntan* 教育科研論壇 6 (2005): 73–74.

Yuan Erti 袁爾涕. "'Wuqi' yu 'wuqi'" "五七" 與 "無期" ["May 7" and "life sentence"]. *Dagongbao* 大公報 (Tianjin), May 7, 1927.

"Yuan Shikai bei po jieshou Riben tichu de 'ershiyi tiao,' Bing quanmian buxia renru fuzhong, woxin changdan" 袁世凱被迫接受日本提出的 "二十一條," 並勸勉部下忍辱負重, 臥薪嘗膽 [Yuan Shikai forced to accept "twenty-one demands" of Japan, encourages subordinates to bear with the humiliation in order to accomplish China's long-term goals, to sleep on brushwood and taste gall]. In Cheng Dong 程棟 et al., comps., *Tu wen 20 shiji Zhongguo shi* 圖文 20世紀中國史 [A pictorial history of twentieth-century China], 10 vols., 2 (May 1915). Guangzhou: Guangdong lüyou chubanshe, 1999.

"Yue wang Goujian" 越王勾踐 [King Goujian of Yue]. In *Xiaoxuexiao chuji yong guoyu duben,* 7:42–43.

"*Yue wang Goujian* guowai maichu tianjia, Chen Baoguo kanhao shoushilü" 《越王勾踐》國外賣出天價, 陳寶國看好收視率 [*King Goujian of Yue* sold abroad for record amount, Chen Baoguo optimistic about TV ratings]. http://www.cctv.com/performance/20060826/101064.shtml (accessed Dec. 25, 2006).

"*Yue wang Goujian* rexiao haiwai, Chen Baoguo zikua biaoyan chuse"《越王勾踐》熱銷海外, 陳寶國自誇表演出色 [*King Goujian of Yue* in great demand abroad, Chen Baoguo praises own performance as outstanding]. http://big5 .xinhuanet.com/gate/big5/news.xinhuanet.com/ent/2006-04/18/content_ 4438399.htm (accessed Dec. 24, 2006).

Zanasi, Margherita. "Globalizing *Hanjian:* The Suzhou Trials and the Post–World War II Discourse on Collaboration." *American Historical Review* 113, no. 3 (June 2008): 731–51.

Zarrow, Peter. "Historical Trauma: Anti-Manchuism and Memories of Atrocity in Late Qing China." *History and Memory* 16, no. 2 (Fall/Winter 2004): 67–107.

Zeng Die 曾迭. "Yue wang Goujian zuo feiji" 越王勾踐坐飛機 [King Goujian of Yue taking an airplane]. *Ren yan* 人言 1, no. 1 (Feb. 17, 1934): 19.

"Zengwenxi shuiku" 曾文溪水庫 [The Zengwenxi reservoir]. In *Guomin xiaoxue guoyu* 12 (lesson 6): 17–19.

Zerubavel, Yael. "The Death of Memory and the Memory of Death: Masada and the Holocaust as Historical Metaphors." *Representations* 45 (Winter 1994): 72–100.

———. *Recovered Roots: Collective Memory and the Making of Israeli National Tradition.* Chicago: University of Chicago Press, 1995.

Zhang Cailiang 張才良, comp. *Li Bai shi sibai shou* 李白詩四百首 [Four hundred poems by Li Bai]. Hefei: Anhui wenyi chubanshe, 1994.

Zhang Daxia 張大夏. *Goujian fuguo* 勾踐復國 [Goujian recovers his country]. Taibei: Liming wenhua shiye gongsi, 1982.

Zhang Geng 張庚. "*Dan jian pian* sui xiang" 《膽劍篇》隨想 [Random thoughts on *The Gall and the Sword*]. In *Lishiju lunji*, 171–77. Reprinted from *Wenyibao* 文藝報 1 (1962).

Zhang Guangnian 張光年. "*Dan jian pian* de sixiangxing" 《膽劍篇》的思想性 [The ideological content of *The Gall and the Sword*]. In *Lishiju lunji*, 178–83. Reprinted from *Wenyibao* 文藝報 1 (1962).

———. "*Dan jian pian* zhi tan" 《膽劍篇》枝談 [A discussion of *The Gall and the Sword*]. *Xijubao* 戲劇報 1 (Jan. 1962): 1–7. Reprinted in *Lishiju lunji*, 184–98.

Zhang Jing 張敬. *Yue wang Goujian* 越王勾踐 [King Goujian of Yue]. Zhengzhou: Henan wenyi chubanshe, 2006.

Zhang Jiugen 張九根. "Zai lishike jiaoxue zhong jinxing aiguozhuyi jiaoyu de changshi" 在歷史課教學中進行愛國主義教育的嘗試 [An attempt to carry out patriotic education in the teaching of a history class]. *Jiaoxue yu guanli* 教學與管理 15 (May 20, 2002): 78.

Zhang Jue 張覺, comp. *Wu Yue chunqiu quanyi* 吳越春秋全譯 [A complete translation of *The Annals of Wu and Yue*]. Guiyang: Guizhou renmin chubanshe, 1993.

Zhang Lili 張麗麗. "Rang zhengzhi ke daoyu chongman meili" 讓政治課導語充滿魅力 [Let political classes be introduced in an appealing way]. *Zhongxue zhengzhi jiaoxue cankao* 中學政治教學參考 10 (2002): 40–41.

Zhang Qiyun 張其昀, comp. *Xian zongtong Jiang gong quanji* 先總統蔣公全集 [The complete works of the late president Mr. Chiang], 3 vols. Taibei: Zhongguo wenhua daxue chubanbu, 1984.

Zhang Qizhi 張奇志 and Zhang Le 張樂. "Zhuanjia xin kaozheng: Taiwan Gaoshan zu gen zai dalu" 專家新考證：臺灣高山族根在大陸 [New research by specialists: Taiwan's Gaoshan people originated on the mainland]. *Minzu tuanjie* 民族團結 7 (2000): 42–43.

Zhang Shuya 張淑雅. "Taihai weiji yu Meiguo dui 'fangong dalu' zhengce de zhuanbian" 臺海危機與美國對 "反攻大陸" 政策的轉變 [The Taiwan Strait crises and America's shifting stance toward the policy of "reconquering the mainland"]. *Zhongyang yanjiuyuan jindaishi yanjiusuo jikan* 中央研究院近代史研究所集刊 36 (Dec. 2001): 232–97.

Zhang Wanyi 張萬儀. "Lu Xun yu Wu-Yue wenhua" 魯迅與吳越文化 [Lu Xun and Wu-Yue culture]. *Xinan minzu xueyuan xuebao (zhexue shehui kexue ban)* 西南民族學院學報（哲學社會科學 版）23, no. 8 (Aug. 2002): 138–42.

Zhang Weiqi 張維祺. *Woxin changdan* 臥薪嘗膽. In *Kang-Ri jiuguo xiju ji* 抗日

救國戲劇集 [A collection of dramas for resisting Japan and saving the country]. Zhongguo Guomindang Hebei sheng dangwu zhengli weiyuanhui, 1932.

Zhang Wenhui 張文輝. "Yue mie Wu de qishi" 越滅吳的啓示 [The insight to be gained from Yue's destruction of Wu]. *Dangfeng tongxun* 黨風通訊 3 (1997): 30.

Zhang Yaojie 張耀傑. "Cao Yu yu Zhou Enlai: Xiju yu zhengzhi de bujie zhi yuan" 曹禺與周恩來：戲劇與政治的不解之緣 [Cao Yu and Zhou Enlai: The indissoluble link between theater and politics]. http://www.dajun.com.cn/caoyu.htm (section 3) (accessed Feb. 7, 2007).

Zhang Yumao 張毓茂. *Xiao Jun zhuan* 蕭軍傳 [A biography of Xiao Jun]. Chongqing: Chongqing chubanshe, 1992.

Zhang Yunnan 張雲南. "Cong 'Wu wang Fuchai de beiju' tan jieli yu shili" 從 "吳王夫差的悲劇" 談借力與失力 [Using "the tragedy of King Fuchai of Wu" as a point of departure for a discussion of using power and losing power]. *Heilongjiang nongken shizhuan xuebao* 黑龍江農墾師專學報 3 (1994): 45–46.

———. "Lun quanli fubai ji qi duice" 論權力腐敗及其對策 [A discussion of the corruption of power and measures for dealing with it]. *Zhoukou shizhuan xuebao* 周口師專學報 12, no. 4 (Dec. 1995): 43–46.

Zhang Zhen 張真. "Gu wei jin yong ji qita: Yu yiwei juzuozhe tan lishiju de yi feng xin" 古爲今用及其他：與一位劇作者談歷史劇的一封信 [Making the past serve the present: A letter to a playwright discussing historical drama]. *Juben* 劇本 1 (Jan. 1961): 62–68. Reprinted in *Lishiju lunji*, 215–28.

———. "Lun lishi de jutixing: Yu yiwei juzuozhe tan lishiju de yi feng xin" 論歷史劇的具體性：與一位劇作者談歷史劇的一封信 [On the concreteness of history: A letter to a playwright discussing historical drama]. *Juben* 劇本 5–6 (May–June 1961): 145–51.

Zhao Cong 趙聰. *Zhongguo dalu de xiqu gaige: 1942–1967* 中國大陸的戲曲改革：1942–1967 [Opera reform on the Chinese mainland: 1942–1967]. Hong Kong: Zhongwen daxue, 1969.

Zhao Huiping 趙惠平. *Cao Yu xiju xinshang* 曹禺戲劇欣賞 [An appreciation of Cao Yu's plays]. Nanning: Guangxi jiaoyu chubanshe, 1989.

Zhao Jiabi 趙家璧. "Zufu: Guan Jigang" 祖父：關吉罡 [My grandfather: Guan Jigang], dated Jan. 18, 2003. http://gzs2.tougao.com/yhgm458/list.asp?id = 64 (accessed Apr. 19, 2007).

Zhao Jingyuan 趙景源. "Cong jiuyiba guonan shuodao yige hao bangyang" 從九一八國南說到一個好榜樣 [Speaking of a good model in reference to the national crisis of September 18]. *Ertong shijie* 兒童世界 29, no. 2 (Nov. 1, 1932): 1–4.

Zhao Jingyun 趙景云. "Jianku chuangye jingshen shi shehuizhuyi benzhi de keguan yaoqiu" 艱苦創業精神是社會主義本質的客觀要求 [The spirit of building something through arduous effort is an objective requirement of the intrinsic nature of socialism]. *Hunan shifan daxue shehui kexue xuebao* 湖南師範大學社會科學學報 25, no. 2 (1996): 14–17.

Zhao Longzhi 趙隆治. *Goujian* 勾踐. Taibei: Huaguo chubanshe, 1953.

"Zheng Chenggong" 鄭成功. In *Xiaoxuexiao chuji yong guoyu duben,* 7:40–41.

Zhengba chuanqi 爭霸傳奇 [A tale of the struggle to become overlord], TV drama. http://tvcity.tvb.com/drama/the_conquest/story/042.html (accessed Feb. 15, 2007).

Zhichishe 知恥社, comp. *Guochi* 國恥, n.d. Reprinted in Shen Yunlong 沈雲龍, ed., *Jindai Zhongguo shiliao congkan* 近代中國史料叢刊 [Historical materials on modern China series], 3 *bian* 編 23 *ji* 輯, vol. 227. Taibei: Wenhai chubanshe, ca. 1987.

Zhiqing 志清 [pseud.]. "Buwang guochi de Goujian" 不忘國恥的勾踐 [Goujian, who didn't forget the national humiliation]. *Minzhong xunkan* 民眾旬刊 4, nos. 16–17 (1934): 17–19.

Zhongguo dianying da cidian 中國電影大辭典 [Dictionary of Chinese film]. Shanghai: Cishu chubanshe, 1995.

Zhongguo geming bowuguan 中國革命博物館 [Museum of the Chinese revolution], comp. *Huangpu junxiao shi tuce* 黃埔軍校史圖冊 [An illustrated history of the Whampoa Military Academy]. Guangzhou: Guangdong renmin chubanshe, 1993.

"Zhonghua minzu wenming shi ke zhuisu dao wannian yiqian" 中華民族文明史可追溯到萬年以前 [The history of the Chinese nation and civilization can be traced back ten thousand years]. *Zhongguo zhigong jiaoyu* 中國職工教育 12 (1997): 24 *(wenzhai* 文摘*)*.

"Zhonghua wenhua fuxing yundong zhi tuixing" 中華文化復興運動之推行 [Carrying out the movement for the rejuvenation of Chinese culture]. *Zhongyang ribao,* July 29, 1967 (reprinted in *Zhongyang ribao: Wushinianlai shelun xuanji,* 141–43).

Zhongyang ribao: Wushinianlai shelun xuanji 中央日報：五十年來社論選集 [Central daily news: Selected editorials from the last fifty years]. Taibei: *Zhongyang ribao* she, 1978.

Zhou Guozhong 周國忠. "Fuchu lishi dibiao de Fan Li" 浮出歷史地表的范蠡 [Fan Li afloat on the surface of history]. *Fujian shifan daxue Fuqing fenxiao xuebao* 福建師範大學福清分校學報 3 (2002): 6–9.

Zhou Hongjun 周宏俊. "Mingren yu zimian lian" 名人與自勉聯 [Famous people and self-motivating couplets]. *Anquan yu jiankang* 安全與健康 5 (1996): 39.

Zhou Shengchun 周生春. *Wu Yue chunqiu jijiao huikao* 吳越春秋輯校彙考 [A critical edition of *The Annals of Wu and Yue*]. Shanghai: Guji chubanshe, 1997.

Zhou Wenqi 周文啓. "Guochi jinianri jingguo zhi ganxiang" 國恥紀念日經過之感想 [Thoughts on the occasion of National Humiliation Day]. *Shenbao,* May 11, 1921.

Zhou Yongzhao 周永釗. "Tan Zhongguo chuantong daode yu peiyang 'si you' xinren" 談中國傳統道德與 培養 "四有" 新人 [A discussion of China's traditional morality and the cultivation of the "four haves" among the new generation]. *Ningbo daxue xuebao (jiaoyu kexue ban)* 寧波大學學報（教育科學版）3 (1998): 29–30.

Zhu Baoqin 朱寶琴. "Ganshou chenggong" 感受成功 [The experience of success]. *Hebei zixue kaoshi* 河北自學考試 10 (1997): 25.

Zhu Jianguo 朱健國. "Bai Hua Zhuhai shuo gudu" 白樺珠海說孤獨 [Bai Hua in Zhuhai talks about solitariness]. *Wenxue ziyou tan* 文學自由談 3 (2003): 70–88.

Zhu Shuangyun 朱雙雲 and Gong Xiaolan 龔嘯嵐. *Woxin changdan: Guoju juben* 臥薪嘗膽：國劇劇本 [Sleeping on brushwood and tasting gall: A Beijing opera libretto]. Hankou: Hankou shi gejie kangdi houyuan hui xuanchuan gongzuotuan, Hankou shi juyeren laojun gongyantuan, 1937.

Zhu Xiang 朱襄. *Baowei Shaoxing ge* 保衛紹興歌 [A paean to the defense of Shaoxing]. In *Shaoxing geming wenhua shiliao huibian*, 443.

Zhu Ying 朱暎. "Jing han yu nei shen jian yu wai: Qian xi huaju *Wu wang jin ge Yue wang jian* de liang ju taici" 精含于內神見於外：淺析話劇《吳王金戈越王劍》的兩句台詞 [The essence is contained within, the spirit is manifested without: A rudimentary analysis of two actors' lines from the spoken drama *The Golden Spear of the King of Wu and the Sword of the King of Yue*]. *Xiju jie* 戲劇界 4 (July–Aug. 1983): 50–51, 80.

Zhu Zhai 朱寨. "Zai tan guanyu lishiju wenti de zhenglun: Jian da Li Xifan tongzhi" 再談關於歷史劇問 題的爭論：兼答李希凡同志 [More on the controversy over the question of historical drama: A response to Comrade Li Xifan]. *Wenxue pinglun* 文學評論 2 (1963): 53–69.

Zhuang Jianping 莊建平, comp. *Guochi shidian* 國恥事典 [A dictionary of national humiliation]. Chengdu: Chengdu chubanshe, 1992.

Zhuge Huazhang 諸葛華章. "Xiao dui nashi de tongku" 笑對那時的痛苦 [Laughing at the sufferings of the past]. *Kaoshi (zhongkao ban)* 考試（中考版）2 (2006): 53.

"Ziqiang buxi de Jiang zongtong" 自強不息的蔣總統 [The unremitting efforts of President Chiang]. In *Guomin xiaoxue guoyu* 9:21–22.

Zou Lu 鄒魯. "Ning fu fei Goujian qie bu pei wei Qin Gui" 寧府非勾踐且不配 為秦檜 [The Nanjing government is not Goujian and doesn't even merit being referred to as Qin Gui]. *Wenming zhi lu* 文明之路 17 (1935): 45–46.

Zuming 祖銘 [pseud.]. "Guochi jinianri ganyan" 國恥紀念日感言 [Thoughts on National Humiliation Day]. *Shenbao*, May 9, 1921.

INDEX

Hundred Flowers Movement (1956–57), 137, 171
Hung, Chang-tai, 51

imperialism, foreign, xix, 152, 228, 253n39; and Boxer Uprising, 48–49; Dutch, 44; Japanese, 40, 41, 44, 60, 61, 64, 123, 225; and national humiliation, 36, 37, 38–39, 40, 44, 49, 58, 69, 84; Russian, 40; in Taiwan, 44, 87, 123
individual, 39, 207, 230; motivation of, 211–17
intellectuals: and CCP, 137, 173, 178, 181, 188, 190, 199, 211; and Mao, 198–99; in post-Mao period, 178, 188, 190, 205, 211, 229, 272n40, 275n70; in Qing period, 21, 36–37
Israel, 237–39, 286n23

Japan: Chiang's concessions to, 72–75; in Goujian story, 55, 56; Goujian story in, 221, 229; imperialism of, 40, 41, 44, 60, 61, 64, 123, 225; in Manchuria, 51, 72, 73; as model, 219; resistance to, 68–76, 231, 251n13; revenge against, 266n60; and Russia, 38, 229, 285n6; in Taiwan, 88, 89, 90; and Twenty-One Demands, 45–48. *See also* War of Resistance
Jewel in the Palace (*Dae Jang Geum;* Korean television series), 223
Jia Fengzhen, 61
Jia Yi, 250n12
Jiang Qing, 199, 272n27
Jiang Tiejun, 257n75
Jiang xiang he (*The General and the Prime Minister;* play), 137–38
Jiang Zemin, 205, 208
Jiao Juyin, 270n5
Jie, King of Xia, 13, 122
jie gu feng jin ("using the past to disparage the present"), 196, 200
jieli (borrowing power), 210
Jin, state of, 11, 19, 24, 75, 164
Jin dynasty, 41
Ji'nan Incident (1928), 61, 68, 69, 73, 257n78

Jiran (Jiyan), 11–14, 26, 30, 245nn23,25
Joan of Arc, xi, xiv, xviii, 233
Johnson, David, 1
Josephus, 286n20
Judaism, xiv, 77, 85, 86, 236–39, 259n109
Jurchens, 41

Kammen, Michael, xv
Kang Ri jiuguo xiju ji (*A Collection of Dramas for Resisting Japan and Saving the Country*), 78
kangzhan, 79, 83. *See also* War of Resistance
Kexuan, 39, 40
Khrushchev, Nikita, 273n45
Khubilai Khan, 43
King Goujian of Yue (*Yue wang Goujian;* television series), 221, 222–24, 225, 284n60
King Goujian of Yue Avenges the Wrong Done to His Country (*Yue wang Goujian xi guochou;* Yu Tianhua), 175–76
KMT. *See* Guomindang
Korea, 38, 223
Korean War (1950), 88, 156, 261n2, 273n42
Kosovo, Battle of (1389), 228–29, 285n19
Koxinga (Zheng Chenggong), 40–41, 44, 45, 53, 116, 252n26
Kuai Dafu, 177, 275n3, 276n4
Kuaiji, Mount, 7, 50, 88, 177, 181; ancestral shrine at, 92, 94; in *The Gall and the Sword,* 162–63; Goujian's defeat at, 2, 3, 23, 24, 99; in Qing period, 39, 40
Kucheng (*The Gall and the Sword*), 159, 162, 165, 167, 171, 274n53
Kulian (*Unrequited Love;* film script; Bai Hua), 188, 190, 198, 277n34

Lagerwey, John, 243nn4,6, 248n55
Lan Hong, 124–26
land reform, 88, 181
language: colloquial, 51, 70, 78, 263n40; in historical drama, 149, 154; in Republican period, 49, 51, 55–56; in Taiwan, 89, 126
Langye (capital of Yue), 28. *See also* Shaoxing

opera *(continued)*
151; Chinese *vs.* Western, 145n; historical, 140, 147, 148–54; Mao Dun on, 145–55; Ming, 145–48; in post-Mao PRC, 220, 222; Qing, 145–46; reform of, 272n27; and ritual, 146, 271n23; in Taiwan, 90, 101–2; televised, 220, 221; Xi Shi in, 101–2, 147, 148, 222, 283n51

Opium Wars, xviii, 36, 53

oral tradition, xiv, xv, xviii, 235

Ottoman Turks, 228–29

Our Great China (Weida de Zhonghua; Tan Zhijun), 99

Our Great Leader (Weida de lingxiu; Tan Zhijun), 99

"Paean to the Defense of Shaoxing, A" ("Baowei Shaoxing ge"), 80

Pan Gongzhan, 84

Past Generation, The (Guoqu de niandai; Xiao Jun), 182

Peasant Resistance (Nongmin kangzhan congshu; collection), 78

Peel, J. D. Y., 85

Peng Dehuai, 166, 174–75, 176, 185, 209; and Hai Rui, 170–71

Peng Sanyuan, 211–12

Peng Zhen, 182

people, common: in Bai Hua's work, 190, 191, 192, 193, 194–95; and CCP, 198, 208, 210; in *The Gall and the Sword,* 157–65, 167, 171, 174; in PRC operas, 148–49, 150–51; in Xiao Jun's work, 182, 184, 187; of Yue, 9, 11, 18–19, 29, 52, 157–65

"People in History Who Achieved Success by Dint of Hard Struggle" ("Lishishang kudou chenggong de renwu"; series of talks; Huang Dashou), 111–14

People's Daily (Renmin Ribao), 200

People's Livelihood News (Minsheng bao), 61

periodicals, xviii; children's, 42; in PRC, 136, 181; Republican-period, 47, 57, 65, 67, 81, 256n72; in Taiwan, 106, 115, 116, 118. *See also* newspapers

Ping, King of Chu, 31, 32, 33

poetry, 41, 80–81, 197, 241n4

politics, xx, 230, 249n4; and art, 139, 143–45, 148, 155, 274n67; and Cao Yu, 155–56, 272n40, 274n67; and drama, 137, 200–201; and history, 134–35, 137, 200–201; liberalization of PRC, 171–73, 178, 202, 226; liberalization of Taiwan, 128; and literature, 105, 155, 202, 271n27, 274n67; in 1960s PRC, 137, 139, 143–45, 148, 155–56, 171–73, 206–7, 272n40, 274n67; in 1980s PRC, 176, 178, 187, 200–201, 202; and opera, 139, 143–45, 146–47, 148; in post-Mao PRC, 205, 226; in Taiwan, 105, 128, 134–35

primers, 53–56, 79, 220, 254n44; in Taiwan, 261n8, 265nn45,46,49. *See also* textbooks

proverbs, 216, 229, 230–31. See also *woxin changdan*

Pu Songling, 224

Qi, state of, 11, 19, 24, 75, 164

Qi Hong, 139, 140, 271n13

Qi Jiguang, 44, 78, 116, 206

Qian Yingyu, 140, 271n13

Qin, state of, 138n

Qin dynasty, 37

Qin Gui, 74, 75, 201, 202

Qin Shi Huang, 84, 117, 131

Qing dynasty, 21, 60, 83; Goujian story in, 37, 39, 40, 86, 228; and Ming, 178, 180, 197n; national humiliation in, 36–41; opera in, 145–46

Qinghua University, 177

Qingshan Opera Company (Shanghai), 139, 140

Qiu Jin, 81, 82–83, 222, 260n126

Qu Yuan, 197n, 206, 208, 279n53

Qu Yuan (play; Guo Moruo), 197

radio, 99, 233; Goujian story on, xviii, 106, 124, 220, 231; in Taiwan, 90, 116, 118

reader-reception theory, 275n75

Red Cliff, battle of (208), 108

Red Guards, 177

Text:	11.25/13.5 Adobe Garamond
Display:	RotisSemiSerif, Adobe Garamond
Compositor:	Integrated Composition Systems
Indexer:	Anne Holmes
Printer and binder:	Thomson-Shore, Inc.